COLONIAL CONGO

Colonial Congo

A History in Questions

Edited by
IDESBALD GODDEERIS, AMANDINE LAURO
AND GUY VANTHEMSCHE

Translated by
SUZANNE HEUKENSFELDT JANSEN

BREPOLS

This book was translated by Suzanne Heukensfeldt Jansen
and proofread by Christopher Uebelhor.

This book was realized in collaboration with
the Royal Museum for Central Africa (www.africamuseum.be)
and published with the support of
Flanders Literature (flandersliterature.be).

© The original Dutch version: 2020, the authors
and Pelckmans Uitgevers nv
© The English translation: 2024, the authors,
Suzanne Heukensfeldt Jansen, and
Brepols Publishers nv

All rights reserved. No part of this publication may
be reproduced, stored in a retrieval system, or
transmitted, in any form or by any means, electronic,
mechanical, photocopying, recording, or otherwise
without the prior permission of the publisher.

D/2024/0095/31
ISBN 978-2-503-59848-2
eISBN 978-2-503-59849-9
DOI 10.1484/M.STMCH-EB.5.127497

Printed in the EU on acid-free paper.

Contents

Foreword   9

1. Why a 'History in Questions'?
Guy Vanthemsche, Idesbald Goddeeris and Amandine Lauro   11

Part I
Key Moments

Introduction
Amandine Lauro, Idesbald Goddeeris and Guy Vanthemsche   25

2. The Congo Free State. Plunder Machine in Service of a Ruthless Leopold II?
Bas De Roo   27

3. Was There a Genocide in the Congo Free State?
Georgi Verbeeck   41

4. Two World Wars. A Turning Point in the History of the Congo and its People?
Guy Vanthemsche   55

5. 1960. The End of the Colonization of the Congo?
Jean Omasombo Tshonda and Guy Vanthemsche   64

6. The Congo Crisis (1960-1963). Proof of a Failed Decolonization?
Emmanuel Gerard   76

Part II
Economy and Society

Introduction
Amandine LAURO, Idesbald GODDEERIS and Guy VANTHEMSCHE   91

7. From Decline to Growth in Population. What Impact Did the Colonization Have on Congolese Demographics?
Jean-Paul SANDERSON   93

8. The Big Conglomerates. How Was a Capitalist Economy Implanted into the Congo?
Frans BUELENS   102

9. Was the Development of the Belgian Congo Only Possible because of Forced Labor?
Julia SEIBERT   114

10. How Did the Congolese Workers Live? The Example of the *Union Minière du Haut-Katanga* (UMHK)
Donatien DIBWE DIA MWEMBU   126

11. Agriculture in the Colonial Congo. A Success Story at the Expense of the Rural Population?
Yves SEGERS and Leen VAN MOLLE   136

12. Infrastructure, Urban Landscapes and Architecture. Traces of 'Development' or Instruments of 'Exploitation'?
Johan LAGAE and Jacob SABAKINU KIVILU (†)   148

13. The Congo, a Colony Heading for 'Development'?
Guy VANTHEMSCHE   160

14. The Congolese Community in Belgium. An Unintended 'By-Product' of Colonial Rule?
Mathieu Zana ETAMBALA   169

Part III
Governance and Power

Introduction
Amandine LAURO, Idesbald GODDEERIS and Guy VANTHEMSCHE   181

15. Repression. Was the Congo a Less Violent Colony after Leopold II?
Amandine LAURO and Benoît HENRIET   183

16. Resistance in the Belgian Congo. The Many Paths of Disobedience
Didier GONDOLA   194

17. Did the Belgian Colonizer Introduce Racism and an Ethnic Identity into the Congo?
Jean-Marie K. MUTAMBA MAKOMBO   205

18. The Colonial State and the African Elite. A History of Subjugation?
Daniel TÖDT   215

19. Women, Sexuality, *Métissage*. Colonization's 'Taboo' Topics?
Amandine LAURO   225

20. Linguistic Diversity. Whose Languages Were Used in the Colony?
Michael MEEUWIS   235

Part IV
The 'Civilizing Mission'

Introduction
Amandine LAURO, Idesbald GODDEERIS and Guy VANTHEMSCHE   247

21. Missionaries. A Human Dimension to Colonization?
Idesbald GODDEERIS   249

22. Health Care. The Jewel in Belgian Colonization's Crown?
Maarten LANGHENDRIES and Reinout VANDER HULST   263

23. Colonial Education in the Congo. More than a Paternalistic One-Way Street?
Marc DEPAEPE and Annette LEMBAGUSALA KIKUMBI   271

24. Colonial Propaganda. The Awakening of a Belgian Colonial Consciousness?
Matthew G. STANARD   280

25. Science. Belgian Colonialism's Accomplice?
Ruben Mantels   291

26. Did the Belgian Colonizer Create, Destroy or Steal Congolese Art?
Sarah Van Beurden   301

27. Animals and the Environment in the Congo. Was Nature Conservation the Same as Nature Protection?
Violette Pouillard   311

Part V
Afterword

28. The Colonial Past through a Belgian Lens. From White Nostalgia to Decolonial Debate
Idesbald Goddeeris, Amandine Lauro and Guy Vanthemsche   323

29. The Colonial Past through a Congolese Lens. From Red Rubber to Red Coltan
Isidore Ndaywel è Nziem   334

30. Photographic Essay
Pedro Monaville   348

Timeline   365

Maps   368

Abbreviations   371

About the Authors   377

Foreword

The Royal Museum for Central Africa (RMCA or AfricaMuseum, Tervuren, Belgium) was established in 1898 as a colonial institute. Housed in a building that is still profoundly marked by Leopold II's presence, it long remained unchanged until a major renovation of both its permanent exhibition and infrastructure between 2013 and 2018. In doing so, the RMCA sought to shift its perspective and become the museum of a history shared by Belgium, Europe and Sub-Saharan Africa. It also embarked on a new way of thinking, working, providing a space for dialogue, and whenever possible, co-creating with African partners and diaspora communities.

One of its mottos, 'Everything passes, except the past', reflects the institution's wish to call on the past to find answers for the present and build the future.

The AfricaMuseum is proud to be a partner in *Colonial Congo. A History in Questions*. It is important for this book, originally published in Dutch and French (2020), to be available to the entire academic community by means of an English version. Two historians from our institute participated, and documents from our archives and collections formed crucial contributions to this collection of essays.

I hope that this book will provide you with some answers to the questions raised. Our endeavour is to continue our work as scientists in questioning the past and present, and to provide material to guide both scientists and the general public in their quest for understanding and empathy.

Bart Ouvry
Director-General
AfricaMuseum

GUY VANTHEMSCHE, IDESBALD GODDEERIS
AND AMANDINE LAURO

1. Why a 'History in Questions'?

At first sight, European colonialism is definitively a thing of the past: in 2023, globally, only a handful of small 'overseas territories' were still controlled (or rather administrated?) by a European country. The vast colonial empires collapsed quite rapidly between 1945 and 1975. Yet the shock wave of colonialism is still tangible. It not only left indelible marks on the former colonies, but also continues to haunt the minds of the former colonizers. In Europe nowadays, many people hold an extremely negative view of colonial rule. Critics primarily focus on the many crimes of the white oppressor throughout the world. Other voices protest against this 'public atonement'. They believe Western self-criticism is wrong and even dangerous. In their view, it discards colonialism's 'positive aspects' and could ultimately even lead to the self-destruction of 'Western civilization'. Moreover, a small, but all the more vocal white supremacist movement goes as far as to proclaim that the 'white race' is 'destined' to rule the world. The colonial past therefore continues to be an ideological issue, and is (once again) about to become a political one. The debate rages in many European countries, and Belgium is no exception. This book, with all due humility, tries to shed light on this issue by bringing to the fore some insights from academic studies into Belgian colonial history.

Motivation: The Continuing Debate about the Belgian Colonial Past

During the Second World War, Belgium sought to enhance its image vis-à-vis the other Allied powers. For this reason, the country emphasized the alleged enormous 'benefactions' it implemented in the Congo, which it represented as a true 'model colony':

> 50 years ago, the population of the Congo was estimated at 30 million, since then the population has fallen to 10 million. Slavery, intestinal wars, and sleeping sickness had made terrible ravages among the native population before the Belgians were able to complete the organization of their colony. The mortality

rate had reached appalling proportions and one wonders what would have been the fate of the black races of Central Africa without the intervention of Europeans. The pacific conquest of the country by Belgium thus had this first and fortunate result in stopping a decay that was threatening to become permanent.[1]

According to the Belgian Government at the time, the 'black races' in the Congo thus owed their survival to the 'peaceful conquest' of their vast territory by the Belgians, whose humanitarian action allegedly had put an end to the dramatic population decline estimated here to be as much as twenty million people… Oddly enough, such figures are still being mentioned today, but from a radically different perspective:

> King Leopold II, a genocidal murdering savage beast, colonized Congo/Zaïre [and] slaughtered 15 million Africans. […] The genocidal events which took place under King Leopold II reign [sic] is [sic] considered one of the most heinous acts of murderous savagery known to man. The barbaric slaughter and mutilation of the innocent people of the Congo, was so [sic] to strip the country of its natural resources in order to build up Belgium.[2]

This quotation obviously does not come from academic sources, but that is hardly relevant here. The blog referred to above expresses a widespread opinion that can be found in countless books, newspaper articles and films. Leopold II's rule in the Congo is depicted as one of the biggest crimes in history. We only need to think of the shock caused by *King Leopold's Ghost*,[3] written by Adam Hochschild at the end of the twentieth century, to which we will return later. This American author estimates Leopold II's rule to be responsible for some ten million casualties. These two diametrically opposed interpretations – the Congo as a model colony or as killing fields – lead to two conclusions.

Firstly, these two contrasting images of the Congo go back a long way. The apologetic text we quoted first was written at the beginning of the 1940s, but follows an extensive tradition of propaganda stretching back to the end of the nineteenth century when Leopold personally set up press campaigns to defend 'his' colony against the criticism it had to endure. On the flip side, the cry of indignation we just cited in fact perpetuates a long tradition of accusations against Leopoldian rule. The earliest examples date from the period immediately following the creation of the Congo Free State in 1885. This 'image war' is therefore as old as the colonization of Central Africa itself.

Secondly, right from the outset, the clash of these two viewpoints has also occurred far beyond the Belgian borders. The first text was published in New York by the Belgian Government's propaganda bureau; the second is from African American circles. Indeed, the fiercest criticism of the crimes perpetrated in the Congo has largely emanated from the Anglosphere, especially the United States. The polemic surrounding Belgium's colonial past is therefore not merely a Belgian or Congolese-Belgian concern. Few aspects of Belgian national history enjoy such global 'fame'…

Over the years, completely contradictory, but seldom verified statements about the colonization of this huge African country have been uttered in different countries. A 'verification process' is therefore essential. This book attempts to chart, as accurately as possible, the actions and experiences of both those who colonized and those who were colonized. In addition to having academic significance, this objective also has a social and political dimension: as we have just seen, the debate about the colonial past reaches far beyond the narrow circle of specialists.

Colonial propaganda of the time still reverberates in many people's minds. This is largely due to the influence of school textbooks, the content of which continues to make itself felt decades on; comics (e.g. *Tintin in the Congo* – renamed *Tintin in Africa* – is still being read); feature films that present a stereotypical image of Africa; the former 'Congo Museum' in Tervuren, in particular before the recent renovation (but according to some, afterwards as well); and so on. The positive image of colonization is still thriving in an (ageing) section of the population: octogenarians who witnessed the last years of the Belgian Congo in situ. Many sincerely believe that they brought progress to the heart of Africa – and some of them did indeed play a role that could be considered 'humanitarian'. They react with great indignation when their actions are equated with Leopold II's malpractices, which are sometimes labelled 'genocide'. To this day, these former colonials, as well as their relatives, friends and sympathizers, are still producing and disseminating publications and opinion pieces that accentuate the 'positive aspects' of Belgian colonization and minimize (or gloss over) the 'negative' ones.[4] Persons who have never been to the Congo, but who are loyal to the dynasty and the country, share the same opinion.

Alongside these traditional pro-colonial networks, an entirely different movement has recently emerged. In August 2018, at the Pukkelpop music festival near Hasselt, a group of young people sang *Handjes kappen, de Congo is van ons* ('Chop their hands off, the Congo is ours').[5] Was it just a stupid joke uttered by tipsy festival goers? This seems unlikely. Somewhat later, a group of Flemish right-wing students asserted that 'the Congo was better off as a colony' and lamented that 'the white man is always being blamed.'[6] Memes with the same message circulate online, albeit less subtly articulated. These recent developments are only the tip of the iceberg, because they express a wider societal evolution: the return of the far right, accompanied, as ever, by violence and abhorrent racism. Beyond organized extreme-right movements, we also witness the rise of 'identitary' sentiments and behaviors opposing the so-called 'multi-culturalist' environment. According to many observers, they stem from a loss of cultural reference points and the fear of being cast aside. In this new social context, the notion of 'identity' often acquires a 'racial' dimension, something which itself is partly rooted in colonial past.

A heterogeneous coalition of people and associations fiercely opposes the advocates of colonialism. They want to eradicate the many legacies of imperial rule once and for all. Their main targets are monuments and other testimonies of the colonial past in public space. They also long to 'decolonize the mind' and to eradicate old racist prejudices that often mould, albeit more or less unconsciously, the thoughts and actions of many of their fellow-citizens. The Congolese diaspora in Belgium and other countries, as is true with all expatriate African communities, inevitably questions the colonial past – a matter of primary concern for them. From this position, some members of this community have thrown themselves into decolonial activism with all their heart and soul. Their actions have political repercussions: the Belgian colonial past and its many legacies are discussed at several different levels of power, from local councils to the Federal Parliament and international organizations such as the United Nations. This aspect is discussed in more detail at the end of this book (see Chapter 28).

In short, sixty years after the collapse of the European overseas empires, colonialism is still a subject of debate in Belgium and elsewhere. But this debate is seldom conducted with in-depth knowledge. Decades of propaganda and counterpropaganda have generated plenty of poor, incomplete or non-informed opinions. So, let us return to the facts, as evidenced by recent scholarly research.

Objective and Method: Communicating the Insights of Academic Research

The colonial past has long been neglected by Belgian historians. Between the 1960s and the early 1990s, few of them had abandoned the apologetic approach. Two figures, however, were outliers. First and foremost, Jean Stengers from the Free University of Brussels (ULB), who patiently analyzed Leopold II's intricate colonial policy, chiefly from a political and diplomatic viewpoint.[7] Jean-Luc Vellut, from the Catholic University of Louvain-la-Neuve (UCL), then broadened the analysis. Having taught at the incipient Congolese universities for many years before returning to Belgium in 1976, he investigated nearly every aspect of colonial history, and still does so. He focuses on life in the Congo itself, while Stengers was mainly interested in the Belgian dimension. Vellut, in other words, is the true trailblazer of modern colonial historiography in Belgium.[8] This field of expertise was pretty much absent from university curriculums, leaving secondary school teachers insufficiently prepared to teach this specific subject. In other countries, especially the United States and the United Kingdom, the history of the colonial Congo generated much more attention in academia. And last but not least, from the end of the 1970s, a first generation of Congolese historians published works of great value about the history of their country.[9] Therefore, long before the end of the twentieth century historiography had built up a broad basic knowledge about the colonial Congo which was eroding the prevailing cliché of colonization as a great 'civilizing' project. The harsh colonial reality, characterized by violence, exploitation and racism, was brought to light... in academic circles.

Paradoxically however, these insights reached the public via different channels. From 1985, this new vision on colonial reality was disseminated by people who were not professional historians. Three people played a prominent role: former diplomat Jules Marchal, who published his first books under the pseudonym A.M. Delathuy,[10] anthropologist Daniel Vangroenweghe, then a secondary school teacher,[11] and finally the author Adam Hochschild, whom we mentioned earlier. While carrying out research of his own, the latter largely drew on Marchal's and Vangroenweghe's works. Thanks to his literary talent, Hochschild succeeded in focusing international attention (once more) on the horrors of 'red rubber', i.e. the systemic exploitation of the Congolese people who, at the end of the nineteenth and the beginning of the twentieth century, were forced to extract this valuable commodity from the wild rubber tree. In 1999, almost simultaneously with Hochschild's book, Belgian sociologist Ludo De Witte published a resounding work on the murder of the Congolese Prime Minister Patrice Lumumba in 1961, incriminating the Belgian Government.[12] Public attention was therefore primarily focused on two bloody episodes from Congolese history. Alas, what occurred in between both events largely remained shrouded in mist.

These books stirred up interest in the colonial past amongst a wide public. The old, pro-colonial certainties, in Belgium and abroad, were shattered. Yet the iconoclastic character of these publications also generated new polemics. The methodology of these titles was not always flawless – some blamed the authors, especially Marchal, for providing too little context or for being too anecdotal. Moreover, these works created new simplifications. Their readers were indignant about colonial crimes, and rightly so, but were often poorly informed. Every sense of nuance was lost; some even included Leopold II in the 'club of mass murderers', with Stalin and Hitler. The term 'genocide' has since commonly been used to label the massacres in the Leopoldian Congo. This polemic context revitalized the counter-offensive of those who defended the 'Belgian colonial achievements.' At the beginning of the twenty-first century, both camps were entrenched in irreconcilable positions.

Beyond this memorial debate, which has its own logic and legitimacy, historical research has its own role to play, not to provide definitive answers to all the hotly debated questions, but to debunk persistent myths and manifest mistakes.

Over the past twenty years, a new generation of historians has followed up the work of the trailblazers and made significant contributions to a fuller understanding of the Belgian Congolese colonial past. Their voices deserve to be heard as well; that is the purpose of this book. It has the – perhaps overconfident – ambition to be a link, or even a conveyer belt, between the world of academic research and the wider public seeking reliable information about the Belgian colonial past. The existence of such a public is proven by the enormous success of David Van Reybrouck's *Congo. A History*, published almost fifteen years ago.[13] This work, with undeniable literary qualities, presents itself in essence as an essay melding the author's personal findings during his travels in the Congo with a wider historical perspective that harks back to the works of numerous historians. Our book, however, has a different intention. It pays tribute to the principle 'from producer to consumer, without intermediaries': the concept of 'short chain', the forte of the new, sustainable economy, can also be applied to the world of academic research…

We therefore gathered a team of authors from a diversity of backgrounds: in addition to Belgian historians (both Flemish and Francophones, quite an exceptional feat!), this volume also features colleagues from the United States, Germany and of course the Congo itself. Most authors hail from the former colonizing country and the three members of the editorial committee are Belgian historians. This imbalance is also, to an extent, the product of history:

we would be poor historians if we did not acknowledge this fact of the situation. The former colonial relationships created dynamics in the field of expertise and knowledge production of which this book is also the fruit. Fortunately, history is not a contest in which the nationality of the researcher dictates to which camps he or she belongs. But while historical research is based on shared methods and techniques, it is also the result of a plurality of sensitivities and approaches. The texts presented in this book do not therefore dovetail with any particular 'camp', school or trend; the authors truly form a representative sampling of historical research into the colonial Congo. They obviously enjoyed complete scientific freedom, and this might explain any possible differences in interpretation the attentive reader will detect here and there. Indeed, historical research does not lead to immutable 'truths', contrary to what non-specialists usually assume. Researchers constantly weigh the clues at their disposal; they are in constant dialogue with their colleagues and always look at the past from different perspectives. Historiography is by nature a dynamic process.

We therefore invite the reader to enter the historian's 'workshop'. From a formal point of view, a handbook or chronological report seemed unappealing. Unravelling the fabric of the past means, first, laying bare the threads with which it has been woven. This then enables a reconstruction of the ways in which they are entwined. We therefore opted for a thematic approach: each chapter covers a specific topic, one of the many 'threads' in this historical fabric. The texts have deliberately been kept short – a challenge for the authors, forcing them to go right to the core of the matter. Each chapter contains cross-references to other parts of the book; this will allow the reader to connect the different topics.

Historical research basically means asking questions. Historians obviously cannot put the past 'on the rack' in order to get answers to their questions, as the inquisitors did, forcing their victims to make coerced false confessions. Anyone who silences or violates the available sources for ideological or political reasons in order to obtain a 'desirable' response is not engaged in historiography, but in propaganda. Researchers only manage to unmute their sources by unrelentingly interrogating the past. We therefore purposely asked the authors to begin their text with a few clearly formulated questions and to also formulate the title of each chapter as a question. This will hopefully help the general reader resolve his queries – even if historians' answers are often more complex than a simple yes or no.

Historical research is not only fostered by continuously asking questions; it is also based on the intensive and critical study of the written, oral or visual testimonies that have been passed down to us. All the chapters in this book synthesize long and meticulous analyses of primary sources. The latter are not mentioned in detail to avoid making this already voluminous book overly lengthy. However, we do list the relevant publications in the bibliography at the end of each chapter. These works, in turn, refer to the primary sources. The footnotes, kept to a minimum, only mention the origin of quotes and quantitative data.

Content: Which Questions, and Which Answers?

To fully grasp the Belgian colonial past, we must, first of all, get rid of the polemical fixation on the Congo Free State, and more specifically on the character and personal actions of Leopold II. Depicting the 'greedy and cruel king' as a devil does not advance any research... To avoid any misunderstanding: Leopold's rule is undoubtedly a key episode of Congolese history. We do not wish to minimize the importance of the massacres perpetrated during the 'red rubber' era; they are obviously not just a footnote in history. It is important however, to place these dramatic aspects into the wider context of the occupation, exploitation and transformation of the Congolese territory, first by representatives of the Congo Free State, then by the Belgian colonial authorities. The thematic breakdown of this book reflects this approach. Most chapters scrutinize the entire colonial era, from the beginning in 1885 up until the end in 1960. This enables the reader to perceive, at a single glance, the profound changes that took place during this period. The Congo of 1955 differed radically from that of, for instance, 1895. However, certain essential traits of the colonial system persisted during the entire seventy-five years of colonial rule.

A first persistent trait was violence. The 'peaceful conquest' mentioned at the beginning of this introduction existed only in the minds of the Belgian colonial propagandists, and of the people who internalized this false image. The armed subjugation of the indigenous population and the implementation of forced labor were long and bloody processes. Of course, this fundamental conclusion inevitably comes with all kinds of provisos. Africans also took part in the violent operations led by Europeans. The latter copied, at least partially and for some time, the violent methods prevailing in this far from peaceful region.[14] The violence of war and subjugation was gradually replaced by a system of 'law enforcement' and repression that was based on routine policing and was less explicitly brutal. But these considerations do not alter the central conclusion: the colonization of the Congo was fundamentally based on violent conquest followed by one society's forced subjugation of another.

A second persistent trait was racism. In the Belgian Congo, people were treated differently depending on the color of their skin. Black people, who were considered inherently inferior to white people, were denied rights possessed by Belgian citizens. They not only underwent all manner of discrimination but were also treated in a way which would be considered inhuman in the 'motherland'. The Central African communities obviously had customs, traditions, cultures and knowledge which differed greatly from those of the conquerors. This enormous chasm 'legitimized' and reinforced the white feelings of superiority. A black person could thus be requisitioned for all kinds of tasks; he or she could be sent to a faraway region against his or her will; and as Lumumba remarked in his famous speech of 30 June 1960, black people were often beaten up and insulted and were always addressed to in the informal *tu* form by white people, while black people had to address their white counterparts with the deferential *vous*. It goes without saying that relations between white and black people could also be permeated with mutual respect, appreciation, solidarity, friendship and even love, but this does not alter the fact that the Belgian Congo, like every other colonial society, was structurally racist. At the time, racism and 'race' were obviously perceived differently than today, but the fact that this perception of the world and of mankind was globally considered 'normal', is of course revealing of the nature of the colonial system itself.

A third persistent trait was the crucial importance of economic factors. It would obviously be too simplistic to reduce colonialism to one single dimension. Political, diplomatic, religious and cultural interests all played a part in the making and functioning of the colonial system. But the insatiable hunger for profit – which was then coyly camouflaged by terms such as 'civilizing mission', 'progress' and 'development' – was most definitely a central aspect of the Belgian presence in Central Africa. Nevertheless, economic policy also went through fundamental changes over the years. The ultra-violent exploitation of the early years gradually made way for more controlled and complex activities. From the 1920s onwards, and especially after the Second World War, the race for profit required massive investments and huge infrastructure. To increase productivity, more care had to be devoted to 'human capital', i.e. the black worker.

A fourth persistent trait was the ambition to reshape the 'native' population and the colonized society. From the outset, the colonial project harbored transformative ambitions. The notion of progress, which had been anchored strongly in European society since the end of the eighteenth century, discovered an enormous territory in the colonies for letting rip its 'pursuit of improvement'. This aspiration concerned both material and immaterial aspects of society. The goal was not only to 'improve' people's living conditions, but also the way they acted and thought, through evangelization, education, teaching new languages, creating new identities, etc. And yet these ambitious projects were not bereft of ambiguity. How could anyone reconcile violence and discrimination with the pursuit of human improvement? Could the extreme racist vision, which regarded non-white people as a subspecies of humanity, be reconciled with the wish to 'elevate' black (or yellow, or brown) fellow human beings to the 'level of their white counterparts'? Did the colonizer always undertake his campaigns to promote progress and civilization without thinking of his own profit? And finally: where was the boundary between pretext and genuine conviction?

These four elements do not constitute a complete list of constants in the colonial system. Yet they do give us a better insight into the themes this book covers. These themes are grouped into four major parts. The first one investigates some important stages in Belgian Congolese history. We will start by examining the essential characteristics of the period in which the colony was set up, in the form of the Congo Free State. This is followed by the period of the two world wars, and finally decolonization and its effects. The second part focuses on social and economic aspects. The implementation of colonial capitalism and the ensuing large-scale infrastructures generated sweeping demographic and social changes, especially in living and working conditions. The third part deals with the governance of colonial society. We will not focus on mere institutional aspects – the political and administrative apparatus of the colony has already been chronicled extensively in other works – but on the relationship between white and black. We will reflect on policies related to gender, race, ethnicity and language, as well as on forms of repression and resistance. In the fourth part of the book, we will explore the so-called 'civilizing mission'. This term encompasses a series of cultural and social activities introduced by the Belgians in the Congo: religious missions, health care, education, scientific research and the conservation of 'indigenous art' and 'wild' nature. Did all those 'accomplishments', spearheads of colonial propaganda, also have a dark side?

The book concludes with a photographic essay and with two chapters mirroring each other and discussing the views of the colonial past of, respectively, the Belgians and the Congolese. These considerations somehow bridge historical research and current discussions about the Belgian Congo. Does this book contain the final words concerning our topic? Of course not: many legitimate questions about the shared Belgian and Congolese past still await answers. But our goal will have been achieved when our clarifications, in turn, trigger new interrogations.

We would like to thank all our authors, especially for the trouble they have taken to be succinct and for the timely delivery of their work. We are also especially grateful to Harold Polis, who took the initiative for the original Dutch edition of this book. It owes much to his criticism and active support; his suggestions during editorial meetings were invaluable.

Notes

1 *Belgian Congo at War*, Belgian Information Center, New York, s.a., p. 20 (this book was published during the Second World War).
2 https://www.bichee.com/cgi-sys/suspendedpage.cgi?link1=read-blog&id=170_weneed-dark-skin-superheroes-for-black-women.html (consulted on 4 October 2023).
3 Hochschild, Adam, *King Leopold's Ghost: A Story of Greed, Terror and Heroism in Colonial Africa*, Houghton Mifflin, Boston, 1998.
4 Some examples: UROME/KBUOL, *La colonisation belge. Une grande aventure*, Éditions Gérard Blanchart, s.l., 2004; de Maere d'Aertrycke, André, e.a., *Le Congo au temps des Belges. L'histoire manipulée. Les controverses réfutées 1885-1960*, Masoin, Brussels, 2011; De Weerd, Guido, *L'État indépendant du Congo. À la recherche de la vérité historique*, Éditions Dynamédia, Brussels, 2015; André-Bernard Ergo's books published by L'Harmattan, etc.
5 https://www.vrt.be/vrtnws/nl/2018/08/20/unia-krijgt-melding-over-racistisch-gezang-op-pukkelpop/ (consulted on 5 November 2019).
6 This refers to a letter to the editor which appeared in *Veto*, KU Leuven's student newspaper, signed by Maxim Goris, the chair of the right-wing Catholic and pro-Flemish student society KVHV: http://www.veto.be/artikel/kvhv-voorzitter-congo-was-beter-af-als-kolonie (consulted on 25 December 2019). See also: https://www.standaard.be/cnt/dmf20180826_03684074 (consulted on 5 November 2019). The person in question is also a member of the extreme right-wing youth association *Schild en Vrienden* ('Shield and Friends'), which not only cultivates a fundamental racism, but is also preparing for the armed struggle 'to defend the white race'...
7 Stengers, Jean, *Congo. Mythes et réalités. 100 ans d'histoire*, Éditions Duculot, Paris-Louvain-la-Neuve, 1989 (a collection of some of his most important articles; second edition: Racine, Brussels, 2005). The complete list of his publications about colonial history can be found in Duvosquel,

Jean-Marie, et al., eds., *Belgique/Europe/Afrique. Deux siècles d'histoire contemporaine. Méthode et réflexions. Recueil d'articles de Jean Stengers*, Le Livre Timperman, Brussels, 2005, p. 33 and 38-42.
8 A volume with some of his most important publications has recently appeared: Vellut, Jean-Luc, *Congo. Ambitions et désenchantements 1880-1960*, Karthala, Paris, 2017 (including a complete bibliography of his works, p. 495-503; second edition in 2021, with index).
9 An overview of these historical works can be found in Vanthemsche, Guy, 'The Historiography of Belgian Colonialism in the Congo', in Lévai, Csaba, ed., *Europe and the World in European Historiography*, Edizioni Plus – Pisa University Press, Pisa, 2006, p. 89-119 (can be downloaded via https://vub.academia.edu/GuyVanthemsche).
10 Delathuy, A.M., *E.D. Morel tegen Leopold II en de Kongostaat*, Epo, Berchem, 1985. Following this work, the same author published a series of titles about other dramatic aspects of the colonial Congo's history. The books by Guy De Boeck were likewise extremely critical about the colonization. See for example De Boeck, Guy, *Les héritiers de Léopold II ou l'anticolonialisme impossible*, Dialogue des Peuples, s.l., 2008, 3 vol.
11 Vangroenweghe, Daniel, *Rood rubber. Leopold II en zijn Kongo*, Elsevier, Brussels, 1985. The publication by Daniel Vangroenweghe of the famous Casement Report about the horrors of the Leopoldian regime (see Chapter 2), took place in 1985, in the academic series led by Jean-Luc Vellut (who also wrote an elaborate introduction for it). This publication did not receive the public response it deserved (série *Enquêtes et documents d'histoire africaine*, Louvain-la-Neuve, 1985, vol. 6). This shows that the academic world was well and truly aware of this tragedy.
12 De Witte, Ludo, *De moord op Lumumba*, Van Halewyck, Kessel-Lo, 1999.
13 Van Reybrouck, David, *Congo. Een geschiedenis*, De Bezige Bij, Amsterdam, 2010 (English translation: *Congo. The Epic History of a People*, Fourth Estate, London, 2014).
14 See Macola, Giacomo, *Una storia violenta. Potere e conflitti nel bacino del Congo (XVIII-XXI secolo)*, Viella, Roma, 2021.

Part I

Key Moments

AMANDINE LAURO, IDESBALD GODDEERIS
AND GUY VANTHEMSCHE

Introduction

Over the past twenty years, the media debate about the Belgian Congolese past has been focused primarily on two specific periods: Leopold II's Congo Free State (1885-1908), and the decolonization crisis (1960-1961) with the murder of Patrice Lumumba, the independent Congo's first Prime Minister. The focus on these two episodes has alas led to a neglect of other – less spectacular, but no less important – aspects of colonial history. The fact remains, however, that these were founding and/or climatic moments in colonial history. In this first part, we would like to take a fresh look at these, and at some other pivotal moments of the colonial era. By adopting a historian's perspective, we do not limit ourselves to the timeframe of the events in the strictest sense, or to the actions of the 'great men', but instead place the episodes in a wider context.

What exactly happened during colonization's initial era, i.e. the Congo Free State established by Leopold II and his all-in-all rather modest flock of officials both in Brussels and on the Congolese territory? How was this odd political entity created and how did it function (Chapter 2)? These questions inevitably lead to the next issue: can the mass violence during this period be considered a genocide? Answering this question involves a twofold investigation, both into the nature of the violence itself, and into the definition (or rather definitions) of the concept of genocide (Chapter 3). It also requires connecting Belgian Congolese history to wider, international historical dynamics. This dimension is discussed in the chapter examining the two world wars (Chapter 4). To what extent can these conflicts be regarded as pivotal points in the history of the colonial Congo? Did they herald a new era, or were they just an intermezzo? What role did they play in the growing protests against the colonial system?

Fifteen years after the victory of the Allied forces, the colonial regime came to an end. For Sub-Saharan Africa as a whole, the year 1960 was indisputably a milestone: within a period of just a few months, some seventeen countries became independent, including the Congo (Chapter 5). What provisions were made for decolonization? Was Belgium prepared to fully accept the political autonomy of its (former) colony? Because the official transfer of power on 30 June 1960, the day of independence, only partially reflects the complexity of decolonization, we will devote the last chapter of this part (Chapter 6) to the years immediately following independence. This enables us to frame the limits of this historical periodization as a question – because independence did not stop the former colonial relationships from continuing, albeit in new guises.

2. The Congo Free State

Plunder Machine in Service of a Ruthless Leopold II?

15 November 1908 was the date that determined Belgian and Congolese history. On that day, the Belgian Government took over Leopold II's Congo Free State. Belgium had to intervene. The position of its King had become untenable. At home and abroad media and activist groups condemned his colonial rule. Forced labor, mutilations, mass murder: Leopold was depicted as a money-grubbing megalomaniac in charge of a violent system of plunder that was ransacking the Congo.

But are these accusations correct? For decades a different narrative dominated. Shortly after Leopold's death, his memory and his colonial rule were rehabilitated and slotted into the 'Belgian civilizing' myth. Colonial government, missions, companies and associations, educational institutions and the press all promulgated the same apologetic and legitimizing discourse (see Chapter 24). According to this version, Leopold and his so-called pioneers charted the rich but primitive Congo and liberated its inhabitants from slavery, then instilled civilization within them. The narrative was that, at the end of his life, the visionary sovereign gifted his colony to the people, and the Belgians continued their civilizing efforts. The accusations directed at Leopold – insofar as these were made – were dismissed as fabrications and exaggerations from British quarters, in an attempt to discredit Leopold and snatch his colony.

The first cracks in this discourse only began to appear after independence. During the 1960s, 1970s and 1980s anthropologists and historians at American, Belgian and Congolese universities examined colonization afresh. They investigated how the colonial system worked in practice and began looking at the past from the perspective of the colonized population. In this way, they deconstructed the colonial myths around Leopold and his Congo Free State. According to these new interpretations, he did not bring civilization to the 'primitive Congolese man or woman'. The 'Congolese' man or woman had never existed and 'primitive' was the last thing they were. Different peoples and communities from the Congo Basin dealt differently with the advent of Leopold's Congo state. That state was far from omnipotent and out of sheer necessity adapted itself to the local context. The colonial system thus took shape in part from the bottom up. According to the researchers, 'civilizing' hardly featured. In practice, colonization meant violent suppression and exploitation for those people who came into contact with the colonizer.

These new academic insights had little impact on the Belgian memory of Leopold and the Congo Free State. The big shift only came around the new millennium with Adam Hochschild's 1998 book *King Leopold's Ghost: A Story of Greed, Terror and Heroism in Colonial Africa* and Peter Bate's 2003 documentary *Congo: White King, Red Rubber, Black Death*. Since then, public opinion has polarized sharply around the figure of Leopold and his Congo state. For some the King is once more an unscrupulous mass murderer who enriched himself at the cost of millions of Congolese lives. Others minimize the colonial wrongdoings and Leopold's responsibility for these, at the same time praising him for other accomplishments such as the architectural stamp he left on Belgium.

Who is right? Did a ruthless Leopold violently ransack the Congo to satisfy his hunger for power, prestige and money? Or is some nuance called for? How was the Congo ruled and exploited in practice? Was so much violent force really used, and if so, why? And what was its impact on the Congolese people? What role did the Congolese play in this colonial system? And how did a Belgian King manage to establish a colonial state in the middle of Africa? In order to answer those questions, we need to go back to the end of the 1860s, to a young King with a huge colonial ambition.

A Colonial Dream...

Leopold II had been dreaming of possessing a colony when he was still Duke of Brabant. Upon becoming King in 1865, he tried to realize these overseas ambitions. He could count on little enthusiasm from the Belgian establishment and population. Yet he was not alone. A group of intellectuals, academics, businessmen, priests, military, civil servants and diplomats shared his dream.

But why did the King and a section of the Belgian elite covet a colony? According to them, overseas expansion would boost the Belgian economy and lessen social tension in the country in the process. What is more, colonization would allow Belgium to expand into a magnificent nation, the center of an empire. Expansion offered many personal opportunities to make a profit and build a career as well, of course, but that was by no means Leopold's and his entourage's principal motive.

But why the Congo? Initially Leopold was not sure what form his overseas project would take. A classic colony that occupied and ruled a territory? A chartered company with exploitation rights? Nor was the King exclusively interested in Africa. He explored possibilities across the globe, from the Philippines to Crete. It was not until the 1870s that he alighted on Africa.

At that point, Africa was the only continent not to have been colonized by Europe. Great Britain, France, Portugal and Spain controlled small enclaves along the coast. The African interior, on the other hand, was one large blind spot for the Europeans. From the 1870s onwards, this suddenly changed. For the first time African colonization became achievable. Modern arms gave the Europeans military dominance. The introduction of quinine meant that they no longer died en masse from malaria. The telegraph, the train and the steamboat made communication and transport significantly faster and cheaper. Driven by geostrategic considerations and the economic potential of the unexplored continent, the European superpowers – established colonial powers such as Great Britain, as well as latecomers such as Germany – took their first steps towards the colonization of Africa. And all of this in the name of civilization and the fight against slavery.

Leopold wanted his share of the African cake and focused his attention on the Congo Basin. Travel accounts from the very first Europeans who had crossed the territory suggested to Leopold that there was a rich, uncultivated region strategically located in the heart of Central Africa. So, the Congo it was to be. But how?

... Comes True

At the end of the 1870s and the beginning of the 1880s, Leopold set up several so-called scientific and humanitarian organizations. These associations were supposed to chart the Congo Basin. In practice, they were the instruments of the colonial policy of their founder and principal funder, Leopold himself. The most important organization was the International Association of the Congo (AIC). It launched military expeditions, establishing posts and concluding treaties with Congolese kings, warlords and chiefs. Leopold thus laid the foundations for his colony in the name of science and philanthropy.

Leopold's AIC was not the only interested party in the Congo. France and Portugal claimed parts of the region as well. Because European interests were also colliding elsewhere in Africa, at the end of 1884 the then superpowers began to look for a solution. During the Berlin Conference diplomats drew up the rules for the colonization of Africa. Their chief concerns were geostrategic and commercial. All these superpowers wanted to secure their grip on this continent with its huge potential.

In the margins of the discussions in Berlin, bilateral negotiations were conducted about the territorial partitioning of Africa. Fortunately for Leopold, countries such as Great Britain feared France and Portugal's protectionist trade policy. In order to obtain the support of the other superpowers, Leopold appointed himself as a vocal champion of free trade. In his colony, traders would pay virtually no tax. No one would be awarded trade privileges. One by one the participating countries recognized the AIC territory as a new sovereign state, to be called *État Indépendant du Congo* or 'Independent Congo State' (generally known as the Congo Free State). Thus, on 1 June 1885, Leopold II, in addition to being the King of the Belgians, became the absolute monarch of a vast colony in the Congo Basin. A state with a territory as large as Western Europe. Belgium fitted into it roughly 75 times.

The Congo in 1885

Leopold's colonial dream finally came true in 1885. But of what exactly had he become sovereign? At the time many Europeans saw the Congo Basin as uncultivated territory full of potential, a kind of clean slate. But was this true? In fact, Leopold and his entourage hardly knew what they got themselves into. Only a few Europeans had crossed the immense region. Gradually it would become clear that the Congo was not the promised land the King and the Belgian colonial circles had dreamed of.

Many factors hampered the development of a colonial government and economy. First and foremost, the impenetrable rainforest, swamps and steep plateaus made large sections of the enormous territory difficult to access. Obviously, there were not yet any roads or railways to transport people and goods over land. Pack animals were not an option either, as they succumbed to the trypanosomiasis parasite, which was passed on by the tsetse fly. Overland transport – of goods *and* Europeans – was done on the backs of porters. Such manpower was absent in many places in the sparsely populated Central African interior. The hundreds of rivers in the Congo offered an alternative in some of the regions. But the many waterfalls and rapids rendered large parts of the Congo Basin unnavigable for European steamers.

Contrary to what the colonial discourse suggested, the Congo was not a clean slate either. The Congo Basin had a sizeable number of societies, each with their own government, economy and culture. Large sections of the vast area were divided amongst different African political powers. In the south, the Chokwe people were advancing, and there were areas where Arabo-Swahilis and Msiri's Nyamwezi held sway. The north was controlled by Sudanese Egypt. Until up into the eighteenth century the centuries old Kingdom of Kongo ruled over the Congo estuary and present-day Northern Angola. And these were only a few of the big political entities. It is also significant that the Congo was not isolated from the rest of the world. Trade networks along caravan routes and rivers connected the interior with Africa's east and west coast and even with the Mediterranean. Slaves, ivory and arms were important commodities. Leopold's colonial enterprise had to adjust in large measure to this Central African reality.

Explore, Occupy and Rule

In 1885 Leopold II became the head of state of the Congo Free State. But how did his colony take shape? What kind of administration did the King form? And what role did the population of the Congo Basin play in this? As soon as the Congo Free State saw the light of day, Leopold organized a number of large-scale expeditions to the farthest reaches of the territory that he claimed. These expeditions tended to involve a handful of European officers and dozens of African soldiers and porters. Local guides led them along existing trade routes and navigable rivers. Step by step the Congo was charted.

The idea behind the expeditions was also to occupy the Congo Basin as quickly as possible. In so doing Leopold wanted to steal a march on competitors such as France, Portugal and Great Britain and present them with a fait accompli. At the end of the 1880s there were no reliable maps of Central Africa. The first colonial border agreements were therefore extremely vague. The newborn Congo Free State was bordered by degrees of longitude and latitude formed by rivers, lakes or river basins, the courses of which were barely known (see map p. 368). Leopold tried to capitalize on this undetermined situation by having as many border regions occupied as possible before expeditions from other colonial superpowers arrived. The King thought: the bigger the colony, the greater the financial gain.

'Occupation' is a grand word. In practice the Congo Free State set up small government posts along the most important access roads and navigable rivers, usually a few days' travel apart. A few white officers and a dozen black soldiers exercised Leopold's authority. Thus, step by step, the expeditions extended the colonial presence. This process progressed slowly and was in fact never completed. Entire sections of the Congo remained beyond the reach of the Congo Free State: not only remote border regions such as Kivu in the east, but also parts of the often barely accessible interior.

By 1908, around a hundred posts had been set up in the Congo Free State, which were manned by a few hundred white officers and officials and some ten thousand black soldiers – the majority from the Congo. This was obviously insufficient to control a territory as big as Western Europe and a population of around ten to fifteen million inhabitants. So how did the colonizer exercise power? To a large extent, the Congo Free State relied on kings, sultans, warlords and chiefs who had ruled the Congo before the arrival of the Europeans. They were incorporated into the colonial system and governed their territory and subjects in the name of Leopold II (see Chapter 18).

Why did some of the Congolese rulers choose the side of the colonizer? Throwing in their lot with the Congo Free State had its advantages. A deal with the colonizer meant military support against internal competitors and hostile neighbors, but also access to arms and Western goods, and a new market for their products such as ivory. Moreover, the colonial government was far from omnipotent. This gave many leaders a margin to continue to rule in their own interest and in that of their people. But most importantly they had little choice. If you did not want to yield, you would be forced to do so sooner or later by the colonial army, the *Force Publique*. During these types of punitive expeditions Leopold's troops tended to lash out with extreme violence. Leaders who followed their own course too strongly suffered an equally violent fate.

The most famous example of unruly Congolese leaders were Arabo-Swahili warlords and traders including the well-known Tippu Tip. Initially, they ruled over the eastern part of the colony in Leopold's name. As long as they paid sufficient taxes in ivory and supported Leopold's expeditions with provisions, porters and soldiers there was no problem. But because some Arabo-Swahili leaders took an increasingly independent line, tensions rose. In 1892 they came to a head. The battles between the Congo Free State and its former allies set the Eastern Congo ablaze for two years. There were thousands of fatalities in both camps and amongst the civilian population. The colonial propaganda machine called the conflict 'the campaign against Arab slave traders' – an argument that is used in Leopold's defense to this day. This can be called ironic at the very least, because the Congo Free State itself recruited slaves and forced them to work as porters and soldiers – 'slave redemption' it was called. Moreover, for years Leopold had relied on Arabo-Swahili leaders to govern the Eastern Congo on his behalf.

The Congo Free State did not by any means bring everyone to their knees and the suppression of uprisings was a constant issue (see Chapter 16). Leaders such as Sultan Sasa in the Northern Uele region for instance continued to challenge central colonial authority. Even if he was officially an officer in the *Force Publique*, his will – and not Leopold II's – was law. It was not until 1912, under Belgian rule, that a military expedition managed to defeat Sasa's army of around 1,500 men and, to some extent, bring the region under control.

Impending Bankruptcy

Leopold's expeditions tried to map and occupy the Congo at breakneck speed. Those Congolese who did not want to take part would have to suffer. But how does the evolution of a ruthless system of plunder fit in this picture? Understanding this requires a look at Leopold's and his colony's disastrous financial situation. Creating a state machinery that had control of the enormous Congo was extremely expensive. Equipping and provisioning expeditions, setting up an army and civil service, constructing government posts, ports, roads and railways, etc.: despite all attempts at cutting costs, the colonization of the Congo cost huge amounts of money. And even Leopold's financial means were limited.

At the outset, the Congo was not the figurative goldmine that Leopold and his entourage had dreamt of. The administration in the colony itself was still in its infancy. The Congo Free State was only able to tax European firms which imported and exported merchandise via seaports such as Banana. But, apart from ivory, there was not yet all that much colonial trade to tax.

For years Leopold largely financed the Congo Free State with his own fortune. This meant he plunged ever more deeply into debt. Both King and colony were on the brink of bankruptcy at the beginning of the 1890s. In the end, Leopold had to appeal to the Belgian Government. In 1890, Belgium lent the King the necessary funds amounting to 25 million francs. This allowed for some brief breathing room. There was a major condition: Leopold had to get his colonial bookkeeping in order. Otherwise, he would have to hand over his colony to Belgium.

A new system of exploitation had to save Leopold's colonial project. The King instituted a ban on the trade of natural resources in virtually his entire colony. From then on, all raw materials belonged to the Congo Free State. In a large part of the Congo, its population had to collect natural resources – first ivory, but before long rubber, predominantly – as a kind of tax in kind or services rendered to the colonial government, which sold the proceeds in European ports such as Antwerp.

But Leopold also conceded a large part of his territory to private businesses (see Chapter 8). Some five companies were given an exploitation and trade monopoly over enormous territories, some bigger than France (see map p. 368). This monopoly had to win over investors – usually from Antwerp and Brussels. As sole buyer, a concession company would, after all, determine the prices, and could thus raise its profit margins considerably. The Congo Free State also benefitted from the concession system. Concession companies had to govern their territory themselves (although they could count on the support of the *Force Publique*), which meant a significant saving for the colonial government. What is more, the Congo Free State – and therefore Leopold as the major shareholder as well – shared in the profits.

Saved by Rubber

The new exploitation systems bore fruit; the colonial government's income grew steadily. The more the concession companies expanded their activities, the more the export of natural resources increased. But true salvation was not yet in sight. Expenses continued to rise. In 1895, the King had to appeal to the Belgian Government once again. The takeover of the Congo became the subject of debate in Parliament. Both the Government and the King were prepared to hand over the Congo to Belgium. But Leopold suddenly changed tack. He continued to hang on to 'his' Congo and procured another emergency loan. The future of Leopold's colonial project remained deeply uncertain, however. How long could this be maintained?

The Congo Free State's shaky financial position did not stabilize until the turn of the century when rubber prices shot up with lighting speed. More and more industrial products began to contain rubber – Dunlop and Michelin's rubber car and bicycle tires, for instance. Rubber production in countries such as Brazil was not able to keep up with the rapidly rising global demand. Moreover, several large producers and commercial firms pushed up the prices artificially by holding back rubber. This was the Congo Free State's salvation. The Congolese forests contained huge reserves. Thanks to the system of concessions and taxes in kind, Leopold's colony produced large quantities of rubber, which were sold for record prices in Antwerp.

The rubber boom provided a balance and even a surplus in the colonial budget. For Leopold this was the moment to pay off his debts and enlarge his fortune once more. He also wanted to invest a share of the colonial proceeds in various construction and urbanization projects in Belgium. With this goal in mind, he created the so-called Royal Domain, an area in the heart of the colony that was approximately ten times the size of Belgium. From 1900, part of the rubber proceeds from this Royal Domain ended up directly in the royal coffers. In addition, Leopold borrowed money in name of the Congo Free State and used these resources for his own urbanization projects in Belgium.

The Congo Free State's rubber system was considered a huge success. France copied and introduced it even into its own Central African colonies. This so-called success did have an extremely bloody underside, however.

Red Rubber

From a position of financial and economic scarcity, Leopold and his entourage developed an exploitation system based on taxes in kind, trade monopolies and concessions. In practice, the population was exploited with violence – to such an extent that Leopold's opponents spoke of 'red rubber', a reference to the Congolese blood that flowed. Why was so much violence used?

Harvesting rubber was not a popular job. The government and the concession companies did not invest in plantations. The Congolese had to look for rubber vines, which grew in the wild, deep in the forest. They produced rubber by scoring into the vine and allowing the extracted sap to harden. They then had to take this rubber to the nearest government or company post, often dozens of kilometers away. During this extremely time-consuming process they were exposed to the full range of the tropical forest's dangers. Meanwhile they were not able to fish or hunt or cultivate their fields. As a result of over-exploitation, the rubber gradually became depleted, and the population had to venture ever deeper into the forest to find new vines.

Because harvesting rubber was so hard to do, no one was keen to pay their rubber tax to the Congo Free State. Selling rubber to concession companies at rock-bottom prices was equally unpopular. And so, both the government and the concession companies used violence on a massive scale to force the population to produce rubber. Burnt-down villages, mutilations, rape, abductions, massacres, raids: when a village did not produce enough rubber, violence would follow. Terror was used to break individual or collective resistance and served as a warning.

The ways in which people were forced to produce rubber, and the amount of violence involved, varied from region to region. And yet the rubber system relied above all on terror and repression. Through a system of bonuses, promotions and fines, colonial officers, officials and concession staff were encouraged to push up rubber production permanently. At the same time, they lacked resources and manpower. Both the government and the rubber companies tried to keep costs down as much as possible. It was not a case of investing, but of plundering. What is more, the nearest government or concession post tended to be a few days' travel away and colonial officials, officers and company staff were largely out on their own. Violence or threats of violence were often the only way to force an entire population to hand over rubber using only a small number of soldiers. Racism legitimized that violence. The Congolese were considered a primitive and inferior race, work-shy toddlers who did not listen, who had to feel the strict hand of the 'civilized white man'.

In order to understand the massive violence, we should also look at the continuation of the nineteenth-century exploitation systems. During the second half of the nineteenth century, large sections of the Congo Basin had fallen into the hands of trade networks such as those controlled by the above-mentioned Arabo-Swahili. These networks linked the Congolese interior with the coasts of the Atlantic and Indian Oceans, and with Sudan and Egypt. In time, the traders created power bases in the Congo. From there, they went on the hunt, looking for slaves and ivory to export. They did not shrink from using violence. The line between trading, raiding and demanding tribute was often wafer-thin. Later, many of the traders, warlords and soldiers, but also the local chiefs who were active in these trade networks threw in their lot with the Congo Free State or concession companies, either voluntary or not. They did the dirty work because the Europeans were only there in small numbers. The violent tactics they had used previously to obtain slaves and ivory were now deployed to amass rubber.

Not all parts of the Congo were hit equally as bad. Yet in many places the impact of this violent rubber exploitation was disastrous. Entire regions were left practically depopulated. On top of the many direct rubber terror casualties, hunger, exhaustion and epidemics took a heavy toll among the weakened population. Many people fled. Birth rates plummeted (see Chapter 7). The crisis not only manifested itself demographically. Everywhere, the rubber regime left behind broken and traumatized societies. The heavy human toll paid by the Congolese population would, in the end, mean the demise of Leopold's colony.

Congolese Resistance and International Criticism

Around 1904, the Congo Free State's exploitation system came under increasing pressure. In many places, less and less rubber was being produced. Overexploitation exhausted the reserves. In some areas there were only few people left to produce it. Resistance grew. The population would sometimes deliberately cut off rubber vines in the hope of being left in peace. More and more desperate people took up arms. The plunder regime had reached its limits.

Moreover, criticism in the West intensified. In 1903, Roger Casement, the British Consul in the Congo, wrote a devastating report about Leopold's violent rule. The report triggered a great deal of debate, first in the media and later even in the British and Belgian Parliaments. In 1904, together with the British journalist Edmund Dene Morel and the Protestant missionary Henry Grattan Guinness, Casement set up the Congo Reform Association. This organization denounced the horrors in the Congo Free State in pamphlets, books, articles and public meetings. Above all, the photos of Congolese people with hands chopped-off unleashed a storm of indignation. The accusations against Leopold's rule of plunder should not be interpreted as a purely Western matter. Congolese individuals and groups would sometimes travel for miles and defy the colonial government and companies to testify against the rubber terror.

Under great pressure, the King tried to put right the situation. A new series of decrees were designed to curb the rubber regime's excesses. Congolese men would only have to work forty hours a month in the service of the colonial government or rubber companies, for instance. These kinds of measures changed little, however, because they were not implemented in practice. In addition, a large-scale media offensive was intended to exonerate the name of the King and the Congo Free State. The accusations were dismissed as a British conspiracy to discredit Leopold's regime and to divest him of his colony.

Under growing national and international pressure, the King decided in the summer of 1904 to send a commission of inquiry to the Congo. He selected the members of the commission himself, however, and personally corrected their final report. Yet the publication of this report, in 1905, heralded the end of the system. The commission of inquiry cautiously recognized the abuses. Its report formed the subject of a great deal of debate in Belgium. Supporters and opponents cherry-picked the information that suited them best. The anti-Leopold camp gradually won ground. Slowly, the conviction grew that the Belgian Government had to put an end to the sovereign's misrule. Meanwhile, diplomatic pressure from abroad also increased.

At the end of 1906 the decision was made. Belgium would take over the Congo. Contrary to the myth that Leopold gifted his colony to Belgium, the King did not let go of the Congo quite so easily. He tried to maintain as much control and power as possible. The difficult negotiations meant that the colony did not end up in Belgian hands until 1908.

Conclusion

It is clear that the Congo Free State was a far from philanthropic venture. The narrative that Leopold II liberated the Congolese population from slavery and later donated his colony to Belgium so that his subjects were able to continue their civilizing efforts, is pure propaganda. This discourse was meant to legitimize the Congo's colonization, but is miles removed from the historical reality.

In actuality, Leopold and his entourage preyed on the Congo in order to enrich themselves and their country, and to increase the international prestige of Belgium and its royal family. Once established, the Congo Free State was difficult to govern and exploit. The Congo was not the colonial horn of plenty some had dreamt of. Nor did the colonial state operate in a vacuum, because the Congo Basin was populated by different societies, each with their own rule, economy and culture. It was impossible for the colonizer to ignore this reality. Colonization was a laborious process. On the edge of bankruptcy, the King developed a system of exploitation based on taxes in kind, trade monopolies and concession companies. In practice, in many places the population was coerced into producing rubber with brute force. For Leopold and a section of the Belgian elite, this system proved to be an enormous financial success. Nonetheless, the Congolese population had to pay an extremely heavy price. Entire regions were left depopulated and completely destabilized.

Do Leopold and the Congo Free State represent colonial evil at its worst? A little nuance is called for here. The explanation for the violent way in which the Congo was looted does not lie solely with a ruthless Leopold and his insatiable hunger for power, wealth and prestige. Despite his central role, the King was only a piece in the total puzzle. A structural shortage of resources and impotence on the colonial side, combined with a racist civilizing philosophy as legitimizing doctrine, also help to explain for the Congo Free State's violent rule of plunder.

It is also essential to take into account the very different ways in which Congolese individuals, groups and communities dealt with the arrival of the colonizer. Some – by their own volition or not – participated in the colonial system, for example as chief, soldier or guide. Others rebelled, fled or cut down rubber vines. Thus, the Congolese contributed to shape the colonial system on the ground – which obviously does not alter the fact that Leopold's Congo Free State installed a violent rule of plunder which devastated countless lives. It is equally important not to generalize about all colonials. It was thanks to the charges made by Congolese *and* Western people, that Leopold's rule was ended. Colonial history is not a black-and-white story with solely black victims and white perpetrators.

Bibliography

Since the end of the nineteenth century, a great deal has been written about Leopold II's Congo Free State. A recent article which explains in a nuanced way why so much violence was used in the Congo Free State, is Roes, Aldwin, 'Towards a History of Mass Violence in the État Indépendant du Congo, 1885-1908', *South African Historical Journal*, 62, 2010, 4, p. 634-670. The underlying financial and politico-economic story is described in De Roo, Bas, *Colonial Taxation in Africa: A Fiscal History of the Congo through the Lens of Customs (1886-1914)*, doctoral thesis, Universiteit Gent, 2016. How the rubber system functioned, is revealed by Vangroenweghe, Daniel, *Rood rubber. Leopold II en zijn Kongo*, Van Halewyck, Antwerp, 2010 (1985). How the Congolese dealt with Leopold's yoke is set out well in Vansina, Jan, *Being Colonized: The Kuba Experience in Rural Congo, 1880-1960,* University of Wisconsin Press, Madison, 2010. Burroughs, Robert, *African Testimony in the Movement for Congo Reform: The Burden of Proof*, Routledge, London, 2018 chronicles the role of the Congolese in the international campaign against rubber violence. And then there is Stengers, Jean, *Congo. Mythes et réalités*, Racine, Brussels, 2005 (1989 reissue). This title explains clearly how Leopold acquired his colony and ultimately gave it up to Belgium. Leopold's role is also analyzed in the following works: Vandersmissen, Jan, *Koningen van de wereld. Leopold II en de aardrijkskundige beweging*, Acco, Leuven, 2009;

Viaene, Vincent, 'King Leopold's Imperialism and the Origins of the Belgian Colonial Party, 1860-1905', *Journal of Modern History*, 80, December 2008, p. 741-790; and Plasman, Pierre-Luc, *Léopold II, potentat congolais. L'action royale face à la violence coloniale*, Racine, Brussels, 2017. The reality of the colonial occupation is depicted by Zana Mathieu Etambala in *Congo veroverd, bezet, gekoloniseerd 1876-1914*, Sterck & De Vreese, Gorredijk, 2020 and *Onderworpen, onderdrukt, geplunderd. Congo 1876-1914*, Sterck & De Vreese, Gorredijk, 2023.

GEORGI VERBEECK

3. Was There a Genocide in the Congo Free State?

Few people doubt that Leopold II's rule in the Congo Free State (1885-1908) was a catastrophe for its inhabitants. Colonial propaganda about the Belgian King who brought the Congolese only 'civilization' and 'progress' (see Chapter 24), has gradually died out. Interestingly enough, contemporaries already knew about the plunder and large-scale violence in the Congo, and it was these facts that played a decisive role in the argument for the transfer of Leopold's Congo Free State to the Belgian Government. At that point the Congo became an official Belgian colony. For a long time – both during the colonial period and afterwards – the flattering picture of Leopold's 'civilizing mission' in Central Africa continued to dominate public memory. But since the ascent of critical historiography at the end of the previous century, and especially as a result of a renewed interest in everything relating to the colonial past since the beginning of this millennium, there is no getting away from it. Leopold II's rule forms a dark page in Belgium's history, and gradually a consensus has formed around this view.

Following years of historical research, the (extremely) violent character of Leopold's regime has been fairly well documented (see Chapter 2). The violence was primarily the consequence of ruthless economic exploitation. With the use of forced labor, reprisals and systemic terror the local population was mobilized to exploit natural resources. This all happened in the context of widely accepted racism, which negated the Congolese population's political, economic and cultural autonomy (see Chapter 17). And this despite a propagated benevolent paternalism, which formed part of the European 'civilizing offensive' (see Chapters 21-27). The occupation itself involved a great deal of violence and plunder, as well as punitive expeditions against rebellious groups and political rivals. Even more than the physical violence that resulted from economic sanctions, various diseases and starvation claimed many lives. All these factors led to general disintegration and a substantial population decline in the entire region. But it is around demographic figures and how they might be interpreted that a scientifically underpinned consensus proves much harder to achieve (see Chapter 7).

Historical research constantly oscillates between 'minimalist' and 'maximalist' estimates of the number of casualties. That the death toll can be in any case estimated to be high, has led to the question as to whether this was a case of *genocide*.

Definition of Genocide

The question of whether something can be described as genocide is essentially relatively easy to answer. In practice, however, new problems of interpretation crop up. The term 'genocide' goes back to the definition the Polish-Jewish legal scholar and lawyer Raphael Lemkin (1900-1959) gave in his book *Axis Rule in Occupied Europe* (1944). Lemkin's ideas were used implicitly by the International Military Tribunal at Nuremberg, and the United Nations adopted his definition at their Convention of 9 December 1948. According to this Convention, 'genocide' concerned 'acts committed with the intention to destroy, in whole or in part, a national, ethnic, racial or religious group'. And according to the Convention this can happen in five different ways by: (1) 'killing members of the group'; (2) 'causing serious bodily or mental harm to members of the group'; (3) 'deliberately inflicting on the group conditions of life calculated to bring about its physical destruction in whole or in part'; (4) 'imposing measures intended to prevent births within the group'; (5) and finally 'forcibly transferring children of the group to another group'.

What strikes the observer on close reading of the definition is that genocide differs in at least three ways from other forms of large-scale violence. The most important one is without doubt the aspect of *intention*, whereby a prior intention to kill an entire section of the population must be established. It is this aspect in particular that, in many cases, often proves to be difficult. Moreover, the definition refers to the 'destroying of groups', which presupposes at the very least a *systematic* approach to the killing of people, and therefore not violence as a kind of 'side effect', or something that 'got out of hand' and creates casualties merely 'randomly' (so-called 'collateral damage'). Finally, it has to involve violence against individuals in as far as they are *classified* as members of a group. They have to be killed not because of their individual acts, but because they are considered members of a group – at least from the perspective of the perpetrators.

In short, genocide differs from other forms of large-scale violence through a unique combination of voluntarism and determinism: *voluntarism* on the part of the perpetrators, who have a clearly worked-out plan and then implement this (or at least attempt to do so); *determinism* at the expense of the victims, who, once they have fallen into the hands of the perpetrators, are no longer able to extract themselves from their fate. It is by no means surprising, therefore, that after the Second World War the Holocaust would be remembered as the 'golden standard' of genocide. No one could doubt the intentional, systemic and global character of the murder of six million Jews by Nazi Germany. There are only a very few other instances in history to which this term could also apply. One particular example is the Armenian genocide under the Ottoman Empire during and shortly after the First World War. It is no surprise that this event also played a significant part in Lemkin's study and interpretation of genocide. But despite the striking similarities between both cases of genocide, a number of equally striking differences can be found, such as, in the Armenian case, the absence of a clearly formulated plan and its non-systemic implementation. It explains why some researchers are rather apprehensive about using the same term for different historical cases and it indicates why there continues to be great resistance from consecutive Turkish governments, for instance, to designate the mass murder of the Armenians as genocide.

The 'stricter' a definition of genocide is used, the more limited its scope. In such reasoning only a handful of historical examples fulfil these precise conditions. Beside the mass murder of the Armenians, the Rwandan genocide in 1994 comes closest to the Holocaust. And then there is another reason why many researchers opt for a limited use of the term 'genocide'. After all, its etymological meaning suggests it must always involve an act of mass-violence whereby the victim group is defined on the basis of belonging to a particular *genos*, in other words, a 'race', nation or people. This seems to lead to the conclusion that genocides in fact occur rather infrequently. The victims first have to be defined 'ethnically', so on the basis of features considered immutable ('race', skin color, morphology, etc.), which blocks the road to possible flight, conversion or adjustment.

It could be argued that the definition of genocide and its adoption at the 1948 UN Convention is rather a product of its time. It was indeed highly colored by the traumatic memories of the Second World War. The United Nations itself sprang forth from the spirit of 1945, a time when a large part of the world was still living in colonial dependence on mainly Western European nations. From a postcolonial perspective half a century later, the UN can be criticized for the bias it has exuded since its creation, but this had not led to the *definition* of 'genocide' as such being substantially discredited. In more recent years, Lemkin's definition of genocide has come under increasing scrutiny, especially in newer 'revisionist' trends in historical scholarship, but it essentially continues to inform the mainstream field of Holocaust and genocide studies. The experience of the Holocaust has indubitably triggered a strong interest in genocides in general – in Winston Churchill's words, genocide before the Second World War would have been a 'crime without a name' – and genocide studies have long after been a form of offshoot from Holocaust studies. Lemkin was very much a product of his time (and marked by his own traumatic experiences), but this does not mean he did not display a great interest in different cases of genocide and mass-violence over the course of history and in his own time.

'Genocide' in Plural

In order to do justice to the many manifestations of mass-violence and not narrow down the perspective to an ethnic dimension, fresh neologisms have been devised over the past few years to shed light on this multiplicity and complexity. 'Politicide' (or 'policide') is a form of violence that is akin to genocide, but aimed at political opponents (the mass murder of communists in Indonesia in 1965-1966, for instance). Comparable is the 'classicide' or destruction of a social class (such as the systemic mass murder of 'class enemies' under communist regimes). 'Democide' is used for the elimination of large sections of a state's own population (for whatever the reason: Stalin's Great Terror in the Soviet Union during the 1930s, the Great Leap Forward and the Cultural Revolution in Communist China between 1949 and 1976, and the Killing Fields in Cambodia during the Khmer Rouge regime between 1975 and 1979, for instance). 'Feminicide' has been used recently to denote the intentional killing of women because of the sheer fact that they are women. The terminological package to describe the different forms of mass violence has thus substantially expanded. A final example would be 'cultural genocide' which refers to the purposeful destruction of a particular social and cultural system, not necessarily its individual bearers. Many further neologisms with the suffix '-cide' (derived from *caedere*, the Latin term for 'to kill') have thus come into being.

Because 'genocide' is usually defined as an intentional and systemic process, researchers have begun to identify different stages in that process. In *Ten Stages of Genocide* (1996) American Law and Human Rights scholar Gregory Stanton defined ten essential phases genocide passes through. The preparatory phase includes processes such as classification, discrimination and stigmatization. This is followed by a phase of practical organization and preparation. Implementation and, interestingly enough, denial (negationism) only feature at the end. The denial of the genocide itself forms an intrinsic part of it: not only do sections of the population need to disappear physically from the face of the earth, the memory of their disappearance must also be wiped out; only then will the eradication be complete. The over-systemic character of Stanton's model can be criticized – and by no means all genocides go through the same stages in the same way – but it does offer insight into the distinctive dynamic that distinguishes a genocide from other forms of mass-violence. In fact, Stanton's framework helps researchers to look at different genocides in comparative perspective.

'Holocaust'

What applies to genocides in general, applies to the Holocaust in particular. Here too there is a kind of sliding scale between a 'strict' and a 'broad' definition. Most historians will be inclined to regard the Holocaust – many prefer the more accurate term 'judeocide' – as a prime example of genocide. The fundamental characteristics of a genocide can be clearly discerned in the destruction of European Jews during the Second World War. No other genocide appears to have effected what the extermination of the Jews has 'achieved': an ideologically motivated, technically-bureaucratically prepared and implemented mass-murder on an industrial scale which was unlimited and only unrealized in full because of practical reasons. Not for nothing did the German historian Hans Mommsen refer to the extermination of the Jews by the Nazis as *Realisierung des Utopischen* ('The realization of the unthinkable').

Within historiography, for years there has been an oscillation between the two extremes. Some historians argue (with good reason) on the basis of these unique characteristics that the Holocaust was an absolutely exceptional historical event.[1] Others (with equally good reasons) seek more deep-seated patterns (of categorization, stigmatization, exclusion, elimination) which do in fact make the Holocaust comparable to other large-scale destructions of human lives. It is precisely because of its strong iconic nature that the term 'Holocaust' is so often used to identify other events. The Holocaust, Tony Judt argued, thus becomes '*the* crime' against which all other crimes in history are measured. It is not unusual to talk about an 'American Indian Holocaust' (with regard to the fate of the indigenous populations of North America), or a 'black Holocaust' (calling to mind the transatlantic slave trade from Africa to the New World). In a polemic sense, a 'red Holocaust' is often used to refer to the death of millions of people during the Stalinist terror or under other communist regimes. Many more examples can be given from modern or contemporary history. To conclude, the fact that activists and some radical interest representatives use the term 'Holocaust' to reinforce their point of view, has led to a genuine inflation in the term's use. For instance, with good reason or not, some people speak of the danger of a 'nuclear Holocaust', and an 'animal Holocaust' (the mass-killing of animals in the food industry), a 'Babycaust' (abortion), or a *Vertreibungsholocaust* (used by extreme right-wing groups in Germany to refer to the flight and expulsion of ethnic Germans from various Central and Eastern European countries after the Second World War).

A Congolese Genocide?

The question as to whether the cruelties of the Congo Free State qualify as genocide depends largely on the way in which the definition has been applied strategically. According to Lemkin's interpretation, which influenced both international law and academic research, it is extremely difficult to define the violence during Leopold's regime in the Congo as genocide. A number of typical distinguishing features as described in Lemkin's classic definition are missing. It is hard to see how there could have been a conscious, intentional and systemically implemented extermination of a clearly defined group of people. In other words, in view of the very essence of the cruelties and terror (i.e. the 'internal logic'), very few or no indicators can be found that might justify the definition of genocide. You cannot say there was an eliminationist ideology or a systemic approach that was essentially targeted at every member of an entire group. The fact that there was a very clear case of racialist thinking (almost inherent in colonialism), cannot be enough to presuppose a more or less coherent *ideology*. What is more, it is not clear whether this worldview, held by many in Europe's nineteenth- and early twentieth-century civil society, would *inevitably* lead to large-scale violence. The violence and terror were also more likely a by-product of economic exploitation than the consequence of a pre-conceived plan to eliminate an entire population. Again, it is worth remembering that the Congolese were considered a labor force first, not members of an 'inferior race' who should all be killed. And finally, *especially* if one wishes to use Stanton's strict systematics, it would be difficult to see how the Congolese case would fit into this.

Not so much the nature as the *scope* of the violence – in other words: the number of deaths – had led some authors to speak of a genocide. So, is the term appropriate here? It remains prudent to bear in mind that the number of casualties, however high it may be, can never be taken as a decisive distinguishing feature of genocide. The number of casualties is largely irrelevant, and even a maximalist estimate does not in itself sufficiently substantiate the claim that there was really a genocide – even leaving aside the fact that demographic calculations about the fatalities in the Congo Free State are usually based on rough estimates (see Chapter 7). It could always be contended that 'incomplete' eradication does *not* have to rule out genocidal intentions – not *all* European Jews, or Armenians, or Tutsis were actually killed. But as previously stated, the merely quantitative dimension is irrelevant for determining whether something should qualify as genocide or not.

An overemphasis on the question of whether the violence in Leopold's Congo Free State can be regarded as genocide can cloud the view of the structure and patterns within which this violence developed. It did not necessarily unfold in a way that corresponds to many people's idea of a mass-murder. Over time, historians have repeatedly refined the image of the violence in the Congo Free State. This violence was not only an extension of economic exploitation, but equally a result of continuing wars and punitive expeditions. Besides, the violence was geographically spread out very unevenly. Some regions were considerably less affected than others. Just as crucial is the role of the colonial regime's indigenous soldiers and henchmen, who greatly contributed to the violence, perhaps more so in the practical execution of the atrocities than the Belgians in charge. The extremely small number of Belgians (and Europeans) present, compared to the total Congolese population, should be borne in mind. In addition, the Congo Free State lacked an efficient apparatus of central governance.

Of course, these are all factors that do not *in* and *of themselves* necessarily disqualify the notion of genocide. The relatively uneven spread of the violence, the cover of war and external aggression, and the involvement of local groups and individuals are factors we know from other genocides. The persecution of the Jews was a more complex story than the emblematic images from Auschwitz suggest. An initial determinant in the Congo was the fact that the dramatic demographic relapse of 1880-1920 was the result of rapidly declining birth rates, malnutrition and disease. These can be directly attributed to colonial occupation and rule but cannot necessarily be reduced to a genocidal policy. The violence was endemic and the economic exploitation was structural – both aspects stemmed from colonization itself – but that does not automatically mean that the deaths of hundreds of thousands (or even millions) were the consequence of a systematic policy. Debating the usefulness of the genocide concept should not obstruct a much more fundamental historical insight, namely that massive violence is (in many cases) inherent in colonial rule as such. And with that notion, historians place it in an even broader framework. Violence and colonization are linked to the fundamental experiences of what Eric Hobsbawm called the 'short twentieth century' or the 'age of extremes'. The German historian Christian Gerlach argued convincingly for replacing the term 'genocide' with 'extremely violent societies', something which might prevent a great deal of terminological confusion. That way, images of Auschwitz can no longer supplant those of 'red rubber'.

Various Voices in Historiography

When exploring academic literature about the history of the Congo Free State, what is most striking is the lack of consensus and persistent terminological confusion. The Congo is also rarely absent from the growing flow of genocide studies. It should be noted however, that these are often summaries which tend to be based on older literature, including testimonials from contemporaries which are not always particularly reliable. The fact that the Congo is frequently included in wide-ranging surveys of historical and more recent genocides does not necessarily mean that compelling proof of a 'Congolese genocide' is being established. (It should also be noted that the term 'Congolese genocide' is often used in a different historical context and in a much wider sense, i.e. to denote the wars in the Eastern Congo after the fall of Mobutu.)

The work of specialized historians, either from Belgium or elsewhere, does not inevitably present a more unambiguous picture. There is again no consensus, and a conspicuous caution about the use of the term 'genocide' is notable. During the 1980s, critical historiography about the Congo gained momentum, with pioneering work by A.M. Delathuy (pseudonym for Jules Marchal) and Daniel Vangroenweghe. The metaphor 'red rubber' to refer to Leopold's terror regime began to be adopted widely. The work of both historians was not welcomed by everyone, and more cautious observers questioned some methodological inaccuracies. Delathuy made an explicit comparison with the Holocaust. Vangroenweghe was generally slightly more restrained, but the suggested number of casualties left little to the imagination. Inevitably, the controversy about the nature of Leopold's regime became linked to the issue of demographic developments in Central Africa, a discussion that is still ongoing.

Historians who speak unequivocally of a genocide are few and far between. Not coincidentally, these are often non-Belgian authors, who do not need to give such strong consideration to still-present colonial nostalgia. In 2003, Robert G. Weisbrod, himself a specialist in Afro-American history and in the role of the Vatican during the Second World War, spoke in no uncertain terms of 'a holocaust before Hitler's Holocaust' (while playing with the difference between small and capital letters). The fact that the entire Congolese population was not killed is insufficient to qualify 'red rubber' as *not* genocide, Weisbrod believed. British author Martin Ewans posited in 2002 that 'Leopold's regime in Africa was synonymous with exploitation and genocide'. US historian Georges Nzongola-Ntalaja expressed himself in similar terms. The 2003 BBC documentary *Congo: White King, Red Rubber, Black Death* to which various Belgian and other historians contributed, referred to 'genocide' as well, admittedly reluctantly and only at the end of the narrative.

And the inventor of the concept of 'genocide' himself? Lemkin's view was by no means limited to Europe alone, and he gave ample space to and had much interest in the violence of European colonizers and settlers in the New World. Unpublished texts from the early 1950s shed light on his view of the events in the German colony of South West Africa (present-day Namibia) and the Congo Free State. The German mass murders of the Herero and Nama peoples carried out in their *Schutzgebiet* ('protectorate') during the period 1904-1908, is presented as a true genocide by many historians. The number of deaths (estimates fluctuate between 50,000 and 70,000) is not comparable in scope to that in the Congo, and the mass murder was the direct result of a military operation (and should therefore instead be qualified as a conventional war crime). But the fact that an explicit *Vernichtungsbefehl* ('annihilation order') had been issued (fairly unique in historical perspective), that the German military command clearly had a *Rassenkrieg* ('race war') in mind and that non-combatants were sent systemically to their deaths strongly argues for the use of the term 'genocide'. For historians who like to talk about a German *Sonderweg* ('special path') there are plenty of reasons to depict the mass murder of the Herero and Nama as a preparation for the industrial murder of European Jews during the Second World War. Colonialism and genocide – including the Holocaust as a culmination – thus form a sliding scale.

Lemkin was insufficiently informed about all the details of the mass violence in Namibia and based his insights largely on the British perception of German colonialism that had arisen after the First World War (the British took over most of the German colonies in 1919, including South West Africa, which was turned into a mandate of the League of Nation, administered by the Union of South Africa). The violence and crimes the Germans had perpetrated were now accounted for by the British as typically German ('Prussian') militaristic traditions, and products of their inadequate colonial structures. The latter would seemingly compare adversely with the benevolent model of colonial rule that the British employed in their own Empire. And Lemkin finally pointed out, in keeping with the position often heard in times of global colonialism, that the Herero had allegedly decided to commit 'racial suicide'. The inability to protect themselves against the genocide, which manifested itself amongst other things in sharply reduced birth rates, was indeed foisted upon the victims themselves.

Lemkin unequivocally described the excesses in the Congo as genocide. However, he did make a glaring overestimate of the demographic drop, and clearly did not base his claims on reliable sources. A striking aspect is that, at the time, both the Namibian and the Congolese issues were met with an international response that was very similar in a number of respects. It was no coincidence that in both cases it was the British especially who levelled strong criticism at what, in their view, were the consequences of disastrous colonial policies in the competing imperial powers. (Conversely, the British had been accused in the international press of wrongdoing against the Boers in South Africa during the 1899-1902 war.) In both cases, Lemkin undoubtedly allowed himself to be influenced by the British perspective. It is notable that, in both cases, the role of the colonized peoples themselves is placed in a very particular light. Lemkin's observation of the events in the Congo were indeed strongly influenced by a Eurocentric and racialist view of the local African population. He emphasized above all the role of the Congolese themselves in the atrocities and the excessive violence. And besides, he showed himself to be a principled supporter of colonization, whereby he took as his starting point that it was only the European civilizing offensive that could save Africa from its indigenous 'barbarism'. He was also full of praise for Leopold II's initial 'philanthropic' objectives when launching his project in 1884-1885. In short, Lemkin's definition of genocide has fundamentally influenced the work of historians and other academics up to this day, but from today's viewpoint, his political and social views would most certainly be qualified as colonialist and racist.

Above all it was popular books, rather than the work of professional historians, that reached a wide audience and fueled discussions about a possible genocide. The 1998 work *King Leopold's Ghost* by the American journalist Adam Hochschild definitively reopened the debate. The book was translated into Dutch and French shortly afterwards and found a wide readership in Belgium, as well as beyond. The author adopted without question the maximalist estimate of the number of victims, but recoiled from using the term 'genocide' – let alone 'Holocaust' – without ifs and buts. Admittedly, it was 'a death toll of Holocaust dimensions', but for Hochschild there was ultimately no genocide in the strictest sense. Nonetheless there had been unprecedented slaughter through human action. 'Sifting such figures today is like sifting the ruins of an Auschwitz crematorium,' wrote Hochschild. A similar caution could be found in the equally popular book *Congo, A History* which appeared in 2010, by the Flemish author and cultural historian David Van Reybrouck. He referred to a '*hecatomb*, a massacre on an unimaginable scale which was not intended, but could have been better understood as collateral damage by a perfidious, rapacious policy of exploitation, an offer on the altar of a morbid quest for profit'. Following the older work of A.M. Delathuy amongst others, Van Reybrouck used a concept that refers to an ancient Greek practice whereby a hundred bulls were sacrificed to the gods. The term is a metaphor for a slaughter on a huge scale, either for a higher purpose or not.

In other words, by far the majority of historians and researchers hesitate to recognize the violence in the Congo Free State as genocide. Likewise, the term 'Holocaust' finds greater acceptance in the media and in public debate than in academic historiography. Most historians will agree with the conclusion by Canadian sociologist Rhoda Howard-Hassmann that there was no genocide, not even when viewed from a retrospective viewpoint. The absence of intention and a methodologically implemented policy are decisive factors for rejecting it as genocide. In Leopold's Congo there was no state, nor any other authority that set its sights on the systemic killing of an entire section of the population. The discussion about the magnitude of the demographic catastrophe during Leopold's rule may be interesting in itself, but in the genocide controversy it is largely irrelevant. The more thoroughly Leopold's regime is examined, the more the absence of the central characteristic of a genocide manifests itself. This also turned out to be the case in a recent study by Pierre-Luc Plasman, who made a searching analysis of the Congo Free State's political structures. He too dismisses the thesis that there had been a genocide, notwithstanding the systemic terror and magnitude of the human catastrophe.

Conclusion

It could be argued, as Guy Vanthemsche quite rightly does, that endless semantic discussions are not always the most useful tools to advance historical understanding. Historians are not expected to engage in this kind of terminological hair-splitting when exploring other topics. No one objects the use of terms such as 'crusade', 'inquisition' or 'witch hunt' when they are used metaphorically in other contexts, and if they do not necessarily refer to dubious practices in the Middle Ages or early modern history. In the case of Leopold's regime in the Congo, it is almost inevitable (and understandable) that quite a few historians fall back on images which suggest at the very least a similarity with or proximity of a genocide, or even the Holocaust. 'Semi-genocidal' or 'comparable to a genocide' are terms which might offer a way out.

But even more advisable would perhaps be to follow historian Christian Gerlach's suggestion, mentioned earlier. The world of the twentieth century – and that of the late nineteenth as a precursor – offered the technical, administrative and psychological conditions for extreme violence. Genocides in the more strict and technical sense are merely exceptional instances of this. The fact that it is so difficult to entirely avoid the reference to genocide has a great deal to do with the political and moral implications of the term. It underlines that, contrary to Belgium's own perception of itself as a small and innocent nation, its history also includes some very dark chapters. It furthermore emphasizes the inevitability of historical responsibility and does not wholly exclude the obligation of a form of reparation. And yet historians could be well advised to use terms as accurately as possible in order to arrive at a well-rounded analysis and interpretation of their sources. For the time being, it seems as if much historical knowledge has been accumulated, but that not everything will ever be fully known.

Bibliography

Genocide studies make up a growing research domain that is relevant for both historians and other scholars. There are a considerable number of commendable introductions that give an overview of historical (and recent) examples. In addition, much attention is traditionally devoted to questions of a theoretical and conceptual nature (what is genocide and how can the concept be defined?). Examples that also discuss the Congolese issue are: Jones, Adam, *Genocide: A Comprehensive Introduction*, Routledge, London-New

York, 2011 (2nd edition); Bloxham, Donald, and Moses, Dirk A., *The Oxford Handbook of Genocide Studies*, Oxford University Press, Oxford, 2010; Barth, Boris, *Genozid. Völkermord im 20. Jahrhundert*, Beck Verlag, Munich, 2006. A good introduction to the question as to exactly what genocide is, is offered by Shaw, Martin, *What Is Genocide?*, Polity Press, Cambridge, 2007. Gregory Stanton's 'ten stages of genocide' can be found on http://genocidewatch.net/genocide-2/8-stages-of-genocide/. Innovative and above all relevant to historians is Gerlach, Christian, *Extremely Violent Societies. Mass Violence in the Twentieth Century World*, Cambridge University Press, Cambridge-New York, 2012. On genocide in an African context: Stapleton, Timothy J., *A History of Genocide in Africa*, ABC-CLIO, Santa Barbara-Denver, 2017. About Raphael Lemkin's vision on colonial violence in Africa (and notably in German South West Africa and the Congo Free State) there is the short but interesting article by Schaller, Dominik J., 'Raphael Lemkin's View of European Colonial Rule in Africa: Between Condemnation and Admiration', *Journal of Genocide Research*, 7, 2005, 4, p. 531-538. About violence in the Congo Free State, see above all: Vangroenweghe, Daniel, *Rood rubber. Leopold II en zijn Congo*, Van Halewyck, Leuven, 2010 (3rd edition) (has also been translated into French); Delathuy, A.M., *Missie en staat in Oud-Kongo 1880-1914. Witte paters, scheutisten en jezuïeten*, Epo, Berchem, 1992. Non-Belgian authors who speak specifically about a genocide are: Weisbrod, Robert G., 'The King, the Cardinal, and the Pope: Leopold II's Genocide in the Congo and the Vatican', *Journal of Genocide Research*, 5, 2003, 1, p. 35-45; Ewans, Richard, *European Atrocity, African Catastrophe: Leopold II, the Congo Free State and its Aftermath*, Routledge, London, 2002. Furthermore, a driver of the debate: Hochschild, Adam, *King Leopold's Ghost: A Story of Greed, Terror and Heroism in Colonial Africa*, Houghton Mifflin, Boston, 1998. In the French translation, the work had been given the subtitle *Un holocauste oublié* ('A Forgotten Holocaust'), causing a controversy in national and international media. Interestingly, the German publisher took a more cautious stance and omitted all references to the Jewish genocide; here the subtitle was *Die Geschichte eines der großen, fast vergessenen Menschheitsverbrechen* ('The Story of a Great, Almost Forgotten Crime Against Humanity'). For the responses to the publication of Hochschild's book, see also: Dumoulin, Michel, *Léopold II. Un roi génocidaire?*, Académie Royale de Belgique, Brussels, 2005; De Mul, Sarah, 'The Holocaust as a Paradigm for the Congo Atrocities: Adam Hochschild's *King Leopold's Ghost*', *Criticism*, 53, 2011, 4, p. 587-606. For more recent literature about the violence in the Congo Free State: Roes, Aldwin,

'Towards a History of Mass Violence in the État Indépendant du Congo, 1885-1908', *South African Historical Journal*, 62, 2010, 4, p. 634-670; Plasman, Pierre-Luc, *Léopold II, potentat congolais. L'action royale face à la violence coloniale*, Racine, Brussels, 2017. Finally, various historical overviews also discuss the question of the 'genocidal' character of the Congo Free State. See for instance (not an exhaustive list): Nzongola-Ntalaja, Georges, *The Congo from Leopold to Kabila: A People's History*, Zed Books, London-New York, 2002; Ndaywel è Nziem, Isidore, *Nouvelle histoire du Congo. Des origines à la République démocratique*, Le Cri, Brussels, 2009; Van Reybrouck, David, *Congo. The Epic History of a People*, HarperCollins, New York, 2014; Vanthemsche, Guy, *Belgium and the Congo, 1885-1980*, Cambridge University Press, Cambridge-New York, 2012. In that context, reference should also be made to a recent monograph by one of the most productive Belgian historians in the field of colonial history and also a most expert voice in the debate about the violence in Leopold's Congo: Vellut, Jean-Luc, *Congo. Ambitions et désenchantements 1880-1960*, Karthala, Paris, 2017.

Notes

[1] Some authors have suggested to distinguish between 'Holocaust' and 'holocaust', whereby the capitalized version refers to the Jewish Holocaust during the Second World War and the latter to other massacres metaphorically compared to the Nazi extermination of the Jewish people in Europe. This text will continue to use the capitalized version 'Holocaust' precisely because of the intrinsically universalizing claim.

GUY VANTHEMSCHE

4. Two World Wars

A Turning Point in the History of the Congo and its People?

Between 1914 and 1918, and once again between 1939 and 1945, Africa was dragged into a world war. For countries across the world, and their inhabitants, these conflicts not only constituted a terrible ordeal, but also an important political, economic, social and cultural breaking point. Did this also apply to Sub-Saharan Africa, which stayed largely out of the firing line? When we focus on the Belgian Congo, the following questions crop up: were both conflicts sensed as something that was happening close by, or far away? Did they really mark the end of an era and the beginning of a new one? And how did the Congolese people experience these wars, which were forced upon them by their white rulers? Were the Congolese spectators or active participants, and were they heroes or victims? All these specific questions are ultimately linked to a more general issue: what role did the Congo play in these two cataclysms? In what follows we would like to shed light in particular on the Congolese dimension of the conflict, which is often overlooked in historiography. For this reason, we will only touch briefly upon the Congo's impact on warring Belgium – however important this may be.

Human Aspect of War

During the First World War, the Congo was not directly affected by combat, except for a few clashes on the eastern border in 1914, the short-lived German occupation of the island of Idjwi in Lake Kivu, and the naval battles on Lake Tanganyika (1915-1916). Apart from these incidents, the armed conflict took place outside Congolese territory. Following a few short campaigns in Cameroon and Northern Rhodesia (1914-1916), the *Force Publique*, the Belgian colonial army, participated in longer campaigns in German East Africa (present-day Tanzania). Thanks to some important victories, it secured a large part of the German colony (occupation of Ruanda-Urundi; the capture of Tabora and Mahenge, 1916-1917). During the Second World War the scene of action was even further removed from the Congo. The *Force Publique* inflicted several defeats on the Italians in Abyssinia (in Asosa, Gambela and Saïo, 1941). A Congolese expeditionary force was then sent to Nigeria (at the time a British colony), and subsequently to Egypt and Palestine (1942-1944), but these soldiers were never deployed during battle. In addition, *Force Publique* military hospitals were active in Somalia, Madagascar and Burma (1940-1946).

In 1914, the *Force Publique* numbered some 15,000 Congolese soldiers and non-commissioned officers. By 1917 this number had risen to 25,000. All things considered, this was a relatively small cohort out of ten million Congolese, especially when taking into account that the *Force Publique* was not only the army, but also the national police force. For the campaign in German East Africa, around 12,000 Congolese troops were mobilized. In total, 1,895 Congolese soldiers lost their lives – more as a result of disease than in battle. But wars cost not only the lives of the military. In order to supply the forces, many porters were put to work, often accompanied by an unknown number of women. Over the total duration of the war, an estimated 260,000 porters were recruited. These men were often forced to leave their villages and had to drag heavy loads over huge distances in atrocious conditions. The death rate in this group was appallingly high: some 27,000 of them died.[1]

On the eve of the Second World War, the size of the *Force Publique* was comparable to what it had been in 1914. The number of Congolese soldiers then amounted to 14,730. In 1942, their number had risen to 34,349. Many thousands of these soldiers had been sent into action outside the Congo: 3,380 in Abyssinia (plus 2,328 porters), around 8,000 in Nigeria (plus 4,000 porters), 7,750 in the Middle East, and a few hundred elsewhere. Notably fewer lives were lost than in the First World War: a 'mere' 440 Congolese soldiers and 240 porters died during these operations, usually as a result of disease.[2]

Judging from these bare figures, it would seem that the world wars in the Congo claimed fewer lives than other ordeals, such as slavery, colonial conquest, forced labor, famines, etc. Each loss of human life in a war is of course deplorable and tragic, but a cynical observer might conclude that the two conflicts in the Congo did not cause a 'demographic bloodletting'.[3]

At any rate, the number of casualties would have been higher if the Belgian Government had deployed Congolese troops on the European front. Unlike the French and British, who sent hundreds of thousands of African and Indian soldiers to Europe during the First World War, the Belgians refused to take that course. This decision did not stem from humanitarian concern, nor from skepticism about the fighting qualities of the Congolese (on the contrary: the

Belgian officers thought highly of 'their' black soldiers, whom they regarded as generally brave and disciplined). Rather, the Belgian authorities feared the long-term effects the arrival of Congolese soldiers in Belgium would have. Their presence in the 'motherland' might indeed tarnish the white man's 'prestige', one of the (assumed or real?) pillars of colonial dominion. If these black servicemen were to see the less rosy side of life in Europe, were to witness white men slaughtering each other and would have to kill whites themselves, then these same soldiers might adopt a much less submissive attitude after their return to the Congo and, who knows, might even become rebellious. Besides, the fear of sexual relations between black soldiers and white women also played a role in the decision to keep the *Force Publique* at a far remove from the European front.

In the end, only 32 Congolese men fought in Europe during the First World War. These men were already in Belgium, volunteered to join the Belgian army and formed part of the 'Congolese Volunteers Corps' (which also included white men) (see Chapter 14). Just like their Belgian colleagues, these Congolese soldiers fared in different ways. Some died of disease; a few were made prisoners of war; others survived the war in good health, or disabled, and/or ill; one or two deserted; three soldiers were found guilty of insubordination.

The Congolese also stayed in Africa during the Second World War. To the great dissatisfaction of some Belgian officers, the *Force Publique* expedition corps stationed in the Middle East was not allowed to take part in the liberation of the old continent, officially because the British refused. But the Belgian Government in exile in London did not insist either on deploying its Congolese soldiers in Europe. Minister of Colonies Albert De Vleeschauwer, in particular, strongly opposed this.[4] So we can only guess what political and psychological effect the entry of Congolese troops in a liberated Brussels in September 1944 would have had...

In both the First and the Second World War, the Congo was of great significance to Belgium. During the First World War, the victories in German East Africa allowed the 'motherland' to show its colors in front of the other warring nations. After the conflict, this military tour de force was even rewarded by the League of Nations with the mandate over Ruanda and Urundi. These two areas captured from the Germans were henceforth under Belgian guardianship. During the Second World War, the Congo had an even stronger determining influence over the fate of Belgium. In June 1940, the Congo joined the British camp and thus continued its fight against Nazi Germany. The decision, which was essentially taken by Governor-General Pierre Ryckmans and Albert De Vleeschauwer, contributed in a crucial way to the establishment and functioning of a legitimate Belgian Government in exile. The 'free Belgium' that sided with the allies continued to exist (and even enjoyed a certain standing) thanks to the Congolese trump card it held. This 'Belgian' dimension of the Congolese involvement leads us straight to the pure 'Congolese' dimension, on which we will focus primarily, as indicated in the introduction.

The War: A Terrible Ordeal for Congolese Workers

Both the Belgian and the British authorities believed that the Congolese were much more useful as workers than as armed forces. Modern wars require enormous quantities of raw materials. The Congo, as an 'inexhaustible' source of natural resources, had to do its part to supply the Allied powers. In the First World War, the exploitation of those resources was still in its infancy, but under the pressure of war, the production of cotton, palm oil, rice, copper and gold increased significantly – amongst others, through coercive measures (one example: the ordinance of 20 February 1917 imposed compulsory sixty days of agricultural work a year; see Chapters 9 and 11). In the Second World War, the by then well-developed mineral and agricultural production was pushed to its limit, for example palm oil from plantations went up from 18,217 metric tonnes in 1938 to 33,869 in 1944; tin from 11,150 metric tonnes in 1939 to 22,300 in 1944; copper from 122,600 tonnes in 1939 to 165,500 in 1944; rubber from 1,014 tonnes in 1938 to 2,095 in 1944, harvested by 'natives' who were forced once again to set to work deep in the rainforest; etc. The Congolese uranium that was used to build the American atomic bombs was already stored in New York at the start of the famous Manhattan Project, the objective of which was to provide America with nuclear arms.

It is obvious that both world wars had a big impact on Congolese life: the economic efforts took a heavy toll, especially during the Second World War. The decree of 10 March 1942 raised the number of days of mandatory labor to 120 a year. Moreover, forced labor for European companies or other production tasks was imposed on an increasing number of Congolese men. The total of Congolese salaried workers rose spectacularly: from 480,000 in 1938 to 800,000 in 1945. For many of them this meant a radical change in environment since they had to leave their villages in order to go and work in (semi-)urbanized centers. Because of this accelerated proletarianization (and urbanization), more and more Congolese were forced to buy products for basic needs from the market. But because of the war the import of consumer goods into the Congo shrank. The result: rising demand was countered by limited supply, meaning prices went up. Moreover, import products also became increasingly expensive because of the devaluation of the Congolese franc in 1941, a consequence of the linking of the Congolese currency to the British pound. In an attempt to halt surging inflation, the Government introduced price controls. But neither these measures, nor the growth of the processing industry in the Congo succeeded in countering the loss in purchasing power. The Congolese living standard, which was already very low, dropped even further. The Government itself admitted that 'the ordinary laborer and the farmer in the forest live in worse circumstances [than in] 1939'.[5]

Because of the war, many Congolese therefore had to work harder for less income. They were clearly the 'social victims' of a conflict in which they were not directly involved. The white population, also affected by the strenuous war effort and by inflation, voiced its displeasure by demanding pay-rises and even by going on strike. But the Congolese – already deeply frustrated before 1940 – expressed their grievances not only by making demands or resorting to all forms of disobedience. They also had recourse to outright revolts or other 'modern' social movements – even if these actions were usually smothered in blood or suppressed by means of other coercive measures (see Chapters 15 and 16). In 1941, the workers of the UMHK went on strike. That same year, riots among the workers of *Géomines* erupted in Manono. In 1945, the dockers of Matadi downed tools. In 1944, a mutiny broke out in the garrison of the *Force Publique* in Luluabourg. All these 'disturbances' showed clearly that a large part of the Congolese population, exhausted by the war effort, was at the end of its tether. It would be wrong to describe these tensions as manifestations of a 'pre-nationalist' striving for independence, but they did open the eyes of the Belgian Government, which began to see that a more 'social' colonial policy was desirable, and even urgently needed.

Political and Cultural Fault Lines?

Starting from this last conclusion, we can ask ourselves which political and cultural developments were set in motion by the two world wars. Were these wars in fact pivotal moments in the history of the country? We should make a distinction here between purely institutional aspects on the one hand, and socio-economic factors and changing mentalities on the other. Before 1914, the Congo was a Belgian colony, and it remained such for a further fifteen years after 1945. The two global conflicts did not immediately cause a rift in the political regime – contrary to what happened in many other colonies, especially in Asia. Having said this, subtle changes could be detected, which did not manifest themselves on an institutional level, but more in the sphere of altered sensitivities, mentalities, perceptions, and actions. After the annexation of 1908, the Belgian Congo was often regarded with skepticism, both internationally and domestically. Many actors and observers doubted whether a small country like Belgium could govern such a huge African colony. After the First World War, that doubt had largely dissipated. To exploit the extensive natural resources of its colony, the importance of which had become even more evident during the war, Belgium invested vast amounts of capital in the Congo. After 1918, the 'motherland' gained more self-confidence and strengthened the psychological and economic ties with its colony. Belgium reinforced its status as a colonizing nation since it had been assigned the mandate over Ruanda-Urundi. After 1945, certain white circles in the Congo called for political reforms, but these did not come about. More than ever, the Congo remained Belgian, and no major institutional changes were implemented. The Second World War thus did not inoculate the 'independence virus' into the Congo, and until 1955 the colonial authorities assumed that Belgian presence in the Congo would be long-lasting. The Congolese themselves gave them little cause to think otherwise, because they did not articulate an autonomous nationalist discourse until 1956 (see Chapter 5).

But as stated earlier, the Belgian authorities were increasingly aware that the over-exploitation of resources, and of the population of the Congo in particular, was not sustainable (see Chapter 13). Economic structures and policies were amended, which had to go hand-in-hand with social reforms. Post 1945 the yoke of suppression and repression pressing down on the Congolese was gradually lightened, without disappearing altogether. The living standard of many Congolese improved, especially in the cities. Because of this material improvement, the hardships of the war were gradually forgotten.

The wars also influenced Congolese minds. The campaigns were still fresh in the memory of the Congolese war veterans and those around them, but recognition of their efforts by the colonial authorities or the 'motherland' was long in coming, or minimal. Material compensation, in the shape of pensions, allowances, etc., was modest, or was paid late or not at all. There was symbolic recognition, in the shape of medals for the 'valiant' (282 Congolese soldiers were awarded a medal for exemplary conduct in the First World War), and later in the shape of sporadic monuments and ceremonies as well. Yet generally, Belgium paid little attention to the war contribution by the Congolese, as soldiers or (to an even lesser extent) as porters or laborers. This led to a dual psychological reaction in the Congolese concerned, and later also in wider circles. On the one hand, through their role in the 'wars of the whites', the awareness grew that they belonged to a national community in the making (the Congolese community, not the Belgian). This was evident from the fact that, in November 1919, the Congolese veterans who had fought on the European front set up the *Union Congolaise – Société de Secours et de Développement Moral et Intellectuel de la Race Noire* ('Congolese Union – Society for Assistance and Moral and Intellectual Development of the Black Race'), the first organization to give a voice to Congolese grievances. One of its founders was Paul Panda Farnana, who is seen as the patriarch of Congolese nationalism. However, amongst other Congolese people, participation in the war and the subsequent lack of recognition led to feelings of resentment towards the Belgian 'bosses', whom they had always defended and served loyally... Nowadays, the Congolese population has no more than a vague memory of the role their country and their ancestors had played in the world wars. But those who keep the memory of the Congolese soldiers alive do so in two ways: these soldiers are sometimes presented in the Congo itself as paragons of dedication and heroism who even to this day are worth imitating; or they are presented as forgotten victims, especially amongst the Congolese diaspora in Belgium, who are working hard for better recognition of their contribution.

Conclusion

The two world wars did not form major fault lines in the history of the Congo. Yet they amounted to more than an interlude. They brought existing tendencies to a head – colonial subordination to Belgium and the Congo's economic exploitation – but added new priorities, especially after 1945, when policymakers switched to more social and 'modern' policies. The Congolese for their part were far more than passive onlookers in conflicts which took place far away from their own country. Indeed, they were assigned an active role, notably as producers of raw materials which proved to be indispensable for conducting these wars. This role – which they were literally forced into – also made them war victims, because they paid a heavy toll for this enormous production effort. The role of the Congolese as military actors was more limited, especially in the Second World War. But in the collective memory, the battles in which they took part and in which Congolese lives were sacrificed – sacrifices which in the eyes of the Congolese were insufficiently recognized by a plainly ungrateful Belgium – had bestowed on these soldiers the status of hero within the embryonic Congolese nation, a nation which is simultaneously embedded in and shaped by Belgian history, but which wanted to free itself from that.

Bibliography

For a long time, historians have focused chiefly on the Second World War. Evidence of this in particular is the pioneering work by Lovens, Maurice, *L'effort militaire de guerre du Congo belge (1940-1944)*, CÉDAF, Brussels, 1975 (*Les Cahiers du CÉDAF*, 1975-1976) and the acts of a colloquium organized by the Royal Academy of Overseas Sciences (*Belgisch-Congo tijdens de Tweede Wereldoorlog*, ARSOM/KAOW, Brussels, 1983). The study by Janssens, Émile, *Contribution à l'histoire militaire du Congo belge pendant la Seconde Guerre mondiale*, 3 volumes, s.l., 1982-1984, is a non-academic source edition. For more details about the impact of the colony on Belgium during the Second World War we refer to Vanthemsche, Guy, *Belgium and the Congo, 1885-1980*, Cambridge University Press, Cambridge, 2012.

Recently we have seen an explosive increase in titles about the First World War, with a source edition (Vanthemsche, Guy, *Le Congo belge pendant la Première Guerre mondiale. Les rapports du ministre des Colonies Jules Renkin au roi Albert Ier 1914-1918*, Commission Royale d'Histoire, Brussels, 2009), but, above all, with many excellent studies, such as the innovative De Waele, Jan, 'Voor Vorst en Vaderland. Zwarte soldaten en dragers tijdens de Eerste Wereldoorlog in Congo', *Militaria Belgica*, 2007-2008, p. 113-132, and the articles from the special issue in the *Journal of Belgian History/Revue Belge d'Histoire Contemporaine*, 48, 2018, 1-2: 'Congo during the First World War'. The works by various Congolese historians have been collected in the acts of a colloquium in Kinshasa (Ndaywel, Isidore, and Mabiala, Pamphile, eds., *Le Congo belge dans la Première Guerre mondiale (1914-1918)*, L'Harmattan, Paris, 2015). Pamphile Mabiala has also published multiple further studies about the *Force Publique*, too many to list here. To conclude, we would like to refer to the following monographs: Brosens, Griet, *Congo aan den Yzer. De 32 Congolese soldaten van het Belgisch leger in de Eerste Wereldoorlog*, Manteau, Antwerp, 2013; Cornet, Anne, 'Le soldat congolais dans la Grande Guerre. Un oublié de la propagande de guerre belge?', *Outre-Mers. Revue d'Histoire*, 1er semestre 2016,

390-391, p. 211-233; Stanard, Matthew, 'Digging in: The Great War and the Roots of Belgian Empire', in Tait Jarboe, Andrew, and Fogarty, Richard S., eds., *Empires in World War One*, I.B. Tauris, London, 2014, p. 23-48.

Notes

1 De Waele, Jan, 'Voor Vorst en Vaderland. Zwarte soldaten en dragers tijdens de Eerste Wereldoorlog in Congo', *Militaria Belgica*, 2007-2008, p. 126-128.
2 The figures are from the studies by M. Lovens and E. Janssens (passim).
3 We should not forget the disastrous impact of the Spanish flu in this either, an indirect consequence of the war, from which, around 1918, the world's entire population had to suffer.
4 Govaerts, Bert, *Ik alleen! Een biografie van Albert De Vleeschauwer*, Houtekiet, Antwerp, 2012, p. 307.
5 *Jaarverslag over het bestuur van de kolonie van Belgisch-Kongo voor de jaren 1945-1946*, Brussels, 1948, p. 9.

JEAN OMASOMBO TSHONDA AND
GUY VANTHEMSCHE

5. 1960

The End of the Colonization of the Congo?

Although a great deal of time had passed since the creation of Leopold II's Congo Free State in 1885, during the 1950s the Belgian colonizers still considered their 'indigenous pupils' unable to govern by themselves the modern country that Belgium had created. Moreover, Belgium used this as justification for its ongoing colonization. Yet history accelerated rapidly around the end of that decade, and by 1958 the end of Belgian sovereignty in the Congo seemed inevitable.

In this chapter we would like to examine the reasons for this shift. We will focus primarily on initiatives by the Congolese population itself. Nonetheless, we should also ask ourselves what exactly the words 'the end of Belgian sovereignty' mean. Did the Belgian Government really intend to give the Congo full independence? Or did it secure a position for itself in which it could continue to influence or even exercise control over this vast African country? In the 24 months that preceded 30 June 1960 – the date that marked the official end of Belgian colonization – a great deal happened: all kinds of maneuvers, abrupt changes of direction and, for some, disillusionment. In other words, the question mark in the title of this chapter is not just some typo. It was placed there deliberately and signifies that the purely legal action that was taken on 30 June is insufficient for comprehending the complexity of the events that took place in the Congo.

The Sudden Breakthrough of Congolese Demands (1956-1959)

For quite some time the Congolese had been airing their frustration and anger in different ways; at times through open revolt, but also through less clearly defined actions (see Chapter 16). But during the second half of the 1950s, their dissatisfaction acquired a political face, in the classical sense of the term. The social group that is usually referred to as *évolués*, was disappointed and frustrated because of the false promises and interminable foot-dragging of the

Belgian colonial policies (concerning the granting of rights, wage demands, etc.; see Chapter 18). In 1956, the politicization of the debate took on a concrete form with the 'Manifesto' published in the journal *Conscience Africaine*, and the subsequent 'counter-manifesto' by the Alliance of the Bakongo (ABAKO). The first document, drawn up by a group of Catholic Congolese (who were inspired by Belgians with the same faith, as it happens), voiced for the first time the wish to politically emancipate the Congo. The second manifesto was sharper in tone and argued for the introduction of a multi-party system in the country, which the authors believed should free itself from Belgium in the near future. The ABAKO had been set up in 1950 as a cultural association for the Kongo people, the largest population group in Bas-Congo, but gradually emerged as a true political party, of which, from 1954 onwards, Joseph Kasa-Vubu was one of the best-known leaders. Another milestone: Patrice Lumumba, a young *évolué*, who had first worked as a post office employee in Stanleyville and then as a sales representative for a brewery in Léopoldville, co-founded the National Congolese Movement (MNC) on 5 October 1958. Together with two other Congolese, Joseph Ngalula and Cyrille Adoula, he took part in the pan-African conference in Accra in mid-December. Under the auspices of the Ghanaian President Kwame Nkrumah, this conference assembled leaders of colonized African countries with the goal to 'offer subordinated people all the necessary help in their struggle for self-determination and independence'. On 28 December 1958 the MNC held its first mass meeting in Léopoldville during Lumumba's journey to Accra. Lumumba, who at the time was considered 'dangerous and difficult' by the Belgians in Stanleyville, stated during that meeting: 'The independence that we demand, may not be seen by Belgium as a gift that it can give to us. We want to assert a right that the Congolese people have lost.' His audience exulted. For the first time in the history of the Congo, a country 'without a history' according to the whites, the crowd chanted: *Dipenda! Dipenda! Dipenda!* ('Independence! Independence! Independence!').

Its aftermath saw a host of other parties being formed in quick succession. Just like the ABAKO, many formations had an ethnic or regional basis. The Confederation of Tribal Associations of Katanga (CONAKAT), under the leadership of Moïse Tshombe and Godefroid Munongo, was set up in the south of Katanga. The General Association of the Baluba of Katanga (BALUBAKAT), led by Jason Sendwe, was active in the north of that province. The African Solidarity Party (PSA) was based in Kwilu and was headed by Antoine Gizenga, Cléophas Kamitatu and Pierre Mulele. The African Regrouping Center (CEREA) was rooted in Kivu and had as its leaders Anicet Kashamura and Jean-Chrysostome Weregemere. The Mongo Union (UNIMO) had its home in the districts of Équateur Province and in the Tshuapa, with Eugène Ndjoku, Léon Engulu and Justin Bomboko as the prime movers. The ASSORECO (later renamed the National Unity Party – PUNA), led by Jean Bolikango, represented solely the Bangala. This fragmentation partly stemmed from the colonial management of the Congo: the 'indigenous' population was not allowed to move around the national territory without permission from the administration (namely a travel visa called a *laissez-passer*), and the Congolese therefore had to carry on living in their original environment. Political formations with a national scope, such as the MNC, were thus very rare. The National Progress Party (PNP) followed this example, but it was founded on the initiative of the colonial authorities. Moreover, the MNC split, because of a dispute between Lumumba and its other co-founders. The break-away would later be led by Albert Kalonji, who restored the new party MNC/K to an ethnic expression of the Luba-Kasaï (Lubilanji).

The authorities expected an uprising among the workers in Katanga, but instead the first disturbances occurred in Léopoldville, followed by Stanleyville. These two popular revolts, the first at the beginning of 1959 and the second at the end of that year, shook the colony to its core. On 4 January, an ABAKO meeting was banned, which led to three days of looting and violence; 42 fatalities and 250 injured were reported officially, all Congolese. The Belgian authorities realized that the situation in Bas-Congo was deteriorating fast, because from a political viewpoint, contact was no longer possible with its population. In the middle of 1959, strikes and violent conflicts broke out in several regions in the Congo, in particular in the provinces of Kasaï and Kivu. In October, events took place in Stanleyville which set ablaze the entire district and intensified the resistance against anything related to the colonial administration. Twenty-six people lost their lives and dozens of people sustained gunshot wounds. On 30 October, the colonial government called for Lumumba's arrest, which meant he was no longer able to go to the MNC conference, due to be held in Stanleyville.

The foundations of the colonial structure seemed to be collapsing. The black community now had its martyrs, and it was no longer the generally anonymous people from the interior who lost their lives during the military 'expeditions' or 'promenades' by the *Force Publique*. Collections were held for the family members of the arrested leaders, in many villages the inhabitants refused to pay tax, and in the province of Bas-Congo branches of the ABAKO mushroomed. All of a sudden, the colonial governance model, which allowed the territorial administrators a great deal of freedom to go even further than the already extremely suppressive laws for the Congolese population, seemed hopelessly antiquated. Because Belgium had not devised a coherent, future-oriented policy, it did not know how to respond to this watershed in its colonial history. It hung on to its image of the black person as a 'mendacious, primitive and lazy charge' who, in less than a century, had been liberated from his 'barbarian state' by Belgian 'geniality'. Because Belgium was imbued down to its subconscious with such colonialist views, it failed to adjust to the changing situation. Just as the Congolese noisily demanded their independence, the colonizer came to a dramatic realization. No changing of the guard had been anticipated, and the Africanization of all institutions (the army, the administration, private companies) was still in its infancy.

The Belgian Response: How to Act in this Explosive Situation?

In this turbulent context it was untenable for the Belgian Government to maintain its wait-and-see stance. White man's prestige had been dealt a blow and political protests only grew. What is more, a decolonization process was underway across the entire Sub-Saharan Africa. On 24 August 1958, General Charles de Gaulle, at the time chairing the French Cabinet, opened the door to independence for the French colonies with a ground-breaking speech in Brazzaville, on the other side of the Congo River. Belgian politicians, under great time pressure and increasingly in panic, had to think about the future of the colony. Governor-General Léo Pétillon was appointed Minister of Colonies on 5 July 1958. He was the confidant of King Baudouin, who, as we shall see shortly, followed his own course in the Congo situation. At the beginning of August, a parliamentary commission was set up. This 'working group' had to explore the political future of the Congo and take into consideration the wishes and grievances of 'both the white and black population of the Congo'. The colonized resented the fact that the group had no Congolese members. The Belgians had imported their political sensitivities into the colony by setting up socialist, liberal and Catholic 'friends circles'; the communists likewise were active in the Congo. But as soon as they were confronted with the pressing problem of decolonization, the traditional Belgian political parties largely put aside their quarrels. Right from its inception the working group was not accepted by the Congolese population, who wanted to express their own opinions about their own future. From the end of 1958, this frustration led to an accelerated politicization amongst the Congolese.

On 6 November that year, Pétillon was succeeded by Maurice Van Hemelrijck. The Minister of the Belgian Congo and Ruanda-Urundi had no experience in the Congolese arena, but thought he could move things along. He wanted to repair *in extremis* the human and moral harm by acting as an intermediary for both the Congolese and the Belgians. He was not unanimously supported by the Belgian political class, however. Some politicians were still opposed to Congolese independence. The Government policy statement of 13 January 1959, which was drafted after the working group had finished, equivocated about the future of the colony. In addition, as luck would have it, it coincided with the unexpected riots in Léopoldville on 4 January. It was a missed opportunity, in other words. But in a radio speech that same day, i.e. 13 January, King Baudouin stated in no uncertain terms that the Congo would most certainly become independent 'without impetuous haste, but also without disastrous dawdling'. The King thus put the contrary Belgian politicians on the spot. The Monarch calmed people's feelings in the Congo and gave the population hope that something would finally change.

That hope proved to be short-lived. Van Hemelrijck's policy could not count on the unanimous support of white public opinion. In financial circles the Minister was dismissed as a 'progressive', and some Belgians in the Congo believed he had adopted too friendly an attitude towards the Congolese. The latter for their part no longer had any confidence in the colonial administration but appreciated Van Hemelrijck's apparent wish to do something about the Congo situation. He did indeed draw up a statement supplementary to the one issued on 13 January, this time with Congolese cooperation and now *with* a precise calendar for the establishment of new institutions, including as a final goal the creation of a Congolese Government in 1960. He also resisted the splitting up of the colony into smaller political entities. However, he ran up against resistance within his own Christian democratic party, and the Government likewise refused to accept his proposals. This explains Van Hemelrijck's resignation on 2 September 1959, whereby he stated himself to be 'disillusioned, battle-weary and disgusted'.

To make matters even more complicated, King Baudouin had his own agenda, because he saw a prominent role in store for himself (or another member of the royal family) in an independent Congo. Complementing this strategy amongst other things was the King's surprise visit to the Congo in the middle of December 1959, an entirely personal initiative; he wanted to keep his finger on the colony's pulse. When Baudouin left Stanleyville on 19 December, he expressed his disappointment in a personal exchange with the Governor of Orientale Province: 'We will leave the Congo behind disgracefully and many people will lose their lives.'[1] It was clear pessimism prevailed in Belgium's highest circles.

At the same time, another – crucial – aspect became clear: the Belgian Government did not want to use violence to restore order in the Congo. The colony was too big, and the resources Belgium had at its disposal were too small. The dramatic experiences in other colonies, which had fallen prey to decolonization wars, stopped the Belgian political parties from deploying the army. The Belgians and Congolese were therefore 'condemned' to a dialogue. On 3 September 1959, the new Minister for the Belgian Congo, August De Schryver, inherited this explosive dossier. He was unable to propose a clear strategy and keep events under control. On 3 November, in the Chamber of Representatives, he announced a 'general consultation' to take place in Léopoldville between 20 and 30 November, shortly before the local Congolese elections that the Belgian authorities wanted to hold in December. This was boycotted by the Congolese parties. When De Schryver traveled to Léopoldville on 21 November, he indicated that the consultation would not take place after all. Instead, he opted for individual talks with the leaders of the cartel that the ABAKO, the PSA and the MNC/K had formed. They simply refused to enter into a 'dialogue' with him and demanded a 'roundtable conference' in Brussels before the December elections. On 26 November the Minister came with a compromise solution: he agreed to the roundtable conference in Brussels, but not until January 1960, so after the elections. Moreover, he did not rule out that the conference would take place alternately in Belgium and the Congo. In the end, these important negotiations were held in Brussels alone. They were attended by 44 representatives from 15 Congolese parties (all accompanied by Belgian advisers, except for the MNC/L) and by the three big traditional Belgian parties (Christian democrats, liberals and socialists). The Belgian authorities counted on the Congolese representatives having little experience and had therefore not prepared sufficiently for the meeting. In so doing, they took a daring gamble, because they hoped to be able to end 75 years of colonialism in one major two-act meeting.

The Two Roundtable Conferences (1960): Full or Limited Independence?

The roundtable conference from 20 January to 20 February 1960 was the first political dialogue between Belgians and Congolese in their colonial history. It was chaired by Albert Lilar, Vice Prime Minister, who had indicated in a government statement of 13 January 1959 that the term 'independence' should be avoided. As soon as the conference started it became deadlocked in a discussion about the program. The Congolese delegates, who aspired to form a true *Front Commun* ('Common Front'), first and foremost wanted clarity about the date of independence. They also demanded the immediate release of Lumumba, who had been given a six-month prison sentence in Stanleyville on 21 January. The Belgian Government agreed to this demand and on 26 January flew Lumumba to Brussels. Upon arrival, he resisted Belgian authority; his release had given him the status of statesman. On 27 January the decision was made to grant the Congo independence in the very immediate future, on 30 June, as the Congolese had proposed. De Schryver concurred with this on behalf of Belgium, amidst applause from the Belgian and Congolese delegations.

This was followed by the crucial debate about the political structure of the future Congolese state. Minister De Schryver proposed that King Baudouin would become the Congo's head of state. Several Congolese leaders, Lumumba amongst them, rejected this. On 16 February Lumumba declared that 'on 1 July [1960] the Congo's head of state should be Congolese, just as Belgium's head of state is Belgian'. Baudouin had set aside his dream of playing a leading role in an independent Congo. The problem of Congolese independence went much further than this specific issue, however. The Belgians wanted to keep control of certain crucial powers (more specifically, defense, finance and foreign affairs) – a proposal that was rejected by the majority of the Congolese representatives, who had obviously set their sights on full independence. During the session of 28 January, socialist Senator Henri Rolin made a statement which everyone agreed with: 'Yesterday, I compared independence with passing on the bunch of keys of the new home that is the Congo. It is my opinion that Belgium should hand over all the keys to the Congolese, and they can decide for themselves how to use these.'

Did the Belgians therefore give up all claims to a position of control in the independent Congo? Not at all, it appears from a 'conversation' on 1 March 1960 in the Prime Minister's office between Harold d'Aspremont Lynden, Prime Minister Gaston Eyskens's Deputy Chief of Staff, and Arthur Doucy, Professor at the ULB and a specialist in African affairs. During that meeting, a comprehensive plan was drawn up for [the] governance of the Congo during the months leading up to independence, but also afterwards. Among the many points discussed in the official report, the following intentions stand out: '[...] 3. Political action. Lumumba must be eliminated. Emphasize his foreign contacts as much as possible. A re-grouping of the moderate forces in all provinces [...]. These parties should be given at their disposal technicians, propaganda tools and funds. In total this would cost 50 million at most.'[2]

In other words, the Belgian authorities wanted to embed themselves in the pro-Belgian black elite in order to secure lasting control over the Congo. In so doing, they behaved like phorid flies, who lay their eggs in the body of their prey, the fire ant, so that these act as a living incubator for their offspring. Confronted by the emergence of cities, presented earlier as outposts of civilization, but now developing into hotbeds of resistance, the Belgian authorities wanted to consolidate the African customary law and traditional structures they believed were the country's only 'stable framework' (see Chapter 18). Dovetailing this was the establishment in November 1959 of the PNP, with the support of the colonial administration (which is why the party was also called mockingly the *Parti des Nègres Payés*, 'Party of the Paid Blacks'), as well as the multitudinous presence of traditional chiefs in its delegation at the roundtable conference in Brussels (which comprised a quarter of the total Congolese representation).

During the roundtable conference, the political structures of the future Congo began to take shape. Inspired by the Belgian constitutional model, a bicameral parliamentary system was introduced (a chamber of representatives, directly chosen on the basis of a male universal single vote system, and a senate, composed of representatives from the provincial assemblies). The essence of the executive branch lay in the hands of the prime minister, who led the government. The president was the head of state and was elected by both assemblies but played a more discreet political role. The Congolese state was unitary but consisted of provinces which had been given their own powers. The promised elections took place in May 1960. They resulted in a resounding victory for the local parties that had fought for independence, in particular Lumumba's MNC, supporter of the unitarian outlook. He became the first Prime Minister of the independent Congo. Joseph Kasa-Vubu, who advocated federalism, was appointed President of the Republic.

An array of problems, which had been raised during the discussion, were *not* resolved at the roundtable conference. This included the apportioning of powers with regard to education, underground resources, etc. Lumumba also broached the statute of the *Force Publique* and was concerned about the presence of Belgian troops in the bases of Kitona and Kamina. Minister De Schryver replied that the *Force Publique* would be at the service of the Congolese Government and that the issue of Belgian soldiers could only be sorted out after 1 July, by means of a technical accord between the Belgian and Congolese Governments. This undecided issue would later form the basis of mutiny within the *Force Publique*, which broke out on 4 July 1960, after the Belgian General Émile Janssens, at that time still in post as its commanding officer, in the presence of his troops, wrote a famous line on a blackboard: *Avant l'indépendance = après l'indépendance* ('Before independence = after independence').

Another sizeable challenge was the Congo's economic situation, which was very worrying (see Chapter 13). The colony was weighed down by a very large national debt. Since 1957, budget deficits had been piling up. These serious problems were discussed during the second conference in the Belgian capital, the 'economic roundtable' (April-May 1960). Initially, the Belgians tried to keep the Congo in their grip via a 'Development Fund', which was to be managed by both Belgians and Congolese. The latter rejected this, because they feared entering into opaque engagements which would have grave consequences for their country. In the wake of this conference, all kinds of relationships were forged between Belgian leaders and members of the Congolese elite, particularly recent graduates who let themselves be guided by purely material advantages.

Very few concrete measures thus came out of this second roundtable conference – except for the promise to disband the so-called 'charter companies', i.e. the semi-public, semi-private companies that controlled large parts of the Congolese economy (see Chapter 8). This disbandment took place on 27 June 1960, three days before independence, with a law that was adopted in the Belgian Parliament. The measure implied that the Congolese Government would lose its control over the UMHK and other large companies, amongst other things. The biggest problem, that of Congolese public debt, had not been settled – nor the many other complex economic and social issues the new Congo would soon have to deal with. Once independence had been proclaimed, the situation became even more complex because of the greediness with which several foreign powers eyed the vast, rich and strategically positioned country.

In great haste, another measure was taken. On 29 June, a few short hours before Belgium handed over power to the new Congolese Government, a Belgian Congolese pact of friendship was signed. This last-minute accord limited, amongst other things, the military actions Belgium was allowed to carry out – a crucial factor in the dramatic events which were to shake up the young African republic not long afterwards...

Conclusion

On 30 June 1960, the independence of the Congo was pronounced with a festive ceremony in Léopoldville. On the face of it, the two peoples, the Belgians and the Congolese, parted peacefully, in the spirit of friendship and harmonious relations. The interlocutors seemed to have succeeded in their intention: during the roundtable conference of January-February 1960 they had reached a unanimously agreed accord in record time and had shaped the political structures of the independent Congo – including trouble-free parliamentary elections. Tragically, in 1959, Congolese blood had been shed when the riots in Léopoldville and Stanleyville were quashed. But compared to the long and bloody colonial wars that the Netherlands, France, Portugal and even Great Britain had waged, Belgium and the Congo came through relatively unscathed. Indubitably, Premier Lumumba's unexpected speech cast a shadow over the cordial atmosphere during the festivities of 30 June. In response to the extremely paternalistic speech by King Baudouin, who eulogized the work of Leopold II and his successors in charge of the colony, the Congolese leader recalled the suppression by colonial rule and the suffering the Congolese population had endured. The incident was indicative of the lasting difference in mentality: while the highest Belgian authorities were still thinking with a colonialist mindset, some Congolese wanted to break completely with the colonial period. Things are seldom what they seem, because behind the apparent success of a consensual independence lurked a reality that was not only much more complex, but even distinctly negative.

The lack of political vision, characteristic of that pursued by the colonial policy, led to the hasty independence of the Congo and lay at the foundation of the chaos that followed. Only as late as 1958 did the Belgian Government attend to the future of the country. At that time, gradual Congolese integration into the exercise of power did not yet feature. Africanization of the policy frameworks did not exist. Everything had to be devised and implemented in great haste. The Belgian Government, taken aback by how suddenly the debate and Congolese actions had politicized and radicalized, wanted, in whatever way, to continue to exercise control over the future Congo.

In the end, the Belgian authorities dropped all the excessively explicit forms of institutional interference. In the spring of 1960, there was therefore no longer any talk of powers which would be 'exclusively for the Belgians', nor about a monarchical union between Belgium and the Congo in the person of King Baudouin or one of his family members. But Belgian political *and* economic leaders (at least some of them) did not give up their ambition to advise or even steer future Congolese leaders from near or afar. This power struggle played out in utmost secrecy, in a twilight zone that formed the scene for all kinds of manipulations and maneuvers that jeopardized the future of the young independent Congo.

The apparent success of the Belgian Congo's decolonization soon turned into tragic, startling mistakes and disillusionments, the consequences of which can be felt to this day. The question as to whether the eventful story of decolonization turned out to be a success or a fiasco, cannot therefore be answered if we stop the analysis at a stroke on 30 June 1960. This moment was but the beginning of a long crisis (see Chapter 6), and in our evaluation we must inevitably take into account the continuing massacres and chaos the Congo experienced after the official end of Belgian colonial administration.

Bibliography

During the 1960s several standard titles about the decolonization of the Belgian Congo appeared, including: Young, Crawford, *Politics in the Congo*, Princeton University Press, Princeton, 1965 and Bouvier, Paule, *L'accession du Congo à l'indépendance*, Éditions de l'Institut de Sociologie de l'ULB, Brussels, 1965. During the middle of the 1970s the following book was published with testimonials by important agents: De Vos, Pierre, ed., *La décolonisation. Les événements du Congo de 1959 à 1967*, Éditions ABC, Brussels, 1975. The economic situation was analyzed by Saïd, Shafik-G., *De Léopoldville à Kinshasa. La situation économique et financière au Congo ex-belge au jour de l'indépendance*, Centre National pour l'Étude des Problèmes Sociaux de l'Industrialisation en Afrique Noire, Brussels, 1969, and also by Marres, Jacques, and Vermast, Yvan, *Le Congo assassiné*, Éditions Max Arnold, Brussels, 1974. During the subsequent years several synthetical works followed, including Vanderlinden, Jacques, *La crise congolaise*, Éditions Complexe, Brussels, 1985, and Etambala, Mathieu Zana Aziza, *De teloorgang van een modelkolonie: Belgisch Congo (1958-1960)*, Acco, Leuven, 2008. Source publications such as *Congo 1959* and *Congo 1960*, Crisp, Brussels, 1960-1961, have enabled easier access to contemporary documents. Amongst the many publications by witnesses of or actors in the decolonization period we would also like to mention Dumont, Georges-Henri, *La table ronde belgo-congolaise (janvier-février 1960)*, Éditions Universitaires, Paris, 1961 and Ganshof van der Meersch, Walter J., *Congo mai-juin 1960*, s.l., 1960.

Notes

1 Leroy, Pierre, *Journal de la Province-Orientale. Décembre 1958-mai 1960*, Presses de la Buanderie, Mons, 1965, p. 177.
2 AfricaMuseum, Vandewalle Archive, 'VDW. Rapports – Notes 1959-1960', copy of a document from the Prime Minister's Cabinet, 2 March 1960, 'Conversation avec Mr. Doucy – 1er mars 1960, notes de Harold d'Aspremont Lynden'.

EMMANUEL GERARD

6. The Congo Crisis (1960-1963)

Proof of a Failed Decolonization?

On 30 June 1960 the Congo became independent, but only a few days after the transfer of sovereignty, the country found itself caught up in a maelstrom of dramatic events that plunged it into chaos and anarchy. Belgium sent troops to its former colony and the Congo severed diplomatic relations with Brussels. The UN stepped in with a full-scale operation. The Congo Crisis, which was to stir up global opinion for years, was born. How did matters reach this pitch? Why was Patrice Lumumba's Government, which had only just taken office, incapable of controlling the crisis? And how could this crisis escalate from a local mutiny into an international flashpoint? In short, what went wrong with decolonization?

Worthless Guarantees

No colony or territory has ever gone through a flawless decolonization process. In any case, from which viewpoint could that process be considered successful? In general, decolonization stands for rupture, not continuity. It brings about a repositioning of the relationship between the new state and the former colonial power, and a power struggle between elites in the new state; this is often accompanied by violence. In the Congo all these elements were present, but the crisis came faster and with more brutality than expected. UN Secretary-General Dag Hammarskjöld and his closest associates repeatedly laid the blame squarely on Belgium and its disastrous Congo politics, before and after 30 June 1960. The international community also considered Belgium's policy generally as a failure, often ignoring the problematic roles of the US, the USSR and the UN.

Any chance for a successful transition obviously depended on the robustness of the existing institutions and on the preparation of the incoming executives. However, in this instance, the institutions were untested and the executives lacked preparation. Two key documents were crucial in the transfer to independence: the provisional constitution and the pact of friendship between Belgium and its former colony (see Chapter 5).

The provisional constitution – the so-called *Loi Fondamentale* – was a Belgian product, approved by the Belgian Parliament, albeit inspired by the resolutions of the January 1960 roundtable conference. It determined the direction of the political struggles that were new to the Congo and not rooted in existing customs or traditions; in other words, the Congo was to have a parliamentary government with two chambers and an inviolable head of state. Actual power-sharing between President Kasa-Vubu and Premier Lumumba, two standard bearers of Congolese nationalism, was in fact not workable and soon led to frictions. The constitutional provisions proved to be little more than a masquerade when President Kasa-Vubu, having been advised by the Belgian Government, gave his own idiosyncratic interpretation of the constitution by sacking Lumumba as Prime Minister. Shortly afterward, the President also dissolved the Congo's Parliament, equally on Belgian advice. From that moment the state survived in a constitutional twilight zone, until it approved its own constitution in 1964. Furthermore, the *Loi Fondamentale* created a unitary state with restricted decentralization of the six provinces. The Congo's unity, created by Leopold II, had been artificially guaranteed by the colonial administration, and was not supported by a public sphere in which a 'Congolese' national awareness could unfold and find expression. The proliferation of political parties, usually based on a regional and ethnic framework, with Patrice Lumumba's National Congolese Movement (MNC) and Antoine Gizenga's African Solidarity Party (PSA) as notorious exceptions, threatened political stability as well as the Congo's unity.

The pact of friendship with Belgium had an even shorter lifespan. The Belgian Government – under pressure from King Baudouin – had insisted it should be signed before independence, as a type of guarantee. This happened at the very last minute on 29 June, before the new Congolese Government commanded full sovereignty. The treaty put the Belgian officials, magistrates and officers – altogether around ten thousand people out of a total of some eighty thousand Belgians in the Belgian Congo – at the disposal of the Congolese Government and in so doing made the new regime dependent on the old colonial administrative apparatus.[1] Belgium would also retain three military bases in the Congo, in Kamina (in Katanga), and in Kitona and Banana (both at the mouth of the Congo River). However, a last-minute amendment to the agreement demanded by Lumumba meant that Belgian troops could only be deployed if the Congo agreed. The violation of exactly that article by Brussels at the beginning of July (see below) rendered the pact of friendship null and void. Neither of the parties would ratify it and it ended up in the waste bin.

In addition to the constitution and the pact of friendship, trust between Brussels and Léopoldville was a third essential ingredient in decolonization. This trust was wholly lacking. Since February 1960, behind closed doors, Lumumba had been branded a communist by Prime Minister Gaston Eyskens's Deputy Chief of Staff, Harold d'Aspremont Lynden, who in so doing voiced the opinion of the UMHK and its CEO Herman Robiliart. D'Aspremont Lynden, who enjoyed the full support of the Prime Minister, set the tone in government circles. His opinion played a crucial role in the events after 30 June. Lumumba for his part was well aware that the Belgians had wanted to keep him out of power after his election victory in May 1960. He also saw how the Belgian Government devised ways to keep the colony's financial assets out of the hands of the new state. His militant speech at the celebration of 30 June was received with indignation by King Baudouin and the top Belgian administrators. When a revolt erupted in the military a few days later, trust was absent on both sides to resolve the breakdown of authority. Belgium and the Congo both accused each other of conspiracy.

Civil Disorder Begins

Indeed, a collapse was not far off. A few days after independence, mutiny broke out in the *Force Publique*, which numbered twenty thousand men. It was still under the exclusive command of a thousand white officers and non-commissioned officers. The Léopoldville and Thysville garrisons refused to take orders any longer and were soon emulated elsewhere in the country. This was the result of the soldiers' unfulfilled expectations, of the Belgian commander Lieutenant-General Émile Janssens's intractable attitude, as well as ethnic tensions among the troops. Lumumba responded by first promoting all soldiers, then discharging Janssens, and after a brief hesitation, by commencing a radical Africanization of the officers' corps of what was henceforth to be called the National Congolese Army (ANC). The Belgian officers were initially tolerated as advisors but had to depart in a hurry a few days afterwards when the ANC came face to face with Belgian paratroopers.

The mutiny was accompanied by violence against the Belgians – both men and women. This caused panic and precipitated an exodus of many Europeans. The Belgian Government sent troop reinforcements to the Congo bases. On 10 July, without waiting for Congolese assent, it decided to deploy the military in Élisabethville and Luluabourg, among other places. Over the following days Brussels flew in even more troops and the intervention grew to around ten thousand troops. The local fires now turned into a blaze. Initially, the white army had to protect the Belgians and their possessions and evacuate them, but from 12 July that command was expanded to a policy of occupation. Belgian soldiers seized strategic locations, even Léopoldville's airport, and in so doing created the impression that Belgium wanted to reconquer the Congo with weapons. In the eyes of the Belgian Government, and more specifically in the eyes of Prime Minister Eyskens, Lumumba's Government was incompetent, illegitimate and non-existent. On 11 July Moïse Tshombe, leader of the provincial government in Élisabethville, used the elimination of the *Force Publique* by the Belgian troops to declare the independence of Katanga. His party, the Confederation of Tribal Associations of Katanga (CONAKAT), had been given mere crumbs in central government. Tshombe referred to the chaos in Léopoldville, labelled Lumumba a communist, and was given immediate support by the UMHK and the highest Belgian military on the spot. The Government in Léopoldville was faced with a fait accompli and offered little resistance. It branded the Belgian intervention as foreign aggression, called on the UN to defend the new country's legitimacy and broke off diplomatic relations with Belgium on 14 July in protest.

The crisis had dramatic consequences for the Government of Patrice Lumumba. Both the army and administration were decapitated by the rushed departure of the Belgians. The secession of Katanga robbed the Prime Minister of vitally needed income. Security and living conditions in the country began to deteriorate systematically. Belgium for its part was faced with the massive homecoming of its citizens from the Congo. During the weeks following the outbreak of the crisis around 25,000 people were repatriated in a *Sabena* airbridge, and some 45,000 Europeans in total left the former colony.[2]

Internationalization

The Congo's call on the UN had far-reaching consequences. Secretary-General Dag Hammarskjöld raised an international force of around 20,000 troops and sent a civil mission to support the Congolese Government. This operation is known as ONUC (United Nations Operation in the Congo). The Swedish diplomat Hammarskjöld enjoyed great authority as the leader of the UN and considered the Congo a test case for the new role of the global organization, which, in 1960, saw its members swell by no less than seventeen countries, sixteen of which were in Africa. The US gave a green light to ONUC in the hope of blocking Moscow. Its mantra was: 'The Cold War out of the Congo, the UN in the Congo.' The American policy caused tensions between Washington and Brussels, which felt abandoned by the US because the UN demanded the withdrawal of the Belgian troops. Paul-Henri Spaak, NATO's Belgian Secretary-General, forced a difficult choice on the American President Dwight Eisenhower: solidarity with the UN or with its NATO partners?

The UN intervention and internationalization of the crisis created a new context, in which neither the Congo nor Belgium were fully in charge of their destinies and saw their own elbow room reduced. Three Security Council resolutions followed, after which Brussels felt that it had to withdraw its troops, including those in Katanga, and that it even had to give up its own three military bases. At the same time, Belgium expanded its support of Tshombe and spurred on Albert Kalonji, another of Lumumba's opponents, to declare independence in the mining state of South Kasai (8 August). After multiple diplomatic maneuvers, the UN finally sent its peacekeeping forces to Katanga, but they did not touch Tshombe and considered the secession an internal Congolese issue. This was a concession to the Belgians, leading to a rift between Hammarskjöld and Lumumba, who abandoned his trust in the UN.

With that, the Congo Crisis took a new turn. American President Eisenhower, both concerned that the failure of the UN operation would open the door to the Soviet Union, and confronted with tensions in NATO, on 18 August gave the instruction to eliminate Lumumba. This galvanized the American CIA, which would send two agents to the Congo over the coming months to kill the Congo's Prime Minister. Now that he could no longer count on the UN, Lumumba tried to force a decision with the ANC itself. He invaded South Kasai and planned to subjugate Katanga as well. He could rely on the logistical support of the Soviets. That support and the numerous civil casualties in Bakwanga (present-day Mbuji-Mayi), the capital of Kalonji's kingdom, were grist to the mill for the UN and the Western powers and provided new arguments to eliminate the Prime Minister.

At the end of August, Lumumba presided over a conference, convened by him, of African states in Léopoldville, and tried to re-enforce his position. His resistance to the UN was not backed by the other states, however. Political opponents of Lumumba, the American Embassy, Belgians in the country conferring with Brussels, and the UN Special Representative in consultation with the headquarters in New York, all acted behind his back. Driven by all these forces, but also under pressure from his own party,

President Kasa-Vubu dismissed Lumumba in a radio speech on 5 September. Kasa-Vubu appointed as the new Prime Minister Joseph Ileo, Speaker of the Senate and one of the authors of the 'Manifesto' that had appeared in the journal *Conscience Africaine* (1956) (see Chapter 5). What was presented as a constitutionally justified intervention by Belgian Minister of Foreign Affairs Pierre Wigny was no more than just a badly executed coup. When Lumumba for his part declared Kasa-Vubu obsolete and was given the support of Parliament, Belgium and the US insisted that the Parliament be shut down, which is exactly what Kasa-Vubu did.

The removal of Lumumba, who continued to consider himself the legitimate Prime Minister, led to a chaotic power struggle. This was battled out among the Congo's politicians, who, in fluctuating positions, were supported or bribed by Belgium, the US, or the UN. On 14 September Colonel Joseph Mobutu, Chief of Staff of the ANC, engineered a new coup; he 'neutralized' Kasa-Vubu and Lumumba, and expelled the ambassadors of a few communist countries. In order to govern the country for the time being, he called on the small group of university students. This resulted in a 'College' of almost forty commissioners. Some came directly from Belgium and brought their Belgian advisors along. Justin Bomboko, a young politician who had graduated from the ULB and had been Minister of Foreign Affairs since independence, was put in charge. No less than 25 members of the College were students or ex-students of the Catholic University of Louvain/Leuven or its Congolese outpost Lovanium in Léopoldville (see Chapters 23 and 25).[3] In order to give the College a semblance of legality, Mobutu accepted a ceremonial role for President Kasa-Vubu.

Mobutu, who owed his political and military career to Lumumba, turned against his mentor, and allowed Belgium and the US to talk him into doing away with Lumumba. Brussels and Washington insisted that he arrest Lumumba, but now ran into a volte-face from Hammarskjöld. In September 1960 the UN General Assembly was the stage of an unprecedented clash between the Soviet Union and the organization's leadership. Soviet leader Nikita Khrushchev demanded Hammarskjöld's resignation because of his role in the Congo. In order to keep the Afro-Asiatic countries on his side, the UN Secretary-General ordered that Lumumba be protected in his residence (but nowhere else). Throughout this time, the return of Lumumba on the political stage (and a great reconciliation) remained a possibility, but this was fiercely opposed by the Belgians and the Americans. When at the end of November, the UN General Assembly recognized Kasa-Vubu's delegation – and not Lumumba's – as official representative, the deposed premier no longer saw a future in Léopoldville. He fled his residence and embarked on the long journey to Stanleyville, where his supporters regrouped. On 2 December 1960, he was intercepted by Mobutu's troops and taken to Léopoldville as a prisoner. By coincidence there was a camera crew at Ndjili airport to record his arrival. Thus, the whole world was able to watch the handcuffed Lumumba being humiliated by Mobutu and his soldiers. These were the last images the world would see of the Prime Minister.

Balkanization

Belgium granted the Congo a unified independence within the borders of its former colony. And yet it almost immediately supported the secession of Katanga, where big economic interests were at stake. Furthermore, Harold d'Aspremont Lynden, who, at the end of July 1960 had been appointed Head of the *Mission Technique Belge* in Élisabethville in order to bolster the Katangese state, also committed himself to the secession of other provinces. This was a way for him to undermine integrated rule and create a weaker confederated regime in which there would be no room for Lumumba. More than once, he reported full of hope to Brussels: the Congo is about to fall apart.

After Lumumba's removal, what really mattered for Brussels was to keep him out of power. This was about the only thing the Belgian ministers agreed on. Other than that, the Government pursued a disjointed Congo policy. Should they opt for Léopoldville once more or continue supporting Élisabethville? Moderates such as Minister of Foreign Affairs Wigny wanted to align with the UN. Hawks like d'Aspremont Lynden, promoted to Minister of African Affairs on 2 September, tried to protect Belgium's imperial privileges and to shore up both Tshombe and Mobutu with military support. Those behind Katanga felt supported by King Baudouin, who used his own channels to spur on Tshombe.

The only way Katanga could survive was with Belgian support and UMHK funds. Behind President Tshombe and his ministers were Belgian chiefs of staff, and all high-level Katangese officials had a Belgian 'advisor'. The regime was propped up by the Gendarmerie Katangaise, the army of the non-recognized state, which had been set up posthaste after the departure of the Belgian troops in August. It was under the command of a Belgian colonel and had a staff of 231 Belgian servicemen, including 204 officers and non-commissioned officers.[4] Most came from the *Force Publique* and were put at the disposal of Katanga's Government by Brussels. From

September 1960 onwards, Katanga increasingly called on European – including Belgian – and South African mercenaries to combat an insurrection in the north of the province by the General Association of the Baluba of Katanga (BALUBAKAT), which had been expelled from the Katangese provincial government and had chosen the side of Lumumba. On 20 September 1960, a UN resolution banned all bilateral assistance to the Congo, including Katanga. Hammarskjöld assumed that by cutting Belgian aid the Katangese problem could resolve itself, but the Belgians disregarded the UN.

Six months after independence the Congo was fragmented. It was not only Katanga (under Tshombe) and South Kasai (under Kalonji) that had broken away. Gizenga, Deputy Prime Minister in the Lumumba Government, had retreated to Stanleyville. After Kasa-Vubu had been recognized by the UN, Gizenga, supported by parts of the ANC, declared his Government legitimate. From Orientale Province, he took Kivu, and with the help of the BALUBAKAT rebels, he invaded North Katanga in January 1961. The regime of Kasa-Vubu, Mobutu and Bomboko was tottering. It oversaw only Équateur Province and Léopoldville Province. Belgium insisted on military cooperation between the 'moderates', i.e. Léopoldville, Bakwanga and Élisabethville, against the 'Lumumbist danger' from Stanleyville.

In that context, on 17 January 1961, with Belgian assistance, Lumumba was transferred from the military camp in Thysville to Élisabethville where he was executed that same evening in the presence of Tshombe and his ministers. Two prominent fellow party members, Joseph Okito and Maurice Mpolo, shared the same fate. The news of their death was not announced by the Katangese Government until 13 February and provoked worldwide protests, aimed at Belgium and the UN. The precise circumstances of Lumumba's end remained a mystery for a long time because the Katangese Government had done all it could to cover up what had really happened and had even destroyed the bodies. The truth only came out little by little as a result of inquiries by the UN (1961), the US (1975), the Congo (1992) and finally Belgium (2001), but also through the work of authors such as Jacques Brassinne and Ludo De Witte. The parliamentary enquiry by the Belgian Chamber of Representatives showed how insignificant the sovereignty of the Congo was to the Belgian Government, and how it had intervened behind the scenes to have Lumumba eliminated. At all costs Brussels sought to avoid freeing the most significant leader in the Congo.

Although the Gizenga regime was recognized by numerous communist and non-aligned countries following Lumumba's assassination, the murders of Lumumba, Mpolo, Okito, and a further seven senior MNC officials who were taken to South Kasai in February and executed in cold blood, led to a shift in power relations. On 21 February 1961 the UN Security Council asked Hammarskjöld to take all appropriate measures to prevent a civil war, using force, if necessary, and demanded that all military and political advisors – read: the Belgians – were to be withdrawn from the Congo. Kasa-Vubu, Kalonji and Tshombe pronounced the resolution an infringement on Congolese sovereignty.

The disappearance of the Lumumbist threat in the end weakened Tshombe as well. At a roundtable conference of Congolese leaders in Antananarivo (Madagascar) he had proclaimed that the confederal formula had prevailed, but during the conference at Coquilhatville (present-day Mbandaka), Kasa-Vubu gained the upper hand. At the end of July, the UN was able to command the conclave at Lovanium University. The remaining Members of Parliament, including many Lumumbists, gathered at the university campus of Léopoldville and decided to form a Government of national unity under Cyrille Adoula, and with the integration of Gizenga. But Tshombe dug in his heels. The UN now tried to put down the Katangese secession. At the end of August, they launched an operation against the mercenaries, and in September they came to blows with the Gendarmerie Katangaise. On 18 September 1961, Hammarskjöld and some of his staff died in a plane crash over Ndola in Northern Rhodesia on his way to negotiations with Tshombe. Since the publication in 2011 of Susan Williams' book about the UN Secretary-General's tragic death, the thesis of an attempt on his life – Hammarskjöld's Africa policy brought him other enemies, not just in Katanga – has been taken seriously. However, to this day no convincing evidence has materialized, and there are no traces of those who may have ordered such an attack. His successor U Thant continued the confrontation and ended the Katangese secession with armed force in January 1963. The Congo was one nation again. Tshombe went into exile in Spain.

Restoration

In April 1961, a new Government led by Théo Lefèvre, a coalition of Christian democrats and socialists, had assumed power in Brussels, with Paul-Henri Spaak, until then NATO's Secretary-General, as Minister of Foreign Affairs. This heralded a change in relations between Brussels and Katanga. Spaak wanted to break through Belgium's international isolation, stop the confrontation with the UN and align more strongly with the US. He allowed support for Katanga to die out. At the end of 1961, diplomatic relations between the Congo and Belgium were restored and in April 1962 ambassadors were once again exchanged. 'Technical assistance' – soon termed 'development aid' – which had been offered in the June 1960 pact of friendship, was resumed, albeit on a much-reduced level. In Katanga it had never ceased; in the rest of the Congo hordes of Belgians had returned after 5 September 1960, to the great dissatisfaction of the UN, which saw no more than the resumption of earlier colonial relationships in Belgian 'assistance'. When ONUC was coming to an end in 1963, Adoula's Government entered into a military partnership agreement with Belgium. The ties between former colony and former metropole were re-established in full, and the Lumumba episode seemed no more than an unpleasant entr'acte in their relations.

In 1964 Tshombe even returned from exile to become the Congo's Prime Minister. Thanks to Belgian military assistance, the Government was able to put down the insurrection in Orientale Province that same year. As if decolonization had never taken place, it was the Belgian officers who led Operation *Ommegang* (after a pageant in Brussels) against the rebels of Stanleyville. But in the end, it was General Mobutu who, as army commander, definitively assumed sole power and sent all the politicians packing, including President Kasa-Vubu. Belgium and the West did not obstruct him in any way.

Conclusion

The Congo became independent on 30 June 1960, but it did not stand on its own two feet. At the time of transition, the nation inherited a decent infrastructure, a developed primary education and a modern health care system (see Chapters 12, 22 and 23), but no administrative, legal and military apparatus that could ensure their continuity. Cooperation with Belgium continued to be an essential factor, but this collapsed following the outbreak of mutiny and Belgian military intervention. Simply in that respect alone, decolonization was an utter failure. The young nation found itself caught up in dramatic chaos that was exacerbated by the internal power struggle and centrifugal forces in the provinces. Patrice Lumumba's recently-appointed Government went adrift, and when it called on the UN, the country became a playing field of foreign powers, and a theatre in the Cold War. For the West, Lumumba, who had been branded a communist but was unaffiliated with either power bloc, had to disappear and be replaced by a reliable regime. This happened only after much violence and bloodshed.

Bibliography

The extensive literature about the Congo Crisis goes back to the 1960s (see Chapter 5), but we will limit ourselves to recent works here. Ndaywel è Nziem, Isidore, *Nouvelle histoire du Congo. Des origines à la République démocratique*, Le Cri, Brussels, 2009, offers a general overview of what happened in the Congo. The Katangese secession tends to be examined from a Western angle. A Congolese perspective on what happened on the inside is: Kabuya Lumuna Sando, Célestin, *Nord-Katanga 1960-64. De la sécession à la guerre civile. Le meurtre des chefs*, L'Harmattan, Paris, 1992. See also Omasombo Tshonda, Jean, ed., *Haut-Katanga*, MRAC, Tervuren, 2018. Two further studies focus on the decolonization years: De Witte, Ludo, *Crisis in Kongo. De rol van de Verenigde Naties, de regering-Eyskens en het koningshuis in de omverwerping van Lumumba en de opkomst van Mobutu*, Van Halewyck, Leuven, 1996 and Etambala, Zana Aziza, *Congo 55/65. Van koning Boudewijn tot president Mobutu*, Lannoo, Tielt, 1999. Indispensable research material about the *Force Publique* mutiny and the Belgian military intervention is Vanderstraeten, Louis-François, *De la Force Publique à l'Armée nationale congolaise. Histoire d'une mutinerie. Juillet 1960*, Académie Royale de Belgique, Brussels, 1993. The killing of Lumumba has been the subject of thorough investigation, which has greatly increased our knowledge about the chaotic first year following independence. Brassinne, Jacques, *Enquête sur la mort de Patrice Lumumba*, doctoral thesis, ULB, 1990, offers essential documentation, but its conclusions were contested by De Witte, Ludo, *De moord op Lumumba*, Van Halewyck, Leuven, 1999. The accusation that the Belgian Government had 'planned' the murder, led to a parliamentary inquiry (2000-2002): *Enquête parlementaire visant à déterminer les circonstances exactes de l'assassinat de Patrice Lumumba et l'implication éventuelle des responsables politiques belges dans celui-ci. Rapport fait au nom de la commission d'enquête par MM. Daniel Bacquelaine et Ferdy Willems et Mme Marie-Thérèse Coenen*, Chambre des Représentants de Belgique, Doc 50 0312/006-Doc 50 0312/007, 16 November 2001. The detailed report by the experts was also published separately under the names of Luc De Vos, Emmanuel Gerard, Jules Gérard-Libois and Philippe Raxhon. A broader international perspective on the killing, with the integration of Belgium, the Congo, the US and the UN, can be found in Gerard, Emmanuel, and Kuklick, Bruce, *Death in the Congo: Murdering Patrice Lumumba*, Harvard University Press, Cambridge MA, 2015. The international character of the Congo Crisis is the subject of increasing attention abroad, also integrating sources from the Soviet period. A good example is Namikas, Lise, *Battleground Africa: Cold War in the Congo, 1960-1965*, Stanford University Press, Stanford, 2013. The death of Hammarskjöld forms an extraordinary aspect of this international context and has aroused much interest with the work of Williams, Susan, *Who Killed Hammarskjöld? The UN, the Cold War and White Supremacy in Africa*, London, Hurst & Co, 2016 (first published in 2011). For the restoration of military cooperation in 1963 we would like to draw attention to Quanten, Kris, *Operatie Rode Draak. De bevrijding van 1800 blanken door Belgische para's in Congo in 1964*, Manteau, Antwerp, 2014. For information about data, we also availed ourselves of two works: Brassinne, Jacques, 'La coopération belgo-zaïroise 1960-1985', *Courrier hebdomadaire du Crisp*, 1985, 1099-1100; Vanthemsche, Guy, *La Belgique et le Congo. Empreintes d'une colonie 1885-1980*, Complexe, Brussels, 2007.

Notes

1 Data about the numbers of Belgians in the Congo: Vanthemsche, Guy, *La Belgique et le Congo. Empreintes d'une colonie 1885-1980*, Complexe, Brussels, 2007, p. 223; data about the number of civil servants: Brassinne, Jacques, 'La coopération belgo-zaïroise 1960-1985', *Courrier hebdomadaire du Crisp, 1985*, nr. 1099-1100, p. 4.
2 Total number reported by the government in *Le Soir*, 2 August 1960. The total number of repatriated people in the *Sabena* airbridge in Vanthemsche, Guy, *La Belgique et le Congo, Empreintes d'une colonie 1885-1980*, Complexe, Brussels, 2007, p. 223.
3 Composition in *Enquête parlementaire visant à déterminer les circonstances exactes de l'assassinat de Patrice Lumumba et l'implication éventuelle des responsables politiques belges dans celui-ci*, Chambre des représentants de Belgique, Doc 50 0312/007, 16 November 2001, p. 943-944.
4 Data about the Belgian servicemen in Katanga in Gerard, Emmanuel, and Kuklick, Bruce, *Death in the Congo: Murdering Patrice Lumumba*, Harvard University Press, Cambridge MA, 2015, p. 167.

PART II

Economy and Society

AMANDINE LAURO, IDESBALD GODDEERIS
AND GUY VANTHEMSCHE

Introduction

It was not only the major geopolitical events that played a part in colonial history, but also long-term structural evolutions and social dynamics. The colonial context acted as a driver for social and economic change and led to new norms and living conditions. This line of approach is central to the second part of this book.

Here again, the topic is not without controversy. This part's first chapter (Chapter 7) examines the effect of colonialism on Congolese demographics and thus ties in with Part I, as the question is bound up with the polemic around the number of casualties under Leopoldian rule. As will be seen, we will run up against the limits of particular forms of historical research. While the brutality of the exploitation regime of the Congo Free State undoubtedly resulted in a significant demographic decline, the gaps in workable data mean that we can only provide estimates for this period, not exact figures. Be that as it may, establishing what is plausible or not is also a way of making progress in this field. As is reflecting on the circumstances in which particular data was obtained.

The more accurate demographic information we have at our disposal from the interwar years was collected largely out of concern for the growing need for manpower in the colonial economy. After some hesitation, the major Belgian financial holdings swooped down on the Congo, in ways that were far removed from the so-called 'laws of the free market'. What were their profits? And at what (social) cost? Three chapters are devoted to these two fundamental questions, which focus in turn on the introduction of industrial capitalism in the colony (Chapter 8), the persistent practice of forced labor (Chapter 9) and the living conditions of the Congolese workers (Chapter 10). It is a euphemism to say that Congolese employees found themselves in a far from enviable position, in stark contrast with the then expansion of social rights in the metropole. Yet, the answers to these questions are not completely monolithic. The working conditions of the 1910s were not those of the 1950s, just as the situation within big companies such as the UMHK (discussed in Chapter 10) was not necessarily representative of the entire Congolese economy.

The workers in the Congolese industrial centers obviously had to eat. Despite (or perhaps due to) the explosive growth of the cities, agricultural production was a crucial issue for colonial authorities. What was the relationship between traditional farming and European agricultural methods – the latter imposed in a brusque and authoritarian way (Chapter 11)? Did this relationship change after the Second World War, when a new rhetoric of 'development' and 'modernization' emerged? Shared across empires at a time when colonialism was seeking new ways to legitimize itself, this new imperative of 'development' went far beyond the agricultural sphere. It also implied a transformation of space and of the building environment, with the construction of a 'modern' infrastructure becoming a flagship for colonial propaganda, as discussed in Chapter 12. From a wider perspective, the concept of 'development' ties in with a frequently recurring question in political debate: can we call the 1950s Congo a 'developing' country, or would 'underdeveloped' country be a better description (Chapter 13)? Finally, while the sweeping socio-economic changes during the colonial era gave rise to an unprecedented movement of people, they also led to new strategies of control of migratory flows. In this part's last chapter, we shift the focus from the colony to the metropole, where, little by little, a Congolese community began to establish itself (Chapter 14).

JEAN-PAUL SANDERSON

7. From Decline to Growth in Population

What Impact Did the Colonization Have on Congolese Demographics?

In 1905, three years before Leopold II handed over the Congo to Belgium, the famous American author Mark Twain published *King Leopold's Soliloquy*. Right in the middle of the international campaign against the crimes in the Congo Free State (see Chapter 2), this pamphlet opposing Leopold II's reign of terror was the first to give an estimate of the number of deaths between 1885 and 1905: ten million. This figure would crop up time and again over the following years. In 1998, the American journalist Adam Hochschild published *King Leopold's Ghost – A Story of Greed, Terror and Heroism in Colonial Africa*, which in the French translation was given the loaded subtitle *Un holocauste oublié* ('A Forgotten Holocaust'). Hochschild too stated that the Congolese population had declined by ten million people. He received a great deal of criticism for his work; issues that were held against him included the fact that he had conducted insufficient checks on the quality and reliability of his sources. Yet this death rate is often quoted by writers, journalists and other analysts.

Alongside this well-known number, different estimates circulate about the demographic state of affairs at the onset of colonization. These estimates have been made both by observers at the time (explorers, etc.) and by contemporary analysts, but raise several questions: what sources of information do we have regarding the size of the Congolese population, and how reliable are these? What can we say with considerable certainty about the evolution of the size of the Congolese population? Can we estimate how big the population was in 1885 and calculate to what degree this dropped after colonization began? In this chapter, we would like to find an answer to these questions and examine whether, based on existing data, the figure of ten million deaths between 1885 and 1908 can be considered realistic.

Counting Subjects: Colonial Sources of Information on Congolese Demography

Historical-demographic literature distinguishes three types of colonial populations, each of which met with a distinctly different historical and historiographic fate: (1) the colonials, who either left the 'motherland' voluntarily or were sent there as 'expatriates' and exercised colonial authority or participated in the colonization – in the case of the Belgian Congo this concerns a fairly small group of people; (2) the colonized, the local population which was subjected to colonial rule; and (3) the 'others', a minority which occupied a half-way position and of which the contours remain rather vague (foreigners who came from other colonies, for example). Fairly extensive literature exists about the colonial cohort; considerably less has been written about the other two. One of the explanations for this is the varying quantity and quality of the available data about the respective groups. Precise figures about the colonizing population were published by the colonial authorities (in the case of the Belgian Congo, in annual reports which were submitted to the Belgian Government). For the other categories, the data are far more fragmentary. They mostly come from colonial censuses, many of them of questionable quality. These censuses were officially introduced in 1891, at the level of *chefferies indigènes* ('indigenous chiefdoms'; see Chapter 18), at least in theory. It is only from the 1920s that the results of these were compiled and published in the annual *Rapports sur l'administration de la colonie du Congo belge*. No official data about the country's total population size exist from before that date.

Censuses consisted in enumerations of colonial subjects subdivided into 'adult women', 'adult men', 'girls' and 'boys'. According to the Ministry of Colonies itself (1925), the aim of these records was to determine the annual contingent of soldiers to be provided for the *Force Publique* (the colonial army), to evaluate 'available' manpower resources, and to forecast how much internal tax could be levied. The censuses were conducted by and for the colonial authorities, with Belgian territorial officers travelling annually from village to village to 'count' the population. The census was a key tool of the colonial bureaucracy; by recording a person in registers, the territorial officer made her or him an official subject of colonial rule and state control.

There are different issues regarding the quality of the collected data, however. The division between adults and children tended to be rather imprecise (young men could pretend to be younger to avoid forced labor for instance, while higher age could be reported for young women involved in early marriages). Some people fled in order not to be registered and to evade forced labor. What is more, in the eyes of the territorial officers, these censuses were yet another responsibility on top of their already extensive range of duties. When we examine the data more closely, we find that certain figures vary widely from year to year: during the first years for which data are available, we see deviations of more than fifty per cent for instance. Only in the period leading up to the Second World War did the quality of the data improve, providing us with useable sets of figures.

Concerning the period before the introduction of administrative censuses and the publication of their results, we can only rely on heterogeneous estimates from explorers and colonial observers. The most famous of these is the one suggested by explorer Henry Morton Stanley in 1885. He made his calculation on the basis of the number of inhabitants of every settlement on the left and right bank of the Congo River (according to him, there were 806,300 people in an area of 4,844 kilometers by 16 kilometers). Assuming a uniform population density over the entire territory on this basis, he extrapolated this number to a population size of 27,697,100 inhabitants for an area measuring 2,726,912 square kilometers.[1]

This method is problematic. On the one hand, questions can be asked about the way in which the first figure was arrived at. Is it an estimate or the outcome of a systematic count? Stanley's text leaves us in the dark about this. On the other hand, the hypothesis of a homogenous population density over the entire territory cannot be maintained in an area as vast as the Congo, with its huge diversity in biotopes and residential habitats. Yet all subsequent estimates have been based on these calculations, which lack a proper foundation for a reliable estimate of the population.

The Generally Accepted Population Evolution

Both the literature from the colonial time itself and more recent publications tend to assume a population decline amongst the Congolese during the first part of the colonial era. This finding is accepted widely for the evolution of the African population size in general and for the Congolese in particular and leads to an evolution model consisting of three chronological phases.

During the first period, from 1885 to 1930, the Congolese population underwent a phase of decline. There are no reliable statistical data, but numerous elements support this hypothesis. At the time of the European conquest of Central Africa, pre-colonial socio-political structures had already been weakened by the slave trade. The situation worsened further still with the arrival of the Europeans. This period was marked by violence, notably in the context of the so-called 'anti-slavery' military campaigns and, later, with the economic exploitation of huge territories (notably the Crown Domain, a vast area where rubber was extracted). This led to countless, well-documented atrocities. However, more than the number of deaths caused directly by these upheavals and violence, it is above all their indirect consequences that go a long way to explaining the population's demographic decline during this period. Quite a large number of people fled from the arable regions, resulting in famines. The general climate of insecurity must also have caused a drop in the birth rate, as happened in other similar contexts. Finally, the arrival of the Europeans went hand in hand with the spread of diseases (smallpox, sleeping sickness, etc.): 'new' diseases which had been brought along by the Europeans, but also diseases already present which spread wider (see Chapter 22).

The second phase, from 1925 to 1945, has been better documented. This probably explains why, depending on the region, more nuanced findings have been arrived at. The Congolese population stabilized during this period at around ten million inhabitants, with a zero or slightly positive growth. According to the prevailing hypothesis, natality remained relatively constant, and mortality decreased through a gradual decline in violence and the first measures on behalf of the local populace (restrictions of forced recruitments, etc.). It is also during this phase that economic and political circles began to worry about the depopulation of the Congo, because it jeopardized the success of the colonial enterprise. It was no coincidence that the first protective measures were those introduced for workers in large mining companies (such as the UMHK) (see Chapter 10).

During the third period, from 1945 onwards, the Congo's population entered a phase of growth. Rising birth and falling death rates meant the population increased to more than fifteen million in 1960. These two evolutions are related to the Congolese people's improved living conditions (less violence, more social measures) on the one hand, and to the development of health care by the colonial government on the other.

Demographic Scenarios

On the basis of existing data and of a detailed analysis of mortality rates between 1935 and 1960 (the period about which fairly reliable data exist), we have been able to map the evolution of the Congolese population between the 1930s and independence, and to come to a figure of 10.3 million people in 1930. This figure is the most reliable estimate of the evolution of the Congolese population for that year and will be used as a departure point for analyzing the previous period.

For previous years, no usable figures are available. Historians and demographers are therefore skating on thin ice. Yet there are some aspects we can take into account. Historical indicators show that mortality rose from 1885 and reached its zenith in 1900, when systemic exploitation in the Congo Free State was at its peak. We can presume a high mortality ratio across the entire country, but even more so within the most affected areas. We can also presume that mortality was already quite high in 1885, considering the political upheavals already underway. After 1900, under international pressure, violence in the Congo gradually diminished. From 1905-1908 onwards, mortality declined, to return around 1920-1925 to the levels probably seen in 1885.

Starting out from these elements, we can come up with an estimate of the mortality rate and of the population's evolution. We have drawn up three possible scenarios. The first one is based on the hypothesis of 20 million Congolese in 1885 and of the halving of that figure in 1930. The second scenario is largely the same but presupposes a population size of 15 million Congolese in 1885. A third scenario does not focus on population size, but on the highest achieved mortality ratios. The aim is to work out which scenarios are more or less plausible by examining the statistical constraints (mainly in terms of mortality) that would need to be imposed on the demographic figures to arrive at the expected result.

Scenario 1 is based on two assumptions:

1. 20 million Congolese in 1885
2. 10.3 million Congolese in 1930

The population decline is supposed to have been the result of a drop in fertility and of an exceptionally big rise in mortality. This combination would have led to a halving of the population. In concrete terms this means that, for the period between 1885 and 1908, we should assume a decline in natality of 39 per cent, with high mortality levels across the entire country. If this is right, around 1885 average life expectancy at birth must have been 9 years for women and 12 for men; between 1885 and 1908, when mortality was at its peak, life expectancy must have fallen to 6 years for girls and to 9 for boys.

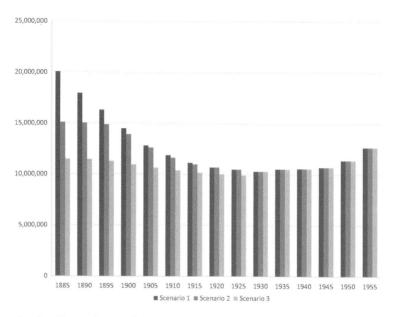

Graph 1. The evolution of the Congo's population between 1885 and 1950 according to three scenarios

The biggest problem with this scenario is the extremely high mortality rate for the entire country. A life expectancy of 8 years is possible in theory and has been found at local level during times of bubonic plague, in clearly demarcated places such as a village or a city. In our scenario on the other hand, this mortality rate applies to the whole of the Congo. Because the country was occupied and exploited in an extremely uneven manner, this means that mortality must have been higher in certain places (in particular in the Crown Domain).

Based on the knowledge that we have about the Congo and Sub-Saharan Africa, this scenario does not look particularly plausible. In the past, extreme situations did occur (for example amongst the indigenous American people during the sixteenth and seventeenth century), but the issue there was microbic shock, whereby the original inhabitants died first and foremost in massive numbers from diseases brought along by the settlers against which they had no resistance. This was not the case in the Congo, where there had been earlier direct and indirect contact between Europeans and the Congolese people, so that the shock effect remained limited.

Scenario 2 is based on two assumptions:

1. 15 million Congolese in 1885
2. 10.3 million Congolese in 1930

Various authors (including Léon de Saint Moulin) estimate the number of Congolese at the beginning of colonization to be 15 million. In terms of natality, we keep here the same hypothetical drop between 1885 and 1908 as in the previous scenario, but for mortality we alter some of the parameters and assume a higher life expectancy, which dovetails better with what had been observed in other places. In 1885, life expectancy would be 22 for women and 23 for men. Over a shorter period, between 1900 and 1908, we should continue to assume a minimal life expectancy (6 years for women and 9 for men). As we have seen in scenario 1, this is not very probable.

Supported by these findings, we have tested a third scenario. In this, we do not try to work towards a particular population size but take as our starting point the presumed evolution of mortality.

Scenario 3 is based on three assumptions:

1. 10.3 million Congolese in 1885
2. Extremely high mortality during the period 1900-1905 (life expectancy of 14 for women and 15 for men)
3. High mortality in 1885 (life expectancy of 22 for women and 23 for men)

Here mortality is still high around 1885, but more plausible in the specific Congolese context. In the wake of colonial exploitation, it reaches its peak during the 1900-1905 period, but this time life expectancy fluctuates around 15 years for the entire country (and possibly lower for particular areas). In this scenario we still see an initial population decline, but it is less drastic: from 11.5 million in 1885 to 10.3 million in 1930. In that case, the European colonization would have caused a population drop of one million people.

Conclusion

This chapter aims to examine the evolution of the Congolese population size at the beginning of the colonial era and thus to make a contribution towards the debate about the demographic consequences of colonization. In a context in which the colonial past is a subject of debates within society, this is not a token exercise. Yet, on the basis of available data, it is hard to come to a definitive number.

Data that were collected before the 1930s are of very little use. Subsequent censuses, however, do allow us to draw up mortality tables for the period 1935-1956 and to delineate scenarios for the evolution of the population size between 1935 and 1956. When doing this, we arrive at a minimum population size of 10.3 million Congolese in the early 1930s. For the period before 1930, we can only formulate hypotheses, and underpin these with contextual elements. They are in keeping with the generally accepted evolution framework: a population drop at the outset of colonialism which then stabilized after 1925. We have translated these elements into evolutions of mortality rates and used them to sketch the possible contours of the Congolese population evolution. For this, we have examined three scenarios.

Scenario 1, a drop of 20 million Congolese in 1885 to 10.3 million in 1930, seems the least likely because of the mortality conditions we have to assume in order to arrive at such a population implosion. Scenario 2, a fall of 15 million in 1885 to 10.3 in 1930, and scenario 3, a fall of 11.5 million in 1885 to 10.3 in 1930, indicate the limits of what is plausible. This margin remains wide, but without more accurate data we cannot sketch a more precise picture. Two things seem certain, however. First, in 1930, the Congo had at least 10 million inhabitants. Second, the population declined sharply between 1885 and 1925-1930. This is partly attributable to a drop in fertility but also and probably before all to increased mortality, which was caused by disease, famine and armed violence. It is impossible to determine to what degree these factors and parameters played a part. What is clear, however, is that we should not only be focusing on massacres or direct victims of the colonizing authorities' representatives, but also on excess mortality caused by 'indirect' deaths (as a result of disease or malnutrition, for instance).

In the complex debate about the impact of Leopoldian rule, it seemed important to us to conduct this exercise in demographic calculation, even if only to determine which different pasts are possible – and plausible. According to the calculations, we arrive at a population decline of 1 to 5 million people. To go one step further requires more research into local population evolutions during the earliest period of colonization. The results of this would lead to more accurate demographic knowledge and to a refinement of the possible Congolese population evolution scenarios during the colonial era.

Bibliography

The era of the Congo Free State as a context of polemicizing demographic estimates has been comprehensively analyzed in Vellut, Jean-Luc, 'La violence armée dans l'État Indépendant du Congo. Ténèbres et clartés dans l'histoire d'un état conquérant', *Culture et développement*, 16, 1984, p. 671-707 (re-published in Vellut, Jean-Luc, *Congo. Ambitions et désenchantements 1880-1960*, Karthala, Paris, 2017); Vangroenweghe, Daniel, *Rood rubber. Leopold II en zijn Congo*, Elsevier, Brussels, 1985; and Hochschild, Adam, *King Leopold's Ghosts: A Story of Greed, Terror and Heroism in Colonial Africa*, Houghton Mifflin, Boston, 1998. In 2007, the *Annales de Démographie Historique* dedicated a special issue to the demography of colonized peoples, in which a number of exceptional methodological challenges were discussed. With respect to the Congolese demography, we refer to the recent monograph Sanderson, Jean-Paul, *Démographie coloniale congolaise. Entre spéculation, idéologie et reconstruction historique*, Presses Universitaires de Louvain, Louvain-la-Neuve, 2018. Also relevant are the publications by Léon de Saint Moulin, for instance his 'Essai d'histoire de la population du Zaïre', *Zaïre-Afrique*, 1987, 217, p. 389-407 and the views of Stengers, Jean, 'Some Methodological Reflections', in Fetter, Bruce, ed., *Demography from Scanty Evidence: Central Africa in the Colonial Era*, Lynne Rieder, Boulder-London, 1990, p. 25-28.

Notes

1 Stanley, Henry Morton, *Cinq années au Congo, 1879-1884. Voyages, explorations, fondation de l'État libre du Congo*, Brussels, 1885, p. 640.

FRANS BUELENS

8. The Big Conglomerates

How Was a Capitalist Economy Implanted into the Congo?

Critics present the colonization of the Congo as a ruthless exploitation for profit; defenders retort that, at most, the Congo was treated a little paternalistically and that the colony was put on a trajectory of economic development thanks to altruistic businesses that did not shirk risk. These are very different views, and this chapter would like to ascertain which of these comes closest to the truth. We will begin by examining the initial robber economy, the construction of the infrastructure and the nascency and evolution of the big holding companies. This will be followed by the most important activities (mining and tropical monocultures), their profitability and the instrumentalization of the Congolese people.

The Robber Economy

When Leopold II acquired the Congo in 1885, he immediately embarked on a gigantic expropriation project. Because the Congo was sparsely populated, it gave the impression that large areas were not being used. Leopold II declared these so-called *terres vacantes* ('vacant lands': pretty much all of the land, and in 1891 extended to include forests, rivers and streams) to be the property of the state. In a Congolese context 'vacant land' did not exist, however, as people hunted and fished across the entire terrain and as the villages would regularly relocate to avoid soil exhaustion.

This land robbery allowed for the assignment of extensive concessions, the sale of land at low prices, or for it to be given away (land grants) or to be taken into exploitation. Leopold II certainly wasted no effort. Following an 1892 decree the Congo was divided into three zones; the Private Domain (which would be exploited by the state), a second area that was to become an official Crown Domain (property of Leopold II, 250,000 square meters) as a result of a decree in 1896, and finally concession areas for private companies. In the latter, private companies were given the temporary right (until the concession ran out) to build a railway line, for example, or to exploit a mine and derive income from this. These concessions would sometimes be accompanied by generous land grants, intended to win over Belgian, but also foreign investors to invest in the Congo.

Because the whole point was to attract capital, many Belgian companies considered Leopold's project a megalomaniac dream, did not believe it had much chance of success, and preferred investing in other countries. Only Antwerp saw opportunities in the trade of tropical products. Through the supply of ivory and rubber in particular, the port of Antwerp was able to place itself amongst the top-ranked global ports, even rivalling Liverpool. Several large Antwerp companies, such as ABIR and *Anversoise*, both established in 1892, became closely involved with the expansion of the Congo Free State into a monopolist trade system with an exploitation regime based on atrocious terror, whereby the population was forced to harvest rubber by force of arms (see Chapter 2). These companies became Leopold II's loyal allies, being able to furnish the Congo Free State with big income since the latter was given a sizeable share package.

Construction of the Infrastructure and Holding Capitalism

Antwerp trade capital was insufficient for the exploitation of the Congo, however. The support of the Belgian holding companies was crucial, first and foremost for investment projects in transport infrastructure (see Chapter 12). The Congolese waterway network was inadequate, and this made the construction of railways vital for the opening up of the interior and the export of raw materials, especially because many mines were located a long distance from the Atlantic Ocean. Railroad construction required huge amounts of money, however. Because the investment carried a high risk and uncertain profit profile and because Leopold II wanted to reduce these, he liberally dispensed land grants and interest and capital guarantees to win over investors. In this way he involved Belgian holding companies in the economy at a very early stage. This also came about as a result of his desire to make the Congo a Belgian project (even though he attracted foreign capital to shore up his unstable international position).

In as early as 1886, Albert Thys, Leopold II's orderly, set up the Congo Company for Commerce and Industry (CCCI). With a modest starting capital of just one million Belgian francs at its disposal, this holding company managed to assemble a small group of directors, some of whom were linked to the *Société Générale*, such as Édouard Despret (later Vice-Governor of the *Société Générale*) and Jules Urban, active in Grand Central Belge, the *Société Générale*'s largest railway exploitation network. The CCCI's first task was to open up the Congo by building a railway. With this goal in mind, they founded the Congo Railway Company (CFC) in 1889, which constructed a railway line between Matadi and Léopoldville over the course of the following ten years. The CFC was not only given full ownership of 150,000 hectares, but also promised a return on capital guarantee of five per cent.

The CCCI was the first holding company to operate in the Congo and never relinquished this head start. It created a host of subsidiaries, which in turn had their own subsidiaries. In 1891, the CCCI embarked on a second large project – in the wake of the CFC two years previously – with the foundation of the Katanga Company (CK), which, by means of a convention with the Congo Free State, had to realize the actual occupation of Katanga as swiftly as possible; this in order to counter British claims to the region. The CK was launched with a starting capital of three million Belgian francs, including British funds. On top of this, it was granted extensive territorial concessions (full ownership of a third of all Katanga land), as well as a 99-year concession for exploitation below ground. But the CK was equally a true charter company. Following the example of the British charter companies, it was also given extensive rights, such as the organization of a police force and jurisdiction, and it thus combined business activities with state functions.

Because the exploitation did not really get off the ground, a typically peculiar Congolese institution was founded, the Katanga Special Committee (CSK). It was a de facto new (semi-official) charter company, which acquired the monopoly over Katanga. It was financed by the government but was able to expand considerably its 'colonial portfolio' (which contained all the government shares in private companies) with share packages in all kinds of enterprises. It was managed by four representatives from the Congo Free State and two from the CK. The latter (the CK) continued to play an active role, and when, in 1910, the CSK's powers were reduced to purely economic ones, the CSK management de facto passed into the hands of the CK. The composition of its board, Albert Thys, Édouard Despret, Léon Lambert, Constant Goffinet and Count John d'Oultremont, show to what extent the interest of government and private enterprises were intertwined. A similar construction would be set up later, in 1927, in other words during the Belgian Congo era, with the *Comité National du Kivu* in the Kivu region.

Other investors were approached in addition to the CCCI. Leopold II managed to convince one of Belgium's wealthiest investors, Édouard Empain, to put money into the Great Lakes region. Empain agreed and, in 1902, founded the Upper Congo to the African Great Lakes Railway Company (CFL). It had a starting capital of 25 million francs and was given four million hectares in land rights by the government, an interest guarantee of four per cent on the capital it had staked and a reimbursement guarantee on the capital shares. Thus, over a total of 12.9 million francs in dividend payments for the period of 1902-1913, 10.1 million francs was paid via the state's interest guarantee. Moreover, the CFL was given a monopoly over the (future) exploitation of all mining resources, and it was able to transfer these rights to subsidiaries, which it would indeed do and as a result of which it evolved into a holding company.

It was a curious situation. The state did the preparatory studies, built the railway line, requisitioned workers for it by force, and even brought in Senegalese laborers and constructed the buildings and workshops. The CFL did not have to do anything with respect to the construction of railways and had only to reimburse the cost of the works and finance the exploitation expenses; but because of the guarantees, these were not risky investments. This construct shows how much Leopold II and his Congo Free State were in need of money in order to fund the colonial project. Here too, we find an interlocking of state and private interests, and the involvement of directors from other holdings. Seated on the CFL's executive board were men such as Edmond Van Eetvelde, Albert Thys, Léon Janssen (*Société Générale*), Édouard and François Empain and Count John d'Oultremont.

Holding Company Capitalism

With the CCCI and the CK, the holding economy had arrived in the Congo. The CCCI grew into the Congo's biggest holding company, but in turn ended up in the sphere of influence of the *Banque d'Outremer* ('Overseas Bank'), founded in 1899, in which the most important Belgian banks as well as foreign capital groups (such as the *Banque de Paris et des Pays-Bas* ['Bank of Paris and the Low Countries'] and the *Deutsche Bank* ['German Bank']) participated, again spurred on by Albert Thys. The *Banque d'Outremer* built a large international portfolio, with chiefly Congolese companies. Gradually, it acquired ever greater control over the CCCI, in particular with the issue of CCCI shares with plural voting rights in 1920 and 1925. When the *Banque d'Outremer* merged with the *Société Générale*, the CCCI found itself inside one of the biggest European holdings (in which it continued to operate as a subsidiary until 1972). This gave the *Société Générale* a major vote in the Congo. It harmonized the activities of all its Congolese subsidiaries with the foundation of the Colonial Interior Committee (CIC). More than ever, the Congo was a travesty of the 'free market'.

In addition to the *Société Générale*, there were several other powerful holdings present in the colony, such as the *Banque de Bruxelles*, the *Empain Group*, the *Cominière* ('Commercial and Mining Company of the Congo'; *Banque Allard* and *Banque Nagelmackers*) and the Lambert group. They maintained numerous mutual alliances, the so-called 'interlocking directorates', whereby the same directors served in multiple companies and thus built up networks. There was little rivalry and much cooperation between these holding companies.

The Congo thus grew into the domain of holding capitalism, in which a limited number of groups ruled the roost. This happened in symbiosis with the colonial state, which received large share packages in quite a number of companies (the so-called 'colonial portfolio' mentioned earlier) in exchange for concessions resulting in mutual interest. An American report formulated it as follows: 'The Belgian Government [...] has obtained shares of stock in all companies engaged in mineral extraction [...]. Business and finance in the Belgian Congo are dominated by a few powerful groups with solidly entrenched interlocking interest.'[1]

The Mining Economy

Already during the Congo Free State, it had become clear that the Congolese soil held large quantities of rare and precious minerals. Businesses realized that the colony might occupy an extremely important position in the global economy. Many capital groups hotfooted it to the Congo: primarily Belgian, but also several foreign investors. It was the start of the new era of mining economy, while the Congo Free State was on its last legs. The population's comprehensive lack of rights, the coercive economy, the 'feudal' obligations, the cruelties and the depopulation of the Congo (see Chapters 2 and 7) resulted in Belgium taking over the colony under international pressure in 1908. Yet many courses that had been set remained in place. A dual economy evolved in the Belgian Congo. Some regions were steered towards export and were given railways and all kinds of facilities. The impoverished indigenous agricultural sector was neglected (see Chapter 11) and was deployed for the supply of manpower and food for the mines. And all of this was run by powerful capital groups.

In 1906, three large companies were set up: the *Union Minière du Haut-Katanga* (UMHK) (see Chapter 10), the International Forestry and Mining Company of the Congo (*Forminière*) and the Bas-Congo to Katanga Railway Company (BCK). Without holding back, they availed themselves of the expropriated lands, including their minerals.

Thus, the UMHK – which would expand into the Belgian Congo's most important mining company – was granted the exploitation rights for the mines in extensive areas of Katanga for a period of thirty years (extended to 1990 in the 1922 decree), as well as the use of waterfalls and agricultural land. The company was founded with capital of ten million francs, underwritten by the *Société Générale* and the British Tanganyika Concessions, with the assignment of a large number of shares to the CSK. *Forminière* – which was to become the biggest diamond producer in the world – received extremely wide concession rights including mining, forestry and plantation rights. It also expanded its activities to neighboring Angola, with the foundation of the Angola Diamond Company (*Diamang*). *Forminière* was also able to attract American capital, from Daniel Guggenheim and Thomas Fortune Ryan amongst others. As with the CFL, all these companies set up quite a few subsidiaries, such as the BCK with the Mining Society of the BCK (SIBÉKA) in 1919, which was primarily active in Kasaï.

Mining resources were not limited to Katanga and Kasaï. In the areas awarded to the CFL, intense mining activity also developed, and was deposited in the care of numerous subsidiaries. In 1922, the Industrial and Financial Auxiliary Society of the Upper Congo to the African Great Lakes Railway Company (*Auxilacs*) was founded, into which the participation in several mining companies was secured. In 1923, the African Great Lakes Mining Company (*Milacs*) obtained all CFL's mining rights. The parent company set about this in a clever way. While the subsidiaries made large profits, the CFL continued to enjoy its interest guarantee and receive state support – a total of 232 million francs in subsidies through state warranties.

The colonial state built up its 'portfolio' chiefly through shares from private companies, but would sometimes take control itself. This was the case with gold, rich veins of which were struck in 1905, especially in Kilo-Moto, in Northeastern Congo. These goldmines were initially exploited along traditional methods, but in 1919 the colonial government incorporated them into the *Régie Industrielle des Mines de Kilo-Moto* ('Industrial Public Company of the Kilo-Moto Mines'), to crank up the return. After this was transformed into the *Société des Mines d'Or de Kilo-Moto* ('Society of the Kilo-Moto Gold Mines') with private capital in 1926, gold mining grew into one of the most lucrative activities in the Belgian Congo. The largest share of the profits went into the colonial coffers and not to private investors, let alone to the local population.

Profit Maximization at the Expense of the African Rural Hinterland

Mining also had an impact on the biggest sector of the economy, agriculture. It dragged a considerable number of workers away from the rural environment. Men were forced to build roads and houses (see Chapter 9) and were put to work in the mines. The remainder of the village populace was forced to produce food and to sell this to the mines for low prices.

In other ways too, rural life stood at the service of capitalist businesses. The colonizing power forced entire regions to grow particular products (see Chapter 11). The compulsory introduction of cotton – to supply the Ghent textile industry with materials – thus led to the Congo becoming the biggest cotton producer in Francophone Africa, and the third largest in the world. The development of the sector was driven by one company in particular, the Congolese Cotton Company (*Cotonco*), founded in 1920. This company evolved into a mammoth, because it was able to profit from its monopoly position, compulsory deliveries and low purchase prices (which were calculated to ensure that the Belgian companies remained competitive).

In the production of palm oil, the British William Lever (Viscount Leverhulme in 1922) of the eponymous Lever Brothers (later Unilever) held sway. As early as 1911, he was assigned an enormous concession area – five circle-shaped regions with a sixty-kilometer radius – and he set up the *Huileries du Congo Belge* ('Oil Mills of the Belgian Congo'), which was renamed Huilever following a merger in 1931. Here too, low labor costs, compulsory deliveries and forced labor were the norm.

In other sectors as well a similar agrobusiness model was applied, from smaller plantations which cultivated coffee, tea, bananas or cocoa, to large-scale cattle ranches and companies which exploited the tropical rainforest.

The monocultures and mining activities shared one disadvantage, they were dependent on the global market and the business cycle: extremely profitable during a cyclical upswing, but very vulnerable during a downturn. This made itself felt during the crisis of the 1930s, when demand and prices collapsed. The average prices paid for palm oil in Liverpool dropped from 37 pounds per barrel in 1928 to 13 pounds in 1933. Yet the state forced the Congolese to continue supplying to *Huileries du Congo Belge*. Resistance by the local population was met with bloody crackdowns, such as during the 1931 Pende uprising in Kwango, when between five hundred and four thousand people lost their lives (see Chapters 15 and 16).

As a result of all this, the system was reformed in 1943 with the establishment of the *Caisse de Réserve Cotonnière* ('Cotton Reserve Fund') which was managed by the Cotton Management Company (COGERGO). The compulsory delivery to one company was abolished and the cotton remained the property of the producer until the point at which it was sold on the global market. The Cotton Reserve Fund was intended to help reduce the influence of fluctuations in prices, like those in the 1930s, on the income of agricultural workers. The proceeds from the sale were paid to COGERGO, however, which partly reimbursed the planters but held back a share itself. The system was geared towards buying agricultural products at the lowest possible prices, and at times up to eighty per cent of the profit went into the Cotton Reserve Fund. In 1958, the fund sat on a massive two million francs.

An Investment that Had to Offer Good Returns

The Belgian Congo retained several systems from the Congo Free State, such as the requisitioning of land. Yet the Belgian takeover brought with it many changes as well. For instance, money made its appearance in the Congo, for the payment of taxes, wages and so on. What is more, the emphasis was placed on sustainable development, with an eye on maximum return. A 1920-1921 report for the Senate expressed it as follows: 'The principle is to equip the colony so that it can give Belgium the yield of which it is capable, like a factory, which one wishes to have produced, must first be set up.'[2]

Profit is what the Belgian Congo indubitably yielded. Granted, this was cyclical, because the sale of raw materials was closely tied in with the general cyclical evolution. During the 1920s and between 1940 and 1960 it showed huge profits, but during the 1930s much less so. General profit margins during the 1920s were 14 to 15 per cent, after 1945, 22 to 26 per cent.[3] This combined data covers numerous companies, and we can only limit ourselves to a few examples here. The CFL cashed in its mining rights via a network of subsidiaries. One of these, *Auxilacs*, produced a profit margin of 15 to 20 per cent even during the crisis years of the 1930s.

In 1960, the SIBÉKA, a subsidiary of the BCK, became the first global diamond producer and managed to pay out 2.05 billion francs in dividends between 1950 and 1960 as well increase its capital to 1.6 billion francs. It did this without asking its shareholders for money, and thus purely by incorporating reserves and revaluation surpluses. The Kilo-Moto gold ended up largely in the National Bank of Belgium. It made Belgium one of the most important global gold producers. But the UMHK outstripped all other companies. During the 1950s alone it paid out 16.9 billion francs in dividends.

Human Beings as Labor Without Rights

Both mining and plantations had much need for workers, who were in very short supply in the Congo and could only be withdrawn from agriculture or imported from other countries. The latter happened in particular in Katanga, a sparsely populated region. From its inception, the UMHK recruited workers from what was then Rhodesia and from 1925 from Ruanda-Urundi (see Chapters 9 and 10).

The Congo Free State worked with sheer forced labor; the Belgian Congo retained this in part (for the construction and maintenance of roads, for instance) while simultaneously using labor forces in the market system (see Chapter 9). It did this through the introduction of monetary taxes which were unrelated to income (unlike all modern tax systems). In this way, the government forced Congolese people to take up wage labor; they would then be able to pay monetary taxes.

During normal market conditions the scarcity of labor would lead to higher wages, but in the Belgian Congo the opposite happened. It was possible to keep wages artificially low because Congolese workers enjoyed little legal protection. Elementary rights, such as freedom of the press, freedom of association (for example in unions) or the right to strike, were entirely absent in the Belgian Congo. Corporal punishment and imprisonment were commonly used methods. Spontaneous strikes were smothered in blood. Resistance leaders were sacked or banned. The colonial administration and the *Force Publique* were at the service of business. While total randomness applied for the Congolese people, the colonizing forces escaped with virtual absolute impunity. The Congo was a colony with an almost totalitarian grip on life. All this was imbedded in a utilitarian *and* racist view of the population. The colonial state, which was closely bound up with business, was able to treat the populace as it wanted, in a brutal way. This translated into a system of apartheid and denial of all possible development of human capital.

The logic of capitalist exploitation (and the threatening shortage of workers) did incentivize some companies to go for higher productivity and increasing mechanization (see Chapter 10). This required skilled laborers. Because European workers were extremely expensive, their Congolese counterparts were used to an increasing degree. This development gained an extra boost during the Second World War. Companies expanded their activities: *Chanic*, established in 1928 and originally focusing on ship repair and assembly, switched to shipbuilding and trained up Congolese workers for this purpose. Quite a few other companies, such as the UMHK, began to mechanize production (and train workers accordingly). Everyone made sure that this training remained limited, however. The colonial ideology, which regarded Congolese individuals as lesser human beings who were inferior to their superior white European counterparts, remained intact.

Conclusion

The Congo's colonization was long presented as a noble act of self-sacrifice, with the aim of 'developing' the country. This version stretches the truth. Rather, Belgian companies were attracted by the enormous potential in tropical products and raw materials. The entire colonial society was organized in such a way that they would be able to realize the exploitation of these to optimum effect. The Congo was organized as a paradise for business, in which many European laws and customs did not apply. The economy was dominated to a great extent by a number of holdings, which formed a power network controlling virtually all large companies. They had a big influence on the colonial administration and were involved in setting the course for colonial policy. The Congo had to 'yield': supply raw materials to the 'motherland', generate income, provide profit to investors and be able to support itself financially. This succeeded. The Belgian Congo became one of the most profitable colonies in the entire world. But this had disastrous consequences for the country and its people on many fronts.

Bibliography

Already during the colonial period several surveys appeared, including Pourbaix, Victor, and Plas, J., *Les sociétés commerciales belges et le régime économique et fiscal de l'État indépendant du Congo*, Imprimerie Van Assche, Brussels, 1899, and Bacq, M., *Les relations financières entre la Belgique et le Congo*, National Bank of Belgium, Brussels, 1943. An overview of the mineral resources was published by the United States Department of the Interior, *Mineral Resources of the Belgian Congo and Ruanda-Urundi. Foreign Minerals Survey*, United States Department of the Interior, Bureau of Mines, 1947.

The influence of the holding companies is a central theme in Lemoine, Robert J., 'Finances et colonisation. La concentration des entreprises dans la mise en valeur du Congo belge', *Annales d'Histoire Économique et Sociale*, 1934, 29, p. 433-449; Delmotte, Louis, *De Belgische koloniale holdings*, St.-Pietersboekhandel, Leuven, 1946; Gonda, J., 'Les holdings coloniales belges et le financement de l'industrialisation du Congo belge', *Revue des Sciences Économiques*, 1956, 105, p. 15-45; Joye, Pierre, and Lewin, Rosine, *Les Trusts au Congo*, Société Populaire d'Éditions, Brussels, 1961. The CIC is analyzed in Vanthemsche, Guy, 'Comment la Société Générale gérait-elle son 'empire économique' au Congo belge? L'action du Comité Intérieur Colonial pendant les années 1930', in Jaumain, Serge, and Bertrams, Kenneth, eds., *Patrons, gens d'affaires et banquiers*, Le Livre Timperman, Brussels, 2004, p. 251-268. A review of all companies quoted on the stock exchange in Buelens, Frans, *Congo 1885-1960*, Epo, Berchem, 2007. An extremely critical review of capitalism in the Congo in Depelchin, Jacques, *De l'État indépendant du Congo au Zaïre contemporain (1885-1974). Pour une démystification de l'histoire économique et politique*, Karthala, Paris, 1992.

In addition, there are the studies of particular companies, such as: Brion, René, and Moreau, Jean-Louis, *De la mine à Mars. Genèse d'Umicore*, Lannoo, Tielt, 2006; Fieldhouse, David K., *Unilever Overseas: The Anatomy of a Multinational 1895-1965*, Croom Helm, London, 1978. A great deal has also been published about the transport sector, such as Huybrechts, André, *Transports et structures de développement au Congo. Étude du progrès économique de 1900 à 1970*, Mouton, Paris, 1970. This author also calculated the rate of profit companies achieved. The same, but for shares, can be found in Buelens, Frans, and Marysse, Stefaan, 'Returns on Investments During the Colonial Era: The Case of the Belgian Congo', *The Economic History Review*, 62, 2009, 1, p. 135-166.

Notes

[1] US Department of the Interior, *Mineral Resources of the Belgian Congo*, 1947, p. 5.

2 *Parlementaire Documenten van de Senaat,* session 1920-1921, nr. 220, Halot report.
3 Huybrechts, André, *Transports et structures de développement au Congo. Étude du progrès économique de 1900 à 1970,* Mouton, Paris, 1970.

JULIA SEIBERT

9. Was the Development of the Belgian Congo Only Possible because of Forced Labor?

The question in the title might surprise some readers: in the collective memory about Belgian colonial history, forced labor immediately evokes the association with the harvesting of rubber during the Congo Free State era. Over the past forty years, Belgian historians have largely agreed that the international protest against the violence in the Congo was a decisive factor in the transition from the Congo Free State to the Belgian Congo and that the annexation of the Congo by Belgium meant a clean break with the practices of forced labor. It is true that in 1908 the Belgian Government tried to develop a new concept for the exploitation of the colony it now had in its possession (*mise en valeur*). For that reason, it enacted a series of laws which would allow the administration to intervene in the colonial economy. Unlike in the Congo Free State – a textbook example of extreme exploitation of workers in the colonial history of the twentieth century – coercion and violence were no longer an option for the mobilization of workers. And the new regulations indeed outlawed the use of forced labor for private enterprises. The introduction of taxes in the colony and a new legal basis for employment contracts were intended to overcome the reluctance of Congolese men and women to engage in wage labor.

But did the end of the Congo Free State really mean forced labor was abolished in the Belgian colony? Was the attempt by Belgian politicians, bureaucrats, entrepreneurs and missionaries to eliminate coercion in labor relations ultimately successful? Or did the violence and forced labor in the colony's mines and on the fields and plantations continue to play a major role afterwards?

Recent studies of the colonial Congo's labor history show that the practice of 'free' wage labor won ground only very slowly and that in many places, from the establishment of the Belgian Congo in 1908 up until independence in 1960, violence was repeatedly used to break the Congolese workers' resistance towards wage labor.

Using various examples, this chapter will demonstrate the central role the labor question played in the economic development of the Congo, and which evolutions entailed the rise of new forms of forced labor and exploitation of Congolese men and women.

The 'Labor Question' as the Biggest Challenge for the Belgian Congo

In November 1908, colonial politicians and businessmen were fully confident that the Congolese people would engage in the colonial economic project. For the Belgian colonial planners it was therefore crucial to integrate a Congolese workforce into a new evolving colonial economy. The authors of the Colonial Charter agreed that the European labor model in the Congo, which was intended to replace extra-economic coercion with contractual relations involving wage workers, could be the foundation for mobilizing workers. With their faith in the liberal economy's universal laws, they were convinced that the Congolese would let themselves be guided by the financial incentive of wages and would abandon their subsistence economy in the villages in order to work in the emerging industries, on plantations or on infrastructure projects. Institutionalizing modern wage labor was intended to bring about an efficient and scandal-free integration of the Congo into the global economy.

All European colonial powers in Africa shared the same experience: the European wage labor model competed with local labor organization and practices, which made it difficult to extract manpower from the local economy. The manager of a British mining company which had had control of the investigation into and exploitation of the Copperbelt in Haut-Katanga since 1902, knew as early as 1906 'that the biggest challenge for the companies in the Belgian Congo consists of making wage labor more attractive to the natives, what is more, making wage labor be a pleasure for the native'. 'Poor working conditions,' the manager continued, 'should be avoided at all costs. The more an employer preserves his workers from illness and death and is able to send them home happy and contented after their work is done, the more successful we [the entrepreneurs] will be and the less our workers will cost us.'[1]

Despite such statements, the terms of employment for the local people were unattractive. This was chiefly due to the poor working conditions and low wages, but also to the new ways in which labor was organized, the working pace imposed and the perception of the value of work, which was novel at that point. The majority of the population in the Belgian Congo were small-scale farmers, requiring a different family and community structure and leading to a work ethic that differed from wage labor relations which were developed in Europe and North America.

Wage labor – the labor model of industrial capitalism – led the Belgian Congo into a crisis, which had consequences for every economic sector in the colony. And because the economic 'value' of the colony was dependent on Congolese workers, the acute wage laborer shortages constituted a danger for the entire Belgian colonial project. This crisis not only affected the Belgian Congo; in other African colonies, too, acute shortage of labor hampered the planned industrialization of individual regions. Solving the problem of labor shortage was the biggest challenge for the colonial planners in Belgium. Without the manpower of hundreds of thousands of men, women, and children, the colonial project was condemned to failure.

In order to combat this shortage in the Belgian Congo, the Belgian colonial state introduced a drastic measure. Contrary to all principles within the recently adopted Colonial Charter, forced labor was reintroduced in 1909. So, the belief in the persuasive power and economic success of wage labor had been short-lived, as more and more Congolese were forced to work against their will in mines, plantations, fields, and road construction. The conditions and consequences of this policy forced labor to move from industry to industry and from region to region.

1909 – Reintroduction of Forced Labor in Road and Railway Construction

On 4 January 1909, a Royal Decree hastily issued by the Belgian colonial administration ordered the forced recruitment of a total of 2,575 workers.[2] These workers had to construct a railway and road for motor vehicles in Uele, Stanleyville and Maniema. To the majority of colonials in charge, these construction plans in the east of the Congo were first order public interest projects, justifying forced labor. Roads and railways were an absolute prerequisite for connecting villages, trade and government posts and the production centers that had sprung up everywhere, and also for connecting them to the existing road network of neighboring colonies.

The Colonial Council briefly debated the question of whether this measure was contrary to the Colonial Charter but decided that the Royal Decree was in fact legal. A few days later it came into effect. The decision was based on a decree from 1887, which had been abrogated. This decree legitimized the forced recruitment of workers for projects that were in the public interest during the Congo Free State era. It formed the legal foundation for the recruitment of tens of thousands of laborers to work on the construction of the railway line between Matadi and Léopoldville, for instance. As early as 10 January 1909, based on this abrogated decree, the Deputy Governor-General ordered men to be transferred from the provinces and districts of Matadi, Stanley Pool, Kwango, Lualaba-Kasaï, Équateur Province, Ubangi, Bangala, Aruwimi, Lake Leopold II and Orientale Province to the planned workers' camps in the districts of Stanleyville and Maniema.

The construction of railways and roads in the east of the colony was the Congo Free State's and pre-First World War Belgian Congo's most important infrastructure project. Between 1903 and 1915, Africans built a total of 731 kilometers of railway. The workers, who, in 1909, had been forcibly recruited under the Royal Decree, were deployed for the construction of the railway line between Kindu and Kongolo. Although, in that year, the Upper Congo to the African Great Lakes Railway Company (CFL) was already employing 5,500 workers – chiefly porters – its management had been unsuccessful in mobilizing more manpower for earthworks, porter services and railway construction.

The history of the decree illustrates how quickly the colonial state was prepared to undermine the labor policy principles laid down in the Colonial Charter. After 1909, the decision was also invoked to legitimize the use of coercion and violence in the recruitment of workers for the expansion of the road network. This is evident from the large number of forced mobilizations of workers for road and rail construction. Thus, an ordinance in January 1919 gave the highest officials from Équateur Province and Congo-Kasaï the authority to recruit a thousand forced laborers and to transfer them for the construction of the port and the station of Ango Ango near Matadi. And six years later, in 1925, six thousand men from Équateur Province and Orientale Province were taken to Bas-Congo to work for the African Construction Company (SAFRICAS) for a year. The mobilization of forced workers for infrastructure projects (see Chapter 12), which was referred to in colonial jargon by the innocent notion of *travaux publics* ('public works'), had become standard practice in the labor policy of the Belgian colonial state.

Forced labor and violence did not disappear with the termination of the Congo Free State. Quite the contrary, in the context of the *travaux publics* they appeared to be acceptable at various points in time in the history of the Belgian Congo.

Mining as a Special Case: From Forced Labor to Stable Labor Force

Forced labor not only gained acceptance in road and railway construction but became an important method for mobilizing workers in other economic sectors of the colony as well. Katanga, the colonial economy's most important region, relied heavily on forced recruitment right up until the 1920s. It was not until then that the largest colonial enterprise, the UMHK, succeeded in establishing a stable workforce in the mining regions of Southern Katanga (see Chapters 8 and 10).

The UMHK was set up in 1906 and grew quickly. In 1912, the company embarked on copper mining in Haut-Katanga; in 1929 it had expanded into the world's second biggest copper producer. This rapid expansion required a large number of workers. The Belgian colonial administration responded by setting up a state recruitment agency in 1909. The Katanga Labor Office (BTK) was tasked with bringing in wage laborers to the thinly populated Haut-Katanga. The agency's success failed to materialize. In 1910, it played a part in the recruitment of 637 workers, but no one had volunteered to come forward for a job in the mines. Soon, the BTK, together with a group of soldiers, recruited the necessary workforce to Haut-Katanga either under pressure by chiefs, or under the direct threat of violence. The fact that even in 1922 just a mere 2,511 out of by now 10,476 laborers were working in the mines of their own volition, shows that also in Katanga, forced recruitment remained the central practice in the mobilization of manpower.

But not only were violence and coercion part of the recruitment process; also working conditions were characterized by exploitation and violence. The poor working conditions in the mines of Haut-Katanga caused many men to desert after just a few days, which fundamentally undermined the use of the BTK. Desertion rates in Katanga were so high that copper production could not be maintained (see Chapter 10). Thus it was often only possible to retain miners at their work places through threat of violence and punishment.

The outbreak of the First World War bolstered the developing system of violence. Katanga was after all of crucial importance to the European war economy. Between 1914 and 1917, copper production in the Congo rose from 103,000 to 229,000 tonnes. While the copper industry's profits went up from 102,085 to 1,603,514 pound sterling, its production costs remained more or less unchanged.[3]

These were tough times for the local people. They may have been spared the Congo Free State rubber terror during the 1890s, but exploitation in the Katanga mines was no less dramatic in the early twentieth century. In fact, this exploitation had an effect similar to that of the rubber harvest. During the first decade of Belgian rule, a total withdrawal can be observed, in particular amongst the Baluba, which in some places led to a total refusal to work. The result was that, in the colonial discourse, the Baluba as a group were soon labelled extremely 'work-shy', 'lazy' and 'unmotivated'. Not a word was said about the fact that their men, women and groups of porters had by then taken care of the mines' food supplies for almost ten years.

Likewise, during the war years, production could only be maintained because the British organized workers from Rhodesia and Angola and the BTK expanded its activities in all directions, and began recruiting men from Kasaï, Orientale Province and Ruanda-Urundi (see Chapters 4 and 10).

When the supply of mobilized workers from Katanga appeared exhausted and the demand for copper became ever greater at the beginning of the First World War, the UMHK's directors began to investigate new ways of mobilizing additional workers. Because they did not manage to get the local people of Katanga to commit to mining for the long-term, in 1920, the UMHK, which was exploiting nearly all the mines by then, together with the BTK decided to change tack and bring in workers to Katanga from far-away regions. Between 1921 and 1925, no less than 96 per cent of all workers had been recruited outside Katanga, 10,112 people in total. Out of the 19,633 people recruited between 1926 and 1930, 1,291 came from Orientale Province, 7,856 from Ruanda-Urundi and 10,846 from Kasaï.

This was a spectacular success for mining and for the Belgian colonial administration. Most of these workers stayed in Katanga for three or even five years, and only a handful left before their contracts expired. There were several reasons for this change in the workers' behavior. Firstly, working conditions had improved and illness and deaths had been reduced. Besides, the UMHK was now pursuing a strategy aimed at encouraging the workers and their families to stay in Katanga for increasingly longer periods.

The fact that in Katanga of all places the working conditions and recruitment methods had changed fundamentally, was chiefly due to the requirements of copper production. Under the concessions of the UMHK, this also had continued to grow steadily after the end of the First World War. Whereas 1,360,303 tonnes of copper were mined in 1923, by 1930 this was totaling 2,603,999 tonnes. Such a rise could only be achieved by the stabilization of the workforce. But more than anything, it was technical development that had been responsible for this spectacular growth. A workforce comprising solely of unskilled, undernourished and sick workers who called it a day after a few months and were then replaced by new unskilled laborers, was not able to carry out the increasingly complex work processes.

The Continuity of Forced Labor in Agriculture

While Katanga had been developing into an island of wage work within the colony during the 1920s, the work conditions in agriculture, on plantations, and in villages continued to be characterized by violence and forced labor until the independence of the Congo. A good illustration of this is the case of palm oil production. In the colonial Congo, this activity was closely tied in with the name of Lever Brothers (see Chapter 8). After long negotiations, the entrepreneur William Lever had been granted the monopoly on the production of palm oil in Équateur Province in 1911, but he had great difficulty finding workers to harvest palm fruits and process the oil. For Lever's company, despite a great labor shortage, processing the first tonnes of palm oil from its plantations a mere few months after signing the covenant, had only been possible thanks to the forced recruitment of local workers. And thus the palm oil industry relied on forced labor from the outset, just as the mining and the construction sectors.

To what degree the company embraced forced labor can be read from correspondence between the Minister of Colonies and the company's directors between 1913 and 1916. In as early as 1913, two years after the agreement about the start of palm oil production was signed, the oil factory's management asked the Minister of Colonies in Brussels to set up a military post in order to force deserters back to work. The 'labor problem' could not be solved without military support, the management of the oil factory in Leverville (present-day Lusanga) declared.[4] In 1913, the then Minister of Colonies Jules Renkin resolutely rejected the company's request. The company built up a private army of hundreds of soldiers. These African mercenaries who were hired and armed by the company's European employers, had to go and hunt down workers. The troops combed the villages and forests to recruit men for three or four months for the harvest of palm fruits. Belgian colonial officials soon reported these practices, which in the end led to Governor-General Fuchs establishing a police station with a force of fifteen soldiers in Leverville on 29 May 1914, ordering it to curb the company's practices.

Despite this reinforced presence of, and purported control by, the colonial government, the local people in the region around Leverville also had to endure the violence dispensed by the company's *capita* ('soldiers') in 1916. A report from that same year by a colonial civil servant named Vanderbosch depicts the violence to which the workers were exposed. The company's private army, which according to Vanderbosch was made up of Bangala and men from Kasaï and West Africa, was deployed increasingly to supervise the works themselves, and even the smallest infringement or attempt to flee would result in extremely violent action against the workers. The consequences of the local male population's forced recruitment were in fact documented in 1930 in a letter by Governor-General Pierre Ryckmans to his wife, in which he describes deserted villages and exhausted groups of workers. Men, women and children who lived in the area around the Lever *cercles* Alberta, Basongo, Elisabetha and Ingende, were forced to work on the plantations.

Forced labor for the production of agricultural products not only featured on plantations, but also occurred in villages and on farm fields. Just as with road construction, the Belgian colonial state was able to find new legal instruments that legitimized forced labor and exploitation of the population shortly after the enactment of the Colonial Charter. A lesson learned from the experience with the palm oil plantations was that Congolese people would only be integrated into the plantation economy with coercion. Even after the end of the First World War, the majority of the rural communities continued to live and work self-sufficiently and independently from the colonial economy. This alarmed the colonial policymakers in Brussels, because from their perspective, a large part of the colony's potential remained unused, namely the agrarian households whose capacity to work, experience and disposal of land to produce agrarian export products and foodstuffs could be utilized. In order to bring about their systemic integration into the colonial economy, a decree was issued in 1917 which legalized compulsory cultivation of food and export crops in the Belgian Congo. The creation of this law can be considered the political answer to the insufficient integration of agrarian households in the colonial farming sector before 1917 (see Chapters 4 and 11).

The idea for this law came from Edmond Leplae, the head of the Ministry of Colonies' Agriculture Department (see Chapter 25). Since taking office in 1913, he sought ways to deploy the existing small-scale agricultural economy of individual villages of families for the economic valorization of the colony. Now that it appeared that the colonial state and private companies such as Lever were not successful in mobilizing farmers as wage laborers for plantations long-term, Leplae believed the cultivation and harvest of cash crops had to be integrated into the living environment of the African farmers and their families. To put it differently, if the local people did not integrate of their own free will into the colonial agricultural economy by leaving their homes and villages to carry out wage labor in the surrounding plantations, the colonial state, together with the local businesses, had to move the production of profitable crops to the villages themselves.

The decree not only legalized compulsory cultivation of specific export crops, but also stipulated that the cash crops could be produced on Congolese farmers' farmland. The so-called *cultures obligatoires* continued to exist until the Congo's independence. The policy of mandatory crops was designed to expedite the introduction of one specific export product: cotton.

Resistance from the Congolese farmers was considerable because cotton production interfered fundamentally with their own, local farming methods. Their acts of sabotage led to ever more repressive systems of *cultures obligatoires*. In order to maintain the production levels of cotton and enforce the policy of forced cultivation, the state introduced a rigid penalty system which, in addition to fines for a bad harvest or an unweeded field, also included corporal punishment in the shape of flogging.[5] Unlike other sectors of the colonial economy, which had been seeing a decline in violence and coercion, the *chicotte* (a leather whip made from a buffalo or hippopotamus hide), fines and other forms of punishment continued to form part of daily colonial life in the context of cotton production. To this day, this continuity of violence in the production of cash crops – first rubber, then palm oil and finally cotton – has left a distinct mark on the collective memory of the Congolese people. Interviews about that era often contain detailed descriptions of corporal violence experienced or observed by the interviewee regarding cotton production.

Up until the Congo's independence, the exploitation of agrarian households was at the base of cotton production. In 1959, following a visit to Kuba villages in Kasaï, a region closely associated with cotton production, historian Jan Vansina concluded: 'Even now, at the end of the colonial period, the larger Kuba villages don't have running water, electricity, secondary education, some don't even have a primary school and not one single form of medical care.'[6] Although, in 1959, 874,000 households with a total of two million people were producing 180,000 tonnes of cotton per year, this had no positive effect whatsoever on the living conditions of the Congolese rural population.[7]

Conclusion

The Belgian Congo's colonial economic development was accompanied by increased extra-economic violence. Industrialization and the resultant expansion of mining, agriculture and the road network, which manifested itself in the landscape as early as during the 1930s in the shape of economic centers and cities such as Élisabethville, Stanleyville and Léopoldville, were only possible as a result of the forced mobilization of hundreds of thousands of Congolese people. Despite the colonial authorities' expectation, the industrial islands, which had been emerging since 1908 in all of the colony's provinces, had not become wage-labor islands. The state and private enterprises had only been able to transform the arid and scarcely populated savannas of Haut-Katanga into a mining center with the help of forced recruitment, surveillance and violence. 136,997 tonnes of copper were produced in the provincial capital of Élisabethville in 1930, while 138,023 people from all parts of Central Africa were living and working there.[8]

Force and violence as tools for mobilizing workers were not limited to the industrial sector, however. Elsewhere, colonial state officials forced entire families to cultivate large quantities of cotton (as well as other products such as cassava, corn and rice). With the introduction of *cultures obligatoires* in 1917, the model of 'free labor' turned out to be an oppression for the rural population as well. The displacement of Congolese farmers from the agricultural market and state intervention in the forced cultivations led to more than one million farmers – one in eight inhabitants of the Congo – growing cash crops between 1920 and 1930.[9] Likewise in road and rail building and in the construction of urban infrastructure, forced labor was omnipresent in the 1920s. Following the takeover of the Congo Free State, Belgium had tried to substitute forced labor with its wage equivalent, but in the end ever more Congolese people found themselves working under the economic and social control of the colonial state. A cautious estimate suggests that, during the 1920s, twenty per cent of the population performed forced labor; a percentage that is only surpassed by a group of companies that used enslaved individuals.

But the history of forced labor in the Congo is also a history of unforeseen consequences: it shows how the 1908 attempt by Belgian politicians, bureaucrats and entrepreneurs to ban force from colonial labor relations had led to *more* violence against the local populations and to a sluggish implementation of wage labor. On the eve of independence in 1960, 1,182,871 men worked as wage laborers and almost a million Congolese households were integrated into the colonial economy as producers of cotton and other cash crops. The history of this mobilization shows how crucial force and violence were for the economy of the Belgian colony.

Bibliography

Many studies exist about forced labor in the Congo Free State as well as a few about forced labor in the Belgian Congo, but there are hardly any compendiums. A summary of research into forced labor in the Belgian Congo can be found in: Seibert, Julia, *In die koloniale Wirtschaft gezwungen: Arbeit und kolonialer Kapitalismus im Kongo (1885-1960)*, Campus Verlag, Frankfurt am Main, 2016. Other important studies that discuss forced labor, wage labor and employment issues include: Henriet, Benoît, '"Elusive Natives": Escaping Colonial Control in the Leverville Oil Palm Concession, Belgian Congo, 1923-1941', *Canadian Journal of African Studies*, 49, 2015, p. 339-361; Likaka, Osumaka, *Rural Society and Cotton in Colonial Zaïre*, University of Wisconsin Press, Madison, 1997; Nelson, Samuel H., *Colonialism in the Congo Basin 1880-1940*, Ohio University Center for International Studies, Athens, 1994; Northrup, David, *Beyond the Bend in the River: African Labor in Eastern Zaïre, 1865-1940*, Ohio University Center for International Studies, Athens, 1988.

Notes

1 Royal Museum for Central Africa, Tervuren, CSK fonds, 622, letter from G. Grey (manager at Tanganyika Concessions Ltd.) to Mr. Cayley about the circumstances in the mining industry in Ruwe/Katanga, 23 April 1906.
2 Cf. 'Arrêté royal du 4 janvier 1909, proclamant d'utilité publique les travaux des chemins de fer du Congo supérieur aux Grands Lacs africains et des routes pour automobiles dans l'Uele', in *Bulletin officiel du Congo belge*, 1909, p. 52.
3 Cf. Perrings, Charles, *Black Mineworkers in Central Africa, 1911-41*, Africana Publishing Company, New York, 1979, p. 33.
4 Report about HCB's operations between 1 July 1912-30 June 1913, cited in Marchal, Jules, *Travail forcé pour l'huile de palme de Lord Leverhulme. L'Histoire du Congo 1910-1945*, part 3, Borgloon, 2001, p. 11.
5 Likaka, Osumaka, *Rural Society and Cotton in Colonial Zaïre*, University of Wisconsin Press, Madison, 1997, p. 45-56.
6 Vansina, Jan, *Being Colonized: The Kuba Experience in Rural Congo, 1880-1960*, University of Wisconsin Press, Madison, 2010, p. 243.

7 Likaka, *Rural Society*, p. 135.
8 This figure was taken from the first official census in the Belgian colony, which was conducted from the beginning of the 1920s. The results of the census were first published in 1930: Ministère de l'Intérieur et de l'Hygiène, *Annuaire statistique de la Belgique et du Congo belge*, 1929-1930, tome 53, Brussels, 1930, p. 240; about copper production: *ibid.*, p. 245.
9 Peemans, Jean-Philippe, *Le Congo-Zaïre au gré du xxe siècle. État, économie, société 1880-1990*, L'Harmattan, Paris, 1997, p. 34.

DONATIEN DIBWE DIA MWEMBU

10. How Did the Congolese Workers Live?

The Example of the Union Minière du Haut-Katanga *(UMHK)*

During the first decades of the twentieth century, the Congo's industrialization led to the translocation of large African population groups who settled closely together around industrial hotspots. Towards the end of the Second World War, an estimated 700,000 Africans worked for European companies in the Belgian Congo.

Colonial literature conveys the impression that these African workers accepted what their employers decided for them with equanimity. They were no more than big children, it was alleged, who did their best for their colonizing superiors. When doctor Léopold Mottoulle, medical affairs advisor at the UMHK, talked about the company's social policy for its African employees, he referred to the colonizer's numerous purely 'humanitarian' achievements for his 'inferior' brother. One of his utterances aptly summarizes his view: 'We only live fully when we live for others.'[1] This adage constitutes the foundation of the paternalistic colonial ideology, which regarded an employer as the father of his African workers. Yet this outlook is too simplistic, because it passes over the important role that the workers themselves played in the improvement of their working and living conditions.

In this chapter, we will examine how these African workers lived. What were their working conditions like? In which way did these conditions evolve? What was the African laborer's attitude towards paid work? How did the employer judge, justify and improve the living conditions of this workforce? What was the role of the African workers themselves in the improvement of their working conditions? Which indicators can we use to find out whether their living conditions did indeed improve?

We search for an answer to these questions by examining one of the colony's largest industrial mining companies. The UMHK was founded by King Leopold II in 1906 to extract copper and other minerals in the southern part of Katanga (see Chapter 8). Its labor policy was considered a 'model' for other colonial companies. It is also the company that is most frequently studied by historians. In many respects, the UMHK occupies a unique position.

In this chapter, we wish to sketch a broad picture of the social history of the laborers who worked for the UMHK, whereby we will take into account both the perception of the company itself and of its African employees. In order to do this, we have made grateful use of the life stories of workers. These have helped us to examine how the workers' social life changed and in which way these workers themselves actively contributed to an improvement in their living conditions. In doing so, we will focus on four indicators: living conditions, social fabric, housing and wages.

Living Conditions

With regard to living conditions, we can distinguish two major periods. The first runs from 1906, the year in which the UMHK was founded, until 1928. This period is characterized by permanent labor migration. At the time, Africans did not consider the city as a permanent place to live. They only stayed for a short time, around three to twelve months, and at the end of their contract they would return to their village to work on the land. During this period, the working conditions were abominable. The Africans worked without appropriate equipment, barefoot, engulfed in dust and smoke. Up until the end of the 1920s they generally carried out their tasks manually: mining was done using pickaxes, transport with wheelbarrows and carts, etc. In 1917, a working day lasted seventeen hours. The workers became weakened as a result of the hard work, excessively long working hours, night shifts and exhausting working conditions deep under ground. The result was a high gross death rate (8.63 per cent in 1914-1916; 4.2 per cent in 1926-1928). The UMHK acquired the reputation of 'people devourer'; the industrialized region of Haut-Katanga a 'country of death'. At the time, work equated slave labor to the Africans: *Kazi ni butumwa* ('Work is subjection, slavery'). The African workers were squeezed like lemons and discarded after a few months. Many fled. In 1913, 87.7 per cent of indigenous workers made a run for it. Between 1920 and 1926, the UMHK saw around seven thousand laborers desert, which amounts to an average of a thousand a year.

The company was forced to change tack and began to pursue a paternalistic policy towards its African workers. This behavioral change was induced by pressure from the colonial government and interest groups, the massive desertion of Africans and the technological innovations that were essential because the ore deposits on the surface were becoming depleted. The UMHK was left with no alternative but to encourage a more permanent African presence in the industrial centers and to improve their working conditions.

Over the course of the second period, from the 1930s, the UMHK began to mechanize its mines, workshops, factories and quarries. The number of manual and semi-manual jobs decreased. What is more, the company shortened the working day, from 07:30 until 12:00 in the morning and 12:30 until 16:00 in the afternoon, set up a health and safety service for its workers, and worked on the professionalization and specialization of its African workers. The drop in the number of injuries due to industrial accidents is an indicator for an improving working climate. This drop began in 1930: 20.2 per cent in 1930, 5.8 per cent in 1940 and 5.7 per cent in 1960.

The Social Fabric

The development of mining in Haut-Katanga went hand in hand with the emergence of labor camps. At first these tended to be constructed at quite a distance from other camps or settlements, and close to the place of work. This meant that the workers did not have to travel very far and made it easier for the company to monitor them. Assisted by the *malonda*, the company police, the camp chief controlled every aspect of daily life and made sure that the laborers did not come into contact with 'corrupting' influences from the outside which formed a threat to productivity. Additionally, the camp chief had to give the workers the sense that they belonged to a distinct community, an obedient, healthy 'big family'. He was soon given the nickname *tshanga-tshanga* ('mixer', from *kutshanga*, 'to mix'). Partly because of the discipline he enforced, the camps resembled barracks.

The workers made friends with people from outside their own tribe or ethnic groups and started to talk amongst each other in a communal language, Kiswahili. Up until the Second World War, the African UMHK employees in Élisabethville did not have their own staff canteen, unlike their white colleagues. They drank their glasses of *munkoyo*, *tshibuku* or *lutuku* in the camp or went into the neighborhoods of Kamalondo or to Kenya to quench their thirst where they came into contact with the local inhabitants. Company management feared that this might have a 'baleful' influence on their productivity, and indeed every day there were many latecomers and absentees. Some relaxation facilities had to be created in the camp itself posthaste. Soon all manner of sports and recreations were organized: football, basketball, athletics, a cinema, a brass band, a bar, etc. Libraries even appeared in every camp, where workers were able to widen their knowledge. Later, the UMHK would also set up youth centers, where a variety of intellectual and sports activities took place for the children of workers.

The company encouraged the workers to organize traditional games and festive dances on Sundays and holidays to avoid homesickness. During these events, workers from the same ethnic background could meet each other and set up tribal societies to safeguard their cultural heritage, defend their interests and help each other. 'Unity in Diversity' was the motto. Thanks to all this, the idea of the 'big family' gradually gained a wider base and a consciousness began to grow amongst the young working class. Important events such as births, marriages and mourning ceremonies were experienced together.

Because the UMHK attached a great deal of importance to the health of its workforce and saw its camps as an environment for social reproduction, it developed a social-medical infrastructure, with hospitals, health centers and maternity clinics for its African employees (see Chapter 22). They also invested widely in the education of African children (see Chapter 23). Everyone began by attending primary school; then the boys went on to technical schools, where they were trained to be future workers for white people, and the girls pursued domestic science in order to become good housewives later on. In addition to schools, *foyers sociaux* sprung up, where adult women learned to sew, iron, cook, clean, and so on. The schools were run by Catholic priests, while nuns specialized in domestic science teaching, the *foyers sociaux*, hospitals and maternity clinics. Together with female social workers, these nuns went from door to door to check on the cleanliness of houses and report back to the camp chief.

In due course, people living in the camp developed their own subculture. They were called *ba mu componyi* ('camp people'), or *ba Union Minière* ('UMHK people'), to distinguish them from the rest of the local population, in particular those in the cities.

Housing

Company policy also changed with regard to housing, in two distinctive periods. During the first (1910-1928), black workers were taken on for a relatively short period and, at the end of their contract, sent back to their villages. The city was a white bastion at the time. The UMHK wanted to avoid building comfortable brick houses, because it would mean a sharp rise in the average cost price per worker. The first workers' houses were therefore rectangular huts which housed twenty people, with all the associated fire and other hazards. Moreover, the huts were replete with vermin, and encouraged the spread of diseases such as pneumonia. It was not until the 1920s that the UMHK decided to erect brick and cement barracks, the so-called Orenstein Blocks. These could accommodate fourteen people, albeit occupying a small floor space (two square meters per person). Later, huts for four, followed by huts for three people were introduced.

During the second period (1928-1960), paternalism gained the upper hand in policy. In order to make the labor camps more appealing, workers' housing had to be improved. The UMHK replaced the Orenstein Blocks and huts with houses. These were concrete initially, but because they were extremely cold during the dry season and very warm during the rainy season, a shift was made to brick houses. From 1934, the company attuned its housing policy to promoting births. Houses were allocated on the basis of the worker's family size. Older houses were converted to make them suitable for large families.

Towards the end of the 1940s, the UMHK became in a sense a victim of the 'success' of its own social policy. The number of lodgings was unable to keep up with the rapid increase in the number of workers. The UMHK had to abandon its policy of keeping the workers out of local cities. At the end of the 1950s, some houses were modernized and new types of dwellings for future UMHK foremen (workers who had been promoted to almost senior staff positions) were built. But the company did not manage to house all of its employees. And despite the increase in habitable floor space, which rose from 4.96 square meters in 1953 to 7.17 square meters in 1960, African workers continued to live squashed together.

Wages

The African worker's pay was much lower than that of his European colleagues. An African would earn twelve francs a *month* in 1910, whereas his European counterpart would have this sum at his disposal each *day*. The ratio between the average wages of the two categories of workers was 1:26 in 1910, 1:65 in 1950, 1:40 in 1954 and 1:33 in 1958. This enormous wage gap can be explained by differences in education and productivity, an incorrect assessment of the African workers' needs, racial discrimination and, because of all this, the generally accepted practice of paying Africans a low wage.

Wages were paid in two ways: in kind and in ready cash. The in-kind pay formed the largest part and comprised food tokens, clothing, housing, medical care, children's school fees, travel costs related to recruitment and moving, access to infrastructure in the labor camps, etc. The second form of pay was meagre and was considered pocket money. For an ordinary worker, in 1920, it would constitute 16.05 per cent of his total wages, and in 1959, 46 per cent. Up until the end of the 1940s, the African workers' monetary remuneration was too low to cover their basic needs. This, together with the far from ideal living conditions, broke the camel's back during the Second World War. The African workers called their first large-scale strike and, following a bloody confrontation involving fatalities (see Chapters 4 and 16), were able to exact a small wage increase. At the beginning of the 1950s, the UMHK's management decided to pay all the wages in money, albeit at first only to specific specialized African workers.

During that same period, African workers' wages rose significantly. The wage index went from 100 in 1950 to 237.50 in 1958, in other words more than a doubling. Because the price index climbed less sharply in 1958, from 100 in 1950 to 120, the workers' disposable income sharply increased, and with it, their social status in the cities. A teacher at a UMHK school, which, from 1951, belonged to the public sector, related that he wore expensive shirts and that his wife was able to buy high-quality fabrics.

The relatively high living standard of the paid worker during the 1950s caught the attention of all kinds of Katangese musicians, in particular Jean Bosco Mwenda wa Bayeke, who sang the praises of paid work. In his opinion, Katanga's joie de vivre was facilitated by paid work which allowed him to buy clothes, food and drinks: *Fura ya Katanga iko wapi he bwana? Fura ya Katanga ni kuvala, kulala, kunywa* ('Where can Katanga's joy be found, sir? Katanga's joie de vivre can be found in beautiful clothes, sleeping well, drinking plenty'). In due course, *Kazi ni butumwa* ('Work is slavery') was displaced by *Kazi ndjo baba, ndjo mama* ('Work is my father, it is my mother'), which testifies to the attraction of paid work.

Yet during the 1958 economic recession, the monetary salary became insufficient again. Because this salary was still only one part of the total wages, many workers had to fall back on food rations to get through to the end of the month.

African Unions

During the Second World War, the Belgian Congo, cut off from its 'motherland', had to find new markets. Spluttering imports caused an increase in living costs; this was intensified by the devaluation of the Congolese franc which, in turn, made these imports even more expensive. Salaries, meanwhile, were still extremely low (see Chapter 4). This situation led to social unrest in places with large concentrations of workers (at the UMHK in Élisabethville in 1941, at *Géomines* in Manono in 1941, in Matadi in 1945, etc.). Workers demanded a wage increase, but their strikes were quashed with violence (see Chapter 15).

In order to prevent new strikes or at least to limit them in number and scale, the colonial authorities and the employers organized frequent contact times during which the workers were able to lay their grievances on the table. From 1946, the colonial administration issued ordinances which stimulated the foundation of local professional associations, and convened commissions to address the problems of the African workers. In the wake of the steadily growing European unions in the colony, who had joined forces in the General Confederation of Unionists from the Congo (CGSC), the colonial authorities allowed the Congolese people to set up their own unions.[2] This led to the foundation of the Association of Indigenous Staff from the Colony (APIC), the Confederation of Christian Trade Unions in the Congo (CSCC) (allied to the Christian union in Belgium, CSC/ACV), which was renamed The Congo Workers' Union (UTC) on the eve of independence, the General Confederation of Unions (CGS; a sub-division of the socialist union in Belgium, FGTB/ABVV), and finally the General Federation of Workers from the Congo (FGTK).

The Governor-General's decision to give Congolese workers their own unions, was a thorn in the side of many big colonial companies, who clung to their paternalistic policy. In this context, also in 1946, Indigenous Works Councils (CIEs)[3] were being set up in companies with at least 250 employees.

Some companies, such as the UMHK, gave these CIEs a wide forum in order to render African unions redundant. The members of the work councils were elected by the workers themselves and put all complaints to the employer. These complaints were about work-related and social issues: the working relations between Africans and Europeans, equipment, overtime remuneration, as well as infrastructure in the camps, rubbish collection, street lighting and lighting in the home, education, child benefits, medical care, food rations and so on. At the CIE's request, company management arranged for recreation rooms to be installed in the workers camps, so that employees could relax after work, and from 1950, they built more spacious homes for the workers. The CIE indubitably contributed to the improvement of social conditions for UMHK workers. In other companies too, white people began to treat African people differently thanks to the CIEs. Nonetheless, these African pioneers, whose status did not offer any legal guarantee, played the role of informer, or rather intermediary between employer and employee, instead of true representative.

Conclusion

The introduction of mining in parts of the Congo set in motion mass immigration. The recently arrived workers had trouble adapting to their new living and working conditions, which were extremely poor and led to high morbidity and mortality. The industry created countless casualties amongst the African workers.

But while their living conditions were still wretched at the beginning of industrialization, they gradually improved thanks to both internal and external factors. Over a timespan of several decades, a company such as the UMHK was mechanized at break-neck speed, while the circumstances of the workers were tackled as well. The working environment became healthier, hygiene, nourishment and housing improved, and a social-medical infrastructure was created.

Under pressure from all kinds of interest groups and the Belgian and colonial authorities, the UMHK was forced to improve the social conditions of its African employees. What is more, the African workers had a clear influence on the company's changing approach. Company management had given them the idea that they belonged to one big family, the workers strove to enhance living and working conditions, to this end organized themselves from the inside and in so doing contributed to the nascency of a worker's identity which transcended regional and ethnic differences.

Taken all together, these factors led to satisfactory results. The labor camps lost the lethally unhealthy character they had during the first years of industrialization when they were intended purely as housing and evolved into centers for demographic reproduction in which large numbers of people lived together, and finally into 'model environments' that were attractive (to a certain extent) to many workers.

An important question is whether the findings for the UMHK can be extrapolated to the whole colony, in other words whether they are representative of the situation in other companies. It appears that the UMHK was considered the model to emulate, especially for big companies. The colonial government itself regarded the UMHK a unique pioneer with a paternalistic policy worth emulating. It is only to a certain extent that the UMHK could however be considered representative of other big industrial and commercial mining companies (such as *Forminière*, BCK, OTRACO in Léopoldville, Kilo-Moto in Orientale Province, *Géomines*, etc.) because although the latter also pursued a paternalistic policy, they invested far less in this. These companies each had their own particular features that impacted the living conditions of their workers in all kinds of ways: more dispersed labor camps (BCK, OTRACO), the deployment of locally recruited workers (Kilo-Moto, *Géomines*), and so on. Small and medium-sized enterprises on the other hand were unable to match the social conditions of UMHK workers because they were unable to bear the enormous costs for housing, food, health and education for the workers and their children. A comprehensive study about this issue has yet to appear. At any rate it is clear that the picture the Belgian colonizing powers and the UMHK painted of the Congolese worker's social 'progress' does not apply unequivocally to rest of the Congo.

Bibliography

Since the beginning of the Congo's industrialization in 1910, quite a number of studies have dealt with the living and working conditions of the UMHK workers. The work by Mouchet, René, and Pearson, Arthur, *L'hygiène pratique des camps de travailleurs noirs en Afrique tropicale*, Goemaere, Brussels, 1922, has the merit that it contains detailed information about the period 1912-1920, in particular as regards hygiene and the construction of African labor camps. Additionally, there are the publications by Léopold Mottoulle, the doctor who for years was the Director of the UMHK medical service and *Département de Main-d'Œuvre Indigène* ('Indigenous Labor Force Department') of the UMHK (notably *Politique sociale de l'Union Minière du Haut-Katanga pour sa main-d'œuvre indigène et ses résultats au cours de vingt années d'application*, IRCB, Brussels, 1946). Mottoulle took stock of the UMHK's social project, which with inordinate optimism he placed in a favorable light. This apologetic nature characterizes all his publications. Other authors have analyzed the workers' social conditions, notably Dibwe dia Mwembu, Donatien, *Bana Shaba abandonnés par leur père. Structures de l'autorité et histoire sociale de la famille ouvrière au Katanga, 1910-1997*, L'Harmattan, Paris, 2001; Rubbers, Benjamin,

Le paternalisme en question. Les anciens ouvriers de la Gécamines face à la libéralisation du secteur minier katangais (RD Congo), L'Harmattan, Tervuren-Paris, 2013. To supplement this literature, we would like to mention the unpublished life stories of UMHK workers which are the result of interviews conducted by Donatien Dibwe dia Mwembu (1990-1996). With regard to the UMHK camps we also refer to De Meulder, Bruno, *De kampen van Congo. Arbeid, kapitaal en rasveredeling in de koloniale planning*, Meulenhoff-Kritak, Amsterdam-Leuven, 1996. For quantitative data we have consulted the annual reports (1937-1960) of the above mentioned UMHK Département de Main-d'Œuvre Indigène, in addition to the works by Perrings, Charles, *Black Mineworkers in Central Africa, 1911-1941*, Africana Publishing Company, New York, 1979, p. 169-170; Joye, Pierre, and Lewin, Rosine, *Les trusts au Congo*, Société Populaire d'Éditions, Brussels, 1961, p. 190; and UMHK, *Union Minière du Haut-Katanga, 1906-1956*, Cuypers, Brussels, 1957, p. 88 and 24.

Notes

1 Mottoulle, Léopold, *Politique sociale de l'Union Minière du Haut-Katanga pour sa main-d'œuvre indigène et ses résultats au cours de vingt années d'application*, IRCB, Brussels, 1946, p. 65.
2 *Bestuursblad van Belgisch-Congo*, 1946, p. 913.
3 Every so often, the Commissions of Labor and Interior Social Progress convened representatives from the government, the employers and African employees. They discussed measures around general working conditions and ways to improve the workers' living conditions.

YVES SEGERS AND
LEEN VAN MOLLE

11. Agriculture in the Colonial Congo

A Success Story at the Expense of the Rural Population?

'Agriculture at the end of the colonial period is sometimes presented as a kind of golden age, during which the production of cotton and palm oil in particular reached a level unequaled ever since. However, we would like to show that it was in the agricultural domain that colonization recorded its greatest failure.'[1]

This quote is from Léon de Saint Moulin, a Belgian Jesuit and Professor at the Université Catholique du Congo at the time. This theologian and historian published numerous studies about the Congo and Zaïre. As an authority on the Congo, he openly expressed his very negative views about the Belgian colonizing powers in general and the colonial agricultural economy in particular. According to de Saint Moulin, local farmers' income rose insufficiently, and the colonial authorities used their agricultural policy chiefly to discipline and safeguard social stability in the rural communities. His critical analysis contrasts sharply with the tone agronomists and other experts tended to employ, for example in the *Bulletin Agricole du Congo Belge*, the bimonthly journal published by the Ministry of Colonies' Agricultural Service. This latter cohort commended the positive effects of the agricultural policy, especially increased production and productivity, the deployment of modern (read: Western) scientific methods and the – in their view – considerable improvement in living conditions within the Congo's rural regions. And when these ambitions could not be realized, they believed the responsibility lay with the Congolese farmers. These clung too strongly to inefficient traditional knowledge, showed no interest in commercially oriented agricultural and food production, and were simply too lazy. The Belgian agronomists had a clear mission in mind in the Congo: upskilling Congolese peasants into modern farmers. Because these would never succeed on their own: *Il est prématuré d'abandonner les indigènes à eux-mêmes, délaissés, ils ne feraient que régresser* ('It is premature to abandon the natives to themselves, since they would only regress if this happened').[2]

In historiography about the Belgian Congo, up until now, relatively little attention has been devoted to the rural environment, the primary sector and food. Socio-economic historians focused primarily on industrial development and the operations of international companies. Themes such as colonial agricultural policy, labor relations on the Western plantations, the development of agricultural research and education, and food supply have only recently become a subject of interest for researchers. Yet, during the colonial era, Congolese society and economy were pre-eminently rural and agrarian by nature, and still are. In 1960, more than seventy-five per cent of the Congolese population lived in a rural environment. Most households were farming households. They tilled the land to meet their own food requirements, cultivated cash crops (such as cotton, palm oil, coffee and cocoa) for export or worked as cheap labor on large-scale plantations run by Europeans.

In this chapter, we will examine in which ways the colonial authorities aimed to integrate traditional Congolese farming into the modern, Western agrosystem. What were the civil servants' and agronomists' original objectives and working methods for optimizing the primary sector? When, why and how did they alter or adjust their strategy? And how did their view on the role of the Congolese farmers evolve? Finally, we will examine the effects in practice. Did the production of food for the local population and export crops increase (proportionally), as planned? Did the standard of living improve in rural regions? Or was de Saint Moulin right when he called colonial agriculture in the Congo *le plus grand échec* ('its greatest failure')?

Congolese versus European, or 'Traditional' versus 'Modern'

In official (annual) reports and accounts about the performance of the agrarian sector in the Belgian Congo, civil servants and agronomists invariably distinguished indigenous or traditional agriculture (*agriculture indigène*) from European agriculture, including concession companies such as the *Huileries du Congo Belge* ('Oil Mills of the Belgian Congo'), plantation owners and settler farmers (*colons*). Historians have long copied this division. But in practice, these two agrarian systems were far more closely intertwined than the sources suggest. The consistent use of this dichotomy reinforced the image of inefficient traditional farming vis-à-vis modern, Western agriculture.

Congolese farming was historically a collective enterprise. The land belonged to the village community and was managed by the clan or village head (the local chief). Families could cultivate their assigned plots at their own discretion. They enjoyed usufruct but had no individual rights of ownership. According to British historian Marvin P. Miracle, before 1908, people living in the Congo Basin grew more than seventy different crops. Typical amongst these were rice, corn, cassava, plantain, groundnuts and soy. Living and eating habits had been tailored to the environment. The women worked on the land, taking care of daily tasks such as sowing, planting, weeding and harvesting. The men focused on hunting, fishing and gathering a wide range of foods. All this provided a varied diet. When, after a few years, the soil became impoverished through a lack of fertilization, they prepared new plots: trees and brushwood were cut down and burnt ('slash and burn'). The ash would then be used as a fertilizer. When the distance between the new fields and the village became too great, the community would decide to move the entire village. This form of semi-nomadic agriculture was common in the pre-colonial era but was discouraged by the colonial authorities because they wanted to tighten their grip on the Congolese population and to control the lion's share of the soil.

Belgian agronomists described Congolese farming as primitive and inefficient. The soil became rapidly exhausted and yields were too low. It was impossible to produce major surpluses, which hampered commercialization. This analysis, however, underestimated regional differences, the particularities of Congolese farming and the local people's agency (their ability to act autonomously, despite the restrictions imposed on them). Africanist Jan Vansina showed that during the pre-colonial period, especially in the west of the Congo, an intensive (inter)regional trade in foodstuffs had existed and that Congolese farmers were definitely able to generate market surpluses. What is more, farmers in the more fertile regions, such as Bas-Congo and parts of Kivu and Ruanda-Urundi, applied more efficient farming techniques and cultivated their farmland on a permanent basis.

In the Congo Free State, a short-term vision on agricultural policy prevailed in order, swiftly and with abundance, to get hold of the lucrative commodities and to cash in on large profits. Even though the colonial authorities recognized the land rights of the Congolese communities, these only applied to the village centers and the surrounding arable plots; they shamelessly appropriated the remainder of the vast territory (*terres vacantes*). These areas were part of the Crown Domain or were granted as concessions to European companies or colonists (see Chapter 2). The Congolese people were compelled – under duress or threat of various sorts of punishment – to supply a fixed annual quantity of ivory and later wild rubber. Rubber, drawn off wild trees (*cueillette*), guaranteed enormous profits from the 1890s onwards. This form of legalized plundering (called *Raubwirtschaft* in German) was accompanied by much terror. Besides, the rubber liana close to the villages soon became exhausted and the Congolese people had to go ever further afield to supply the demanded yields. As a consequence, they had less time to grow their own food or to hunt, which brought about malnourishment, physical weakening and increased mortality (see Chapters 2 and 7). The Congo Free State devoted little attention to structural development of the primary sector. The available resources and manpower were limited and the small group of civil servants and agriculturalists in the region possessed little field knowledge. The first botanical gardens, experimental fields and stations, intended to study the climate and the soil in order to boost the cultivation of native and non-native crops, were by 1908 still in their infancy (see Chapters 25 and 27).

Mandatory Cultivation

Belgium's takeover of the Congo in 1908 heralded the dawn of a new agro-economical era. The economic opening up and speedy valorization of natural resources continued to occupy a central place in colonial policy. The Catholic Minister of Colonies, Jules Renkin, assigned a leading role to the primary sector, not only to generate profits and to achieve financial independence for the colony through the export of cash crops, but also to provide enough food for the fast-growing population in the urban and industrial centers. Could both objectives be realized, considering the shortage of manpower?

The Ministry of Colonies' Agricultural Service, set up in 1910 and led until 1933 by Professor Edmond Leplae, an agronomist at the Catholic University of Louvain/Leuven, outlined a multi-track policy. The service initially stimulated and supported the settling of Belgian farmers in the colony, in Katanga in particular. These *colons* had to literally 'take possession' of this rich border region (the British for a while disputed the Belgian Congo's eastern border), produce food for the industrial workers and serve as an example for the Congolese farmers. When, during the First World War, contacts between the colony and the metropole were less smooth, the Belgian Parliament was not able to exercise its control over colonial policy and demand for cotton needed by the Allied troops peaked, precisely then did Leplae manage to introduce a system of compulsory cultivation (*cultures obligatoires*). He did so through the Decree of 20 February 1917, based on the advice of Belgian agronomists and therefore appearing to have scientific legitimacy.

His aim was to step up the production of export crops such as cotton and palm oil. Farming experts determined for each region what and how much should be produced, according to population size, soil fertility, climate and types of crops. The sale of the harvest would enable local people to meet the tax liability imposed on them by the colonial authorities. Indigenous people were also forced to work a specific number of days for the colonizing forces, as porters and for the construction of roads and railway lines, for a fixed, low wage; initially a maximum of 60 days a year (in practice often many more), during the Second World War up to 120 days and from 1957, 45 days (see Chapter 9). Belgium was not the only colonial power with a program of compulsory cultivation. Such systems also existed in British, French and Portuguese colonies, but nowhere else was the forced agricultural production as widespread and drastic as in the Belgian Congo. In the Dutch East Indies, the *kultuurstelsel*, the system of forced farming, had been abolished in as early as 1870, partly after heavy criticism by the author Multatuli in his novel *Max Havelaar*.

Officially, the *cultures obligatoires*, also euphemistically called *cultures éducatives* ('educational cultivation'), were a response to the purported Congolese laziness or the rural population's inability to provide for its own food and take up modern Western agricultural practices. In reality, they first and foremost generated profits for the Western, chiefly Belgian companies, such as the Congolese Cotton Company (*Cotonco*), which had a monopoly and bought the harvested cotton for fixed low prices (see Chapter 8). The system of compulsory cultivation was much-criticized, not only in Belgium, but also internationally, for example by the International Labor Organization (ILO) in Geneva. In 1957, it was comprehensively assessed and reformed, but not abolished. The system, introduced initially as a temporary measure, thus outlived all controversy right up to independence. From an economic perspective and in the short term, compulsory cultivation was a success. Between 1920 and 1948, the export of cotton fibers rose to 51,000 tonnes, that of palm oil from 7,624 to 110,387 tonnes. The production of food crops for the local population, however, was less abundant. Compulsory cultivation disturbed the lives of hundreds of thousands of families in the Congolese countryside. The remuneration for their work was trifling and did not always end up in the right hands, because they were paid out via the local chiefs. What is more, when the assumed production quotas were not achieved, harsh punishments followed.

Officially, it was the colonial authorities' aim to integrate local farmers into the capitalist agrosystem, but in practice they curbed the fast development of a dynamic Congolese farming class. It was difficult for Congolese farmers to get hold of farmland, they were not allowed to employ farmhands, hardly had any capital to invest and were given little access to credit or modern knowledge. During the economic crisis of the 1930s, all attention and resources went into supporting European farming. Yet in some regions, in particular around the cities in Bas-Congo and Katanga, local farmers managed to produce for the commercial market, but these were exceptions.

The Agricultural Service also focused on research. In order to be able to better steer the colony's agro-economic and agrotechnical developments, the colonial authorities wanted to attract more science-based knowledge. There was a growing awareness that the colony's natural riches were not inexhaustible, even though the colonial economy continued to run on extreme exploitation of natural and human resources. Research had to propose structural improvements and offer solutions for problems. For this reason, the state established experimental plantations and research stations spread out over the entire colony. These had three goals: to conduct (fundamental) scientific research that could generate new knowledge and insights for the benefit of private farming initiatives; to operate as commercial players (their crops were sold and profit went into the public purse); and to serve as an example to convince national and international companies and individuals to invest in the Congolese agro-economy.

At first, agronomic research encountered numerous problems. The available budget and the number of researchers were extremely limited, bureaucracy hampered the development of a dynamic research context, and the recruitment of skilled and experienced personnel continued to be an issue. Staff turnover in colonial agricultural administration was extremely high. When the global economy began to pick up again in the middle of the 1920s, many officials started their own farms or plantations. Others began to work for private companies, which paid much better. Leplae, supported in this by Minister Renkin, believed the Government's plantations and experimental stations thus forth should operate even more as private companies, in order to be able to act more flexibly with regard to wages and technical insights. As a result, the Public Enterprise of the Plantations of the Colony (REPCO) was set up by Royal Decree in 1926, after the example of *'s Lands Caoutchouc-bedrijf* ('The Country's Caoutchouc Company') in the Dutch colony of Java.

In the beginning of the 1930s, the Great Depression put an end to the economic boom. The oversupply of colonial products on the global market led to sharp price drops, falling wages and rising unemployment in the Congolese industry and on its plantations.

In rural regions, the situation became even more difficult because many workers returned from the cities to their native villages. Added to this, the global crisis in the Belgian Congo was reinforced by internal, structural problems. The colonial authorities initially responded with measures that were intended to have effect in the short term. Thus, transport costs for agricultural products were reduced significantly and a temporary Fund for Agricultural Credit was set up as a mechanism to help farmers get through this difficult period. However, according to historian Bogumil Jewsiewicki, these initiatives benefitted primarily the export-oriented plantations and the *colons*. In other words, the colonial authorities shifted the effects of the crisis onto the local rural society. What is more, the Congolese rural sector suffered a great deal more under the economic recession than did the countryside in other colonies such as Gold Coast and Uganda, where agrarian production was in the hands of indigenous producers and the impact of the crisis less severe.

The System of *Paysannats Indigènes* (Indigenous Peasantry Scheme)

Nonetheless, the economic crisis of the 1930s gradually caused a shift in the Belgian Congo's agricultural policy. Colonial circles argued increasingly for supporting indigenous agriculture in a way that was scientifically underpinned. A whole range of proposals were considered: smoother access to farmland, modern tools and credit, the provision of education, and the abolition of compulsory cultivation. These ideas were largely legitimized by the speech given by Crown Prince Leopold in the Senate in 1933 following his long journey through the Congo. In this, he broke a lance for the establishment of *paysannats indigènes*, or an independent Congolese farming class, and a reorganization of research into tropical farming.

Because revenue was disappointing and the government no longer saw it as its responsibility to run commercial plantations, the REPCO was shut down and, on 22 December 1933, replaced by the National Institute for the Agronomic Study of the Belgian Congo (INEAC). As a scientific mission, the new institution's task was to support not only European commercial agriculture, but also Congolese farmers. Shortly before the Second World War, INEAC deployed some eighty experts, the majority of whom were in possession of a university degree. It organized training courses for the Agricultural Service's agronomists and technical personnel and aimed for a more rational implementation of compulsory cultivation. At the same time, INEAC reinforced cooperation with private companies. An important new responsibility was the reorganization of indigenous farming, on a scientific basis. The goal was to motivate the Congolese farmers to farm individually (and thus no longer collectively) and to adopt modern Western methods, without breaking entirely with helpful time-honored practices.

INEAC soon began to experiment with *paysannats indigènes*. In 1937, six families took part in the trial project. Although the impact was minimal at first, it initiated an important new phase in colonial agricultural policy. During the Second World War, some more *paysannats* were set up, involving dozens of families: in 1941 in Turumbu (near Léopoldville) and in 1942 close to the station of Bambesa (in Orientale Province). After the war, the *paysannats* system went up a gear. Fundamental to this was a successful cooperation between INEAC and cotton giant *Cotonco*, which was increasingly facing soil exhaustion and erosion. In 1944, in his book *Afrique, terre qui meurt* ('Africa, dying ground'), colonial scientist Jean-Paul Harroy had sounded the alarm because of the shortcomings and negative effects of the European farming methods on the black continent. It was not the traditional practices, as many Western agronomists claimed, but colonial imperialism that had disturbed the equilibrium between soil, fauna, flora and human activities, he argued. In 1946, *Cotonco* proposed to INEAC that it would extend the *paysannats* system near the station of Bambesa to seven thousand square kilometers and include almost 50,000 Congolese people into this form of agricultural colonization. At the end of 1948, more than 5,000 plots had been divided amongst families. Through the experiments of the previous years, the staff of INEAC had acquired the necessary expertise to further develop organized agricultural colonization both in a theoretical and practical sense.

How did the agronomists proceed? Families who agreed to participate, were allotted a plot of farming land. In many cases, these plots belonged to the local community, in accordance with tradition, but the colonial authorities wanted to develop them more efficiently. Taking into account climate and soil conditions, the INEAC experts drew up a cultivation plan that the Congolese farmers had to follow. In most cases this involved a combination of food crops and cash crops. The most important were cotton, coffee and also palm oil and rubber, depending on the region. The cultivation plan tried to incorporate long periods when the land would be left fallow to increase soil fertility. The location and placement of the *paysannats* was given considerable thought: usually along a road, so that the harvests could be promptly transported to cities and industrial centers. The introduction of individual plots simplified the distribution of high-quality sowing seeds and young plants and the monitoring of workers. These workers were also encouraged to live on or near their plots. In short, the entire system was designed to make them develop into capable, independent farmers.

The motives behind the *paysannats* system were both economic and social. For the time being, the colonial authorities wanted to modernize farming techniques in order to increase production, make the Congolese peasants work in a more market-oriented way, let their income increase and thus limit rural exodus. Much attention then went into the expansion of the transport infrastructure, school construction and the setting up of medical facilities, social centers, etc. Besides, the authorities hoped to discipline the Congolese farmers through individual land use. Yet not everyone was equally delighted with the *paysannats*. The large plantations, settler farmers and industrial companies feared the competition of a successful Congolese farming class in the agricultural, food and labor markets.

From the early 1950s onwards, the colonial authorities stepped up their operation. In the Ten-Year Plan (1949-1959), 25 billion francs had been reserved for the development of the colony (see Chapter 13). More than half of this amount went into the expansion of transport infrastructure, and the actual agricultural program could only count on 1.4 billion francs, barely half of which was earmarked for stimulating Congolese farming itself. Yet the ambition was to integrate into the *paysannats* system no fewer than 500,000 Congolese farmers and their families (altogether around 2.5 million people or a quarter of the entire population) by 1959. This did not work out; in 1959, only around 210,000 farmers and their families participated. And meanwhile the system of compulsory cultivation continued to exist.

The *paysannats* were devised top-down by colonial agronomists and technical personnel. It took quite some effort to convince Congolese farmers to take part and to move to the new plots. In order to achieve smoother acceptance of the system, *conseils de paysannats* were launched, intended to facilitate a dialogue between experts and farmers. In practice, this did not work either, and in some regions gentle force was needed through the so-called *travaux d'ordre éducatif* ('educational work'). This coercion only led to an increase in the rural exodus, especially amongst (young) single men. The system also increased pressure on women, who took on the lion share of the farming. For now, little information is available about the income of the *paysannats* farmers. This is said to have been two to three times higher than that of other Congolese farmers or day laborers on European plantations, but doubts exist about the representativeness and accuracy of the available data. In any case, it is clear that, all in all, the improvement of indigenous farming and rural living conditions remained limited until independence and the ambitious expectations were not fulfilled.

Meanwhile, the rural population continued to be the crucial link in the colony's industrial exploitation and lucrative export economy. The available figures are testament to this. The share of food products in 'European agricultural production' in the Congo halved during the 1950s from 7 to 3.5 per cent, in favor of industrial crops for export (such as palm oil, cotton and coffee), which, in 1959, accounted for an impressive 96 per cent of proceeds. In 'indigenous agricultural production' the share of industrial crops increased as well, from 16 to 24 per cent. Moreover, it was the yields of the export crops in particular that improved. It is no surprise therefore that, in order to feed the growing urban and industrial Congolese population, during the 1950s, increasingly greater quantities of food crops needed to be imported.[3]

Conclusion

The evolution of the Belgian Congo's agricultural policy illustrates the colonial authorities' arduous quest to mold the colony's primary sector and rural society on a Western model. Many obstacles had to be negotiated, and this happened with varying success. Colonial agricultural policy got no further than a sub-optimal compromise. In many cases, this was the result of a difficult balancing act between diverse and evolving objectives, views and interests. On the whole, the government's initiatives and measures only partially achieved the ambitions set and generated countless unwelcome effects which the authorities were not always able to monitor or control. (Field) expertise was limited, especially during the early years, and financial resources were insufficient.

A striking feature is that the objectives and achievements of the agricultural policy during the colonial period changed a number of times. Historian Piet Clement distinguishes three major phases. During the first phase, legalized plundering was paramount (the Congo Free State). This was followed by a phase in which economic exploitation was the prime objective and the indigenous people were deployed in the capitalist agrosystem, without any say whatsoever, through the compulsory cultivation scheme. The third phase began in the 1930s, partly in response to the economic crisis, but also because the structural problems required a long-term solution, such as the rural exodus and rapid soil exhaustion due to monocultures, which in turn endangered food supplies for the Congolese people. Agronomists and consultants increasingly felt compelled to hark back to tested local practices. As a consequence, an exchange took place between the two cultures, whereby European agronomists turned to traditional farming practices and Congolese farmers set to work according to so-called rational advice. This interaction created new, hybrid knowledge which was implemented above all on the *paysannats*. The support of INEAC in the organization of the *paysannats* is an apt demonstration of how the colonial authorities used agricultural science to legitimize and realize their economic and social plans, and how scientists involved themselves in the colonial logic in order to underpin economic exploitation and develop rural society.

On the eve of independence, the Congolese rural regions had to contend with countless problems. The flourishing cities exerted a great pull, especially amongst young men. In some regions, food production remained below expectations, which led to shortages, even malnourishment, and necessitated the import of food from neighboring countries. In other words, Léon de Saint Moulin unarguably put his finger on it. Just as in the metropole, industrial interests prevailed in the Belgian Congo. The limited interior spending power and the shortage of rural workers curbed the development of a powerful Congolese agriculture. Then *paysannats* could have turned the tide, even though, according to de Saint Moulin, they had been set up in the first place to safeguard social stability in the countryside (following a period of unrest and revolts) and to offer a response to rural exodus. But they did not get off the ground properly. In his opinion, the prejudices and attitudes of the agronomists and civil servants were the biggest sticking point, even at the end of the 1950s. They continued to typify Congolese farmers as incompetent and lazy, he believed. They still approached them as children *à qui on pouvait tout dicter* ('to whom one could dictate everything').[4]

Bibliography

Documents and visual material about rural society and the agro-economy in the Belgian Congo can be found in the archives of the former Ministry of Colonies, now held at the National Archives of Belgium. This also houses the sizeable archive of the scientific institutions REPCO and INEAC. Personal archives of prominent colonial civil servants and researchers are kept, amongst other locations, at the AfricaMuseum in Tervuren, for example, those of Jean Lebrun, Floribert Jurion and Pierre Staner. A valuable work about the Belgian Congo's rural society, based on writings by INEAC staff members, has been compiled by Drachoussoff, Vladimir, Focan, Alexander, and Hecq, Jacques, *Le développement rural en Afrique centrale. 1908-1960/1962. Synthèse et réflexions*, 2 volumes, King Baudouin Foundation, Brussels, 1992. Agricultural and rural policy has been described in detail by Mokili Danga Kassa, Jeannôt, *Politiques agricoles et promotion rurale au Congo-Zaïre 1885-1997*, L'Harmattan, Paris, 1998. An analysis of fundamental and applied agrarian research is presented in Menge, Wemo, *Transfert du savoir agricole au Congo-Zaïre. Héritage colonial et recherche agronomique*, L'Harmattan, Paris, 2001. A few historians focus on the importance of the agricultural economy in the former colony; see for example Clement, Piet, 'Agricultural Policies and Practices in the Belgian Congo. The Origins and Implementation of the "Indigenous Peasantry" Scheme (1917-1959)', in Vanderlinden, Jacques, ed., *The Belgian Congo Between the Two World Wars*, ARSOM/KAOW, Brussels, 2019, p. 83-128; Segers, Yves, Van Molle, Leen and Kerckhofs, Stephanie, '"C'est par la science qu'on colonise". The relationship between the Great Depression and agricultural policy in the Belgian-Congo', in Vanderlinden, Jacques, ed., *The Belgian Congo Between the Two World Wars*, ARSOM/KAOW, Brussels, 2019, p. 159-189; Segers, Yves, and Vekemans, Charlotte, 'Settler Farming, Agricultural Colonization and Development in Katanga (Belgian Congo), 1910-1920', *Historia Agraria*, 2020, p. 195-226.

Notes

1 de Saint Moulin, Léon, 'Les essais de modernisation de l'agriculture du Zaïre à l'époque coloniale', *Zaïre-Afrique*, 202, 1986, p. 83.
2 'Comment les Bantous du Congo belge s'acheminent vers le paysannat. Communication faite au Congrès de la Société indigène, Paris, 1931', *Bulletin Agricole du Congo Belge*, 22, 1931, 4, p. 578.
3 *La situation économique du Congo belge et du Ruanda-Urundi en 1959*, Ministère des Affaires Africaines, Brussels, 1960, p. 34-35; N'Dongala, E., 'La production vivrière au Congo pendant la période 1960-1966', in *Indépendance, inflation, développement. L'économie congolaise de 1960 à 1965*, Mouton, Paris, 1968, p. 750-751.
4 de Saint Moulin, Léon, 'Les essais de modernisation de l'agriculture du Zaïre à l'époque coloniale', *Zaïre-Afrique*, 202, 1986, p. 96.

JOHAN LAGAE AND
JACOB SABAKINU KIVILU (†)

12. Infrastructure, Urban Landscapes and Architecture

Traces of 'Development' or Instruments of 'Exploitation'?

In his 2010 exhibition *Congo (belge)*, renowned Magnum photographer Carl De Keyzer presented some hundred images of traces in the Congo left by Belgium's colonization of the territory. His photographs depicted bridges, schools, churches, hospitals, houses, hotels, factories and prisons (see Chapter 30). The panorama compiled was at times disconcerting because of the ramshackle state of the colonial-built legacy. As a result, the exhibition was misunderstood. Despite the photographer's different agenda, it was often mistakenly interpreted as a nostalgic project. Nevertheless, *Congo (belge)* remains a remarkable testimony, demonstrating the considerable amount of construction work 'little Belgium' undertook in the Congo. Mapping the traces of colonial construction activity across the entire Congolese territory allows us to close a gap in nineteenth- and twentieth-century architectural history, as well as to make a correction in this history which thus far has remained far too Eurocentric. The traces in question are also an invitation to re-evaluate the notion of 'heritage'. To whom do they belong these days? Do they really constitute a 'shared heritage', as, for instance, the International Council on Monuments and Sites (ICOMOS) suggests? What memories cling to these stones? And what does their future look like: should they be restored, or rather demolished?

The relevant, yet complex question of the Congo's architectural colonial heritage is not, however, what we will address here. Rather we will discuss how infrastructure, urban landscapes and architecture can serve as a powerful starting point for the writing of an alternative history of the Congo's colonial past. How did colonization transform the Congolese landscape and what does it say about the way in which 'development' or 'economic activity' (*mise en valeur*, here also referred to as 'exploitation') was implemented? How was the colonial city laid out and what does this teach us about colonial society's segregation? What kind of buildings did the Belgians build in the Congo? As these buildings formed the setting of the 'colonial encounter' in all its complexity, we need to have a good understanding of how they 'functioned'. By examining types of cities, buildings and interiors, we can thus obtain a nuanced insight into colonial mechanisms of domination and their effects – which, in colonial daily life, were not always as clear cut as it first appears. Just as in other colonial territories, colonialism in the Belgian Congo was a complex phenomenon in which numerous protagonists – Africans, Europeans and others – had a role to play. Structuring our analysis of the colonial urban and built environment on three levels (territory, city, building), we propose a reading of colonial history that goes beyond the traditional dichotomy of 'active colonizers' and 'passive colonized'.

The Transformation of the Territory between 'Development' and 'Exploitation'

Colonization first and foremost involves a territory's 'penetration', followed by its 'occupation' and finally its 'exploitation'. The extractive economy that formed the basis of Leopold II's Congo Free State and later also of the Belgian Congo (see Chapters 2 and 8), required an extensive infrastructure: a network of railways and roads, often monumental bridges, ports and airports which served as gateways to the 'motherland', large industrial sites with warehouses, factories and labor camps, as well as vast plantations some of which were attached to centers for agricultural research (see Chapter 11). Even the urbanization of the colonial territory ran largely along an economic logic: most cities were primarily nodes of production and/or reservoirs of labor.

The Bas-Congo region is a case in point, illustrating to what extent the extractive economy led to a fundamental reorganization of the territory and a radical transformation of the landscape, alongside the massive construction of buildings erected by the colonial state or the – Catholic as well as Protestant – mission organizations. From the end of the nineteenth century onwards, Bas-Congo was served by the notorious railway line between Matadi and Kinshasa. This iconic 'iron road', which became a symbol for the 'penetration' of the territory that Leopold II had set in motion, formed an alternative to this region's unnavigable section of the Congo River. It constituted a true 'lifeline' for the colonial economy, or as Stanley put it: 'Without [this] railway line, the Congo is not worth a penny.'[1] From the 1920s, as part of the development program initiated by the then Minister of Colonies, Louis Franck, the entire line was furnished with impressive railway infrastructure, stations, maintenance workshops and numerous, often large-scale labor camps. During this same period, Matadi and Kinshasa's port infrastructure also took shape. Over the years, more sites were added to the economic landscape of Bas-Congo, including a cement factory in Lukala, established in 1921, and Moerbeke's immense sugar plantations, two enterprises that are still active to this day. During the interwar years, a road network was constructed, resulting in the opening up of production sites even further away. In the 1950s, power pylons appeared, supplying the prime economic nodes and urban centers with electricity from Zongo's gigantic hydro-electric power stations, and heralding the transformation of this natural environment into an industrial landscape – even though this region never became the 'Ruhr area of the tropics' that some had been fantasizing about during the 1920s (see Chapter 13).

Constituting a direct consequence of a policy aimed at 'economic exploitation' as well as serving an agenda of 'development', all this infrastructure was built on land that was no *terra nullius* or no-mans-land. Rather, these territories were by and large already inhabited, farmed or organized by different ethnic groups and crossed by trade routes dating from long before the arrival of the Belgians (see Chapter 2). In Bas-Congo, as elsewhere in the colony, the transformation of the territory and the landscape thus had to be negotiated with local rulers, in practice primarily with the traditional chiefs (see Chapter 18). Some of these tried to extract personal financial gain from the new situation caused by the colonization, while others adopted a more ambivalent attitude. The 'economic exploitation' also entailed a large demand for manpower, which often was impossible for the local population to meet. More than the radical transformation of the landscape, the extractive economy and ensuing recruitment of workers had major and destabilizing consequences which fundamentally changed the flows of people and goods in Bas-Congo, either by force or otherwise (see Chapter 9). Because roads, railways and rivers did not suddenly come to a stop at the outer edges of the colonial territory, these conduits often crossed its borders. As such, we need to study Belgian colonization in Central Africa in a more transnational perspective.

The Segregated Colonial City: Plans versus Reality

The fundamental change in mobility that was put in motion by Belgium's colonization can be seen most clearly in the Belgian Congo's cities. Especially after 1945, they attracted many rural people who were exhausted from the war effort (see Chapter 4). But in the norms and forms of colonial urban planning. Since the Congo Free State era, groups occupying an intermediary position in colonial society furthermore had been voicing their opposition to urban planning practices. Playing a crucial role in the urban economy and often maintaining closer ties with the African population, Greek, Portuguese, Italian, but also West African or 'Asiatic' small traders had a tangible influence on the development and planning of colonial cities. In many instances, their intervention would halt the implementation of a planned urban project.

Recent research into colonial policing in African cities, including in the Belgian Congo (see Chapter 15), shows that racial segregation in daily life was far from a matter of course. It had to be enforced continuously, often through coercion and the use of force. Mobility between the white and black city, for instance, was governed by colonial legislation, with a curfew for both white and black citizens, amongst other things. Yet this control proved hard to implement. The *zone neutre* often appeared more porous than legislation suggests; at times it even operated as a contact area. Moreover, city life constituted a break with the traditions of rural populations. From the 1930s onwards, the 'African city' was called the *centre extra-coutumier* ('centers not subject to customary law'). The colonial city thus established a new kind of space that enabled and even encouraged the emergence of a particular urban culture in which all actors, not just Congolese or Belgian, had a role to play. Even remarkable subcultures emerged within urban colonial society, the 'Bills' in postwar Léopoldville being a case in point (see Chapter 16). Our research into the sanitary alleyways (*ruelles sanitaires*) in Lubumbashi – narrow paths along the rear boundaries of the plots in the 'European city' – reveals another example of the complexity of colonial urbanity. These alleyways were built from as early as the foundation of the city in 1910, so that African domestic servants – the so-called 'boys' – were able, without being seen, to remove waste and household refuse which did not fit the image of the 'clean' colonial city. Soon, however, these passages became places where these servants could meet, even if briefly, and escape the 'all-seeing eye' of colonial rule. It did not take long for the local authorities to see the alleys as a 'threat to public security'. Yet the plans to remove these circulatory structures from the townscape remained largely unimplemented. If you visit Lubumbashi today, you can still find traces of these alleyways. They remind us that the daily reality of the colonial city was not a question of 'subjugated' and 'subjugators', but was rather produced through a continuous, if obviously inequal, process of negotiation between urban actors. In other words, studying the colonial city requires a moving away from the all too simplistic paradigms that have long dominated historiography about the Belgian Congo, such as that of the 'active colonizer' and 'passive colonized'.

The 'Colonial House', a Place of Separation and Encounter

Racial segregation in the urban environment also became noticeable on the scale of the individual building. In South Africa, apartheid manifested itself quite openly on the outside of buildings, which had clearly separated entrances for black and white people. Although this was not always as conspicuous in the Belgian Congo, similar 'petty apartheid' strategies can be found in the separate circulatory arrangements for Africans and Europeans in the European city's offices, hospitals, shops and even houses.

It is important to study these buildings from a plural perspective, so that we can critically examine the 'developmental logic' that they appear to embody while revealing their, at times, contradictory character. The extensive network of schools, hospitals and houses that the *Office des Cités Africaines* ('Office of African Districts') built during the 1950s, for instance, obviously constituted an impressive infrastructure reflecting the idea of the 'model colony' vehiculated by postwar propaganda (see Chapter 24). In some cases, these spaces offered Africans opportunities for social mobility, but they generally remained instruments of a paternalistic colonial policy that aimed to retain a clear division and hierarchy between black and white. The majority of these buildings were in keeping with 'welfare colonialism' as had been introduced in the Congo on the basis of the Ten-Year Plan (1949-1959) (see Chapter 13). But this policy also entailed the construction of a network of disciplinary institutions, such as prisons, psychiatric hospitals and relegation camps (see Chapter 15). In other words, through architecture, we can examine in a tangible way what Nancy Hunt called the Belgian Congo's 'nervous state'.

Be that as it may, the 'colonial encounter' continued to be an ambivalent theme, because in daily life, colonization took shape in all kinds of encounters between groups and people who, at times, stepped outside the boundaries and constraints of colonial power. The 'colonial house', a term which, in sources of the time, was reserved for the colonizer's place of residence, illustrates how complex the colonial regime of 'living apart together' could be, from the era of the Congo Free State right up to independence. In the colonial house, all kinds of forms of segregation based on race and gender were distinctly palpable, but these could occasionally be transcended, as becomes clear when investigating an evolution in architectural typology. From the 1920s, the 'tropical bungalow', which formed the standard house in the early days of colonization, was replaced by the 'villa'. The bungalow was characterized, among other things, by a veranda which ran around the entire house whereas the villa was more in tune with a Western house in its appearance, while being characterized by a clearer separation between living and servants' quarters. This change was not only prompted by progress in building techniques; it was chiefly the result of growing criticism of the veranda. Indeed, from the beginning of the twentieth century, some official sources presented this particular space as a *refuge des paresseux*, a refuge for lazy people. It was true that often the veranda of the tropical bungalow presented a 'not very civilized' image of habitation, with a white bachelor hanging his washing out to dry or having a drink with his friends, sometimes in the company of his *ménagère* (literally 'housekeeper', often also 'concubine', see Chapter 19). In a telling detail: during the 1950s, a colonial magazine still referred to this kind of veranda from the pioneering days as a *whisky barza*.[3]

When, around the 1920s, the European spouse made her entrance into the Belgian Congo, this brought about a fundamental shift in relations with African domestic servants (the 'boys'). The veranda was considered problematic in this context, as it offered direct access to all the rooms and thus carried with it 'too great a promiscuity', in the words of an engineer from 1921.[4] Just as cities in the Belgian Congo were split up into separate areas for blacks and whites, the principle of racial segregation also impacted the organization of the colonial home. In Léopoldville, for instance, the 'boys' were no longer allowed to sleep on the premises of their master; and in Élisabethville, where the urban culture was strongly influenced by the example of the British colonies in southern Africa, domestic servants were housed in an extremely modest shack at the back of the garden, called the *boyerie*. The 'boy' might be indispensable for making the life of his master in the colony easy and pleasant, but he had to be discreet, or better still, remain invisible. From the interwar years onwards, a separate room was therefore introduced in colonial homes, marked as *office* ('scullery') on the building plans. This term was borrowed from the typical layout of a bourgeois house in the 'motherland'. It is a room between the living room and kitchen/laundry room, screening the house owners not only from cooking smells and noises, but also from the boys' 'indiscretion'.

Over the years, the rules for this colonial regime of 'living apart together' became increasingly codified, in the form of handbooks for women leaving for the colony, for instance. Yet these rules were not fixed nor absolute, and could, in practice, be adapted depending on the views and mentality of the homeowner and his family. Many testimonies suggest that racial segregation in day-to-day life tended to be a rather relative concept. White children frequently played with their black servants' counterparts in the garden. For adults, transcending racial and gender barriers tended to be more difficult, as is evident from studies into miscegenation and prostitution in the Belgian Congo (see Chapter 19). At any rate, it is important not to minimize the unequal conditions underlying this regime of 'living apart together' and not to downplay the 'petty apartheid' as a mere form of 'social contract', as some ex-colonials claim still today. The *Vocabulaire de ville d'Élisabethville* by André Yav, a testimony from the 1960s written by a former domestic servant, contains unsettling passages about the wretched living conditions of a Congolese father being accommodated with a large family in a *boyerie*. In these 'single-room houses', there was no privacy whatsoever, which led to awkward situations 'when getting up and going to bed'. Although the *boyeries* often had two extra rooms for the domestic servant to live in, Yav wrote, 'the "white man" preferred to use these as a chicken shed or rabbit hutch'.[5]

Conclusion

Infrastructure, urban planning, architecture – research into these three domains demonstrates that the colonization of the Congo was a complex phenomenon that was experienced by all those involved in different, divergent and sometimes contradictory ways. The fact that Belgium made a large effort to build many houses, schools and hospitals dovetailed with the idea that colonization had a 'civilizing mission', or, post-1945, that a policy of 'development' was pursued. Yet these efforts were on the whole directly related to the colony's economic exploitation. The intention was primarily to efficiently organize the extractive economy. In addition, architectural heritage in the former Belgian Congo reflects quite plainly the racial segregation which was standard throughout the entire colonial era. The bipartite layout of the colonial city, just like the separated circulation of white and black people in buildings, showed to what degree the color bar pervaded all aspects of daily life in the Belgian Congo. Yet, a discrepancy often appeared to occur between urban plans and the reality on the ground. This was primarily the result of the colonial authorities lacking the necessary financial resources, or due to difficulties caused by the terrain, or because of resistance by different protagonists within colonial society. Research shedding light on colonization from a spatial perspective thus illustrates that different realities existed in which a multiplicity of actors played a role. That is why it is important to go beyond frameworks of analysis that are too simplistic, and produce schematic narratives of 'active colonizers' versus 'passive colonized'. We should also acknowledge the existence and impact of groups and individuals who occupied an intermediary position. Furthermore, as certain connections and flows crossed the borders of the colonial territory, viewing the history of the colonial Congo in a purely Belgian Congolese perspective is too reductive. Because the present-day debate about the Congo's colonial past appears to be characterized by increasing polarization, it is both salutary and urgent to examine the complex colonial situation in the Belgian Congo through an analysis of colonial spaces and their use.

Bibliography

During the 1990s, Bruno De Meulder launched the investigation into colonial space in the Congo with his occasionally provocative works: De Meulder, Bruno, *De kampen van Kongo*, Meulenhoff-Kritak, Amsterdam-Leuven, 1996 and De Meulder, Bruno, *Kuvuande Mbote. Een eeuw architectuur en stedenbouw in Kongo*, Houtekiet, Antwerp, 2000. The research field was widened through the studies by Johan Lagae into the architects who had worked in the Congo, an overview of which has been included in Van Loo, Anne, ed., *Repertorium van de architectuur in België van 1830 tot heden/Dictionnaire de l'architecture en Belgique de 1830 à nos jours*, Mercatorfonds, Antwerp, 2003. With regard to urban and architectural heritage, we refer to the websites wikinshasa.org and www.urbacongo.info, and to the publications by Johan Lagae and Bernard Toulier, in addition to those by Yves Robert and his colleagues at the École de La Cambre/ULB. Jean-Luc Vellut, Léon de Saint Moulin, Jacob Sabakinu Kivilu and Côme Khonde Ngoma di Mbumba likewise conducted studies into the history of Congolese cities, even though the spatial aspect does not always loom large. The analyses by Nancy Hunt and Didier Gondola are extremely useful. Since 2000, important research has been conducted in Lubumbashi into the 'urban memory' by historian Donatien Dibwe dia Mwembu among others. The work on Kinshasa by anthropologist Filip De Boeck continues to be an extremely important reference. Since 2007, the two authors of this chapter have been collaborating on architecture and urban history, including as supervisors for doctoral research by Luce Beeckmans, Sofie Boonen, Robby Fivez and

Simon De Nys-Ketels, see Lagae, Johan, and Sabakinu Kivilu, Jacob, 'Producing New Spatial(ized) (Hi)stories on Congolese Cities: Reflections on Ten Years of Collaboration between UGent and Unikin', *Afrika Focus*, 31, 2018, 2, p. 87-106 (available online on https://ojs.ugent.be/AF/article/view/9920). To conclude, we would like to mention a few additional publications by the authors of this chapter. By Johan Lagae: 'In Search of a "comme chez soi": The Ideal Colonial House in Congo (1885-1960)', in Vellut, Jean-Luc, ed., *Itinéraires croisés de la modernité au Congo Belge (1920-1950)*, CÉDAF-L'Harmattan, Tervuren-Paris, 2001, p. 239-282; with De Keyser, Thomas, and Vervoort, Jef, *Boma 1880-1920: Colonial Capital City or Cosmopolitan Trading Post?*, A&S Books-MRAC, Gent-Tervuren (cd-rom), 2005; with Toulier, Bernard, eds., *Kinshasa*, Civa, Brussels, 2013 (Collection Villes et Architecture), with a contribution by Jacob Sabakinu Kivilu. By Jacob Sabakinu Kivilu: 'La dynamique de l'espace du Bas-Zaïre. Quelques données d'analyse sur les voies de communication de 1855 à 1938', *Cultures et Développement*, 9, 1979, 2, p. 247-259; 'Chemin de fer et intégration à l'économie capitaliste au Bas-Zaïre', in Jewsiewicki, Bogumil, and Chrétien, Jean-Pierre, eds., *Ambiguïtés de l'innovation. Sociétés rurales et technologies en Afrique centrale et occidentale au XXe siècle*, Éd. Safi, Sainte-Foy-Québec, 1984, p. 266-295; with Obotela Rashidi, Noël, eds., *Engagements historiques et méthodologiques sur le Congo-Kinshasa. Regards, calculs, pratiques urbaines et sociales. Mélanges offerts au R.P. Léon de Saint Moulin*, MRAC-L'Harmattan, Tervuren-Paris (in print).

Notes

1 This by now legendary statement by H.M. Stanley is often quoted without precise acknowledgment. Stanley expresses this opinion on several occasions in his writing, often differently phrased. See for example: Stanley, H.M., *The Congo and the Founding of the Free State*, part 1, Sampson Low, Marston, Searle and Rivington, London, 1885, p. 463; and Cornet, René Jules, *La bataille du rail. La construction du chemin de fer de Matadi au Stanley Pool*, L. Cuypers, Brussels, 1947, p. 30. For the historical context of this statement, see Nicolaï, Henri, 'L'image de l'Afrique centrale au moment de la création de l'État Indépendant du Congo', in Stengers, Jean, ed., *Le centenaire de l'État Indépendant du Congo. Recueil d'études – Bijdragen over de honderdste verjaring van de Onafhankelijke Congostaat*, ARSOM/KAOW, Brussels, 1988 (in particular p. 20 and note 34).

2 Chalux, *Un an au Congo*, Librairie A. Dewit, Brussels, 1925, p. 110 and p. 24.

3 'In so far as it ever existed, the time of the idling colonial and the "whisky-barza" has gone, and our grandparents no longer need to fear that the family's black sheep will set out for Africa.' Stienon, Jean, 'L'Architecte au Congo belge', *La Revue Congolaise du Bâtiment et de l'Industrie*, 1953, 10, p. 22.
4 Engineer Habig in *Le Matériel colonial*, 1921, 12, p. 347.
5 *'Vocabulaire de ville d'Élisabethville* d'André Yav', in Jewsiewicki, Bogumil, Dibwe dia Mwembu, Donatien, and Giordano, Rosario, eds., *Lubumbashi 1910-1920. Mémoire d'une ville industrielle*, L'Harmattan, Paris, 2010, p. 45.

GUY VANTHEMSCHE

13. The Congo, a Colony Heading for 'Development'?

In the beginning of the twentieth century, colonization was justified with a dual argumentation. The colony made the 'motherland' more prosperous and powerful, on the one hand; on the other, the colonized populace obtained 'civilization' in exchange for labor and natural resources. However, 'civilization' was (and still is) a vague notion emphasizing immaterial aspects (ideas, attitudes, ethics, artistic expressions, and so on) while discarding the socio-economic dimensions. Yet colonialism had a profound impact on the latter: the occupying authorities introduced a monetary and tax system; they dragged adult men away from their homes to carry goods or to work in mines or on plantations; they created a repressive market economy with forced cultivation and unilaterally enforced prices and wages, etc. (see Chapters 8, 9 and 11). But what societal model did the colonizers have in mind in the long run? To put it differently: what would (or should) the Congo look like in the future, more specifically, in the socio-economic sphere? Would it be exploited at will till the end of time? Or was it destined to become an exact copy of the 'motherland', or some different and novel type of society? The classical colonial rhetoric remained extremely vague.

Over the course of the 1940s this lacuna was filled to some extent. From then on, the authorities proclaimed that they (also) wanted to 'develop' the colonized territories. Why this change in discourse? What did the new concept of 'development' entail exactly? Were those words turned into deeds – was a new colonial policy effectively pursued? And if so, did this strategy succeed? Or to put it more pointedly, was the Congo gradually turning into a 'developed country' *thanks to* its colonization?

Critics of Industrialization in the 1920s and 1930s

By the 1920s, plans to industrialize the colony already existed, even before the notion of 'development' emerged. A spectacular example was Colonel Pierre Van Deuren's ambitious project for the lower reaches of the Congo River. Gigantic infrastructure works around the rapids would create an inexhaustible source of hydroelectricity, and this energy would generate flourishing chemical and metal industries (see Chapter 12). 'If our projects are carried out, Bas-Congo is destined to become one of the most prominent centers of [economic] activities in the world.'[1] This techno-optimistic prediction never materialized: despite the construction of the Inga Dams, in the 1960s and 1970s, Bas-Congo never became the 'tropical Ruhr [region]' Van Deuren had dreamt of.

But aside from such plans, the colony's rapid 'industrialization' was a hotly debated topic during the interwar period. This term, however, did not refer to the growth of (still marginal) manufacturing industries, but to the substantial investments by large companies that produced commodities for the global market (copper, tin, gold, palm oil, coffee, and so on; see Chapter 8). Some colonial circles worried about this evolution, fearing that unbridled capitalist investments would entirely disrupt Congolese society. Excessive recruitment of workers, whether forced or not, was considered a mortal peril, both literally and figuratively, since village communities were robbed of their vital forces (see Chapter 9). This rural environment was the Roman Catholic's mission territory par excellence (see Chapter 21); many missionaries were therefore critical of the Belgian capitalists' unrestrained investments. As fervent 'indigenists' – defenders of the 'unspoiled' Congolese rural community – they wanted to clamp down on wage labor within the Congolese population, and therefore on the establishment and/or expansion of large enterprises.

But in other circles too, many were worried about the dramatic fate of the Congolese. Occasionally such criticisms were echoed publicly, especially in Parliament, for example when socialist leader Émile Vandervelde denounced social abuses in the Congo. But on the whole, such criticism was voiced behind closed doors. Catholic senior civil servant Octave Louwers, for instance, did not mince his words in internal memos: 'In the capitalist system of exploitation, the social and material improvement of the natives is not the essential objective of the development of our country, as set out in our Colonial Charter. [...] The most important goal is the exploitation of the country's resources for the profit of capitalist companies. [...] The natives get no more than the crumbs that fall off the table.'[2] In countless Belgian colonial meetings, the former interim Deputy Governor-General Colonel Alexis Bertrand argued tirelessly for a more humane social policy for the 'natives'. Even the renowned Governor-General Pierre Ryckmans expressed this view. On leaving his post in 1946 and returning to Belgium, he declared: 'Our natives in the villages do not have much; their living standard is so low that not only can it not be lowered, it is also already below survival minimum. [...] the masses are poorly housed, badly dressed, ill-nourished, at the mercy of diseases and a premature death'.[3] And this criticism came from a high-ranking and unimpeachable source! Obviously, half a century of intense capitalist activity had brought nothing (or very little) to the ordinary Congolese man or woman, who lived in abject material misery (see Chapter 10).

'Development' as a New Leitmotiv (End of the 1940s)

Unsurprisingly, this painful diagnosis was silenced by the ever-triumphant Belgian colonial propaganda machine (see Chapter 24). But it did reverberate in Belgian colonial circles. The international context made it all the more critical. After the Second World War, the world suddenly looked very different. During the conflict, the colonial powers had been dealt some telling blows, not only in Europe, but also in their overseas territories (see Chapter 4). Many colonies, even prominent ones (e.g. British India), became independent. The new superpowers (the United States and the Soviet Union) were both anticolonialist, albeit for different reasons. The colonial powers could count on little understanding in the recently created United Nations. On the contrary, they found themselves in the dock. Their colonial policy was relentlessly criticized by other nations, more specifically ex-colonies. From then on, the colonizers had to 'account' for their actions in (what remained of) their colonial empires. In this respect a new factor was of overriding importance. During the second half of the 1940s, a new concept was catching on globally amongst economists, opinion formers and politicians: the inseparable twin concepts of 'development' and 'underdevelopment'. While in a handful of rich nations economic prosperity seemed to soar, growing unstoppably, the majority of the planet remained stuck in poverty. Closing this gap was a new task for politicians – at least in theory.

In short, during the second half of the 1940s, colonial dominance could no longer be promoted with the woolly justification of 'bringing about civilization'. The old argument that colonization was good because it (only) benefitted the 'mother country', had become obsolete. Henceforth, the colonized society was to be the prime beneficiary of colonization. More specifically, it had to be lifted out of 'underdevelopment' by the benevolent and altruistic 'motherland'. The colonial government thus had to pursue a 'development policy' offering clear advantages for the colonized population and society.

This realization had also registered within Belgian colonial circles just after the war. It confirmed and even reinforced the negative diagnoses such as those by Ryckmans. Moreover, the exiled Belgian Government had survived the war thanks to the existence *and* the support of the colony. Belgium thus had a moral and material debt with respect to the Congo. The Belgian authorities recognized that reality by stepping up their medical-social action, which was still very poor at the time. For this reason, the Fund for Indigenous Wellbeing (FBEI) was set up in 1947 (see Chapter 22). But that was not all. Two years later, the Belgian colonial authorities launched an ambitious 'Ten-Year Plan for the Economic and Social Development of the Belgian Congo'.

The Ten-Year Plan (1949-1959) and the Colony's Modernization

A few years earlier, the big colonial brothers, France and Great Britain, had already launched a distinctive development policy for their colonies. Belgium could not lag behind. The groundwork for an all-encompassing development plan began in 1947. Two years later the document was completed. Its authors started from a painful assessment: the Congo suffered from structural shortcomings, which could and should be remedied by targeted actions.

First, the economy was much too focused on the export of a handful of primary commodities; as a result, it was too sensitive to cyclical economic trends. The 1929-1930 crisis had dealt heavy blows to large-scale exporting businesses and consequently to the many Congolese employed by them. Second, inland agriculture was in a ramshackle state. It was in urgent need of support and reform, more specifically through the expansion of the so-called *paysannats*, a system intended to make the Congolese farmers more independent, modern and productive (see Chapter 11). Third, the Congolese processing industry was far too weak and had to be stimulated. The Congo should eventually export more and import fewer manufactured goods. Likewise, Congolese traditional crafts had to be supported. Fourth, serious social problems had to be addressed through programs for housing, hygiene and education. The authors of the Ten-Year Plan even expressly proclaimed that they had put the interests of the Congolese people first (*La primauté des intérêts indigènes*). But to fulfil all these objectives, large-scale investments had to be made in transport infrastructure and in public utilities (electricity networks, for instance). Meeting these objectives required huge amounts of money. The authors of the plan anticipated no less than 25 billion Belgian francs in expenditure over ten years. So on average 2.5 billion per year – a considerable sum, especially when compared to the Belgian Congo's total public expenditure (which, in 1947, amounted to 3.7 billion).

The 'Positive' Effects of the Ten-Year Plan

The Ten-Year Plan had a certain propagandistic effect. In international forums, Belgium was now able to justify its dominance over the Congo with a fashionable argument: it was 'developing' its colony and enhancing the wellbeing of its subjects. Whether this argument actually convinced the anticolonialists is doubtful; moreover, the answer to this question falls outside our scope. More importantly, did the Plan indeed 'develop' the Belgian colony? Before answering this question, let us examine the financial aspects.

First, costs were running out of control. In 1958, the Ten-Year Plan had cost around 50 billion francs, double the planned amount. What was this financial manna spent on? In 1959, expenditure for transport and telecommunication had gobbled up almost half of the resources (46.3 per cent). Expenditure on water distribution and electricity (11.7 per cent), housing (6.1 per cent) and health care and education (14.6 per cent) improved the living conditions in the colony. Expenditure on public administration (7.3 per cent) gave the Congo an evident stamp of 'modernity' during the 1950s: brand-new buildings and public resources dovetailed beautifully with the image of the future-focused, healthy colony that the authorities wanted to present. Remarkably, only a paltry 6.4 per cent went into agriculture – we will come back to this shortly.

Second, these figures only relate to public investments. 'Ten-Year Plan' was in fact a misnomer: it had nothing in common with the eponymous plans launched by the so-called communist countries. In the Congo, there were no compulsory investments in specific sectors, there were no enforced production objectives, etc. In reality, the Belgian colonial development plan was no more than a coordinated program of public spending over the longer term – in itself not a bad achievement for a government used to short-term thinking and acting.

Attracted by the public spending programs *and* by favorable prices for primary commodities on the global markets, private capital also flowed into the colony in vast amounts: no less than 66.5 billion francs between 1950 and 1957 – a multiple of the public funds. This double supply of (public and private) capital led to a true surge. Between 1946 and 1957, the Congolese economy grew by an annual average of 7 per cent, an impressive achievement internationally. Productivity in the private sector doubled in less than ten years; twice as many goods were produced using the same input of labor. This also had a positive effect on the purchasing power of the Congolese. It doubled over the course of the 1950s, boosting internal consumption. In the cities, the standard of living of the black wage earners rose, while medical and hygienic conditions also improved. This also stimulated the Congolese manufacturing industries. Textile factories, breweries, building firms and so forth enjoyed a notable increase in their production.

Negative Aspects of this Evolution

Underneath these spectacular achievements, the Ten-Year Plan also had important shortcomings. Despite its boom, the Congolese economy remained unbalanced and lopsided. While the production of consumer goods undeniably thrived, the Congo was and remained chiefly a producer of primary export goods. The considerable public investment in transport infrastructure (especially the railways) had even reinforced the economy's predominant orientation towards foreign markets. The Congo's economic health was still largely determined by the global economic cycles. The spectacular growth of the 1950s was in fact largely built on quicksand.

Another fundamental weakness of Congolese society, the stagnation of traditional African agriculture, was not remedied either. On the contrary, the problems of this crucial sector became ever more acute. During the 1950s, production of foodstuffs for the Congolese rose by 1.7 to 1.9 per cent a year, while the population was growing by an annual 2.5 per cent. The Congo was therefore no longer able to feed itself. As a result, more food was imported (from 116,000 tonnes in 1955 to 211,000 tonnes in 1959) (see Chapter 11). Economic 'progress' remained largely limited to a few 'modern' agglomerations: the rural communities, where most people still lived, did not enjoy the rise in purchasing power. Consequently, the cities attracted increasing numbers of people. During the late colonial period the towns were bursting out of their seams. In addition, unemployment began to rise.

Last but not least, the Ten-Year Plan induced a financial hangover. Impressive sums had been raised *and* spent, but they were not a generous 'gift' from the 'motherland' to its colony. Avaricious Belgium had refused to chip in financially for Congolese development. Despite all the propaganda, the Ten-Year Plan was no 'development aid' *avant la lettre*. Quite the reverse, the Congo financed its 'development' with its own public financial resources. The budgetary surpluses of the end of the 1940s melted away like snow and in 1959, the Congolese Government was dealing with gaping deficits. The plan was also financed by loans. The Congolese public debt increased twelve-fold, from 3.7 billion francs in 1949 to no less than 46 billion in 1960. When the Congo became independent in 1960, it carried a heavy debt.

Conclusion

Did colonization result in the 'development' of the Congo? Undoubtedly, the country changed rapidly under colonial rule and impressive economic growth figures were indeed recorded, especially during the 1950s. This expansion also generated a trickle-down effect: the material lives of many Congolese improved. They consumed more and their housing became more comfortable as a result of colonization. One should not forget, however, that in these respects the Congo of the 1950s contrasted strongly with the previous era, when the picture was undoubtedly gloomier. The final years of Belgian rule were by no means representative of the entire colonial history.

From a broader perspective, it is also clear that colonization was responsible for other, far less 'positive' effects. As elsewhere in the 'Third World' – this concept had only recently been coined – the economy was facing painful disruptions and lasting imbalances, which could not be eliminated with the wave of a magic wand. Even a totalitarian colonial regime without freedom of expression, trade unions and political opposition was unable to do so. The seemingly 'omnipotent' colonizer had reached the limits of the changes it had set in motion over the course of the preceding decades in an abrupt, even brutal fashion. From the onset of colonization, it had given priority to the export of primary commodities, at an extremely high 'social cost' (a euphemism for the ruthless exploitation of the Congolese workers). This fundamental trend, i.e. the focus on export, persisted, despite the lucid diagnoses by the authors of the Ten-Year Plan and by various economists and sociologists at the end of the 1950s. Colonialism had set in motion other, associated, evolutions such as nascent urbanization and the crisis of local agriculture. This ultimately resulted in the burgeoning rift between 'city' and 'countryside'. The latter was submerged in a deep crisis, while the urban centers were confronted with entirely new problems such as overcrowding and inadequate public infrastructure.

During the 1950s, the optimism of the Ten-Year Plan (and of colonial propaganda) was able to conceal all these budding problems. The sky still appeared to be the limit. Apparently, the Congo was gradually becoming a 'developed' country, or at least a kind of 'African Brazil', but at the end of the 1950s the stargazing colonizer was overtaken by reality. The burden of debt exploded, precisely *because* of the Belgian policy. Rural communities were no longer able to feed themselves. The new infrastructure reinforced the imbalanced nature of the economy, which was too strongly focused on the export of raw materials. Social tensions mounted, also in the cities, where part of the African population enjoyed better living conditions. But full stomachs do not necessarily lead to fulfilled minds. Quite the reverse, since other types of aspirations – political participation, an end to European racist attitudes, upward social mobility – emerged in exactly those circles, partly because of the social changes triggered by the Belgian authorities and capitalists (see Chapters 5, 17 and 18). On the eve of independence, the Congo displayed all the features of a country wrestling with 'underdevelopment', another concept emerging at that time. Disastrous postcolonial policies undoubtedly reinforced these pre-existing tendencies, yet they did not create them out of the blue.

Bibliography

The documents regarding the genesis and implementation of the Ten-Year Plan are in the archives of the former Ministry of Colonies, now kept at the National Archives of Belgium (Cuvelier Depot, Brussels). The plan itself appeared in print: *Plan décennal pour le développement économique et social du Congo belge*, De Visscher, Brussels, 1949. A critical analysis of the plan can be found in Vanthemsche, Guy, *Genèse et portée du 'Plan décennal' du Congo belge (1949-1959)*, ARSOM/KAOW, Brussels, 1994 (the pdf can be downloaded from https://vub.academia.edu/GuyVanthemsche). Just before, or immediately following decolonization, a number of works offered a thorough overview of the Belgian Congo's economic situation after the Second World War: Bézy, Fernand, *Problèmes structurels de l'économie congolaise*, Ires-Nauwelaerts, Leuven-Paris, 1957; Baeck, Louis, *Economische ontwikkeling en sociale structuur in Belgisch-Kongo*, KUL-CES, Leuven, 1959; Lacroix, Jean-Louis, *Industrialisation au Congo*, Mouton, Paris, 1967. The following works were published more recently: Peemans, Jean-Philippe, *Le Congo-Zaïre au gré du xxe siècle. État, économie, société 1880-1990*, L'Harmattan, Paris, 1997; Huybrechts, André, *Bilan économique du Congo 1908-1960*, L'Harmattan, Paris, 2010.

Notes

1 Van Deuren, Pierre, *Aménagement du Bas-Congo*, s.l., 1928, p. 243.
2 1933 Memo from Louwers to Prince Leopold (the later Leopold III), cited in Dufour, Julien, *Pour une autre colonisation. Le discours du prince Léopold au Sénat, le 25 juillet 1933*, MA thesis, UCL, 2007, appendix II, p. VIII.
3 Ryckmans, Pierre, *Étapes et jalons*, Larcier, Brussels, 1946, p. 205.

MATHIEU ZANA ETAMBALA

14. The Congolese Community in Belgium

An Unintended 'By-Product' of Colonial Rule?

Today, the Congo is a major country of origin for migrants in Belgium, both in terms of new arrivals and established communities. Yet this has not always been the case. As a host country, Belgium differs from other colonial metropoles because, for a long time, it kept its doors shut to its (former) imperial subjects. Whereas one can easily find staple dishes such as bami or nasi goreng in the Netherlands and chicken tikka masala in Great Britain, there are few options for Congolese cuisine in Belgium. Belgians have adopted couscous from Morocco and doner kebab from Turkey, but are far less familiar with moambe and chikwangue.

This chapter discusses Congolese migration into Belgium during the colonial era. How many Congolese individuals came to Belgium? For what reasons and under which circumstances? How were they received? How long did they stay? And what traces did they leave?

Exhibitions and Educational Projects during the Congo Free State

An early cohort of Congolese people wound up in Belgium because of the world fairs held in the country at the end of the nineteenth century. In May 1885, an initial twelve-strong group of Congolese arrived for the Antwerp World Exhibition at the invitation of the Royal Geographical Society of Antwerp. Masala, a 'linguister' or interpreter-intermediary between the local chiefs from the Vivi area (near Matadi) and white traders, was the best known. When he left the mouth of the Congo River, the *Association Internationale Africaine* (AIA) claimed the region; by the time he left Antwerp in September 1885, the area belonged to the Congo Free State.

Some years later, the administration of the Congo Free State took the initiative to bring over more than 160 Congolese people for the Antwerp World Fair in 1894 and to house them in a barbed wire fenced reconstructed 'indigenous village'. They had to act out their daily life in the Congo and thus kindle enthusiasm for the colonial project (see Chapter 24). The initiative was a success, and four years later, during the 1897 Brussels International Exposition, more than 260 Congolese individuals were transported to Tervuren to be exhibited in three facsimile villages. These projects cost human lives, however. In 1894, four Congolese people died at Stuivenberg Hospital. They were buried in the cemetery of Kiel, which has been closed for almost a century. In 1897, a further seven Congolese individuals did not survive their Belgian adventure. Their graves have been preserved outside the St John the Evangelist Church in Tervuren. For the Congolese, it has become a *lieu de mémoire*, a place of remembrance.

Exhibiting foreign, 'wild' and subjugated or colonized people had become a normal phenomenon in Europe. It was done in exhibitions, zoos or circuses, in which shows involving exotic people alternated with performances with animals. Not surprisingly, such phenomena are referred to as 'human zoos'.

Shortly after Masala had returned to Vivi, Nsakala left the same region to travel to Belgium. He accompanied the Belgian officer Lieven Vandevelde as his 'boy' and thus found himself in Ghent where he spent two years at secondary school. Nsakala was the first in a long line of Congolese boys who were transferred from the Congo to the 'motherland' by Belgians in order to be educated. Paul Panda Farnana (1888-1930) was the most famous example. He studied in Mons and in Nogent-sur-Marne (near Paris), became a state agent in the Belgian Congo, but returned to Belgium before 1914. He volunteered in the First World War and was a prisoner of war in Germany and Romania. The house in Ixelles/Elsene where he lived for many years now bears a commemorative plaque with his name.

Most Congolese schoolchildren in Belgium were taken to the 'motherland' in an organized and institutionalized way. This program was initiated by Abbé Van Impe, a priest in the Ghent Diocese and Director of the St Luigi Gonzaga Institute in Gijzegem (Aalst), who founded the *Werk der Opvoeding van Congolese Kinderen in België* ('Organization for the Education of Congolese Children in Belgium') in 1888. The boys ended up in his school, while the girls were dispersed amongst the boarding schools of sister congregations throughout Flanders; in Leuven with the Annonciades, in Gierle, Diepenbeek and Maaseik with the Ursulines, and so on.

In 1900, the Congo Free State administration in Brussels decided to terminate Van Impe's project, and apart from a few exceptions, all the children were returned to the Congo. One of the girls who stayed in Belgium made history. Marie Ibanga had initially been placed with the Ursulines in Diepenbeek. When she received a religious calling in 1903, she was transferred to the Missionary Sisters of St Francis Mary in Gooreind, who had been active in the Congo since 1897. She died in September 1906, just a few weeks after she had made her profession. She was the first Congolese nun in the history of the Congo.

Growing Restrictions in the First Decades of the Belgian Congo

Traces of the first Congolese who wanted to stay permanently in Belgium can be found a few years before the outbreak of the First World War. In October 1911, the newspaper *Le Soir* wrote about two *superbes nègres* ('splendid negroes') roaming around the Namur Gate in Brussels. Their age was estimated between 18 and 24 and they were making a living doing odd jobs. In its edition of 13 December 1913, *Le Journal du Congo* noted half a dozen Congolese men who sold products such as *acacia purgatif* and *sucre de canne cuit* ('cooked cane sugar') against coughs and bronchitis on the *Place Sainte-Catherine* fruit and vegetable market. Some spoke Dutch. These street-traders were even mentioned by name, for example Antoine Boimbo, Jean Mavungu and Pierre Sumbu. They had all worked on ships sailing between Matadi and Antwerp as boilerman, cook or *blanchisseur de linge* and had chosen to seek new opportunities, especially in Brussels and its environs. They were not always successful, and some Congolese individuals sought material assistance from public welfare, the forerunner of the Public Center for Social Welfare (CPAS).

The very same *Le Journal du Congo*, in 1912, had conducted a racist campaign against the small Congolese community trying to build a future in Belgium (see Chapter 17). Its reporter was convinced that educating them morally and intellectually would have little effect; it would not elevate them to a higher rung on the social ladder. Besides, he criticized the colonials who had brought the Congolese to Belgium, because they had not taken into account that the Congolese people had only just emerged from so-called 'barbarism' and would not be able to resist all that Western 'luxury'. He believed repatriation measures should be taken to prevent Congolese people from continuing to live in wretched and penurious circumstances. But he also pointed to the danger of them coming into contact with 'negative' aspects of Western civilization in Belgium and, upon their return to the Congo, spreading dangerous ideas. The above reactions show that present-day stereotypes about the Congolese community are hardly new.

When the First World War broke out, most Congolese men volunteered to fight at the front (see Chapter 4). After the war, on 30 August 1919, a group of them founded the *Union Congolaise, Société de Secours et de Développement Moral et Intellectuel de la Race Congolaise* ('Congolese Union – Society for Assistance and Moral and Intellectual Development of the Congolese Race') in Brussels. This association devoted itself to granting material assistance to Congolese individuals who were in need or unwell, as well as to adult education. Sections were set up in Liège, Marchiennes-au-Pont, and other places. The great driving force behind this emancipatory movement was Paul Panda Farnana, mentioned earlier. Although the Congolese Union was patronized by King Albert and Minister of Colonies Louis Franck, it was not fully trusted in Belgium. In 1924, the Franciscan Stanislas Van de Velde was asked to take care of the Congolese in Brussels.

A notable difference from the Congo Free State years was that the door was now closed on educational projects. While a small number of Congolese individuals had been able to study for a degree in Belgium, by the interbellum years sailors and those in other jobs requiring only temporary stays formed the largest groups of Congolese in Belgium. In Antwerp, Father Alfons Cruyen, former Scheut missionary in the Congo, had been appointed Chaplain of *Ndako ya Bisu* ('Our House'), where sailors from *Compagnie Maritime Belge* ships could enjoy 'healthy recreation'. This project, in addition to Van de Velde's, was actually intended to keep the Congolese out of communists' hands. In fact, this kind of paternalism was the trademark of Belgian colonization.

New Groups in the Postwar Period

After the Second World War, Belgium had to contend with a new category of Congolese visitors. In 1953, the Minister of Colonies decided to invite, every two years, a limited group of around fifteen Congolese individuals from different regions and ethnic backgrounds for an introduction into Belgian society. The idea behind these educational trips was to acquaint them with Belgium's 'great' culture and industry, but the colonial authorities also wanted to make the Congolese aware that their road to independence would be an extremely long one.

The individuals involved tended to be loyal collaborators with the colonial authorities (see Chapter 18). On 29 April 1953, landing at Melsbroek airport were, among others, the *Mwata Yamvo* ('the great Balunda Chief'), Henri Bongolo (former Second World War fighter and Chief of Léopoldville's *centre extra-coutumier*, the area that was not subject to customary law), Antoine-Roger Bolamba (poet and Chief Editor of *La Voix du Congolais*, a paper for the *évolués*, or Congolese elite in the making controlled by the authorities) and Joseph Kiwele (music teacher at the St Boniface Institute in Élisabethville and founder of the famous children's choir *La Chorale à la Croix du Cuivre* ['Copper Cross Choir'], which was invited to perform at the 1958 World Fair). The Congolese group spent two months travelling across Flanders, Brussels and the Walloon provinces. They visited the coast, cathedrals, abbeys, museums, model farms, ports, mines, factories and so on.

From 1955 onwards, a tour of this kind was organized annually. In 1956, Patrice Lumumba, the future Prime Minister of the independent Congo who would later be murdered, formed part of this chosen cohort. These first trips were intended for a select few Congolese. But in 1958, in the context of the World Fair, a larger number of Congolese individuals were given the opportunity to visit Belgium.

The Belgian Congo's exhibit at this 'Expo 58' did not exactly break new ground; it was imbued with colonial stereotypes. Belgian colonial and missionary achievements were housed in several pavilions and, just as in 1894 and 1897, an 'indigenous village' was constructed to showcase Congolese folklore. The organizers wanted to exhibit the results of the Belgian civilizing mission and show a respect for positive aspects within African cultures. But the Congolese protested against the 'indigenous village', a true 'human zoo', which they regarded as demeaning. Some were also critical of the paternalistic manner in which they were treated in their residence, the Reception Center for African Staff (CAPA) in Tervuren, fitted out specially for the purpose. Like adolescents, they had to be 'home' by 10 pm and apply for a permit if they wanted to receive visitors. The experience in Belgium – including the confrontation with racism and the insight that white Europeans performed manual and service duties – inspired some to work toward decolonization.

The 1950s was also the period during which Belgians saw Congolese footballers play in their stadiums for the first time. The best-known trailblazer was Léon Mokuna, who, after his initial stay in Europe for Sporting CP (Lisbon, 1954-1956), was transferred to the Buffalos (KAA Gent) in Ghent in 1957, and from 1961 played for KSV Waregem. Other Congolese footballers followed, including Raoul Lolinga who went to Sint-Truiden, Remi Yamukanda and Julien Kialunda to Saint-Gilloise (and Kialunda subsequently to Anderlecht), and Paul Bonga Bonga to Standard Liège. These football players also had to deal with racism and were often viewed as a circus attraction.

A further pull factor was education. Thomas Kanza, a young teacher from Luozi (Bas-Congo) enrolled at the Catholic University of Louvain/Leuven's Institute for Applied Psychology and Pedagogy in 1952. Having graduated, he spent an additional year at the College of Europe in Bruges. Another Congolese teacher, Henri Malutama, completed his studies at the Nivelles Normal School at the same time. During the subsequent years, several Congolese students arrived to attend university in Belgium, primarily at the (then still bilingual) Catholic University of Louvain/Leuven and the (Francophone) Free University of Brussels (ULB). Many of them became politicians. For example, former Louvain/Leuven students included Albert Mpase, Marcel Lihau, Mario Cardoso, Albert Bolela and Paul Mushiete; Justin Bomboko, André Mandi, Claude Mafema and others attended ULB.

Meanwhile in 1954, Lovanium University had been founded in Léopoldville, followed in 1956 by the State University of Élisabethville (see Chapters 23 and 25). But when it became clear that independence would come about sooner than generally expected, and people in colonial circles believed that the development of the young state was only possible with an elite educated at university level (see Chapter 18), this resulted in a sharp increase in Congolese students receiving grants. By way of illustration: in one decade, the number of grant-aided Congolese students in Louvain/Leuven rose from 19 in the academic year 1959-1960 to 346 in the academic year 1969-1970. These Congolese students formed the base of the Matonge neighborhood, the so-called African heart of Brussels. During the colonial period, this district in Ixelles/Elsene was home to a few (white) colonial associations, such as the *Royale Union Coloniale Belge* ('Belgian Colonial Royal Union'; from 1912) and the *Union des Femmes Coloniales* ('Union of Colonial Women'; 1950s). Congolese students moved into the area in the 1960s, gradually followed by other Africans, and in their wake, dance halls, restaurants, hair salons and barbers opened up. In the past decades however, numerous Congolese moved out, which means that Matonge does not offer a truthful representation of Congolese life in Belgium. Quite the reverse; some fear that it has become a contemporary 'human zoo'.

Another group that came to Belgium during the years before and after decolonization were the mixed-race children who had African mothers and Belgian fathers. Many were removed from their mothers and villages by Catholic institutions and colonial authorities to be raised and educated in orphanages or boarding schools. Some were transferred to Belgium where they were adopted by Belgian families, housed with foster families or placed in institutions. A resolution about their segregation approved by the Belgian Chamber of Representatives on 29 March 2018 lists some of these institutions by name: Home Bambino in Schoten, Bloemendaal Castle in Bruges, the St Anna site of the Works of the Reverend Froidure at The Cabin in Rhode-Saint-Genèse/Sint-Genesius-Rode, the Home of Father Desmet in Schaerbeek/Schaarbeek, Le Pilote Home in Woluwe-Saint-Pierre/Sint-Pieters-Woluwe, the Œuvre d'Adoption Thérèse Wante in Ottignies, the Home Betty in Chimay and the Château de l'Horloge near Namur. This resolution led to an official apology by Prime Minister Charles Michel a year later, because in addition the Belgian Government had revoked the Belgian nationality of many of these mixed-race individuals, who were disadvantaged for the rest of their lives by forged (or absent) birth certificates and/or changed identities (see Chapter 28).

Conclusion

In other colonial empires, decolonization involved major emigration to the colonial metropoles (a third of Suriname's population settled in the Netherlands, for example). Moreover, these had been much quicker to admit an elite from the colonies onto European territory (think of Gandhi and Nehru, who had studied in the United Kingdom, or Ho Chi Minh who lived in France). Belgium, by contrast, kept its doors shut to colonial migration. This barely changed during the first decades following Congolese independence. The number of Congolese students in Belgium, however, did increase. In 1984, 624 students of Congolese origin studied in Brussels: 554 at the ULB, 21 at the VUB, 30 at the *Facultés Universitaires Saint-Louis*, 12 at the Faculty of Protestant Theology and 7 at the Royal Military Academy. But these are low numbers compared with those from neighboring countries. What is more, most graduates returned to the Congo/Zaïre (although some left their children in boarding schools and later allowed them to continue their studies at Francophone universities).

The number of Congolese in Belgium only began to mushroom from the 1990s onwards. Many fled the political chaos in the latter Mobutu years and the wars in the aftermath of the 1994 Rwanda genocide, and applied for political asylum. The Congolese diaspora increased even further through chain migration. This evolution is also visible in associations and clubs. Student organizations such as *Le Cercle des Étudiants Zaïrois de Leuven* ('Circle of Zairean Students in Leuven') quietly faded away or are being marginalized. Associations with names such as *Totelema* (Lingala for 'Let us Rise!'), in which asylum seekers play a prominent role, are taking their place. Numerous Congolese prayer groups have sprung up in Belgian cities such as Antwerp, Liège and Charleroi. Far fewer, but all the more notable are the Catholic Congolese priests who are gradually being entrusted with Belgian parishes. Most of these black missionaries are in Walloon Brabant, mainly because of the proximity of the UCL, where these priests prepare for their PhD in Theology.

The Congolese in Belgium continue to experience a lower standard of living. However, one should not generalize; in 2018 Congolese entrepreneurs founded the Léopards Club, an apolitical and private circle of Congolese businesspeople that organizes conferences about economic and financial activities in the Congo and promotes Congolese art.

These are all recent phenomena, however. During the colonial period and the first decades after independence, Congolese migration to Belgium was limited to specific groups and contexts, such as participants in world fairs, students, and elite groups on excursion. Just as in the colony itself, the Belgian Government retained control over the Congolese presence in the 'motherland' at all times. Another similarity with the Congo itself is racism. Up until far into the twentieth century, Congolese individuals were seen as exotic curiosities, and to this day they have to contend with discrimination. The older generation of this diaspora was focused almost exclusively on the political and socio-economic problems in their native country, to which they hoped to return. The second generation goes all-out for full integration into Belgium and demands the same social and economic opportunities as their Belgian contemporaries. But they are also fighting for a much more critical look at the colonial past in Belgian history books, in which they find the roots of the racist behavior they have to contend with today (see Chapter 28).

Bibliography

In 1993, I attempted to outline the Congolese presence in Belgium in my book *In het land van de Banoko. De geschiedenis van de Kongolese/Zaïrese aanwezigheid in België van 1885 tot heden*, Steunpunt Migranten – Cahiers nr 7, Leuven. Banoko is the nickname Congolese people gave to the Belgians who colonized them, and means 'uncles'. It is not meant pejoratively and refers more to a 'joking relationship'. A few years later, in 1995, in an article titled 'De meester bleef meester en de slaaf is leerling geworden: reflecties over wit-zwart stereotypen en vooroordelen', *De Gids op Maatschappelijk Gebied*, nr. 6-7, I tried to explain the historical relationships between black and white people in general, and between Belgians and Congolese in particular. It is based on an analysis of the information about the Congo disseminated in some Flemish newspapers. In 'Brève histoire de la diaspora congolaise', *Politique*, nr. 65, June 2010, I expanded on Matonge, amongst other neighborhoods.

Further publications about present-day Congolese migration to Belgium include Schoonvaere, Quentin, *Studie over de Congolese migratie en de impact ervan op de Congolese aanwezigheid in België. Analyse van de voornaamste demografische gegevens*, Studiegroep Toegepaste Demografie UCL en Centrum voor Gelijkheid van Kansen en voor Racismebestrijding, Brussels, 2010; Demart, Sarah, 'Congolese Migration to Belgium and Postcolonial Perspectives', *African Diaspora*, 2013, 6, p. 1-20; and Cornet, Anne, 'Migrations subsahariennes en Belgique. Une approche historique et historiographique', in Mazzochetti, Jacinthe, ed., *Migrations subsahariennes et condition noire en Belgique. À la croisée des regards*, Academia-L'Harmattan, Louvain-la-Neuve, p. 39-64. The resolution by the Chamber of Representatives can be found online: https://www.lachambre.be/FLWB/pdf/54/2952/54K2952007.pdf. The Belgian Parliament also tasked *CegeSoma* to conduct an in-depth historical study into the role of the civic and ecclesiastical authorities in the treatment of mixed-race people during the colonial era in the Belgian Congo and in Ruanda-Urundi. While awaiting the results, more information can be found in Ghequière, Kathleen, and Kanobana, Sibo, *De bastaards van onze kolonie. Verzwegen verhalen van Belgische metissen*, Roularta Books, Roeselare, 2010, and – about Rwanda – Heynssens, Sarah, *De kinderen van Save. Een geschiedenis tussen Afrika en België*, Polis, Antwerp, 2017.

Part III

Governance and Power

AMANDINE LAURO, IDESBALD GODDEERIS
AND GUY VANTHEMSCHE

Introduction

The exercise of colonial authority also relied on a state apparatus and institutional structures. The Belgian Congo's political administration was organized according to a centralized pyramid structure. The very top was occupied by the all-powerful Ministry of Colonies in Brussels, right at the bottom stood the *chefferies indigènes* ('indigenous chiefdoms'), with multiple levels in between (general-government, provinces, districts and territories), each with their own prerogatives. On paper, this structure gave the impression of a coherent organization and a well-oiled machine. In practice, the situation was far more complex. During the fifty years of Belgian rule in the Congo, there were frequent tensions and reorganizations which often tended to be driven by adaptations to changing circumstances rather than by a proactive policy vision. Be that as it may, the colonial administrative structures throughout the entire period were organized along an axis of power that formed the core of all exercise of colonial rule in the nineteenth and twentieth century, namely race. How were these structures implemented over the Belgian colony's entire territory? What was their (potentially specific) relationship with racism, colonized elites and resistance movements in a country that constituted almost an entire continent in itself, with a large cultural diversity and multiple pre-colonial histories?

The distinction between colonizers and colonized people (which, as we will see in several chapters, intersected with other categories such as gender or ethnicity) was a fundamental political tool for the colonial authorities. This was not an 'informal' distinction, but a differentiation that was cast in official statuses conferring different (political and legal) rights. It was this distinction in particular that enabled the routine deployment of repressive violence, which did not end with the fall of the Leopoldian regime, as the first chapter of this part shows (Chapter 15). Although violence was at the heart of the colonial enterprise, we should not forget that colonial rule was vulnerable, and far less omnipotent than its protagonists liked everyone to believe. First, it was constantly undermined by colonized people themselves, as demonstrated by the contribution about resistance (Chapter 16). Far from being passive subjects, the Congolese developed a wide range of strategies to challenge and circumvent the colonial system. Colonial power was also undermined by its own contradictions. While the colonial enterprise was based on the denial of the capacity of colonized people to govern themselves, the limits of colonial control led the Belgian authorities to rely on African auxiliaries for the day-to-day exercise of power. The ambiguous relationship between the prerogatives delegated to 'traditional' chiefs and the cautious (and slower than elsewhere) formation of a new elite of *évolués* is also the topic of a contribution (Chapter 18). These analyses provide a reminder of the extent to which the appropriation of European norms and values rarely took the forms colonial rule had hoped for, and at times even had a counterproductive effect.

Finally, various chapters illustrate the limitations of an approach in which colonial society and governance would only be considered through the prism of a 'stand-off' between colonized and colonizers: beyond the relations that transcended the boundaries of these categories, each group was divided by differences of gender, ethnicity, or language (Chapters 17, 19 and 20). These differences formed both an instrument of power for the Belgian authorities (within a divide and rule strategy) and a framework of mobilization for the colonized populace.

AMANDINE LAURO AND
BENOÎT HENRIET

15. Repression

Was the Congo a Less Violent Colony after Leopold II?

'We have not forgotten that the law was never the same for the white and the black, that it was lenient to the ones, and cruel and inhuman to the others.' This is how Patrice Lumumba summarized the judiciary repression in the Belgian Congo in his historic speech of 30 June 1960. The newly appointed Congolese Prime Minister thus shed light on a fundamental feature of colonial regimes: the existence of distinct laws for the colonizers and the colonized, each having to answer to a different legal status. Later in his speech, Lumumba continued: 'Who will ever forget the shootings which killed so many of our brothers, or the cells into which were mercilessly thrown those who no longer wished to submit to the regime of injustice, oppression and exploitation?' Lumumba evokes here a different guise of the colonial repression, one that has less to do with the racialized legal order than with the observation that the colonial power shamelessly brushed aside its own laws when feeling threatened. These two fragments illustrate the multifaceted nature of repression and law enforcement in the colonial context. They rested on other legal provisions than those prevailing in Belgium, as well as on the resort to illegal violent means.

These aspects are not specific to the Congo, and Lumumba could have certainly levelled the same criticism against other colonial powers. However, the will of Belgian colonial authorities to fashion themselves as 'an exemplary colonizer' adds an extra weight to these accusations. Indeed, Belgian colonial actors relentlessly promoted the Congo as a 'pacified' colony, where the use of violence remained a very last resort. The burden of the Leopoldian past still weighed heavily when the Congo officially became a Belgian colony in 1908, and the authorities claimed to have put a final end to the brutal repression prevalent in the infamous Congo Free State. However, can we effectively speak of a 'clean slate' between the new regime and the Leopoldian Congo? How did the colonial state respond to the popular uprisings and daily defiance of the Congolese people that punctuated its history? Were the structures for maintaining law and order radically different from those in Belgium, in terms of mechanisms (police, army, etc.) and spaces (prisons, etc.)? And how did they evolve over time?

The *Reprise*, a Transition in Repression?

At the turn of the nineteenth and twentieth centuries, international criticism of the regime of the Congo Free State brought to light the scale of the violence inflicted on the Congolese people by colonial agents, and in particular by the *Force Publique* (see Chapter 2).

Created in 1885, the colonial armed force was both an army of conquest and an internal police corps. Its bloody interventions (euphemistically called 'police operations' or 'expeditions to maintain order') were aimed to nip in the bud any form of rebellion. However, in a context of structural confusion between legal-rational governance and the imperatives of economic productivity, any reluctance to work or any drop in production was potentially considered insubordination, thus justifying repression by the armed forces. As a Belgian critic denounced in 1906, it was a system that 'made the same civil servants responsible for obtaining rubber and ensuring public order.'[1] A year later, another prominent figure of the Congo Free State – who had himself notoriously been involved in acts of violence against the Congolese – summed up the political climate of the time: 'The Congo needs rural wardens, police officers and gendarmes. Soldiers should not have been involved...'[2]

Criticism led the 'new' Belgian authorities, from 1908 onwards, to assert their ambition to surround repressive interventions by the *Force Publique* with legal safeguards. However, these intentions had little effect. Although some magistrates were receptive to the complaints of the Congolese and were keen to put an end to the system of impunity that had prevailed until then, the day-to-day maintenance of order still resulted in numerous acts of violence. It should also be remembered that the work of surveillance and repression was not entirely in the hands of agents of the colonial state. On the one hand, in certain agricultural or mining concessions, private entrepreneurs recruited their own mercenaries, or tried to mobilize the contingents of the *Force Publique* assigned to them as their private militias. On the other hand, a series of powers were devolved to 'traditional' chiefs, which entailed a partial delegation of the exercise of violence: chieftaincies were endowed with police and judicial powers, and could set up their own forces to maintain order (see Chapter 18). This raises the complex question of the role of intermediaries in the implementation of repression. In the

Congo, as in most other colonial contexts of the same period, the law enforcement bodies were mainly made up of locally recruited agents supervised by a small minority of European officers. For the most part, they were mobilized through 'levies' of men imposed by colonial authorities on traditional chiefs. As a result, in the 1910s and up until the interwar, the bulk of the *Force Publique* contingent was made up of men from the social margins of the traditional Congo, who did not necessarily have a stake in perpetuating the old order. Nevertheless, Belgian authorities never stopped worrying about the loyalty of their intermediaries.

Maintaining Order on a Daily Basis

Because colonial domination did not rely on the population's adherence to the authority of the state, the maintenance of order relied more than in other contexts on the use of violence. At the same time – and paradoxically – law enforcement bodies were undermanned: the police grid was insufficient to effectively supervise extensive regions and their large number of inhabitants. These two characteristics helped to shape policing practices that differed from those that prevailed in European metropoles at the time, not only when it came to repressing major uprisings, but also in the more 'ordinary' aspects of police work.

At the end of the First World War, the government of the Belgian Congo tried to find an answer to the security challenges inherent to the 'economic valuation' (*mise en valeur*) of the colony. The priority was no longer to stage large-scale demonstrations of military force. In 1919, the *Force Publique* was reformed and divided into two groups: 'camped troops', responsible for the external defense of the colony, and 'territorial troops', entrusted with the maintenance of order and with daily policing activities. In the 1920s, the Belgian authorities also created the first civilian police corps, which worked independently from the *Force Publique* and were primarily deployed in urban areas. The idea was to be able to respond more 'effectively' to the new forms of crime and protest that were emerging in towns and cities, and that could threaten the safety of Europeans. In practice, however, the division between military and civilian domains remained porous until the end of the colonial period: 'civilian' police officers, for example, were mainly recruited from the ranks of former soldiers of the *Force Publique*. As was the case in most of the colonies, the priority of law enforcement was much less to prevent and suppress criminality among colonized communities than to defend colonial interests.

These specificities had two consequences. Firstly, they lend a very martial guise to police activities, particularly because they allowed for the expeditive use of violence in 'everyday' interactions with colonized communities. However, this brutality should not give the illusion that police surveillance was omnipotent. In the 1950s, for example, in the heart of the capital, the police officers themselves confessed that they no longer dared venture into certain neighborhoods at night. And while Congolese notables on the *Conseil de Cité* – a consultative body on urban issues – constantly denounced the absence and ineffectiveness of the police in the city's African quarters, colonial authorities proudly announced at the time that Léopoldville had as many police officers (around 800) as the city of Liège… without mentioning that, in the 1950s, the Congolese capital had twice as many inhabitants as the Walloon city. Secondly, these characteristics also led the police to crack down on a very broad spectrum of 'disorders'. These were not limited to the 'classic' crimes and misdemeanors, but also included a whole series of contraventions of the colonial order, in a context where the boundary between 'ordinary' delinquency and political dissent could prove porous. This latter dimension was also at the heart of the particularities of the judicial system.

Colonial law indeed envisioned a series of offences attributable only to the so-called 'indigenous' populations. For the most part, these misdeeds were related to the control of Congolese mobility (travelling without the required *pass* was deemed a punishable offence), labor (deserting a job site was also punishable), participation in 'compulsory work' in rural areas, as well as health screenings and disciplinary control in the broadest sense (compliance with provisions on segregation, alcohol consumption, failure to pay taxes, etc.). Many of these breaches of colonial order were also punishable under criminal law in ways that contradicted the principle of the separation of powers. Territorial administrators (public servants representing the 'executive' power) were indeed granted with judicial prerogatives, acting among others as judges in the colony's police courts. Finally, colonial law also provided for specific penalties for the colonized, in the form of corporal punishments, inflicted in particular with the *chicotte*, the whip made from rhinoceros or hippopotamus skin that for a long time symbolized the repressive might of the colony. Colonial law was harsh on those who broke it. Congolese convicted of serious crimes could be sent to the gallows. Between 1931 and 1953, 127 Congolese were hanged, whereas in mainland Belgium, death sentences had been commuted to prison terms since the end of the nineteenth century (with the notable exception of wartime and postwar periods).

The 'Disorder' of Extraordinary Repression

In times of real or imagined crisis, the maintenance of order in the Belgian Congo took on a different guise. When the colonial administration was faced with a threat perceived as 'existential', the violence of its response exceeded its self-imposed rules envisioned to curtail the exercise of its repressive power. Law enforcement agents shot on sight, fustigated extensively, and sent convicts to the firing squad 'to set an example'. These operations exposed the anxiety of civil servants, who regarded episodes of insubordination as endangering the very survival of the colony, as demonstrated by the repression of several major episodes of protest, including the largest rural revolt of the interwar period (see Chapter 16).

In 1931, a rebellion broke out in the Kwango District. It was linked to the fallout from the Great Depression, which heavily impacted palm oil production, the region's main economic activity. The already meagre wages of Congolese workers were drastically reduced, while poll taxes increased. Against this tense backdrop, a new millenarian movement emerged, the *Tupelepele*. Local men and women claimed to have been visited by the spirits of their ancestors, who told them that the Belgian occupation would soon come to an end. On 8 June 1931, territorial agent Maximilien Balot, who had been sent to the region, was murdered and dismembered by *Tupelepele* followers, who then shared his remains among local communities. Balot's murder was a spectacular event, a reversal of colonial violence that sent a wave of panic through the administration. The *Force Publique* was deployed in the district. The objective assigned to the officers? To 'pacify' the region and collect the body parts of the murdered civil servant. The military response had to be orderly; the soldiers were instructed not to use their weapons, outside of cases of extreme necessity. However, the operations were carried out in complete disregard of these instructions, as noted by a Senior Colonial Magistrate, Judge Eugène Jungers. In an inflammatory report penned in November 1931, he mentioned having met Congolese 'terrorized by the military operation and especially by the systematic and brutal application of the *chicotte*' during police interrogations. Fustigations were carried out 'with such cruelty that many of the victims died', he wrote. Jungers also mentions the 'pointless and unnecessary deaths' of Congolese shot at point-blank range as they tried to get away from the fighting. According to him, the 'pacification' operations claimed more than 500 victims.

The experience of the Second World War was also marked by the brutal repression of other episodes of revolt. From May 1940 onwards, the Congolese economy was articulated to the Allied war effort, which entailed an extreme pressure in terms of production (see Chapter 4). In the mines of Haut-Katanga, the work pace increased without any pay raise. In December 1941, strikes broke out in Jadotville and Élisabethville, two of the region's main economic centers. They were quickly and violently put down by the *Force Publique*. In Élisabethville, 48 strikers were shot dead by soldiers. During this period, conflicts also broke out within the *Force Publique* itself. In February 1944, a battalion of over 600 soldiers stationed at Luluabourg refused to follow their officers' orders, and seized control of the camp for several days. A group of mutineers among them also killed three Belgians during their flight. The authorities' response to the Luluabourg mutiny resulted in 26 executions, most of which were carried out in public. In both Katanga and Luluabourg, the colonial state deployed its repressive power arm with ostentatious brutality. Shooting strikers or bringing mutineers to the firing squad on a public square were spectacular demonstrations of its authority, designed to nip in the bud any longing for sedition. Behind this line-up of corpses, however, one can see the action of a helpless state that has no other weapons than its capacity for violence to keep its colonial 'subjects' in line in times of crisis.

In the 1950s, the *Force Publique* was aware of the strengthening of anticolonial sentiment and the security challenges it entailed. Confidential directives and even an 'emergency plan' were drawn up to deal with the possibility of riots. Contrary to the idea that the authorities were unaware of the dissent broiling in the colonized population right up to the last minute, the archives of the law enforcement bodies reveal the anxiety of certain officials faced with the threat of unrest, particularly in the light of the insurrectionary movements that were breaking out in other parts of Africa. Military experts kept abreast of the new operational techniques deployed against rebels, whether in the context of the Mau-Mau revolt in Kenya or in the French-dominated Maghreb, where a *Force Publique* study mission was even sent in 1957, at the height of the Algerian War of Independence. Given the extreme brutality of colonial repression in these contexts, one might wonder about the 'lessons' that were learned.

The outbreak of riots in Léopoldville in January 1959 did not completely take those responsible for maintaining order by surprise (see Chapter 5). Their clumsy and bloody repression contributed to the three days of 4, 5 and 6 January becoming a crucial turning point in the march towards decolonization, almost as much as the uprising itself. Only after a major military deployment (1,400 police and 1,500 soldiers) and the massive resort to lethal weapons did the colonial authorities manage to regain control of the capital.

The violence of the rioters was also tellingly directed against the representatives of law enforcement. Initially, the police opened fire to free up policemen engulfed by the crowd; the rumor that 'black people were being killed' then spread like wildfire, increasing the anger (and the numbers) of the rioters. However, most of the shots were first fired to protect the European parts of the city, and then to regain control of the African areas. The uprising's official toll counts 42 casualties (all African) and 250 injured. However, this figure was disputed by some observers. While it is reasonable to assume that the death toll was underestimated, it is difficult to be more precise on the basis of the currently available evidence. In the aftermath of the riots, and on the eve of the Government and royal declarations opening a path towards independence, in a singular echo of the events at the beginning of the century, Belgium saw old ghosts reappear: the international press made headlines of the violence of its repression (in the United Kingdom, *The Times* even mentioned the fanciful figure of 200 deaths, including several Europeans), while in the metropole, left-wing MPs called for a parliamentary commission of enquiry on the repression of the riots.

Prison and Relegation: The Many Faces of Confinement

At the crossroads between the punishment of 'ordinary' crimes and the repression of resistance, the practice of confinement in the Belgian Congo took on different guises, and was particularly embodied in different spaces: the prison, obviously, but also the camp.

Detention was not unknown in pre-colonial Central Africa, but it was rarely used as a penalty: reparation, corporal punishment or banishment were the main methods of judicial settlement. Europeans often liked to present 'their' prison as an improvement on pre-colonial methods of repression (executions, mutilation, etc.). This discourse, which maintained that prison was a relatively 'gentle' form of punishment for Africans, in turn served to justify a carceral regime that was harsher than in the colonial metropole, particularly as it was combined with other repressive practices, such as corporal punishment, shackling and forced labor.

The first colonial prisons date back to the end of the nineteenth century, but their development began in earnest in the 1910s. In practice, the prisons took on very different forms. The six large 'central prisons' in the colony were the ones that most closely resembled Belgian institutions, even in their architecture. It was in these establishments that European prisoners were incarcerated.

African prisoners were also jailed in the many district, chiefdom and territory prisons and other 'annex prisons' scattered throughout the territory, whose facilities were generally rudimentary. The disparity in the spaces (and therefore the conditions) in which Congolese prisoners were held was, however, mitigated by the almost systematic imposition of 'chores' on them. Until the end of the colonial period, prisoners constituted a pool of labor force from which the colonial authorities did not hesitate to draw, including for heavy construction work (building roads, for example), which, paradoxically, meant that prisoners had to leave the prison on a regular basis. After the Second World War, the emergence of less brutally repressive and more 'redemptive' views of the prison experience led to calls, particularly from the Belgian metropole, to reform the organization of Congolese penitentiaries. These criticisms were also based on concerns that the deplorable conditions of detention might act as a breeding ground for further opposition to the colonial regime, given the large number of Congolese who passed through prison.[3] However, these reforms only concerned the central prisons, and remained limited in scope.

Throughout the colonial period, the state also mobilized another form of incarceration, with no equivalent in the metropole: the relegation. This procedure consisted of a deportation coupled with a house arrest, forming together a kind of internal exile. It is particularly illustrative of the confusion of state prerogatives in a colonial context: relegation was indeed a sanction handed down by the administration (by the 'executive' branch) outside of any judicial procedure. As such, it was neither subject to appeal nor limited in time.

Promulgated from 1910 onwards, relegation was initially used mainly against rebellious notables and troublemakers, affecting a few hundred people in its first decade of application. From the 1920s onwards, it took on a completely different scope. Relegation became the main repressive tool levelled against followers of the messianic movements that were developing in the interwar Congo (Kimbanguism, Kitawala, etc.) (see Chapter 16). The increasing use of relegation (which concerned several thousand people from the interwar period onwards) entailed new practical adjustments. The convicts were settled in ad hoc 'relegation villages', where they had to build their own homes and provide for their subsistence. In the mid-1940s, the wartime context led to the formalization of camps aimed more specifically at political prisoners deemed as 'dangerous', paired with stricter surveillance regime and with the use of forced (agricultural) labor as a tool of repression. One nevertheless has to note that in terms of punishment, the colonial power did not always have the means to match its ambitions. Ironically, the sometimes lax surveillance of relegated villages contributed to the dispersal of a series of ideas (linked to messianic movements, among others) far beyond the region where they emerged.

Conclusion

The overview of repressive practices in the Congo outlined in this chapter highlights a set of institutions, customs and rules which, when taken together, offer stark contrasts with the model in the metropole. First of all, the maintenance of order in the Belgian Congo pursued its own objectives: to defend colonial interests, to maintain the racial hierarchy essential to its political survival, and to nip in the bud any protests that might jeopardize the colony or threaten its facade of tranquility. To achieve these objectives, the very principles of the rule of law had to be adapted: different laws had to be envisioned for colonizers and colonized, administrative and judicial functions had to be merged, and ad hoc disciplinary institutions had to be tailored for the specific needs of the colony. Belgium's takeover of the Congo was therefore not accompanied by the advent of a 'metropolitan' model of repression in Central Africa, but rather by adaptations to an already existing apparatus. Although these changes were significant, they did not 'pacify' the colony, and violence continued to permeate relations between the state and the Congolese.

However, this coercive repertoire did not entirely stifle Congolese people's capacity for action. Some took advantage of the limited window of opportunity offered by the judicial system to assert their rights. Various episodes of brutal opposition to colonization also run through the history of the Congo. While these multifaceted revolts were violently repressed, they revealed a recurring tension in the use of violence by 'nervous' colonial authorities. The administration feared that the violence inherent in colonial rule would be turned against it. In the field, mutinies, strikes and local uprisings were seen by government officials as a threat to their existence, as well as being harbingers of large-scale uprisings. They would therefore require swift suppression, even at the cost of bloody and disorderly action. Colonial officials' obvious anxiety about the potential for revolt among the colonized was one of the driving forces of their repressive practices.

Bibliography

Among the many studies on this topic, we would particularly like to mention the pioneering work by Jean-Luc Vellut, who during his career has examined closely the use of violence during the period around the *reprise*, anticolonial resistance and its repression, and the use of capital punishment. All these investigations have been collected in one volume: Vellut, Jean-Luc, *Congo. Ambitions et désenchantements*, Karthala, Paris, 2017. Also deserving of special attention are the publications by Dembour, Marie-Bénédicte, 'La chicotte comme symbole du colonialisme belge?', *Canadian Journal of African Studies*, 26, 1992, 2, p. 205-225, and 'La peine durant la colonisation belge', in *La Peine/Punishment, Recueils de la Société Jean Bodin pour l'histoire comparative des institutions* ('Mondes non-européens', part 4), De Boeck Université, Brussels, 1991, p. 67-95. More recently, the police and 'day-to-day' forms of law enforcement have been covered in Lauro, Amandine, 'Suspect Cities and the (Re)Making of Colonial Order. Urbanization, Security Anxieties and Police Reforms in Postwar Congo (1945-1960)', in Campion, Jonas, and Rousseaux, Xavier, eds., *Policing New Risks in Modern European History*, Palgrave, New York, 2016, p. 57-85, and 'Maintenir l'ordre dans la colonie-modèle. Notes sur les désordres urbains et la police des frontières raciales au Congo Belge (1918-1945)', *Crimes, Histoire, Sociétés*, 15, 2011, 2, p. 97-121. Although Anne Cornet's work deals with the Belgian mandate region in Rwanda and Burundi, it contains illuminating lessons about 'special offences' which also apply to the Congo: Cornet, Anne, 'Punir l'indigène: les infractions spéciales au Ruanda-Urundi (1930-1948)', *Afrique et Histoire*, 1, 2009, 7, p. 49-73. For more information about the penitentiary institutions and banishment we refer to: Bernault, Florence, ed., *Enfermement, prison et châtiments en Afrique. Du 19e siècle à nos jours*, Karthala, Paris, 1999; Piret, Bérengère, *Les cent mille briques. La prison et les détenus de Stanleyville*, CHJ Éditeur, Lille, 2014; and Dewulf, Valentine, 'Enfermement administratif et répression coloniale. Formes et pratiques de la relégation au Congo belge (1910-1960)', *Revue Belge de Philologie et d'Histoire*, 97, 2019, 2, p. 1-36. Historiography about the repression of the big revolts displays many gaps and is somewhat dated (we are thinking above all of the works by Louis-François Vanderstraeten, in particular 'La Force Publique et le maintien de la "Pax Belgica" 1944-janvier 1959', in *Recueil d'Études Congo 1955-1960*, ARSOM/KAOW, Brussels, 1992). A somewhat out-of-date monograph by L.-F. Vanderstraeten describes the 'pacification' of Kwango and has recently been placed in a wider perspective by Henriet, Benoît, 'Des ethnographes anxieux. Pratiques quotidiennes du pouvoir au Congo belge, 1930-1940', *Vingtième Siècle*, 140, 2018, 4, p. 41-54. See also Mabiala Mantuba-Ngoma, Pamphile, 'Bula Matari et son Congo (1885-1960): coloniser dans la peur', in *La société congolaise face à la modernité (1700-2010). Mélanges eurafricains offerts à Jean-Luc Vellut*, L'Harmattan/MRAC, Paris-Brussels, 2017, p. 33-60.

Notes

1 Vermeersch, Arthur, *La question congolaise*, Bulens, Brussels, 1906, p. 142.
2 Charles Lemaire (1907), cited in Marchal, Jules, *E.D. Morel contre Léopold II. L'Histoire du Congo 1900-1910*, L'Harmattan, Paris, 1996.
3 Between 1945 and 1960, a period for which fairly reliable figures exist, depending on the region and year, approximately 2.5 to 7 per cent of the male population would have been locked up in prison, a percentage that was much higher than in Belgium itself. Dewulf, Valentine, *Les barreaux de la justice. Institutions, réseaux, acteurs de l'enfermement carcéral sous la colonisation belge (1908-1960)*, doctoral thesis, ULB, 2023, p. 126-133.

DIDIER GONDOLA

16. Resistance in the Belgian Congo

The Many Paths of Disobedience

Not so long ago, Congolese resistance to colonization was still described in two rather antinomic ways. Belgian colonization was either depicted as a kind of *Pax Belgica*, i.e. as a long, calmly flowing river in which the Congolese people kept paddling without a care in the world under the benevolent, paternalist gaze of the familiar colonial trinity (the state, Catholic missions and Belgian companies); or it was presented as a dystopian, suffocating 'empire of silence' where even the slightest subversive impulse raised anxiety and was mercilessly stymied. Regardless of the different views on Belgian colonialism, the consensus seemed to be that anticolonial resistance movements had been confined to two distinct periods: first to the colonial conquest, which in some parts of the vast territory continued well beyond the 1920s, and second to the post-World War II era.

For those who see the Belgian Congo as an 'empire of silence', a kind of Orwellian universe created by the Belgians in the tropics, the first period was marked by forms of 'primary resistance', sometimes even armed ones, the most emblematic being that waged by the Bapende in the Kwango region between May and September 1931. At the time, resistance first and foremost meant battling against the occupation, notably because the occupying forces made no attempt to disguise their totalitarian ambitions nor their plans to wipe away local customs and exercise political control through an unprecedented form of governance based on poll tax, compulsory cultivation and forced labor. As for the second (post-World War II) period, historians regard it not so much as an era of overt and violent resistance, but rather as a period of adjustment, in which conflicts between the colonizers and the colonized revolved more around the pace of 'modernity' which gained momentum mid-way through the 1930s, than around a resolute rejection by the Congolese people.

But how, and above all why, did the Congolese challenge the colonial 'march of progress'? How is that this colony, forged by the so-called 'genius' of the Belgians and their self-proclaimed successful colonial combination of capitalism and paternalism, experienced a deluge of dissent in so many places? Why did the 'Belgian Bantu', the 'most *bourgeois* Black in the whole of Africa',[1] bite the hand that fed him and, at the end of almost a century of 'great work' by the Belgians in the Congo, turn his anger against his alleged benefactor?

Facing the Severed Hands

It is easier to answer these questions when we place them in a wider historical perspective. Coveted for its enormous wealth, the Congo Basin, as many studies have stressed, has been routinely pillaged for almost half a millennium, and has known repeated cycles of ruthless violence which followed the rhythm of evolutions in the global economy. Such an unbearable violence has led not only to militant vigilance but also to literary voyeurism, to which writers such as Joseph Conrad, Mark Twain, Arthur Conan Doyle, V.S. Naipaul and even Aimé Césaire have succumbed. It was precisely from here, starting with Henry Morton Stanley's travelogue, that the Congo earned its literary sobriquet of 'heart of darkness' (which gained currency in the English language through Joseph Conrad's eponymous novel, *Heart of Darkness*). On the other hand, perhaps it is because this violence was so atrocious and propels us into the deepest doldrums of hell and the heart of horror and revulsion that literature has taken it up with such a vengeance; as if it wanted to stem the blood gushing out from all sides of this horn of plenty, from a territory that was materialized as the playground of the most powerful economic interests.

Because Congolese history has witnessed a litany of bloodshed, starting with the sixteenth century and the slave trade that plagued the Congo Basin, resistance – in its many forms and folds – is virtually part of the Congolese genetic makeup. When, at the end of the nineteenth century, the thumping boots of the *Force Publique* startled the villages of the Équateur region, there was already a long genealogy of resistance among Congolese people. As Daniel Vangroenweghe has written, never before 'did such an exploitation elsewhere by a state or a head of state lead to such monstruous cruelty as those registered in Leopold II's Congo under the rule of concessionaries who were fully under the control of the sovereign' (see Chapters 1 and 2).[2] But what can you do when hands are being severed? How do you revolt when the ABIR (Anglo-Belgian India Rubber Company) militias take women hostage and rape them in order to force men to harvest wild rubber deep in the rainforest? What action could apparently defenseless villagers take against this violence, which sowed chaos and fear throughout, hit the vulnerable sections of the population most, and made centers of resistance shrink away to just a few pockets? Scattered over vast territories, living in autonomous villages, often without the protection of a centralized state and therefore without an army, the first reaction of these villagers was to flee. This strategy, often used successfully during raids by Arabo-Swahili slave traders, certainly enabled them to escape the violence inflicted by colonial troops, but it did little to spare their home. Villages were burnt to the ground in retaliation, and thus not only disappeared from the landscape but also from the collective memory. The soldiers commandeered manpower for the rubber and ivory trade, to carry goods, but also to facilitate their own food supplies. Soon it became standard practice to use food as a means of pressure to settle disputes between Congolese peasants and colonial authorities.

As a last resort, the Congolese turned to armed resistance. Different examples of this can be found. In response to the abuses of the colonial agent Eugène Rommel, who cracked the whip in Kasi, in the Cataractes District (Bas-Congo), and who set up the infamous 'Baka Baka' camp (to which he deliberately gave a Kikongo name, so that the populace would understand instantly his abduction and concentration scheme), an extremely fearless armed faction emerged throughout the region. Led by Chief Nzangu, the rebels tried several times to negotiate with Rommel to free the women he was holding hostage. When their attempts came to nothing, they organized a lightning ambush and succeeded in storming the camp on 5 December 1893. Rommel was killed and the 'Baka Baka' camp ransacked and set on fire. Although the colonial authorities applied a scorched earth policy, pockets of resistance followed in its wake, including a series of mutinies among the *Force Publique* Batetela contingent in 1895, after the great Tetela warlord Ngongo Lutete was accused of treason by the Belgians and executed. The 1931 Bapende insurrection mentioned above went down in history as the fiercest act of opposition.

God is Not White

Even in the sphere of healthcare, the colonizing powers strived to keep an eye on, control and 'master' the Congolese people through medicalization. In line with the colonial doctrine *mens sana in corpore sano* ('a healthy mind in a healthy body'), the Belgians intended to transform the Congolese into obedient subjects. This explains why religious movements opposing colonial rule, in which *ngounza* ('prophets') were attributed thaumaturgic powers, aroused irrepressible enthusiasm among their followers. It was because of this dual ambition – messianic and thaumaturgic – that these movements soon came under intense colonial surveillance and repression.

For the Congolese, resistance could also mean knocking the white Jesus from his cross and replacing him with a black one. Here again, this spirit of indiscipline must be considered through the prism of the *longue durée*. As early as the end of the sixteenth century, the figure of Black Christ on the cross had acquired a place in the collective consciousness of the Kongo people (the inhabitants of the region around the lower reaches of the Congo River), following conversions to Catholicism by Portuguese Catholic missionaries who had followed in the footsteps of explorer Diogo Cão. The copper crucifix with the black Jesus, of which several examples have been preserved to this day, is the testament of an iconographic appropriation rooted in the religious landscape of Kongo culture. Around 1700, in the strong hands of prophet-healers Apollonia Mafuta Fumaria and Kimpa Vita, it became a powerful symbol of resistance against the Catholic orthodoxy imposed by the Portuguese. Apollonia Mafuta Fumaria went so far as to proclaim that Christ and Mary were in fact Kongo and to deplore the instrumental use of the Bible by Portuguese missionaries. Declared a heretic, Kimpa Vita was burnt at the stake on 2 July 1706, but her resistance movement, which placed at its center the existence of a black Christ and therefore of a black God, was emulated by others and inaugurated a messianic genealogy in which centuries later, Simon Kimbangu and Simon Mpadi were going to be the leading figures. The first was a famous prophet who, in 1921, saw his death sentence converted into life imprisonment by the 'mercy' of the Belgian King and spent thirty years in jail until his death in 1951. His crime? Claiming a black church outside the ruts established by missionaries. He preached, sung songs – some of them subversive – and healed the sick. People deserted their work sites to converge on Kamba, the 'New Jerusalem' of Bas-Congo, some hoping for salvation, others to be cured. Mpadi for his part was a former Salvationist who took over Kimbangu's torch and founded the *Mission des Noirs* ('Mission of Black People') in 1939, a movement that was modelled after certain facets (such as the khaki uniforms worn by the faithful) of the Salvation Army. Like Kimbangu, Mpadi strove for an independent black church. But he also went further: he advocated the revaluation of 'African customs', including polygamy, preached a kind of liberation theology and exalted martyrdom by encouraging his followers to accept arrest, prison sentences and even death if necessary. The popular fervor generated by this umpteenth incarnation of the resistance movement which emerged in the eighteenth century with

Kimpa Vita, was rooted in the vision of a purely African church, stripped of the colonial straitjacket. Despite – or rather thanks to – the colonial repression, the 'Kakists' continued to offer resistance even when deprived of their leader, as they were strengthened by a millenarian eschatology which predicted the end of colonization. The song that was sung during 'Kakist' meetings in Yakoma in the north of the Congo, where Mpadi was staying in August 1945 having escaped from prison once more, offers a good example:

> In three years' time the earth will burn
> The whites who remain will become blacks
> They will be our servants, our porters
> We will make them carry loads
> We will make them climb palm trees
> As they have made us do
> We have suffered too much; we will make them suffer[3]

The millenarian effervescence was only enhanced by the arrest and incarceration of black prophets (see Chapter 15) and it fueled the 'alarmist noises' and rumors which, during the Second World War, spread through the colony like wildfire. It was whispered that the Belgians would disappear soon and, as some hoped, be replaced by German troops. Mpadi himself, who missed no opportunity to inflate his aura amongst his followers, led them to believe that Germany supported him in his spiritual and political fight. That was all that was needed to light the fuse. Colonial authorities took the rumors seriously and immediately resorted to hard repression. The colony was quickly cordoned off. Colonial rulers waged a fierce battle and decapitated the movements by arresting their prophets and prophetesses. But the popular fervor was not going to disappear overnight. On the contrary, pockets of passive resistance grew into full-blown insurrections. For the first time, these even spread to the cities and inspired several strikes, such as at the UMHK in 1941, amongst the railway workers of the Upper Congo to the African Great Lakes Railway Company (CFL), the workers of Léopoldville and in the port of Matadi in 1945. Within the *Force Publique*, unrest grew as well, which escalated into mutiny in 1944 and threatened the colonial order in Kasaï and Katanga, two provinces which were regarded as milk cows for the colonial economy (see Chapter 4).

Weapons of the Weak

Apart from strikes and insurrections, which, it should be emphasized, continued to spring up sporadically in the post-World War II urban landscape, there was a plethora of less spectacular, more 'ordinary' resistance practices which would deserve further research, as they challenge the conventional definition of the 'political'. With them, we are entering the territory of rumors, humor, evasion and subterfuge – in short, what the American anthropologist James Scott has described as 'hidden transcripts' or 'weapons of the weak'. As long as we confine 'what's political' to visible actions, argues Scott, we will find that dominated groups remain excluded from it, except for the rare moments when they express their overflow or despondency directly and in an ostensible manner. But in doing so, Scott continues, we miss the wide grey zone between submission and rebellion. By fixing our focus too much on the coastline of the 'political', Scott concludes, we lose sight of the enormous continent silhouetted against the horizon.[4]

This resistance of the weak, often too muted and disguised to be recorded in the annals of history, was played out far from the spotlights. There, in the blind spot of the dominant culture or behind the opaque screen of derision, the weak wielded their weapons. Colonial sources generally paid little attention to these resistance strategies and to the myriad of other (sometimes inconsequential) gestures of disobedience that punctuated the daily experiences of colonialism for the populations who were both hypnotized and disoriented by the *trompe-l'oeil* dazzle of the cities where they lived. After all, Africans living in what was known in the bizarre and condescending parlance of the time as 'extra-customary centers' were supposed to marvel at all the rapid progress being made – which they were expected to jump at the chance to participate in. They were expected to be grateful to colonial authorities for having freed them from their so-called savage customs. And yet, under the guise of galloping modernity, with their brand-new spruce houses, tarmacked roads, mobile cinemas and *foyers sociaux* ('social homes'), these colonial cities were similar to a modern Cronos, the Greek God who devoured his children.

There was a flipside to this coin: the curfew, the *chicotte* and the insults, the most common of which was 'dirty macaque'. 'Yes, that's what the whites said', a certain Damas Tshiautwa explained during an interview with journalist François Ryckmans. His words echo those of Patrice Lumumba, who suffered the same fate at the hands of a white woman in Léopoldville: 'Macaque! Hey! Macaque! Get over here, will you!'[5] However – and somewhat paradoxically –, despite the smoke and mirrors, the colonial city exerted a magnetic pull on Congolese people. The city seduced and eventually devoured many of the countless migrants who got entangled in its web, as the popular culture of the time often lamented. It swept them into a vertiginous civilizational maelstrom, as if it were some kind of nirvana. But for those who managed to haul themselves up onto the highest rung, the so-called *évolués* – the scarce Congolese who were able to pocket either a *carte du mérite civique* ('civil merit card') or an *immatriculation* ('registration') (see Chapter 18) – bitter disappointment awaited before long.

Educating the Congolese to make them understand and accept the blessings of colonialism became everyone's business. Africans were deluged with 'good' advice so that they would be able to 'evolve' as best as they could in the city. From cradle to grave, they were pursued by an arrogant, paternalistic gaze. For all these reasons, resistance by the urbanized Congolese was not expressed along the beaten track but rather followed circuitous routes. Black workers rarely responded to the infernal work rhythm imposed on them by going on strike, for instance. Much more often they flitted from job to job, resorted to chronic absenteeism or simply quit without telling their employer. Their behavior towards their boss would be obsequious and polite, but behind his back they could sabotage the machines in order to slow down the working pace. They dawdled, dragged out finishing a task for as long as possible and invented comical nicknames for their employers, as historian Osumaka Likaka has shown, to then poke fun at them under their noses. The state of chronic inebriety of some workers, which seemed to preoccupy the authorities, can similarly be seen not only as an escape but also as a way to pull the wool over colonial capitalism's eyes. Even though the 1911 ordinance which forbade 'people of the black race' to consume fermented or distilled drinks between Saturday afternoon and Monday morning remained in force until the 1930s, alcohol flowed freely in the *flamingos* and other places of entertainment in the large Congolese cities. Because wine was reserved for those who had been through the *immatriculation* process or for holders of a *carte du mérite civique*, on Friday nights, Léopoldville's partygoers took the last boat to Brazzaville to go dancing, drink themselves legless and breathe a little air of freedom *Chez Faignon*, especially after 1946, when African inhabitants of Brazzaville gained access to European clubs.

Indépendance Cha Cha

Although all of these weapons of resistance could do little more than scratch the self-complacent veneer that gave colonialism its gleaming arrogance, there were other forms of – less visible – 'infrapolitical' actions that targeted the colonial system explicitly. These were not inspired by the *évolués*' formal anticolonial discourse that emerged late in the colonial era. In fact, it was the other way round. In their political battle, the *évolués* fell behind, while musicians, so-called 'delinquent' youths and *femmes libres* ('free women', i.e. young, unmarried women, the queens of Léopoldville nightlife), were on the vanguard. In other words, the *évolués* who, at the end of the 1950s, launched the fatal salvo which put an end to colonial rule, did not invent the anticolonial wheel. On the contrary, they picked up issues that had already been brewing in African neighborhoods for some time and followed the rhythm set by what was being whispered and imagined in the streets, at markets, in bars, stadiums and improvised cinemas, which were springing up from Léopoldville to Élisabethville.

Who remembers, for example, that Patrice Lumumba, during the period before his political career took off, made a name for himself in the bars of the capital as commercial director of the *Brasserie de Léopoldville*? In June 1957, he was taken on by the brewery with a specific mission: to restore the reputation of the Polar beer brand, which had been the subject of public rumor. It was the beer of the whites, some said; what is more, it could make men impotent. Lumumba grabbed the bull by the horns and went to bars where he met 'free women', the big influencers of the time, and became acquainted with the twilight world of nightlife in which, thanks to their charms, these women had been upending gender roles and had the men dancing to their tune since the 1940s. 'Free women' organized themselves in *sociétés d'élégances* with suggestive names such as *La Rose*, *La Violette*, *La Reconnaissance* or *Diamond*, and painstakingly guarded their financial and sexual autonomy (see Chapter 19). They obviously did not give Lumumba any formal lessons in politics, but by interacting with them, he could begin to sense the sheer extent of the people's political aspirations which, by the end of the 1950s, developed regardless of age or gender and emerged from both the *évolués* and the masses.

Within the mass of city dwellers, there was a group that made no secret of its striving for independence: the young 'tropical cowboys'. As early as 1936, they could be found in Élisabethville, Jadotville and above all Léopoldville, where, inspired by the cinematic exploits of Buffalo Bill (their eponymous hero), they organized themselves into gangs of 'Bills'. They demanded independence from all the hierarchical structures erected by colonization: school, work, Church. Aware that the Belgians were infantilizing and animalizing Congolese men, they rebelled against the illusory masculinity into which the *évolués* allowed themselves to be forced. The Bills played sheriff and macho in their respective neighborhoods, defended the boundaries of their fiefdoms with as much fervor as they guarded the hymens of 'their' girls, and came to frequent blows with competing gangs. When riots broke out in Léopoldville in January 1959 (see Chapter 5), these *enfants terribles* were on hand to orchestrate the uprising and spread the ferments of indiscipline and popular vindictiveness throughout the capital's neighborhoods. When the 'Bills' went for the interracial state secondary school in the district of Ngiri Ngiri, the crown jewel of Belgian gradualism, they summed up their anger in one word: 'independence'. Chalked on walls, doors and school blackboards, it was signed with *Écumeurs du Texas* ('Texan robbers').

And then there were the Congolese musicians. The heart of the capital and by extension of the entire colony beat to the rhythm of their rumbas. They did not only capture the grievances of the street, but also acted as griots. Thanks to the photos of Franco de mi amor and other musicians of the time taken by Jean Depara, the 'Bills' home photographer (see Chapter 30), all kinds of subversive night-time scenes in which musicians, *évolués* and a handful of white people threw parties with 'free women' in Léopoldville's *flamingos* have been preserved for prosperity. These musicians defied the curfew to add luster to evenings girded by a blush of subversion, and crossed further boundaries by striking up risky relationships with European women in Brazzaville. Their indocility culminated in 1954 with the song *Ata ndele* ('Sooner or Later') by Adou Elenga. Composed in mourning and pain, during the *matanga* ('vigil') of a deceased friend, this lament rang like a tocsin to the ears of the colonists: *Ata ndele, ata ndele, ata ndele, mokili ebokaluka; ata ndele, ata ndele, ata ndele, mondele akosukwama* ('Sooner or later... the world will change, sooner or later... the white men will be wiped away'). The song was banned, and its author locked up in Léopoldville's Ndolo prison. A musician as a political prisoner! And what a musician, probably the least literate of them all!

Conclusion

The tinder box of pent-up colonial frustrations blew up throughout the vast territory of the Congo, seventy-five times the size of Belgium but where, on the eve of independence, 100,000 Belgian colonials kept some fourteen million Congolese individuals at bay. The Belgians compensated for their numerical minority, even more problematic because of the colony's enormous size, with an ideology and mechanisms of control and repression that were far more totalitarian than elsewhere in Africa. For this reason, and also because the Belgian colonization by Belgium was yet another one in a long string of ordeals afflicting the region, the Congolese sought refuge in daily, perennial and protean forms of resistance. Ultimately, if the colonial edifice remained virtually intact until the late 1950s, it was not because the Congolese resisted in vain, but because for every gesture of resistance there was a gesture of collaboration. Janus had two faces.

Bibliography

Hot on the heels of independence, an impressive corpus discussing the traditional forms of resistance materialized, including: Lemarchand, René, *Political Awakening in the Belgian Congo*, University of California Press, Berkeley, 1964; Young, Crawford, *Politics in the Congo: Decolonization and Independence*, Princeton University Press, Princeton, 1965; Weiss, Herbert, *Political Protest in the Congo: The Parti Solidaire Africain during the Independence Struggle*, Princeton University Press, Princeton, 1967; Verhaegen, Benoît, 'Les premiers manifestes politiques à Léopoldville (1950-1956)', *Les Cahiers du CÉDAF*, 10, 1970; Mulambu-Mvuluya, Faustin, 'Contribution à l'étude de la révolte Pende, mai-septembre 1931', *Les Cahiers du CÉDAF*, 1/71, 1971; and Vellut, Jean-Luc, 'Résistances et espaces de liberté dans l'histoire coloniale du Zaïre: avant la marche à l'indépendance (ca. 1876-1945)', in Vellut, Jean-Luc, *Congo. Ambitions et désenchantements 1880-1960*, Karthala, Paris, 2017, p. 165-213. As yet, few studies have been devoted to infrapolitical acts of resistance. Nonetheless, art historians, anthropologists and historians such as Filip de Boeck, Johannes Fabian, Christraud Geary, Didier Gondola, Charlotte Grabli, Nancy Hunt, Maëline Le Lay, Amandine Lauro, Katrien Pype, Charles Tshimanga, Sarah Van Beurden and Bob White have each in their own way shed light on the interface between politics and popular culture. We refer in particular to: Gondola, Ch. Didier, *Tropical Cowboys: Westerns, Violence, and Masculinity in Kinshasa*, Indiana University Press, Bloomington, 2016; Gondola, Ch. Didier, '"Bisengo y a la joie". Fête, sociabilité et politique dans les capitales congolaises', in *Fêtes urbaines en Afrique. Espaces, identités, pouvoirs*, Karthala, Paris, 1999; and Hunt, Nancy R., *A Nervous State: Violence, Remedies, and Reverie in Colonial Congo*, Duke University Press, Durham, 2016.

Notes

1 D'Ydewalle, Charles, 'Orages à Léopoldville', *Revue des Deux Mondes*, 15 February 1959, p. 697.
2 Vangroenweghe, Daniel, *Du sang sur les lianes. Léopold II et son Congo*, Didier Hatier, Brussels, 1986, p. 22.
3 Cited in Kabongo, Tshijuke, 'Les cultes africains comme manifestation de la résistance au colonialisme belge (1920-1948)', *Présence Africaine*, 104, 1977, p. 57.
4 Scott, James, *Domination and the Arts of Resistance: Hidden Transcripts*, Yale University Press, New Haven, 1990, p. 199.
5 Cited in Ryckmans, François, *Mémoires noires. Les Congolais racontent le Congo belge, 1940-1960*, Racine, Brussels, 2010, p. 84.

JEAN-MARIE K.
MUTAMBA MAKOMBO

17. Did the Belgian Colonizer Introduce Racism and an Ethnic Identity into the Congo?

Coming up with a definition of 'racism' that everyone will agree with is far from easy. Nevertheless, what we can say is that racism is an amalgam of feelings, opinions, prejudices and attitudes based on an assumption that there is a hierarchy between groups of people who are divided into 'races'. In the Belgian Congo, just as in other colonies, this theory was not short of adherents. The notion of 'race' even took up a central position in the power relations within colonial society. Belgian colonizers followed theories of social evolutionism and racial determinism which had caught on in the second half of the nineteenth century. In fact, 'race' was constructed as a 'biological' concept: a handbook from 1945 aiming at preparing Belgian women for life in the colony still claimed that 'science tells us that the brain of a black person weighs a little more than a monkey's, yet 800-1000 grams less than that of a white person. The shape of his skull is different as well, as are his reflexes.'[1] Colonial racism was also based on the view that a hierarchy existed between 'cultures'. So-called 'primitive' or 'backward' societies were placed at the bottom of human evolution; at the top stood Western society, which was considered the most advanced form of human civilization. Between these two extremes lay an entire spectrum of intermediate stages labelled according to an elaborate taxonomy: *évoluants* ('evolving citizens'), *demi-civilisés* ('semi-civilized people'), *évolués* ('evolved people', who supposedly came closest to the ideal of the civilized white individual), and so on (see Chapter 18).

Was the Belgian colonizer racist? This may seem a redundant question, but it was the subject of intense debate during the colonial era. After the Second World War in particular, when racial theories were being dismissed with increasing frequency and colonialism was being debated internationally, racial segregation, which formed the core of colonial policy, and its vocabulary, led to many discussions. In 1955, Governor-General Léo Pétillon stressed that black and white people in the Belgian Congo lived 'together', not 'alongside' or 'apart from each other'. The Government at the time did not want to talk about apartheid, a term for which they preferred to leave the patent to South Africa. Yet an unmistakable colored dividing line ran across the Congo's colonial society. Did this 'color bar' have legal foundations? In which form did it manifest itself in society and daily life? And how did people oppose it?

From the nineteenth up until the middle of the twentieth century, the term 'race' was also used for further subdivisions that would later be referred to with the term 'ethnicity' or 'population group'. Here too the Belgian colonizers created several categories they could use to give preferential treatment to particular groups or to play them off against each other to their own advantage. How were 'ethnic' differences in the Congo devised? And to which degree did this approach contribute towards the emergence of new identities that differed from those in the precolonial era?

Racial Discrimination in Writing

The least we can say is that colonial society was not egalitarian. 'The white person's floor is the black's ceiling' captures the relations. The issue was not just unspoken practices in the margin of the law. Quite the opposite, racial discrimination was simply permitted in many circumstances, and was even incorporated formally in official legal provisions and standardized administrative practices. The colony's entire legal basis rested on the distinction between 'indigenous people' and 'non-indigenous people' (*indigènes* and *non-indigènes*). Depending on one's status, one had very different political rights and would come under a separate legal and disciplinary system. 'Indigenous people' were subjected to specific measures that applied exclusively to Congolese individuals. They were only allowed to travel within the country with a *passeport de mutation*, were given specific punishments not applicable to their 'non-indigenous' counterparts, and had limited access to particular forms of education, jobs and hierarchical levels (see Chapter 15).

Concerning employment, legislation covering what was called 'engagement in service' differed, depending on whether the labor contracts were for European or African workers. The remuneration laid down in such a contract varied widely as well. In the private sector, the worst paid European employee in a company usually received a higher wage than his best-paid African counterpart. In the public sector, Congolese employees were in a different administrative framework from Europeans. The regulation of European civil servants in Africa, reformed in 1948, introduced four categories, equivalent to hierarchical 'ranks'. The positions in the lowest category (*agents territoriaux, rédacteurs*) were intended for non-university educated Europeans at the beginning of their professional career. Congolese clerks, who started working as soon as they had left secondary school, had to wait at least 24 years before they would be able to make it to adjunct (*agent territorial adjoint* or *rédacteur adjoint*). Within the *Force Publique* (the colonial army), the highest rank a Congolese soldier could attain was that of first sergeant major. The colonial authorities announced the introduction of officers' training for Congolese students as late as in December 1958, the first class of which would graduate as lieutenants in… 1968.

This discrimination also stemmed partly from a thorough code of conduct drummed into representatives of the colonial state. This is clearly reflected in the colonial authorities' official guide which appeared in 1930, the *Recueil d'instructions à l'usage des fonctionnaires et agents du service territorial du Congo belge* ('Handbook for civil servants and agents in territorial service of the Belgian Congo'). This guide stated explicitly that 'civil servants must make every effort to safeguard the prestige of the white race in general – within the boundaries of the law and regulations'.[2] Colonials had to uphold prestige, and with it the illusion of their own alleged racial superiority. The officials also had to take care of their demeanor and language; they were not allowed to show any disagreement in the presence of black people and had to avoid everything that might ridicule the white race or lower its esteem. Even Belgian soldiers who served in the Congo had to follow these rules: 'Only a relationship based on service is allowed; no intimacy, no friendly relations. We do not shake their hand, except for in the most exceptional circumstances: an encounter with a high-ranking chief or an older non-commissioned officer who is being decorated and so forth.'[3]

The Congolese and Racial Discrimination

Some Congolese people were critical of these racist practices from the beginning. Shortly after the First World War, Paul Panda Farnana, one of the rare Congolese individuals to have been educated in Belgium and a trailblazer of anticolonial criticism, denounced 'the moral sophism which suggests that the black person is no more than a big child, just a kid'.[4] He also condemned Congolese people being put on show in trade and world fairs (see Chapter 14). Many years later Patrice Lumumba confessed what a shock it had been when, in 1947, he crossed the Congo River for the first time to go to Brazzaville, the capital of the French Congo. He was thirsty, and after hesitating for a long time, went into a café occupied by white patrons only, and was served by a European waitress. He was so dumbfounded that he ordered just a glass of mineral water which he did not even finish. Afraid that they were going to throw him out once they had spotted the mistake, he made sure he left as quickly as possible. The fact that he had been served without any problems left a deep impression on him: this kind of thing would be unthinkable in Léopoldville...[5] For visitors from the French colonial empire it was the other way round. Jacques Rabemananjara from Madagascar, travelling through Élisabethville in 1939, was almost denied access to his hotel and its restaurant. When he insisted, he was called a troublemaker. In other words, also during the interwar years, segregation in the Belgian Congo was notably stricter than in the French colonies.

During the 1950s, the Congolese elite (see Chapter 18) denounced this discrimination and the many concrete practices it translated into. Three years after his visit to Brazzaville, Patrice Lumumba was able to muster the courage to question racial discrimination in an article for the newspaper *La Croix du Congo* (albeit, to be on the safe side, hidden behind the acronym 'P.L.'): 'Why are there separate cemeteries for white, mixed-race and black people? Why in all the churches are there seats reserved for white people, but never for their black counterparts? To God, all people are equal, irrespective of their race. Situations such as these seem unjust to us. There should be just as many seats or pews for black people as there are for white.'[6] The editors shrugged it off with a joke: 'This question may seem pertinent, but it is not! It bespeaks of an ill-considered opinion.'

The contrast with the French colonies increasingly became a seedbed for criticism. During a conference for former Christian school pupils in 1952, Antoine-Roger Bolamba, Chief Editor of *La Voix du Congolais*, a journal aimed at *évolués*, reported about his trip to Dakar, where he had represented the Congo at the World Assembly of Youth: 'Nowhere that demeaning racial discrimination: all residential areas, hotels, cinemas, places of worship, markets, etc., are simply mixed.'[7] In saying this, Bolamba concurred with the anonymous informants of the Belgian socialist Omer Prion, who said in as early as 1947: 'Life is much better in the French Congo... The French are more humane, less imbued with racial prejudices; in French Africa, skin color is far less important than here.'[8]

A visit to the 'motherland' could likewise open people's eyes. In 1949, the former seminarian and permanent union representative Jacques Massa traveled to Belgium for the first time, at the invitation of the Belgian Christian union. While he was there, he spoke a few words of Dutch, which was welcomed with applause. Back in the Congo, he was not allowed to enter a bar on Boulevard Albert I. Massa began to read the papers with different eyes and condemned the writing of the *Courrier d'Afrique*, one of the main newspapers of the colony, that still in the 1950s published articles with statements such as: 'We can no longer allow black nurses to give white women injections', or: 'Black people, who are always drenched in sweat, have no place in the same queue as white people.'[9]

The End of Racial Discrimination

Some Congolese individuals were given the opportunity to travel abroad, to Belgium or other colonies, from the 1950s. This raised their awareness of the discrimination at play in their own country. Racism increasingly served as a catalyst for resistance against the Belgian colonizer, and many *évolués* were unhappy about the meagre 'privileges' they were granted piecemeal (see Chapter 18).

During the 1950s, restoring 'human relations' between black and white people became one of the Government's chief concerns, at least officially. In 1951, Governor-General Eugène Jungers summarized it in a phrase for the Cabinet which would later go on to lead a life of its own in *évolués* circles: 'The hand extended too late risks being declined'. The next Governor-General, Léo Pétillon, supported a 'Belgian Congolese community' from his appointment in 1952. With this somewhat vague notion, he wanted to reform social relations between black and white people and allow the country to evolve into a greater colonial mix; what this project could mean in terms of concrete institutional reform has always remained unclear though. After everything the *évolués* had been through, they considered this Belgian Congolese community as no more than a hollow phrase, a bogus project, a mere palliative. At the end of June 1956, just when the 'Manifesto' appeared in the journal *Conscience Africaine* (see Chapter 5), the bishops of the Belgian Congo and Ruanda-Urundi took up an open position regarding racial issues: 'Differences in pay that are only based on race are inequitable [...]. All people are fundamentally equal because they are the same by nature and have the same destiny, because they are all saved by Jesus Christ... Racism, for whatever reason, is always reprehensible' (see Chapter 21).[10] The popular uprising of 4 January 1959 accelerated the situation. By the middle of March 1959, Governor-General Hendrik Cornelis signed fifteen documents which put a stop to the most conspicuous forms of discrimination. In its wake, dozens of discriminating measures were eliminated from the law (the segregation of cities, the different legal statuses and so on). The decolonization process had been set in motion by then, however.

Ethnical Groups: New Identitary Frameworks Marked by Colonization?

The prospect of independence led to new tensions, related to differing group identities which themselves were affected by the historical dynamics of colonization.

Over the course of a long history, within the borders of present-day Congo, divergent cultural, political and ecological entities took shape: from the savanna communities and centralized kingdoms of the Kasaï uplands to the hunter-gatherers in the tropical forests and the lakeside communities in the northeast. From the onset of colonization, the Belgian colonial authorities tried to grasp this heterogeneity by classifying the entities into well-defined 'tribes' or 'ethnic groups' that were clearly demarcated geographically, were each given their own cultural and linguistic identity and were assumed to be homogenous. Occasionally, these sub-divisions more or less corresponded with existing pre-colonial entities. In other cases, they formed a tight straitjacket for far more flexible and dynamic realities which were difficult to classify within the rigid category of 'tribe'. Be that as it may, these ethnic groups became a central fact in Belgian policy. It is no surprise therefore, that different actors instrumentalized the identity frameworks created.

In the Équateur region, for instance, the ethnonym 'Bangala' only emerged in conjunction with colonization. Explorer Henry Morton Stanley was the first to launch the term in 1877; before him, there had been no tribe called 'Bangala' and not one single black person considered him or herself to be a member of it. The Europeans used the ethnonym for small communities on the right bank of the Congo River, and later expanded it to other population groups in the region between Bolobo and Stanleyville, on both sides of the river. The ethnonym comprised a collection of extremely heterogeneous elements: not only fishing communities who had lived for centuries on the banks of the Congo River, but also groups of Sudanese origin (Ngbandi, Ngbaka, Mbandja) and a few Bantu minorities (Ngombe). The label was ultimately stuck onto some fifteen population groups in Équateur Province to the north of Coquilhatville, especially in the districts of Ubangi and Mongala and in the regions of Bolomba and Bomongo in Équateur District.

This classification had concrete consequences, for example for military recruitment campaigns. The colonial administration saw the Bangala 'ethnic group' as a 'martial race', eminently suited to warfare. Bangala men were thus much in demand as recruits for the *Force Publique*. Because of this, Lingala grew into the official language within the *Force Publique* and later became the most-used indigenous language within Équateur Province and Léopoldville education and bureaucracy (see Chapter 20).

The privileged position of Lingala triggered other dynamics; it led to a reaction amongst the Bakongo, the people on the lower reaches of the Congo River, for example. Their leading association, the Alliance of the Bakongo (ABAKO), which would later become a significant political player in the decolonization process (see Chapter 5), initially aimed for the integration, preservation, perfection and dissemination of the Kikongo language. The ABAKO was founded by Edmond Nzeza-Nlandu and was initially supported by Catholic missionaries in the region (see Chapter 21). The latter saw parallels between the concerns of the Kongo population group and the cultural and linguistic problems in Flanders. Moreover, 'the ABAKO seemed the best antidote against protestant or Kimbanguist-inspired political messianism'.[11]

In some cases, these ethnic classifications also served as a basis for preferential treatment to particular groups or putting others at a disadvantage for political reasons, either inspired by the ancient adage of 'divide and rule' or because some population groups had the reputation of being more loyal to colonial rule. This policy fanned certain rivalries. In Kasaï, for instance, the Luba group had enjoyed privileged ties with the colonizing forces since the turn of the century. They were given easier access to educational institutions and auxiliary posts within colonial bureaucracy, to the disadvantage of the Tetela and Lulua, who lived in the same region. During the 1950s, this policy came under increasing pressure. When Luluabourg took over from Lusambo as the provincial capital of Kasaï in 1950, the colonial authorities moved their high-placed Luba functionaries to Luluabourg, even though it was situated in Lulua territory. Incensed, two Lulua intellectuals, Augustin Mutapikayi and Laurent Kapuku wrote a letter to the provincial government in June 1951. They felt humiliated because even on their own territory 'Baluba strangers' were given preferential treatment, and they insisted that the Belgians redress this 'disadvantage'. They were received by the Provincial Governor, but it turned out to be an intimidating experience. The Belgians had decided to change their provincial capital but saw no reason not to continue with existing personnel. Why make things unnecessarily complicated?

On the eve of independence, ethnic tensions in the province of Kasaï deteriorated into open violence.

The institutionalization and rigidification of ethnic frameworks were also a source of tension in many Congolese cities where, as a result of labor migration, many population groups of diverse origins lived alongside each other (see Chapter 12). In the mining region of Katanga, for example, discord grew between the self-declared 'true Katangese' who joined forces in the Confederation of Tribal Associations of Katanga (CONAKAT, founded in 1958), and the so-called 'Kasaïans' (who were given the nickname 'Mocassins'). The latter were a minority group that had ended up in Katanga because the company directors preferred to recruit workers from the Lomami District, which had been incorporated into the province of Katanga during the first decade of the twentieth century. The political openings at the end of the colonial period, and in particular the first urban council elections in 1957, proved a catalyst for latent antagonisms, with the 'native' Katangese contesting the privileged entry of the 'Kasaïans' into politics, and demanding to be represented only by themselves (in the new local councils, for instance).

Conclusion

Racism manifested itself clearly in the color bar, which remained in place throughout the entire colonial era. This color bar was based on organized and controlled forms of segregation and was reinforced in daily life by unwritten rules, which denied black people access to places reserved exclusively for their white counterparts. During the 1950s, a small number of Congolese individuals were given the opportunity to travel abroad (including to Belgium). There, they became acquainted with greater openness, which spurred them on to expose the behavior of the colonials in the Congo. In the colony itself, the 'paternalistic' policy was intended to smooth racism's sharp edges, yet the discriminating practices remained in place and were increasingly called into question by the Congolese themselves and by a few Belgian leaders (who tried to propose corrective action). This met with great resistance, because racial categories were one of the foundations justifying the existence of the colony. Colonial society was a diverse one: it was 'easier' to govern it using all kinds of neatly defined categories and classifications, 'racial' as well as 'ethnic'. Colonial rule gave preferential treatment to specific groups over others and contributed to consolidate powerful identity frameworks; as such, in many cases, it strengthened – or even in some cases stirred up – the grounds for ethnic tensions.

Bibliography

The problematic relations between black and white people are discussed in a book which is somewhat dated: Burns, Alan, *Colour Prejudice*, Allen & Unwin, London, 1948. In addition, I consulted three of my earlier works. Firstly, Mutamba Makombo, Jean-Marie, *Du Congo belge au Congo indépendant 1940-1960. Émergence des 'évolués' et genèse du nationalisme*, IFEP, Kinshasa, 1998. The second book, *Patrice Lumumba correspondant de presse (1948-1956)*, which appeared in 1993 in Brussels in the series *Cahiers Africains*, and in 2005 in Paris with L'Harmattan, describes Lumumba's thoughts about racial discrimination after his stay in Brazzaville in 1947. *L'Histoire du Zaïre par les textes*, part 2 (1885-1955) appeared in Kinshasa with Edideps in 1987 and with Éditions Universitaires Africaines in 2007, and elaborates on the initial manifestations of the latent tension between the Bena Lulua and Baluba in 1951 and all kinds of racist prejudices in the period 1953-1954. Two titles zoom in on the conflict between the Lulua and the Baluba: Chomé, Jules, *Le drame de Luluabourg*, Éditions Remarques Congolaises, Brussels, 1960; and Kalanda-Mabika, A., *Baluba et Lulua. Une ethnie à la recherche d'un nouvel équilibre*, Éditions Remarques Congolaises, Brussels, 1959. Mumbanza mwa Bawele wrote two illuminating articles about the identity of the Bangala: 'Y a-t-il des Bangala? Origine et extension du terme', *Zaïre-Afrique*, 13, 1973, 78, p. 471-483; and 'Les Bangala du fleuve sont-ils apparentés aux Mongo ?', *Zaïre-Afrique*, 14, 1974, 90, p. 623-632. Donatien Dibwe dia Mwembu assessed the Katangese-Kasaïan conflict in 'L'état de la question du conflit Katangais-Kasaïens dans la province du Katanga (1990-1994)', in Jewsiewicki, Bogumil, and N'Sanda Buleli, Léonard, eds., *Les identités régionales en Afrique centrale. Constructions et dérives*, L'Harmattan, Paris, 2008. On the subject of the *Force Publique*, Pamphile Mabiala Mantuba-Ngoma recently published *Les soldats de Bula Matari (1885-1960). Histoire sociale de la Force Publique du Congo belge*, Kinshasa, Éditions Culturelles Africaines, 2019.

Notes

1. Cited in Coméliau, Marie-Louise, *Demain, coloniale!*, Éditions Zaïre, Brussels, 1945, p. 132.
2. Ministère des Colonies, *Recueil à l'usage des fonctionnaires et des agents du service territorial au Congo belge (Rufast)*, Weissenbruch, Brussels, 1930, p. 59-60.
3. *Information et conseils à l'usage des militaires des Forces métropolitaines en service au Congo Belge*, Direction de l'Information et de l'Éducation des Forces armées, s.l., 1957, p. 43.
4. Letter from Paul Panda Farnana to the Minister of Colonies of 28 June 1924, in Tshitungu, Antoine, et al., *Paul Panda Farnana. Une vie oubliée*, Africalia, Brussels, 2014, p. 51.
5. Clément, Pierre, 'Patrice Lumumba, Stanleyville 1952-1953', *Présence Africaine*, 1er trimestre 1962, p. 57-78.
6. P.L., 'Rubriques Questions – Réponses', *La Croix du Congo*, 24 December 1950, p. 4.
7. *La Voix du Congolais*, 79, October 1952, p. 609.
8. Omer, P., 'Congo 1947', *Les Cahiers Socialistes*, 16-17, July 1947, p. 116.
9. Interview with Jacques Massa, December 1978.
10. *La Croix du Congo*, 8 July 1956, p. 4.
11. Verhaegen, Benoît, 'Les premiers manifestes politiques à Léopoldville (1950-1956)', *Les Cahiers du CÉDAF*, 10, 1971, p. 9.

DANIEL TÖDT

18. The Colonial State and the African Elite

A History of Subjugation?

Without local intermediaries, a colonial regime would have been unthinkable. The number of Europeans in situ was small. By themselves, they would barely have been able to maintain colonial rule on African territory. The colonial authorities therefore introduced intermediaries into the administration – either by force or otherwise –, both in the Congo and in the rest of colonial Africa. But how did the colonial state mold its African intermediaries? How did both sides relate to each other? What degree of influence and latitude did the African elites have? What advantages did they gain from their intermediary position between the colonial state and African society? Who used whom, for whose interests?

The discordant and ambivalent history of the relationship between the Belgian rulers and the Congolese intermediaries shows that there were limits to the colonizer's power, and that it was characterized by unwanted side effects. After all, it was the representatives of the theoretically subservient and loyal elite who, in 1960, fought for political independence. Within an extremely short period of time, they transformed from cornerstones to pall bearers of colonial rule. The Belgian protagonists viewed the result of their elite policies in the same way as Victor Frankenstein did his creation in Mary Shelley's novel.

Research into the Belgian Congo has long focused primarily on the so-called 'modern' elite and its part in decolonization. Only during the past two decades have the various forms of cooperation by African elites become the subject of historical studies. The history of the so-called 'traditional' elites, however, who were close to the colonial state but lost influence in the postcolonial state, remained relatively underexposed.

Crucial for the African elites' position of power was whether the colonial state opted for direct or indirect rule. In the first instance, the foreign rule was based on a European-led administration of a newly defined territory; in the second case it would delegate powers to local authorities within existing territorial areas. Indirect rule had been regarded as typically British as illustrated by the supporting role of the maharajas in colonial India; direct rule dominated in

French and Portuguese Africa. Belgian colonial politicians preferred the indirect rule model but in fact it was not only local reality that adapted to these two principles of governance; these governance principles also adapted themselves to local reality. The Congo Free State and the Belgian Congo were characterized by a historically variable and hybrid way of exercising power that was challenged by historical protagonists. This meant that the African elite's position and scope was subject to historical change.

Orchestrated Indirect Rule: Traditional Elites as a Colonial Invention

The annexation of the territory constituting the later Congo Free State rested on treaties between European and local rulers. The latter transferred rule over their territories to the Congo Free State, usually without awareness of what effect their assent would have on their sovereignty. Yet in 1891, the so-called indigenous political units were recognized as an integral part of the government of the Congo Free State. But how meaningful could this be given that violent conquest, the slave trade and associated regional power shifts had largely wiped out the sort of political structures that might have served as the vehicles of indirect rule? Out of sheer necessity, the colonial authority created the so-called *chefferies indigènes* ('indigenous chiefdoms') and appointed corresponding chiefs to serve as the Congo Free State's representatives and subordinates. Quite ironically, in many places these loyal intermediaries did not enjoy any traditional authority over their populace before the arrival of the Europeans. They were handed a medal by functionaries of the Congo Free State during solemn ceremonies as a visible token of their newly won power. In exchange for discharging their duty to recruit workers forcibly – in rubber production, for example, with its high cost in human lives – these decorated chiefs were provided with soldiers and weapons. Violence, in other words, replaced this orchestrated form of indirect rule's missing legitimacy.

Around 1900, the Congo Free State had 450 chiefs at its disposal, who were thus in the majority vis-à-vis the 300 European functionaries. Despite their mostly random appointments, following a decree in 1906, these chiefs became responsible for the *droit coutumier*, African customary law, and gained authority over a supposedly culturally and linguistically homogenous group with its own laws and customs. What was being regarded as a kind of natural tribal system ultimately consisted of flexible alliances which were now taking shape as administrative units (see Chapter 17).

When Belgium took over the Congo Free State from King Leopold II in 1908, the new colonial state was keen to show its abhorrence of the internationally condemned terrors, including with respect to policies for local elites. It therefore tried to restore the traditional authorities. In 1910, the Ministry of Colonies appointed *sous-chefferies* ('sub-chiefdoms') alongside *chefferies*. These extremely small-scale regions henceforth had to constitute the new integral parts of the modern governing state. Apart from that, not much changed: the various chiefdoms were headed by a chief, who himself was under the authority of the colonial state. How these chiefs were appointed was locally very different. Sometimes the Belgian functionaries opportunistically leant on *chefs coutumiers* ('traditional chiefs') and emphasized the latter's authority; elsewhere they appointed chiefs at their own discretion and without knowledge of local power relationships, whereby they preferred subservient candidates over established authorities and/or ignored local succession tradition.

The colonial state demanded loyalty and efficiency from its chiefs in the execution of the administrative tasks they were assigned. These consisted of recruiting workers and soldiers, collecting taxes and crusading against customs considered 'primitive' by missionaries and colonial officials. The chiefs also conducted censuses and forced their populace to cultivate and sell particular products. Last but not least, they passed sentences on their subjects according to the *droit coutumier*, or African customary law, which in the dual legal system was only used for the African population and on the basis of which the colonial state enacted extremely repressive regulations and obligations; for the European population, Belgian criminal and civil law applied. The chiefs were recompensed in different ways for their activities: a salary from the state, a share of tax income and fines levied, and payments from companies for workers supplied. As interchangeable intermediaries, they functioned as pivots in foreign rule. In the eyes of the subjects, they embodied the colonial state; whereas to the colonial state, they were the subjects.

In 1917, there were no fewer than 6,095 *chefferies* and *sous-chefferies*. We should therefore visualize the political map of the Belgian Congo as an ever-changing patchwork. A splintered region such as Bas-Congo comprised no less than 126 *chefferies*; the Kuba Kingdom in Kasaï, almost twice as big, consisted of just one *chefferie* and continued to exist as a form of indirect administration within its own borders, despite colonial rule. The Kuba King took advantage of his administrative and patronage structures and retained his power. He remained subservient to the colonial state but was an equal partner within the local government. The fact that Kuba sculptures were admired by the avant-garde from the 1890s onwards also gave the King an international aura of inviolable traditional authority.

Besides the Kuba Kingdom, similar political systems continued to operate in other parts of Kasaï, in a few regions near Lake Kivu, and in Katanga. This does not mean that they were all equally respected by the colonial regime. Quite the contrary; the former Lunda Kingdom was split up over several territories.

Yet the idea of indirect rule reigned supreme during the interwar period. Louis Franck, the first liberal Minister of Colonies (1918-1924), in particular warmed to this approach, which was gaining popularity in British Africa through the publications by Frederick Lugard, the former Governor-General of Nigeria. Franck's argument for the revitalization of what he considered political units was no coincidence: he was a proponent of cultural autonomy for Flanders. In 1921, he merged the subdivided administrative units into *grandes chefferies*. In order to reduce the large number of *chefferies*, he consolidated the smaller *chefferies* into so-called *secteurs*. These were headed by a *chef de secteur* ('sector chief') who had his own budget, taxes and far-reaching powers. On behalf of the colonial state, he also exercised power, up to a point, in the domain of jurisdiction and repression.

Indirect rule was also attractive for financial reasons. During the economic crisis of the 1930s, the number of districts, territories and areas ruled by African leaders was scaled down drastically, through territorial reform in 1933. Towards 1935, the number of *chefferies* had been halved to 2,496, while 57 *secteurs* had been formed. At the same time, the European colonial functionaries meddled increasingly in the affairs of *chefferies* and *secteurs* and took over budget management, amongst other things. In 1950, there were only 476 *chefferies* left while the number of *secteurs* had risen to 517.

Nonetheless, the close involvement of the African elite in the governance of the colony met with fierce resistance as well. In regions with a considerable European population, such as the industrialized parts of Katanga, colonial agents thought that the chief should only supply manpower and by no means be involved in governance. The Catholic mission congregations, who had the authority to provide education (see Chapters 21 and 23), opposed Minister Franck's plans to give the sons of chiefs an administrative education in schools established especially for the purpose. Some missionaries refused to baptize the future bearers of indirect rule, because they regarded them as advocates of unchristian and banned practices such as polygamy.

Indirect Rule with Cultural Tools: The Colonial Invention of a Modern Elite

After 1945, an educated elite often described as 'modern' sprung up in the Belgian Congo: the so-called *évolués*. These were Congolese people who had been trained as office-clerks, teachers or priests. Because of a lack of universities, seminaries were indeed the highest form of education Congolese individuals were able to enjoy, but only one in twelve graduates – until 1945 some 1,300 students – entered into the service of the Church. For the new elite, feigning that you wanted to devote your life to God was a way to attain higher education and more lucrative positions.

In late colonial Africa, the emergence of an educated elite culturally oriented towards Europe was by no means unique to Belgian-controlled territory. The *lettrés* in the Francophone colonies occupied a similar position, as did the 'educated Africans' in areas under British rule and the *assimilados* or *civilizados* in Portuguese Africa. But the collective term *évolués* in the Belgian Congo was a particularly striking expression of cultural Darwinism, which pre-supposed universally applicable levels of civilization, and legitimized and consolidated political and social hierarchies within the colony. A highly developed and civilized European culture was positioned at the top; African culture at the bottom was seen as its alleged primitive and wild counterpart.

Estimates from 1947 suggest that there were just 40,000 *évolués* amongst 750,000 wage earners. They worked as office-clerks in the colonial administration or for companies, as medical assistants, teachers or foremen. Out of a total population of more than ten million people, this seems a small number, but if you compare this with the 35,000 Europeans who were in the Congo, it is immediately obvious that *évolués* played a key role in the upkeep of the colonial state.

Post-Second World War developmental colonialism in particular (see Chapter 13) needed educated elites who had sufficient knowledge of administration and technology for its modernization programs. The colonial state not only tried to shape these modern elites to its vision, but equally to control them. The formation of an elite was also intended to rebut the international community's accusation that Belgian colonial policy had failed to develop the Congolese population culturally and politically.

For the colonial state and the missionaries, the small circle of African intellectuals was both a spearhead and an advertisement for a steadfast civilizing mission. Little by little the *évolués* had to make the ideal of monogamous families, civic virtues and gender roles socially acceptable. Just as with the working classes in Belgium, colonial society had to be pacified via a bourgeois vision of values and lifestyle. Under the banner of developmental colonialism, then, the colonial state increasingly relied on the use of soft power, on indirect rule by cultural means.

The colonial state's elite policy relied above all on journals and associations. As early as the 1920s, mission orders stayed in touch with their former pupils through these channels (see also Chapter 21). Club life kept the educated elite together and showcased bourgeois civilization through lectures and debates. Alongside the older *La Croix du Congo* ('The Cross of the Congo'), closely linked to the missions, a new magazine appeared in 1945, *La Voix du Congolais* ('The Voice of the Congo'), made 'by the Congolese for the Congolese'. Although the monthly was published and controlled by the government, it gave the *évolués* a voice. *La Voix du Congolais* showed what was uppermost in *évolués* lives and minds, how they commented on events and developments in their country, as well as their demands.

Quelle sera notre place dans le monde de demain? ('What will be our place in the world of tomorrow?') is how, in March 1945, full of expectation, the author Paul Lomami-Tshibamba summarized the African elite's question regarding its position in future colonial society. It strived for a special legal status, improved living conditions, a bigger voice and greater recognition. This particular legal status for the *évolués*, which would protect them from the *droit coutumier*'s randomness and methods of coercion, was the topic of heated debate as far back as during the 1920s. The plan foundered on two issues: how far should legal equality with the Europeans go, and, in particular, what in fact characterized the African elite? The Belgian colonial ideologues believed it was their striving for perfection – and with it the assumption that they were still not yet perfect and therefore not ready for emancipation.

Colonial law in the Belgian Congo equated legal assimilation with cultural assimilation. But the recognition of cultural equality between Europeans and Africans would have shaken to its foundation the colonial society's hierarchy, legitimized with cultural differences considered immutable. This problem led to fierce debates about the status of the *évolués* involving numerous commissions, African authors, European missionaries and settlers as well as colonial functionaries. The outcome was meagre, however. While Belgian colonial reformers took their lead from the legal system of the French Empire, in practice they lagged behind it. When, after a laborious process, the Minister of Colonies decided to introduce the *carte du mérite civique* (1948) and a revised *immatriculation* (1952), the African population of the *Union Française* – and thus on the other side of the Congo River – had already been granted civil rights.

It is no surprise therefore that the reforms were a disappointment to the African elite. They did not meet in any shape or form the demand for legal equality for which the African elite had been campaigning for years. Those who requested a new status had to subject themselves to a meticulous inspection by the predominantly European awarding committee, and conform to the ideal image of the *noirs perfectionnés* ('refined blacks') the *évolués* themselves had cultivated in their journals. In order to be accepted officially into the African elite, a Congolese man had to convince he was a 'civilized', well-educated worker and loyal, monogamous husband. His wife needed to show they were leading a petit bourgeois lifestyle and family-life following European example as she would have learned from the Belgian chaperones in the *foyers sociaux* ('social homes'). Most Europeans in the colony would surely have failed to meet the requirement for morally impeccable behavior at all times.

The number of people in possession of the *carte du mérite civique* and of those 'immatriculated', including their wives and children, altogether came to a mere 2,325. In other words, the awarding committee regarded less than 0.02 per cent of Congolese individuals as 'sufficiently civilized'. Its criteria were strict: a successful application could fail over insufficiently clean cutlery.

The few successful candidates were invested during official ceremonies. These were different than in previous times: medals had been hung around chiefs' necks, whereas the modern elite were given a certificate. Photos of these ceremonies would appear in the press, which was supposed to illustrate the close cooperation between the modern elite and colonial rule. They affirmed the existing colonial hierarchy, however, because the celebrated *évolué* family tended to be flanked by a European functionary and a chief, who, as an extended arm of the colonial state, continued to keep a close watch on the educated elite's ambitions. The celebrated *évolués* did not have any equal rights, and had to subordinate themselves and swear allegiance to the colonial state, which, despite all their efforts, firmly curtailed their career perspectives and social participation. The holders of this status were not even safeguarded from legal and day-to-day racist discrimination.

This new elite's discontent became a self-fulfilling prophecy. The irony of the Belgian Congo's decolonization history is that the colonial state was always afraid of the ascent of a well-educated, but embittered elite, but that it itself ended up creating this as a result of half-baked reforms after the war.

Challenging and Overcoming the Colonial Regime: Transformation of the Modern Elite

The school funding controversy that erupted in Belgium during the 1950s, led to the politicization of the Congolese elite. Some *évolués* were frustrated about the limited opportunities for progressing to higher levels in mission schools and sided with the liberal Minister of Colonies; others remained loyal to the Catholic community. At any rate, their voices were sounding more assertive and increasingly critical of the colonial regime. The *Conscience Africaine* and ABAKO manifestos from the summer of 1956 were the opening shots of a battle that would lead to independence (see Chapter 5).

To pour oil on troubled waters, the Minister of Colonies introduced forms of political participation in some cities. The mayoral elections of 1957 and 1958 laid bare the ethnic, language-related and regional chasms amongst the African populace. The *évolués* became ever more fragmented: many, for electoral gain, increasingly presented themselves as the spokespersons of their own specific groups. They no longer wore three-piece suits but flaunted themselves with a spear in hand or a leopard skin draped around their shoulders. In other words, the *évolués* branded *detribalized* during the interwar period reinvented themselves as *retribalized*. In so doing, they removed a weapon from the arsenal of colonial power, which had created the tribes and traditional chiefs. While, up until then, such designations had been an instrument for the perpetuation of European occupation (see Chapter 17), the African elite now used it to defy colonial rule. Political ethnonationalism sharpened social tensions, which in some places deteriorated into violence. In Kasaï, it was remarkably enough the Kuba King who, together with King Baudouin, defused the bloody conflicts between Lulua and Luba. The colonial regime regarded the traditional chiefs as moderate and loyal forces. Within Congolese politics, the modern elite, increasingly also developing an international network, had long stolen a march on the chiefs. The PNP's election promises to protect the existing order alongside the traditional elite and Belgian protagonists, contrasted in a hopelessly out-of-date fashion with the pan-African, anti-imperialist and nationalist ideology of Patrice Lumumba's MNC.

The African elite did not accept minor changes or vague promises about independence. The Belgian powers not only lost their grip on the *évolués*' 'character development', but also had to relinquish control over the country's political development, paradoxically to an elite which had once been so loyal (see Chapter 5).

Conclusion

In the independent Congo, the *évolués*' transformation into the political elite happened at breakneck speed, and many junior civil servants in the colonial administration rose to become ministers. In essence, this elite had first served the colonial state, then conquered it and finally inherited it. The metamorphosis of its first Prime Minister, Patrice Lumumba, is paradigmatic for that first generation. In 1954, as a model *évolué* and young postal clerk, Lumumba had sung the praises of the explorer Henry Morton Stanley and the Belgian civilizing mission. Six years later, after King Baudouin's independence ceremony speech, he mercilessly broke with the Belgian colonial regime.

The former *évolués*' soaring careers implied an equivalent deep plunge. The African elite, which could fall back on little political experience, landed in the middle of one of the Cold War's biggest proxy conflicts in Africa. The Congo's late- and postcolonial crises indubitably have their origin in the shaping of the Belgian Congo's elite. This is a paradox, because the African elite's limited size, internal divisions and somewhat ill-preparedness were not so much a failing, as a success of the colonial state's elite policy, which wanted to exclude the African populace as long as possible from political emancipation, higher education and posts of responsibility. The chaos and the power vacuum, about which Belgian politicians had warned in the event of accelerated independence, was a side effect of that elite policy. It sowed subjugation and reaped insurrection.

Bibliography

A standard work about the history of the *évolués* is Mutamba Makombo, Jean-Marie, *Du Congo belge au Congo indépendant. Émergence des 'évolués' et genèse du nationalisme*, Publications de l'Institut de Formation et d'Études Politiques, Kinshasa, 1998. Recent publications about the educated elite include: Monaville, Pedro, *Students of the World. Global 1968 and Decolonization in the Congo*, Duke University Press, Durham, 2022; and Tödt, Daniel, *The Lumumba Generation. African Bourgeoisie and Colonial Distinction in the Belgian Congo*, De Gruyter, Berlin, 2021. Further articles about the topic can be found in Tousignant, Nathalie, ed., *Le manifeste 'Conscience africaine' (1956). Élites congolaises et société coloniale. Regards croisés*, Publications des Facultés Universitaires Saint-Louis, Brussels, 2009. Since the 1960s, the *évolués* have been discussed within the political history of the Belgian Congo, by Crawford Young and Michel de

Schrevel amongst others. However, they lose sight of some aspects that do not have immediate political consequences. More recent studies shed light on the educational institutions, gender roles and family models of the elites, such as those by Nancy Rose Hunt, Gertrude Mianda and Charles Tshimanga. Exhaustive biographies exist about the people who represented the first generation of politicians, in particular those about Patrice Lumumba by Jean Omasombo and Benoît Verhaegen. By contrast, the literature about the traditional elite is less extensive. Aside from older classic studies by Andrzej Zajączkowski and Edouard Bustin, several up-to-date works examine the bearers of indirect rule, such as Vansina, Jan, *Being Colonized: The Kuba Experience in Rural Congo, 1880-1960*, University of Wisconsin Press, Madison, 2010; and Loffman, Reuben A., *Church, State and Colonialism in Southeastern Congo, 1890-1962*, Palgrave, Basingstoke, 2019.

AMANDINE LAURO

19. Women, Sexuality, *Métissage*

Colonization's 'Taboo' Topics?

The classic accounts of the history of Belgian colonization in the Congo have long presented colonial expansion as a 'men's business'. Whether the discussion centered on Belgian decision-makers or on their Congolese political opponents, protagonists in history books are predominantly male. Over the past decades, however, new studies have come out which shed light on the gender dimension of Belgian colonialism. They examine women's experiences of colonization, colonial interventions in the private sphere and how colonialism affected masculinity. From the exaltation of the triumphant virility of explorers to the 'moral' conversion preached by missionaries, from *grand* 'civilizing' discourses on the condition of African women to debates about the role of white women, gender matters, closely interwoven with issues (and representations) of race, have been at the heart of colonial projects – of their self-legitimization arguments as well as of their practices of power.

Following on from a few recent controversies (around mixed-race children and colonial sexual violence for instance), these newly rediscovered issues are sometimes branded 'taboo topics' or 'secrets' of colonization. Yet they were discussed intensely during the colonial era, either in political debates or in heated public discussions. Gender, sexuality and 'morality' matters featured regularly in parliamentary interventions, international congresses or in the press; because they constituted an important part of the 'civilizing mission' and of the definition of racial boundaries, they preoccupied a wide range of colonial actors. As objects of governance, they also gave rise to interventionist measures based on the disqualification of indigenous gender models and on the promotion of new norms modelled on a European, bourgeois and Christian template. This program was nevertheless subjected to multiple interpretations and transgressions. Which policy measures were taken, and how did these evolve over time? How did they relate to the colonial Congo's particular political economy? Which concrete effects did measures related to gender, sexuality and family have on the Congolese population, besides rhetorical discourses about women and the 'civilizing mission'? And was the Congo somewhere where, sexually, nothing was out of bounds for the European colonizers?

The Early Colonial Period: Civilizing Rhetoric and Gender Violence

From the first years of the colonization onwards, the 'civilizing' rhetoric employed by the Congo Free State to project a positive image on the international stage used gender issues. In official discourses, 'civilizing' also equated 'liberating' Congolese people (and in particular Congolese women) from their so-called 'primitive' familial customs, which were regarded as a reflection of their 'excessive' sexuality. Behind this philanthropic facade, in practice, few initiatives were taken. The 'civilizing mission' was, after all, not Leopold II's regime's priority. Congolese women were not spared the Congo Free State's extreme brutality. While women were not forced to harvest rubber or to carry out porterage duties, other constraints weighed heavily upon them. The responsibility of resupplying Europeans and their auxiliaries laid mostly on their shoulders, in a context in which the subsistence of the community was already made more complicated by the hoarding of men in the service of the newly imposed *corvées*. Women were also prime-targets for hostage-taking strategies carried out by agents of the regime as an 'encouragement' for men to work harder. And finally, women were the principal victims of the sexual violence that was part and parcel of Leopoldian violent strategies of conquest and coercion. Not much information exists about this, but in 1904-1905, for instance, thirteen Congolese women testified to the commission of inquiry that had been sent to the Congo to investigate the acts of violence during this period (see Chapter 2).

At the beginning of the twentieth century, the vast majority of colonizers in the Congo were men. In 1900, there were only 82 European women, compared to 1,105 men. Because the region had the reputation of being 'the white man's grave' and because the colonial occupation came about in a war context, the presence of women did not seem expedient. Out of the few dozens of women who made it to the Congo during this initial period, most were missionaries (see Chapter 21). From the 1890s, the Sisters of Charity from Ghent founded various establishments in Bas-Congo and Kasaï including a hospital, an orphanage and a girls' school. Gradually, the number of female religious orders in the Congo grew. Nuns' primary task was to support the evangelizing work of the male congregations by providing care and education for Congolese women and girls. In a way, this subordinate position mirrored the gender-based divide of the colonial education policy: girls' education was focused on domestic skills and aimed above all at molding wives and mothers for the (male) elites and auxiliaries of colonial rule (see Chapter 23).

In Moanda, on the west coast of the Congo, the largest boarding school (known at the time as a *colonie scolaire*) was built for this ambition. The institute served as a training college for the wives of the initial Congolese catechists and clerks, who were educated in the neighboring male missions. At the same time, the history of this boarding school shows how even within such a well-oiled project, tensions generated by the agency of Congolese women surfaced: in the mid-1890s, Moanda had to close its doors for a few months because of rumors that young pupils were involved in relationships with Europeans, and shortly after the turn of the century, the mission also came under judicial scrutiny after several girls ran away.

The Maternalism of Belgian Colonization

Up until the end of the colonial era, this view on girls' education remained largely intact. The paternalism of the Belgian colonial policy is often discussed, but maternalism too formed an essential part of Belgian 'civilizing' and social control strategies in the Congo. By attempting to impose a new model of family life and gender roles based on the Christian bourgeois ideal of the nineteenth-century 'motherland', Belgian authorities aimed to encourage the emergence of a European way of life in the privacy of home and to make women the vehicles for espousing the colonial regime's new values.

With the annexation of the Congo in 1908, this civilizing discourse gained new zeal. The ambition was to 'elevate' Congolese women who were portrayed as 'enslaved' by practices such as polygamy and by the hard labor of agriculture they traditionally assumed. On the eve of the First World War, a Belgian Jesuit priest summarizes this well: 'To concern Belgium with the fate of black women is therefore to interest it in a crucial element of the big problem our country has to solve: the civilization of its Congo.'[1]

This view was widely shared across empires at the time. Within colonial Africa, some specificities of the Belgian regime outlined a distinctive configuration that influenced the ways in which women were 'targeted' by the colonial government: the central role of the Catholic Church and its privileges, the unrivalled scale of demographic anxieties (marked by eugenic overtones) and a punctilious concern for bourgeois exemplarity. For educational policy this proved to be an explosive cocktail. In combination with the Belgian colonial administration's structural distrust towards the emergence of a colonized elite, it resulted in an extremely slow and scant schooling of girls. On the eve of independence, less than ten per cent of girls went to school; not one single woman was amongst the hundred or so Congolese students who were enrolled at the country's two universities; and only one woman in the entire colony had completed secondary education successfully (as opposed to some eight hundred men) – this was Sophie Kanza, a trailblazer, who in 1966 also became the first female Congolese minister. Up until the end of the colonial era, Congolese women remained to a great degree excluded from wage employment. Even domestic service remained monopolized by men (the so-called 'boys'). In rural areas, although many women worked the land, they remained largely excluded from the colonial government's agricultural development projects (involving new techniques, cash crops, etc.; see Chapter 11). In urban areas, women were de facto relegated to the margins of the formal economy.

The fact that education placed so much emphasis on domestic science and good mothercraft has a lot to do with strongly biopolitically-colored hygienist and demographic anxieties. After 1908, and even more so during the interwar years, Belgian authorities partly blamed the Congo's demographic decline (see Chapter 7) on a low birth rate, which was itself presented as the result of a moral crisis and of 'traditional' practices such as lengthy breastfeeding. Mining companies, philanthropic associations and missionary initiatives (and to a lesser extent medical and social public services) promoted improvements in mother and children's health by setting up infant welfare centers and offering courses in hygiene and childcare (see Chapter 22). In the 1920s and 1930s, when the debate about manpower and its threatened shortage took center stage on the political agenda, the education of African women into 'good' mothers was seen as an important part of the solution. Even charities led by European women made no secret of the connections of these concerns: as one of them argued in 1930, 'caring for the child while educating the mother is a duty. We need workers, the colony's wealth depends on it.'[2]

European Women, African Women: A Colonial Feminism?

It was against this backdrop that European women turned out to be useful allies for colonial leaders. From the interwar years onwards, they came to the Congo in ever increasing numbers, albeit on a limited scale: just before the Second World War they only made up a third of the colony's European population. During the 1920s and beyond, European women were handed a double mission: a moralizing and a 'civilizing' one. The first consisted of contributing to the stabilization and respectabilization of colonial society. Through their presence, the practice of interracial concubinage – white men living with Congolese women – was to decline in favor of bourgeois family lifestyles more in line with the metropole's model. The second, the 'civilizing mission', was aimed at colonized women, more specifically at the protection of mother and child.

This occurred both in a philanthropic and professional context. Women volunteers founded organizations such as the *Ligue de Protection de l'Enfance Noire* ('League for the Protection of Black Childhood'; 1912) and the *Association pour la Protection de la Femme Indigène* ('Association for the Protection of the Indigenous Woman'; 1926). From its foundation in 1923, the most important association of Belgian women in the Congo, the *Union des Femmes Coloniales* ('Union of Colonial Women'), also organized a series of activities for Congolese women, even though it was primarily intended as a social and solidarity network for colonial women. Many European women took part in smaller-scale initiatives and assisted in hospitals, orphanages and other institutions run by nuns. Up until the end of the 1940s, social work for women remained largely in the hands of mission sisters, who were increasingly aided by African auxiliaries. Lay social work took off after the Second World War in particular, alongside a greater professionalization of the sector. It played a key-role in the development of a network of *foyers sociaux*, a type of domestic science school for (adult) Congolese women in the cities, the aim of which was to create an 'evolved' female elite.

These activities mirrored those practiced in nineteenth-century Belgium for working-class families, when bourgeois pater/maternalist philanthropy had to make up for the lack of social protection. While this model was completely out of step with Belgian twentieth-century social evolutions, in the Congo, it continued to prevail for decades. In a wider perspective this helps explain the European women's not-so progressive view on the emancipation of African women, which was being constantly postponed: this view never broke away from the colonial model and from its patronizing maternalism, and reflected the Eurocentric stereotypes of the period. Yet this did not stop some colonial women (and on occasion some feminist associations in the metropole) from criticizing colonial authorities and the limits of their initiatives in favor of Congolese women (in the sphere of education or equal rights for instance). But these criticisms were raised in the name of a feminized 'civilizing mission' and European women never quite departed from the idea that African women were minors who needed to be guided along the path to 'evolution'.

Interracial Sexuality and *Métissage*

In practice, the colonizers themselves turned out to not always respect the 'evolved' moral standards of respectability and virtue they were at pains to propagate. Up until the interwar years, men often lived in concubinage with Congolese mistresses, who were referred to by the euphemism *ménagères* (literally 'housekeepers', often also 'concubines') in the colonial vocabulary. For most of them, these relationships were short-lived and illegitimate. They lasted as long as the European partner was in the Congo, and rarely led to an official marriage. Interracial unions were never forbidden by law in the Belgian Congo, but official marriages were advised against and remained an exception.

Over the course of the colonial era, tolerance towards such relationships and their visibility evolved considerably. At first, the colonial authorities turned a blind eye. They did not even stumble over the way in which these relationships came into being – i.e. either in a context of violent predation whereby the 'right of the conqueror' also applied to women's bodies, or in a context of 'negotiation', whereby local chiefs would offer women, often slaves or women with a low social rank, to colonizers as a sign of allegiance or to seal an alliance. The racist stereotyping of African women as hypersexual, lascivious and willing creatures, as well as the myth that the tropical climate exacerbated sexual impulses, contributed to the permissive atmosphere around these relations, even when they involved very young girls. After the *reprise* and even more from the interwar years, Belgian colonial authorities, which wanted to assume a respectable image, adopted a less broad-minded attitude towards these *ménagères*. Interracial sexuality was increasingly considered as a moral and racial transgression, which tarnished the colonizer's 'prestige'. However, this growing disapproval affected not so much the occurrence of these relationships as their visibility; from the interwar years, colonials were merely urged to exercise greater discretion.

Another reason why these relationships were considered problematic was that they were seen as dangerous sources of 'contamination', most notably because they might produce mixed-race children. We do not have exact figures, but during the 1930s, at least a few thousand children must have been born from these mixed relationships, and during the 1950s the number amounted to more than ten thousand. Colonial society was based on racial distinctions. By their very existence, mixed-race children jeopardized these distinctions. As such, they presented colonial authorities with a number of political and legal issues. Should these children be assimilated into the group (and status) of Europeans because (according to the view prevailing at the time) they had 'white blood' in their veins? Should they be treated, on the contrary, as 'natives', on the basis of the argument that their 'African' biological traits would remain dominant anyway? Or should they be given an intermediary status, especially created for them? The Belgian colonial government never made a definitive choice for any of these options.

Paternal recognition played a key role in the possibilities opened to mixed-race children. Without this recognition, it was impossible for a child to acquire the status (and rights) of a European. While some fathers did recognize their child(ren), this remained the exception. Many children lived with their mother and held a range of positions within their African family, depending on the kinship system in force in their area, and obviously also on their personal situation. Gradually, the colonial state, with the support of missionaries, began to develop interventionist policies and to encourage (and in many cases to compel) the placement of these children in missionary-run institutions. Some of these 'specialized' in the care of mixed-race children, such as the 'special schools' of Kabinda and Lusambo or the Save institute for *mulattos* (located in Rwanda, but also taking in children from the Congo and Burundi). On the eve of independence, the marginalized position of these children, shaped by the segregation policy of colonial authorities, became a source of concern for the missionary hierarchy, in a context of political and ethnic tensions that left little room for in-between identities. This led the religious authorities of Save, with the support of the colonial administration, to organize the transfer of mixed-race pupils from the institute and from neighboring schools to Belgium. In principle, the mothers had to give their permission for this 'evacuation', and most (but not all) did so, either because they were convinced that this was the best option for their child, or because they had no other choice, and possibly also without anyone explaining to them what exactly it was they were giving their permission for, namely a definitive separation. While the fate of the children of the institute of Save has received a great deal of media attention (see Chapter 28), what happened to the thousands of other children who stayed in the Congo, is (still, and to an even greater extent) little-explored.

Challenging Gender Norms, Challenging Colonial Domination

Although colonial policies offered Congolese women limited room for maneuvering, they never resigned themselves to the limited roles they had been allotted.

Women were not absent from movements opposing colonial rule, even though as yet too little is known about their participation. In 1915, for instance, Maria Nkoy, a young woman renowned as a powerful healer, was the driving force behind a major uprising in the Western Congo. She opposed a string of colonial constraints (taxes, forced labor, etc.). In the tense situation during the First World War, she also prophesized the Belgian defeat against the 'Germani'.

More generally, many colonial initiatives aimed at Congolese women did not work out as colonial ideologues had hoped. Often, complex dynamics involving rejection, negotiation and appropriation materialized. In cities in particular, Congolese women found unexpected opportunities. Although their presence in urban centers had been long advised against by the colonial authorities, from the 1920s onwards increasingly greater numbers of women settled there. They embarked on professional activities that went counter to the gender norms of colonial rule, of 'traditional' African societies, and of the new male elites trained at European schools. Many women, whether married or known as a 'free woman', began independent economic activities in the fringes of colonial control (petty trading, food production, transactional sexuality, etc.). When these cities grew exponentially after the Second World War, women also shaped urban culture through their activities and investments in new forms of sociability and popular culture (musical creation, fashion, entertainment, and so on) (see Chapter 16).

During the 1950s, ever more women's associations aimed at recreation and/or mutual aid emerged. While they did not have political ambitions *per se*, they nevertheless challenged colonial as well as Congolese norms and often escaped colonial supervision. Although *évolués* men often talked about the position of women who, as indicators of 'progress' and 'civilization' continued to be an important political battleground, they hardly ever gave those directly concerned a voice. Aside from a few exceptions (such as Andrée Blouin, who was active within Patrice Lumumba's MNC), the presence of women in formal decolonization movements (political parties, etc.) remained limited. During discussions about the practical modalities of independence, Belgian colonizers and Congolese leaders agreed that women, despite their new social role and their potentialities for mobilization, would not be given the right to vote.

Conclusion: A Selective Visibility

On the eve of decolonization, colonial authorities still listed the 'advancement of women' as one of their 'civilizing' priorities. But the great visibility of this theme proved deceptive. As during the entire colonial era, the staging of the Congo as a 'model colony' was still illustrated by falling infant mortality rates, photos of the bourgeois home interiors of *évolués* (see Chapter 30) or articles about the first qualified assistant-nurses. Yet the reality was a great deal more ambiguous. Colonizers were in fact never entirely loyal to their official 'civilizing' program. Firstly, a strong 'indigenist' movement existed amongst colonial policymakers, who feared that too brusque a 'liberation' of women would undermine the Congolese social order and who therefore continued to pursue a policy aimed at preserving 'traditional' family customs. In rural areas, the colonial state supported the application of customary law in family and conjugal disputes law. Despite the official interventionist rhetoric, polygamy was only banned in 1950. Secondly, some official 'civilizing principles' clashed throughout the entire colonial era with the daily practice of colonial exploitation. While in principle, women should not be coerced into forced labor or 'obligatory crops', for instance, colonial constraints linked to tax pressures, increased migrant labor, and production demands placed on export crops all meant that in practice women had to take on a workload made heavier by its invisibilization and by the lack of official acknowledgement. As with many other issues around gender and sexuality in colonial contexts, it is less a matter of 'taboo' than a matter of selective exposure.

Bibliography

Diverse actors of the colonial society were preoccupied by women and 'morality' issues, from explorer and army officer Charles Lemaire (*Africaines: contribution à l'histoire de la femme en Afrique*, Bulens, Brussels, 1897), to the first Congolese journalist Antoine Bolamba (*Les problèmes de l'évolution de la femme noire*, L'Essor du Congo, Élisabethville, 1949), or to the Haitian anthropologist Suzanne Comhaire-Sylvain (*Femmes de Kinshasa hier et aujourd'hui*, Mouton, Paris, 1968). During the past thirty years, several historians have been working on these topics. A bibliographic overview can be found in Lauro, Amandine, 'Women in the Democratic Republic of Congo', in *Oxford Encyclopedia of African History*, Oxford University Press, Oxford, 2020. Unmissable are the publications by Nancy R. Hunt, one of the trailblazers in this field of study, alongside those by Gertrude Mianda, Didier Gondola, Anne Cornet, Catherine Jacques and Valérie Piette, who have covered a variety of aspects. More recent publications include Bouwer, Karen, *Gender and Decolonization in the Congo: The Legacy of Patrice Lumumba*, Palgrave, London-New York, 2010; Heynssens, Sarah, *De kinderen van Save*, Polis, Kalmthout, 2017; and Lauro, Amandine, *Sexe, race et politiques coloniales. Encadrer le mariage et la sexualité au Congo Belge 1908-1945*, Éditions de l'Université Libre de Bruxelles, Brussels, 2024 (awaiting publication).

Notes

1 Vermeersch, Arthur, *La femme congolaise. Ménagère de blanc, femme de polygame, chrétienne*, Dewit, Brussels, 1914, p. 5.
2 Van den Perre, Louise, 'La protection de la femme indigène', *Troisième Congrès Colonial National,* Brussels, 1931, p. 193.

MICHAEL MEEUWIS

20. Linguistic Diversity

Whose Languages Were Used in the Colony?

In contrast with other European colonizing nations, Belgium needed to find solutions to not one but two problems in developing a linguistic policy for its overseas territories. The first was uniquely Belgian and was related to horizontal communication, i.e. which language to use in the different forms (spoken, written) and domains (education, administration, etc.) of official communication amongst white colonizers. After all, both Dutch- and French-speaking Belgians were involved in the colonial project. The second question, which other colonizing countries also had to answer, was what language to use in vertical communication, i.e. in the communication between colonizers and colonized. Here the issue was whether it was best to use French or a Congolese language.

This contribution reflects on the different choices that were made in these matters. How was the horizontal language question resolved, if at all? To what degree did it constitute a divisive issue for the Belgian community in the Congo? How did the Congolese respond to these quarrels amongst the Belgians? And regarding the vertical communication, how should we perceive the gradual introduction of more Congolese languages? Did this really reflect a respect for the existing, pre-colonial linguistic realities of the Congo, as is often assumed?

Horizontal Communication: Hegemony of French

When, in the second half of the 1870s, Leopold II launched his colonial project in Central Africa, Belgian official structures were operating solely in French. This meant that the occupation of the Congo also began with French, and not Dutch, as the official language among Westerners. This was more an organic corollary of the Belgian linguistic reality at the time than an explicitly formulated decision.

Gradually, Flemish-sensitive politicians and thinkers objected to this de facto dominance of French in the Congo Free State. In 1908, this led to the inclusion of a specific article on language rights for Belgians working in the Congo in the Colonial Charter, the organic law which organized the take-over by the Belgian state of the Congo. This article 3 stipulated that general decrees and statutes had to be drawn up in both French and Dutch, and that, no later than five years after the Colonial Charter, decrees had to have been issued that guaranteed the language rights of all Belgians in the colony.

By 1913, no such decree had yet been drafted. This led to repeated further protest from Flemish Movement sympathizers both in Belgium and in the Congo. This protest snowballed from the 1940s onwards, due to the increase of the number of Flemish people working in the Congo and more specifically the number that had been able to study in Dutch in Belgium. It was not until 1957 that the first – and only – language decree appeared, which gave Flemish defendants in courts in the colony the right to be heard in Dutch. Later attempts to create a similar language decree for administrative, rather than only judicial, procedures did not get finalized before the end of colonization.

Vertical Communication: Assimilationism, Differentialism, Metropolitanism

From the 1880s up until roughly the end of the First World War, the colonial regime planned the linguistic and cultural assimilation of the Congolese. The idea was that they should be absorbed ('assimilated') as quickly as possible into Belgian 'civilization' and language, read: the French language. To this effect, between 1887 and 1906 circulars and decrees stipulated that only French should be used in oral communication with Congolese soldiers, laborers, and children.

The majority of the white people who were working on the ground did not find this feasible. Many came from Flanders, or from countries where languages other than French were spoken, and therefore had insufficient command of French to implement the assimilation plans. For Catholic missionaries, assimilationism was also at odds with what the Propaganda Fide in Rome had been ordaining since the seventeenth century, namely that, globally, they should avoid cultural Westernization and use 'local' languages in their work as much as possible (which did not mean that, right up until the end of colonization, no missionaries in the Congo held assimilationist ideas). Moreover, from the beginning, some prominent Flemish missionaries supported the emancipatory Flemish struggle in Belgium. For some, this struggle meant more than a mere abhorrence of the French language; it was also rooted in the nineteenth-century romantic assumption that each language was divinely assigned to 'its people'. Missionaries thus considered it their duty to protect the 'essential specificity' of the Congolese 'tribes' and their languages against any type of outside influences (see Chapter 21).

Increasingly after 1908, the position won ground that the depopulation of large parts of the Congo, which was considered disquieting from an economic standpoint in particular, could be reversed by avoiding 'psycho-cultural deracination', in other words by countering attempts at assimilation. Instead, the policy should rely on the principles of 'differentialism', also called 'adaptationism' or 'indigenism', linked to the colonial system of indirect rule (see Chapter 18). Differentialism was based on the assumption that the intellectual capacity of Africans was fundamentally too different ('inferior') to allow them to assimilate Western culture and language. Colonization therefore had to be adapted to the Congolese's 'own language and culture'. The colonizer's duty was to screen off this linguistic and cultural 'authenticity', albeit after this 'authenticity' had been carefully defined and selected by the white rulers.

Louis Franck, Minister of Colonies between 1918 and 1924, collated the emerging differentialist viewpoints in a new explicit 'indigenous policy'. Franck himself had become a differentialist because of his Flemish-sensitive background in Belgium, his personal friendships with South African apartheid thinkers, and an admiration for the American system of racial segregation. During his term in office, colonial congresses were held in Brussels and Paris, at which the differentialist theories were further developed and explicated.

In 1922, Franck set up a commission to streamline the educational methods which up to that point had evolved in nonuniform ways according to the preferences of each local mission (see Chapter 23). The commission drew up agreements, the so-called De Jonghe conventions, between the Belgian Government and the – primarily missionary – schools for Congolese children subsidized by the state. The draft for the first program agreement was initiated in 1924, the last adjustments were made in 1956. From the first 1924 draft, in the spirit of differentialism, it was stipulated that French was only allowed as a subject in the last years of primary education and as medium of education in the (extremely rare) secondary schools, but that the medium of education in primary schools should be a Congolese language.

A discussion quickly emerged as to which Congolese language should be chosen for this. Presently, more than 230 are accounted for academically, a number highly underestimated in those days. At any rate, Franck and his allies thought that there were too many Congolese languages to be practicable, amongst other reasons for the production of schoolbooks. They proposed that a limited number of 'vehicular languages' (also called *linguae francae*, 'intertribal' or 'interethnic' languages) should be used, even if these had to be actively imposed on Congolese who did not speak them. Some even suggested that the vehicular languages should be limited to a single one for the entire colony; either Lingala (as Franck himself contemplated for a while), or another language. The prevailing belief, however, was that four vehicular languages that had spread in the years of the Congo Free State (see below) should be used, according to the region: Swahili in the east, Kikongo in the southwest, Lingala in the west and north, and Tshiluba in the central part. A (vocal) minority, the so-called radical indigenists, were altogether opposed to the use of any vehicular language, in any context. They regarded imposing them on the Congolese as unacceptable in principle, and advocated instead the use of the smaller, locally restricted native languages (also called 'tribal', 'ethnic' or 'vernacular' languages), as they considered these to be culturally more 'authentic'. They did argue, however, that the number of these smaller languages had to be actively reduced by the whites. This was to be done by steering them towards bigger language units using interventionist methods of linguistic unification and standardization and making these unified and standard language forms mandatory. The Commission for African Linguistics, set up in 1950 in order to advise the Minister of Colonies on linguistic issues, opted for the radical-indigenist position. The advice of the Commission was rarely acted upon, as its work was usually considered too academic to be able to be converted into a workable language policy.

Following the heydays of differentialism, the educational convention of 1948 again created more space for French as a teaching language in primary schools. This was because the expanding administrative apparatus required ever more Congolese clerks with a command of French. In theory, the opportunities for the Congolese elite to receive school education in French became greater when, in 1950, they were allowed access to schools for Belgian children, where French was the medium of instruction. The liberal Minister of Colonies Auguste Buisseret (1954-1958) also arranged for more state schools to be introduced, in which the metropolitan (Belgian) educational programs and French as the teaching language had to be implemented. But all this only had a very limited effect. In 1957, the Congolese made up a mere 4.05 per cent of the total number of children in primary schools with a metropolitan regime and secondary schools combined.[1] The Belgian colonizer indeed always adhered to the logic *le danger n'est jamais d'enseigner trop peu, c'est d'enseigner trop* ('the danger is never to teach too little, it is to teach too much'), as the colonial educational specialist Albert Maus noted.[2]

French, just like other 'higher' socio-economic competencies, was to be taught only to the number of Congolese 'required' to keep the colonial administration up and running (see Chapter 23).

New Languages, New Language Forms, New Linguistic Boundaries

The differentialist option to focus on Swahili, Lingala, Kikongo, and Tshiluba, which are still the four 'national' languages of the DR Congo today, did not plug into an old, pre-colonial reality, but rather into fairly new sociolinguistic realities that had evolved during the Congo Free State. Indeed, during those early years, civil servants, members of the military and more missionaries than is generally believed were already convinced that it was impossible to conduct all vertical communication in the large number of Congolese local languages. Therefore, many instead preferred to work with one of the four languages, a preference which in fact strongly influenced their geographical diffusion and, in some cases, even their coming into being.

In pre-colonial times, Swahili was only used in a tiny trading area between the Lualaba River and Lake Tanganyika, namely as a second language in contacts between local inhabitants and travelling salesmen from the coasts of East Africa. Only in the second half of the 1870s did it start its spread across the east and northeast of the Congo, after some decades under the language name Kingwana. Colonization and Catholic mission efforts, primarily those of the White Fathers, were essential in this. During the first decades of the twentieth century, the Belgians also disseminated it as a language for vertical communication in the southeastern mining region of Katanga.

The late 1870s likewise witnessed the emergence, in the southwest of the Congo, of Kikongo ya Leta out of existing varieties of Kikongo. This happened in the context of the highly disruptive European caravan routes between the Atlantic coast and Pool Malebo (the former Stanley Pool). Kikongo ya Leta means 'the language of the state', which is telling about the degree to which the Congolese recognized that it differed in form and function from their own Kikongo varieties. Another meaningful name was Kibula-Matari, 'the language of the state people'.[3] It was and is also known as Fiote, Ikeleve, Munukutuba and Kituba.

In the west and northwest of the colony, in the centers of Léopoldville (established in 1881) and Nouvelle-Anvers (1884) among others, the first European occupiers and Catholic missionaries chose the pre-colonial trade language Bobangi, in preference to local native languages, as medium for vertical communication. In their eyes, these centers were burdened by an unmanageable linguistic diversity, as they housed Congolese from many different regions and languages, who either had been brought there by force or had come to live there of their own volition. From this early colonial use of Bobangi as a lingua franca, Bangala came into being, which was renamed Lingala after 1901 (see Chapter 17). What is more, from 1884 onwards Nouvelle-Anvers played an important role in the emergence and growth of the colonial army, the *Force Publique* (which officially saw the light in Boma in 1886). This led to Bangala and later Lingala becoming the army's official language. In the 1890s, military campaigns were organized from Nouvelle-Anvers to the Northeastern Congo in order to vanquish Islamic trade competition from East Africa and the Sudan. In the wake of the *Force Publique* campaigns, the troops disseminated Bangala/Lingala to these northeastern regions, where, around 1900, the language had firmly established itself.

In Central Congo, also during the time of the Congo Free State, a simplified Tshiluba *de traite* sprang up from extant Tshiluba varieties. This Tshiluba *de traite* was also called Kibula, Chituba or Kituba, which led to a confusion over names with the other Kituba.

In addition to the vehicular languages, colonization and missionary activities also affected the landscape of the local native ('ethnic', 'tribal') languages. The missionaries who were opposed (or over time became opposed) to the vehicular languages and preferred working with these smaller languages, did not simply 'describe' these languages. They took decisions, often on purely pragmatic grounds, about where one language started and another began, and thus unwittingly played an irreversible role in the delineation and re-categorization of languages and their speakers. They also made choices, depending on the location where they happened to be working, about which variety of a language should be used for Bible translations, schoolbooks and written standardization, and what name it should be given. This led to lasting perceptions of 'the superior standard form' (that of the missionaries) of a Congolese language versus its 'inferior dialects'. For these choices, the missionary-linguists seldom followed original African relationships, which in any case were fluid and context-dependent. They instead started out from an imagination of Africa as composed of timeless, territorially confined, monolingual 'tribes' or 'ethnicities', an assumption that only very rarely matched pre-colonial flexible realities. This laid the foundation for a Western knowledge about African languages and their speakers which was fed, and at the same time shaped by a colonial gaze. This knowledge was used by the colonial administration to categorize the Congolese into stable and controllable ethno-linguistic units. The insight that the colonial human and social sciences 'created the study object rather than discovered it', and the recognition that in essence there was 'not one single scientific enterprise about colonial issues which escaped being of benefit to the colonial rule', is of great significance here.[4]

The normative, prescriptive grammars and dictionaries that the missionary linguists published 'for', rather than merely 'about', both the vehicular and the local languages, led to all kinds of well-defined perceptions amongst Congolese. The language forms that the missionaries proposed were identified by Congolese as Mission language, Bible language or Lofafa (literally: 'Missionarese'). With these labels they indicated the distance between how missionaries spoke and wrote their languages, and how they themselves spoke them. Following a tour through the Congo to chart the existing Bible translations, the international Bible specialist Eugene Nida concluded: 'It is not infrequent to find natives who say... "Oh that is the way it is in the Bible, but no one says it that way."'[5]

Congolese Voices

The above-mentioned Congolese reflections about white missionary language forms were not the only ones. The Congolese took a stand regarding all aspects of colonial language policy and practice. They were, for instance, very explicit about the Flemish demands for a bilingual administration, mentioned above. The so-called *évolués*, the colonial category of a Congolese elite (see Chapter 18), were vehemently opposed. They had learned very little Dutch, if at all. The language had only been included in the educational program since 1948, and only from the fourth year of secondary school, to which only a small minority of Congolese pupils could progress. What is more, the program was not applied to the letter everywhere. A demand for Belgian bilingualism for Congolese civil servants would mean a brake on their socio-economic emancipation. During a meeting of the Government Council in 1957, Gaston Diomi, Lumumba's later political associate, concluded the following: *Imposer la connaissance du flamand, alors que ce n'est pas l'intérêt des Congolais serait pur colonialisme* ('It would be pure colonialism to impose knowledge of Flemish, as it is not in the interest of the Congolese').[6]

There were also strong views about how the exposure to French in school education had been limited since the policy of differentialism. From 1945 onwards, Congolese intellectuals called for a reduction in the role of Congolese languages as medium of instruction and for using French instead from the first year of primary education. They voiced these opinions using various channels, including their journal *La Voix du Congolais*. As early as 1945, Léon Ilunga complained that *l'instruction que nous recevons en général fait de nous de simples auxiliaires* ('the instruction we receive in general reduces us to mere helpers'), and therefore asked *que la langue française soit généralisée* ('that the French language be generalized').[7] They argued that the colonizers, with their choice of Congolese languages, purposively held them in isolation and in a subordinated socio-economic position.

Conclusion

The question as to whose language was to be used in the Belgian colonial context had many layers, and the range of answers formulated to it had various consequences. Firstly, the question as to which language was to be used for horizontal communication – Dutch or French – not only divided the colonizing minority, but the debate also led to the socio-economic exclusion of the Congolese. Secondly, it is too easy to posit that one of these two Belgian languages, French, was symbolically and categorically rejected by the Congolese. Towards the end of colonization, some claimed and appropriated the language, in particular in their demands for participation in decision-making, emancipation and prosperity. French thus became one of the many languages that make up the Congo's linguistic landscape today, although it certainly does not bring about social equality. Thirdly, the choice of which Congolese languages to use in the colonial vertical communication amounted more to an attempt to control a linguistic diversity considered unmanageable than to an unconditional respect for pre-existing African realities. Language standardization, grounded in white authority over black languages, linguistic steering, targeted selection, and enforced dissemination via education and mission activities, all fundamentally altered the linguistic landscape of the Congo. Language boundaries were presented as converging with ethnic-cultural-territorial ones in order to keep the Congolese human diversity in check. Four selected, heavily modified and in some cases even newly devised Congolese vehicular languages were actively disseminated. Via all such avenues, language and colonialism were interwoven in much more complex ways than appears at first sight.

Bibliography

The debates and studies about the position of Dutch in the Belgian Congo have been summarized, and supplemented with transregional analyses, in Meeuwis, Michael, 'Taalstrijd in Afrika: het taalwetsartikel in het Koloniaal Charter van 1908 en de strijd van de Vlamingen en Afrikaners voor het Nederlands in Afrika tot 1960', *Wetenschappelijke Tijdingen*, 75, 2016, p. 27-61. Bert Govaerts conducted a series of fascinating detailed studies, such as Govaerts, Bert, 'De Universiteit van Elisabethstad (1956-1960). Arena van het laatste Vlaamse gevecht in Belgisch-Congo', *Wetenschappelijke Tijdingen*, 69, 2008, p. 107-146. A book that broadens the subject of Flemish linguistic and cultural rights in the colony into a discussion about intercultural paternalism in postcolonial Flanders is Ceuppens, Bambi, *Congo Made in Flanders?*, Academia Press, Ghent, 2003. For information about vertical colonial language policies and language and missionizing in the Belgian Congo, good sources are: Fabian, Johannes, 'Missions and the Colonization of African Languages: Developments in the Former Belgian Congo', *Canadian Journal of African Studies*, 17, 1983, p. 165-187; Errington, Joseph, *Linguistics in a Colonial World*, Blackwell, London, 2008; Meeuwis, Michael, 'The Origins of Belgian Colonial Language Policies in the Congo', *Language Matters*, 42, 2011, p. 190-206. For overviews of the evolution in the use of Congolese languages in colonial school education, the best sources to consult are: Vanhove, Julien, 'L'œuvre de l'Éducation au Congo Belge et au Ruanda-Urundi', in *Encyclopédie du Congo Belge*, part 3, Brussels, 1953, p. 749-789; Lupukisa, Wasamba, 'Problématique du bilinguisme et du plurilinguisme au Zaïre', *Langues africaines*, 5, 1979, p. 33-44; Nsuka, Yvon, 'Les langues africaines et l'école. L'expérience de la République Démocratique du Congo', in Ndaywel è Nziem, Isidore, *Les langues africaines et créoles face à leur avenir*, L'Harmattan, Paris, 2003, p. 35-43. Historical interpretations of the dissemination of the four vehicular languages can be found in Meeuwis, Michael, 'The Lingála-Kiswahili Border in North-eastern Congo: Its Origins in Belgian Colonial State Formation of the Late Nineteenth and Early Twentieth Centuries', *Africana Linguistica*, 12, 2006, p. 113-135; Fabian, Johannes, *Language and Colonial Power: The Appropriation of Swahili in the Former Belgian Congo*, Cambridge University Press, Cambridge, 1986; Mufwene, Salikoko, 'La créolisation en bantou. Les cas du kituba, du lingala urbain, et du swahili du Shaba', *Études créoles*, 12, 1989, p. 74-106. Congolese individuals articulated their views on language and the colonial language policies in their journal *La Voix du Congolais. Par les Congolais, pour les Congolais*

(1945-1959), amongst others, which was controlled by the *Bureau de l'Information Indigène*, but was afforded a great deal of freedom of expression over linguistic issues. Discussions of these views can be found in Meeuwis, Michael, 'Afrikaanse perspectieven op koloniale taalpolitiek in Belgisch Congo tijdens de jaren 1950', *Mededelingen der Zittingen van de Koninklijke Academie voor Overzeese Wetenschappen*, 55, 2009, p. 111-121; Meeuwis, Michael, 'Bilingual Inequality: Linguistic Rights and Disenfranchisement in Late Belgian Colonization', *Journal of Pragmatics*, 43, 2011, p. 1279-1287.

Notes

1 Depaepe, Marc, and Hulstaert, Karen, 'Creating Cultural Hybridity by Exporting Metropolitan Structures and Cultures of Schooling and Educationalization?', *European Educational Research Journal*, 12, 2013, p. 201-214 (p. 206).
2 Maus, Albert, 'Le nouveau programme de l'enseignement libre', *Congo*, 19, 1938, p. 490-525 (p. 500).
3 *Bula-Matari*, literally 'the breaker of rocks', was initially the epithet Henry M. Stanley had been given by the Congolese. It became a designation for the whites and the colonial state in general.
4 Poncelet, Marc, et al., 'Les sciences d'outre-mer', in Halleux, Robert, et al., eds., *Histoire des sciences en Belgique, 1815-2000*, Brussels, 2001, vol. 2, p. 235-265 (p. 235-236).
5 Nida, Eugene A., 'Some Language Problems in the Congo', *Congo Mission News*, 145, 1949, p. 14-16 (p. 15).
6 Report of the Governors' Council meeting of 21 December 1957.
7 Ilunga, Léon Georges, 'L'enseignement dans le Congo de demain', *La Voix du Congolais*, 1, 1945, p. 175-176 (p. 175).

PART IV

The 'Civilizing Mission'

AMANDINE LAURO, IDESBALD GODDEERIS
AND GUY VANTHEMSCHE

Introduction

The 'civilizing mission' was a core feature of colonial argumentation. It was wielded by all nineteenth- and twentieth-century colonial empires, both in the rhetoric used to legitimize colonization and in concrete policy measures that were intended to transform the colony's territory and society. The notion is based on the belief that European civilization was superior to that of colonized societies. Western countries would therefore have had the responsibility to elevate so-called 'inferior' societies to a higher level of civilization, if necessary by coercion. This responsibility was the 'white man's burden', as British writer Rudyard Kipling formulated it at the end of the nineteenth century: confronted with 'primitive' peoples not able to 'develop' themselves, Europeans had the 'duty' to do this for them. In practice, the humanitarian overtones of the 'civilizing mission' were often a cover for self-interested ambitions and stood in sharp contrast to the violent exploitation that accompanied colonial expansion.

To confine ourselves to this observation, however, is to fail to consider the links between 'civilizing' projects and the economic and political motivations behind colonial expansion. The situation in the colonial Congo shows clearly that these dimensions were interwoven and did not necessarily contradict each other: (forced) labor could be justified as a 'civilizing' strategy (as a first step to encourage the development of a 'modernized' wage-labor force), while educational policy was aimed at creating compliant workers rather than educated citizens.

Which forms did this 'civilizing mission' take on in the Belgian Congo? How important was this ambitious statement of intent in the official rhetoric about colonization's 'benefactions'? Beyond *grand* declarations, in which concrete projects did it find shape, and with what results? The first chapter (21) of this fourth part explores the perhaps most obvious actors in this 'civilizing mission', the missionaries. They played a (purportedly disinterested) key role in health care and education, the themes of the two following contributions (Chapters 22 and 23). Just as in many other fields, research shows that here too the reality was quite different from what the ambitions of the self-proclaimed 'model colonizer' suggested. It highly contrasted with the polished, but partial image that was spread by colonial propaganda, a well-oiled machine that is the subject of Chapter 24.

Over the course of the twentieth century, both the civilizing discourse and the concrete projects resulting from the 'civilizing mission' went through a far-reaching evolution. After the Second World War, there was less and less talk of the *mise en valeur* (an expression referring both to exploitation and 'improvement') of the colony, and increasingly of 'welfare' and 'development' instead. But did this changing vocabulary cover what was in fact happening? These new attempts at legitimization played a key-role in the expansion of 'colonial sciences' (Chapter 25). This expertise was deployed in various fields (culture, technology, even ecology), but at whose service (and to whose benefit) did this happen exactly? Chapters 26 and 27 show how, in environmental conservation as well as in cultural policy, the colonial authorities succeeded in gaming this new lexicon for their own interest and in setting themselves up as 'protectors' of African art and fauna.

IDESBALD GODDEERIS

21. Missionaries

A Human Dimension to Colonization?

To this day, famous Belgian missionaries such as Father Damien and Sister Jeanne Devos continue to inspire because they were close to ordinary people and gave their lives for their ideals. Does this also apply to the missionaries in the Congo? Or should we see them as a cog in the colonial system? And how can we evaluate their activities? Were they very successful? Were they appreciated? The answer to those questions is not unequivocal and depends on individuals, institutes, approaches and eras.

A Polemic Initial Period

Mission has been part of Christendom from its earliest days, and was closely bound up with the voyages of discovery and colonialism in the early modern era. Missionary work faded during the Enlightenment, but boomed again during the nineteenth century thanks to romanticism, religious revival, new Western expansionism and the drive to civilize. Belgian missionaries set out for the United States (Pieter-Jan De Smet), British India (where, in 1864, Belgian Jesuits were assigned the whole of Bengal) and China (the initial destination of the first Belgian mission congregation, the Scheut Missionaries, established in 1862). From the end of the eighteenth century, Protestants likewise focused on missionizing overseas areas and founded an array of new institutes (the Baptist Missionary Society in 1792, for example). David Livingstone traveled to South Africa in 1840 as an Anglican missionary.

From the late 1870s, Protestant missionaries also settled in the Congo. These were primarily British, American and Swedish, and they were supported by Leopold II in their endeavors. The Belgian King feared that French congregations would extend French influence in the region. In 1865, Spiritans, or Holy Ghost Fathers, had made their way to Bas-Congo, and, from 1878 onwards, the Missionaries of Africa (commonly known as the White Fathers, founded by the (French) Archbishop of Algiers in 1868), began to explore the area between Lake Tanganyika and the upper reaches of the Congo River. Leopold tried to cut them off at the pass, not only by involving Protestants, but also winning over Belgian Catholic missionaries for his colonial projects. He only managed to do so after years of lobbying, right up to the Vatican, which in 1888 established an apostolic vicariate, or missionary diocese, in the Congo. The first Scheut Fathers arrived in the Congo at the end of that year, the Jesuits in 1893, the Trappists in 1895. They were given all kinds of privileges by the state, such as free transport, land concessions, workers, military protection and children liberated from slavery whom they were allowed to raise as Catholics. When, from the mid-1890s onwards, Protestants expressed increasingly negative views about the administration of the Congo Free State (and in so doing joined in with international criticism; see Chapter 2), the Catholic missionaries benefitted even more. Up until after the Second World War, many Belgians considered Protestants fifth columnists who wanted to undermine Belgian rule.

These first missionary groups were modest in numbers, because many individuals died after a few months or years. In 1908, there were seven male and six female Catholic congregations with 233 priests and 102 sisters, spread out over 56 mission stations.[1] During the nineteenth century, hundreds of new female congregations had been founded, partly inspired by the role Protestants gave to women, but also by new social needs such as the expansion of education and health care. Several of these 'new' congregations – including the Sisters of Charity of Jesus and Mary (Ghent/Lovendegem, 1803), the Sisters of Notre Dame de Namur (1804/1809) and the White Sisters (1869) – sent missionaries to the Congo from the 1890s onwards. They were often less visible because they were more dispersed, but also because they were overshadowed by their male counterparts. After the First World War, practically all congregations – in addition to priests and nuns also brothers, who were mostly engaged in teaching – were active in the Congo.

The mission congregations developed diverse strategies for converting Congolese people to Christianity. Led by Victor Roelens, the White Fathers created a theocratic state in the Eastern Congo. They developed a state currency, legislation and militia, and tried to convert local leaders who, just like Roman Emperor Constantine and the Frankish King Clovis, would go on to convert their own subjects to Christianity. In Kasaï, between 1902 and 1909, Scheut Father Emeri Cambier procured more than 12,000 terminal sleeping sickness patients for an average price of between three and five francs (around twenty to thirty euros) and baptized them as they lay dying.[2] His confrères in Bas-Congo and Équateur Province and the Jesuits in Bas-Congo focused primarily on children, and instructed them to become catechists, teachers of religion, and/or fathers of

Christian families. At first, missionaries founded school colonies together with the state but from the turn of the century onwards they created their own structures: the Scheut Fathers built school chapels and Christian villages, the Jesuits so-called 'chapel farms'. These were auxiliary missionary stations on the edge of villages, where Congolese children received primary education, provided for themselves with farming and stockbreeding, and often carried on living there after they completed their education. There were several hundred chapel farms in total, and by analogy with abbeys in medieval Europe and *reducciones* ('settlements') in colonial South America, the Jesuits hoped that these would expand into Christian model villages.

These systems came under fire in the Belgian media, were condemned by the commission of inquiry that had been sent to the Congo to investigate the acts of violence (1904-1905; see Chapter 2), and led to frequent parliamentary debates. The accusations were harsh. The socialist party journal *Le Peuple* spoke of child theft, because not all children were redeemed slaves or rescued orphans, but often simply taken during government raids or punitive expeditions. They were not allowed to leave school colonies or chapel farms, had to provide labor for free, received very little education (which was mostly religious), and were subject to a strict disciplinary regime, with corporal punishments that were often harsher than was legally allowed. Moreover, there was doubt about who owned the land and about consent from the surrounding villages. Under penalty of custody these were compelled to provide *chikwangue* (a type of fermented bread made from cassava) and forced labor. Jules Marchal, who, under the pseudonym of A.M. Delathuy, between 1988 and 1994 published three books about the missions in the early colonial Congo based on government archive material, even talks of concentration camps, hecatombs and a Holocaust (a questionable term, see Chapter 3). He calculated that in the school colony of Kimwenza (close to present-day Kinshasa) 1,200 children died between 1893 and 1899, and that 5,000 children lost their lives in Scheut school colonies (1,000 out of the 1,500 children in New Antwerp, for instance), often as a result of sleeping sickness (see Chapter 22).[3] He furthermore blames several congregations for not having offered any resistance to the excesses of Leopold II's regime. However, because of his limited source material and not very analytical methodology, his books should be approached with the necessary caution.

The missionaries and various Catholic politicians and opinion-makers dismissed the accusations as defamation by Protestants and Freemasons and set up campaigns to refute them. Such polarization between Catholics and anticlericals was not unusual at the time, and it is difficult to distinguish truth from lies in the detailed discussions. At any rate, between 2002 and 2010, theologian Wim François and historian Anne-Sophie Gijs proved on the basis of letters and reports in Jesuit archives that not all charges held water and that the 1904-1905 commission of inquiry accepted some of the accusations without verifying them. What is more, some missionaries condemned the rubber terror. Most did so only behind the scenes, out of pragmatism and patriotism, but in 1906 Jesuit Arthur Vermeersch published a critical book about Leopold's system which partly convinced the Catholics to accept the Belgian takeover of the Congo Free State two years later. Yet the missions cannot be entirely exonerated on account of this. Some Jesuits themselves (J. Van Heede, for example) admitted that the commission of inquiry's criticism of the missionaries was not altogether undeserved. Others continued to make a stand for Leopold II (for instance, Auguste Castelein in 1907). Also of some significance is the fact that François and Gijs took their research only up to 1908, while during the first years of the Belgian Congo intense smear campaigns were still being conducted in the newspapers and in Parliament, marshalled in particular by socialist leader Émile Vandervelde. It is not clear to which degree these were based on rumors.

Catholic Monopoly

It was not only the First World War that led to these storms abating. The Church itself recognized that it would be better to apply different strategies, not least because the first decades had yielded at best some twenty thousand converts.[4] Moreover, Protestant missionaries and their less aggressive approaches threatened to gain support amongst the Congolese people. The Jesuits transformed their chapel farms into regular mission stations. As was the case in all the other societies, these grew into large complexes with, alongside a church and living quarters, schools, clinics, dispensaries, a *procure* ('logistical center') and a farm.

The missionaries increasingly turned their focus to adults, with the idea that they might act as an edifying example to their children. Initially, they found an especially willing ear amongst outsiders who had lost their ties with their families and society and as a result made the drastic choice to convert: ex-slaves, migrant workers, victims of the social and political disintegration colonialism was causing, but also young men who felt trapped in the rigid social structures of their community, and young women who had fled polygamy, domestic violence, exploitation or witch hunters, for instance. Gradually, the Congolese settled on Christianity for other reasons as well, such as education and access to knowledge (see Chapter 23), (limited) social promotion and material benefits, and medical care (see Chapter 22). Also important is the role of African go-betweens such as translators, intermediaries, catechists (amongst Catholics) and evangelists (amongst Protestants). This local workforce settled in the villages and was visited by a missionary (the 'travelling father') only a few times a year.

The renowned historical anthropologist Jan Vansina stresses that Christianity was much less alien to many Congolese people than might be expected. Some had heard of it, because, since the end of the fifteenth century, the Portuguese had been active in Bas-Congo (where King Nzinga Nkuwu had himself baptized in 1491), and European missionaries had only left the region as late as in the 1830s. Others drew parallels with their own faith. They saw God as the highest nature spirit (and gave him their own names), Bible stories as his revelation (as in dreams) and Communion as a collective rite for renouncing sorcery. Some elements were new but could be accommodated. Many Congolese believed in reincarnation, for instance, but were open to the idea of a hereafter, especially in a climate in which death was so omnipresent. Other aspects were more problematic. For instance, personal salvation was at odds with the anti-individualist world view. All in all, numerous Congolese interpreted Christianity in their own way, for example sticking prayers and Bible texts in amulets for invocations. The first generation of missionaries turned a blind eye to this, but their successors were much more orthodox and banned sacrifices and other practices. In response, a number of Congolese set up their own prophetic movements, in which they incorporated selected Christian ideas and translated these into an African setting. The best-known examples are Kimbanguism, Mpadism and the Kitawala ('watchtower'; see Chapter 16). Not only the missions, but also the Belgian Congolese authorities denounced this syncretic messianism and utopian protest as sectarian heresy, and accused the Protestants of being at the root of it.

The Catholic missionaries were indeed given the government's full support. As early as 1906, the Congo Free State concluded a convention with the Vatican and committed itself to donating land to missions in exchange for scientific research and education in the national Belgian languages (in practice only French, which meant that non-Belgian Protestants were put at a disadvantage; see Chapters 20, 23 and 25). During the 1920s, the cooperation between Church and state was sealed with several accords, which would hold out for some thirty years and usher in a golden age for Catholic missions. The state handed over the organization of education almost entirely to the national – i.e. Belgian – missions. These received funding, which in 1929 was forty times higher than in 1924.[5] The colony held on less to the separation of state and Church than the 'motherland', and non-Catholic Ministers of Colonies recognized the role of missionaries. Mission schools were cheaper than state schools because the input from missionaries was almost free; moreover, they endorsed the national interest. Up until after the Second World War, Protestants did not receive any funding, were not allowed to issue diplomas and were thus permanently weakened. Many companies also delegated education and other services to Catholic missionaries.

This did not mean that the relationship between missions and authorities was always perfect. The missionaries remained suspicious, in particular after the liberal Governor-General Maurice Lippens, in the early 1920s, tried to undermine their position by placing all Christian villages and schools that were dependent on missions under African chiefs (eventually, he was called back and dismissed). His contemporary fellow party member, Minister of Colonies Louis Franck, created a less extensive system of indirect rule, but this likewise could count on little support from the missions, because 'tribe-alien' Christian villages did not want to become subordinate to 'traditional heads' (see Chapter 18). British historian Reuben Loffman labels the relation between Church and state as 'competitive co-dependency'. Both needed each other: the Church for protection and financial support, the state for moral legitimization and concrete expertise. But both also tended to have opposing viewpoints. During the interwar years in particular the Church proved to be the strongest: missionaries applied their own rules (banning ritual dancing, for example) and influenced the local government's policies and decisions (for instance the creation of *chefferies* and the punishment of witch hunters).

This is not surprising, because in 1935 there were scarcely 600 administrators in the Belgian Congo and at least 2,300 missionaries, so almost four times as many.[6] Around half of these were nuns. They were given specific tasks, such as teaching domestic skills, giving pre-marital instruction to couples, maternity care and nutritional guidance, and did so in separate institutions like *foyers sociaux* ('social homes'), dispensaries and maternity clinics. Sisters were also important in the propagation of new role patterns and standards, such as caring, domesticity and chastity. They worked at the invitation of and under the authority of priests, who acted as their spiritual leaders and confessors, and who were the only ecclesiastics allowed to preach the Gospel. Only gradually were some mother superiors, such as Annonciade Anselma Ulens, able to wrest more autonomy and steer their own course.

The missionaries not only actively spread a new religion, but also indirectly transformed Congolese society. With their interest in local languages and oral traditions and their typical colonial fascination with classification they created new languages and identities (see Chapters 17 and 20) and contributed to the fragmentation of the country, more than to its national integration. The ethnic fault lines even conformed to the congregations, which tended to compete amongst themselves about methods and all kinds of other issues (and therefore partly subdivided the colony into dozens of parishes and prefectures, each of which were assigned to a particular congregation). Several Missionaries of the Sacred Heart (in particular Edmond Boelaert and Gustaaf Hulstaert) championed the Mongo. Jesuits such as Jozef Van Wing supported the Bakongo, even though their French speaking confrères in the Kwango region used another, more simplified form of Kikongo. Scheut Fathers in Léopoldville identified with Lingala, but in so doing frustrated ethnic groups they had promoted in other provinces, such as the Yombe (Leo Bittremieux) and the Luba (Auguste De Clercq). An explanation for this focus on ethnic identities can often be found in many of the missionaries' Flemish nationalist background. Some 85 per cent of the Belgian missionaries in the Congo came from Flanders.[7] Many of them made connections between experiences in the Congo and back home. They saw language as an important vehicle for an 'authentic' cultural awareness and did not want to disrupt this by the dissemination of French. An equally important motive was that knowledge of French would help the Congolese in their social advancement, and many missionaries – who idealized village life – wanted to protect them from industrialization and modernization. Some even explicitly resisted the capitalist holdings which lured away manpower and disrupted rural society.

Alongside these so-called indigenist or adaptationist missionaries, there were many assimilationists, who strived for a transition from Congolese cultures into Western 'civilization'. Jean-Félix de Hemptinne, the Benedictine Bishop of Katanga, even believed that Congolese paganism had to be destroyed in order to make way for Christendom (and during the Second World War was suspected of sympathizing with King Leopold III and his German-friendly stance, partly because he opposed the Belgian Government in London). De Hemptinne was also close to companies such as the UMHK which made him a standard-bearer for modernity. This could also be said of another well-known missionary, Scheut Father

'Tata' Raphaël de la Kethulle de Ryhove, who advanced vocational and secondary education (and sporting activities) in Léopoldville and thus became a key figure in the development of the new capital.

Just as during the initial period, missionaries differed widely in their vision and approach. The first generation often had strong racist beliefs. Victor Roelens wrote instructions for White Fathers in 1938 in which he called black people underdeveloped, unstable, selfish, proud and lazy. Barely ten years later, Franciscan Placide Tempels, in his much-read study *Bantu Philosophy* (1945-1946) argued the opposite, namely that black people were not primitive races but had developed their own wisdoms and world view. Black intellectuals later accused him of white supremacy, because it was yet again a European who had helped Africans formulate their thoughts. During the 1950s however, Tempels laid the foundation for a community, the *Jamaa* ('family'), in which he barred inequality and hierarchy, and in 1962 he distanced himself from his own bestseller.

Tempels's ideas did not go down well with some of his priors. He returned to Belgium in 1946 and only re-settled in the Congo when a new apostolic delegate – the Vatican representative – had taken office in 1950. Yet it would be wrong to depict the Church leadership merely as a conservative factor in mission history. Popes Benedict XV (in the apostolic letter *Maximum illud*, 1919) and Pius XI (in the encyclical *Rerum Ecclesiae*, 1926) argued for the implant of a local and sustainable Church and the creation of a local clergy, thus inspiring a progressive missiology in Leuven led by the Jesuit Pierre Charles. The first seminary in the Belgian Congo was set up as early as 1905. In 1917 Stefano Kaoze was the first Congolese novice to be ordained after some four centuries (five years after the first Congolese Protestant minister, Thomas Paku of the Christian Mission Alliance).

The Laborious Decolonization

In 1960, there were more than six hundred Congolese priests.[8] Yet this does not mean, as is often argued, that the Church was better prepared for independence than the colonial government because it had made an early start with training an indigenous clergy. Although religious education and training priests was high on the agenda, the Africanization of the Church in the Belgian Congo should not be overrated. Quite a number of congregations were reluctant to open themselves up to Congolese seminarians or were discouraged by their superiors in Europe, and initially worked with separate institutes. The Jesuits, for instance, created the Saint Joseph Brothers of Kisantu and only set up a noviciate for African priests in 1948. Compared to several other Central African countries, the proportion of Africans among the total number of priests was low: 14 per cent in 1961, against 24 per cent in Gabon (ex-French), 35 per cent in Uganda (ex-British) and 32 per cent in Ruanda-Urundi.[9] The first Congolese auxiliary bishop was not ordained until 1957 (Pierre Kimbondo), the first Congolese actual bishop until July 1959 (Joseph Nkongolo), and it would take until 1988 for the full episcopate to become African. Furthermore, during the 1950s, quite a few missionaries behaved in a somewhat paternalistic and authoritarian manner towards their black confrères, and the rules applied to black priests were different from those for their white counterparts.

At the same time, the climate changed after the Second World War, and some missionaries took an active part in this. The Jesuits Joseph Guffens and Jozef Van Wing supported the request from educated black people for an expansion of secondary and higher education. Several congregations created alumni societies and evening-course groups, which played an important role because political parties were banned. Missionaries were also involved in a whole array of Catholic-specific organizations, such as youth clubs and unions, in part to steal a march on the growing competition from the left. Yet the shift was far from smooth. Many missionaries had difficulty adjusting to the new zeitgeist. They explicitly resisted all these new initiatives and even created their own unions. It was no surprise, therefore, that the Young Christian Workers (JOC/KAJ), with its more urban and democratic slant, was critical towards the old missionary methods. The youth organization's activities in the Belgian Congo had been given a big boost by Monseigneur Jozef Cardijn's visit to the colony in 1953.

Likewise, as a result of measures introduced by some Belgian government coalitions without the Christian democrats, the missions saw their privileged position crumble. In 1946-1947, state schools for white children were established, and in 1954-1958, this network of official or neutral schools was expanded to include black children, while subsidies for mission schools were reduced to 45 per cent of the resources (though this did in fact increase; see Chapter 23). Quite a few missionaries figured out that they would be better off making overtures to the Congolese rather than to the government. White Father Guy Mosmans managed to persuade the bishops to distance themselves from the colonial policy in an official statement in June 1956, and to grant approval for the political emancipation of the Congolese. A few days later the Scheut affiliated weekly *Conscience Africaine* issued the first Congolese political manifesto (see Chapter 5). In line with what Jef Van Bilsen had proposed half a year earlier, it demanded emancipation within thirty years, and was therefore soon superseded. Nonetheless, it broke fundamentally with the past.

Not all Church authorities shared this vision. Pope Pius XII agreed with decolonization but did not want it to happen too quickly for fear of a communist advance. During the second half of the 1950s, several top-ranking officials – including Pietro Sigismondi, the Secretary of Propaganda Fide (responsible for the mission regions) and the former Apostolic Delegate in the Belgian Congo – frequently manifested their displeasure towards the Belgian Ambassador for the Holy See about Belgian promises to the Congolese nationalists. It was only during the second half of the 1950s that the Belgian Congo was converted from a mission region into an independent ecclesiastical structure with its own hierarchy (whereby all vicars apostolic – apart from one all white – automatically became bishop). This was later than elsewhere in Central Africa and was hastened by the new pontificate of John XXIII from October 1958 and the events in the Belgian Congo itself.

In January 1959, revolts had broken out in Léopoldville (see Chapter 5). Alongside shops run by Greek and Portuguese traders, mission posts were the main target. This was partly because the demonstrators had been pushed back into indigenous residential districts where the missionaries were the most visible Belgians. It also shows that many Congolese continued to associate missions with colonial rule. Moreover, they felt neglected, because the missions were not able to meet the growing demand for education due to staff shortages, among other things. The Church stressed even more strongly that it distanced itself from the independence process, but it was to no avail. During the Congo Crisis, rebels killed dozens of missionaries, including in Kongolo in 1962 and Stanleyville and its surrounding area in 1964. Yet their congregations have remained active in the former colony. In 2020, there were still some hundred missionaries living in the DR Congo. Some receive considerable recognition: when the Jesuit Léon de Saint Moulin died in October 2019, he was posthumously elevated to the Order of National Lumumba-Kabila Heroes. An academic session was organized in the cathedral of Kinshasa with the vice-chancellors of the capital's three main universities, and his funeral was conducted by Cardinal Fridolin Ambongo Besungu and attended by various politicians. Conversely, during the past decades hundreds of Congolese priests have begun to work in Belgian parishes. The importance of

African religious individuals was also underlined by the beatification of the Congolese martyrs Marie-Clémentine Anuarite Nengapeta in 1985, Isidore Bakanja in 1994 and Francesco Spoto in 2007.

Conclusion

In 1960, more than thirty per cent of the Congolese people were Catholic (and almost ten per cent Protestant). This is an impressive proportion: around a fifth of all Catholic conversions in Africa and Asia combined took place in the Congo (and in the Belgian mandate and trust territory of Ruanda-Urundi).[10]

On the other hand, a majority – including, in 1960, among particular communities such as the Kuba even more than 75 per cent – continued to adhere to their own religion.[11] Anthropologists often emphasize the continuity in Congolese culture before and after Christianization. Cambridge University mission historian David Maxwell is more nuanced: conversion was a watershed and it was the subsequent generations above all that developed a dialectic with ancient customs. In the end, the missionaries did not achieve cultural hegemony and did not succeed in fully colonizing the African communities' consciousness. The Congolese historian Flavien Nkay Malu concludes that the local populace were no passive receivers of the faith, but instead negotiated their new identities.

The missionaries certainly made an important contribution to the opening up and development of the Belgian colony and left a big stamp on Congolese society in various domains. Giving a final assessment is difficult. The Congolese themselves are divided: they used *aussi méchant qu'un Père* ('as angry as a clergyman') as a proverb, but as recently as 1997 named a sports stadium after 'Tata Raphaël'. Amongst the Belgians, anticlericals such as the socialist Prime Minister Achiel Van Acker were full of praise, while missionaries themselves were at times critical. It is at any rate clear that the missions in the Belgian Congo were part of a colonial system and that many missionaries turned a blind eye to its excesses, but it is also obvious that many reacted against this. Missionaries were indeed full of contradictions. They brought 'progress' and 'civilization' but turned against 'modernity' and materialism. There were big individual differences, because many missionaries had strong characters and because they developed diverse careers as fundraisers, organizers, scientists, teachers, architects, rural developers or parish priests, to name but a few. At the same time, they were subject to collective evolutions from triumphalist clergymen with long beards who threw up neogothic buildings, to progressive aid workers who felt very strongly about humility, respect and reciprocity.

Equally important is that, to many Belgians, missionaries were the face of colonialism, not only through family connections, but also through their fundraising, their youth work (among the Scouts and Chiro Flanders as well as specific organizations such as the Eucharist Crusade) and their propaganda through magazines, exhibitions and so-called 'good works' (collecting foil or bottle tops for the missions, for instance). Missionaries also had a big impact on the Church, to which they initially endowed a great deal of prestige – after the nineteenth-century conflicts with liberalism and socialism, and before the emerging secularization during the 1960s – and which they later brought into contact with interculturality and globalization.

Today, this Church is under fire for its sexual scandals. Belgian missionaries, too, hit the headlines in this respect (for example Jan Van Dael in Brazil, Eric Dejaeger in Canada and Luk Delft in the Central African Republic). Sources about the Congo contain scattered traces of covered-up cases. A.M. Delathuy in particular makes occasional reference to missionaries who were called back to Belgium because of illicit sexual relations. The most sensational case was that of Scheut Father Emeri Cambier, who founded the mission in Kasaï in 1890, but in 1913 was accused of the murder of a child that he was said to have fathered with an African woman. Although he was acquitted, he was not allowed to return to the Congo. It is difficult to find out the full facts behind such stories, and partly for that reason sexual abuse is not (yet?) a central theme in the mission history of the Congo.

Bibliography

Vanthemsche, Guy, 'De verhouding tussen de katholieke kerk en de staat in koloniaal Congo (1885-1960)', in De ruysscher, Dave, De Hert, Paul, and De Metsenaere, Machteld, eds., *Een leven van inzet. Liber amicorum Michel Magits*, Wolters-Kluwer, Mechelen, 2012, p. 197-242, gives a good overview of the missionaries' relations with the Belgian and colonial authorities, and provides an excellent bibliography (including references to the cited works by Delathuy, François and Gijs). Additionally, there are several parts of Ceuppens, Bambi, *Congo Made in Flanders? Koloniale en Vlaamse visies op 'blank' en 'zwart' in Belgisch Congo*, Ghent, Academia Press, 2003, which are very relevant, as are the articles in *Trajecta. Tijdschrift voor de geschiedenis van het katholiek leven in de Nederlanden* by Jean

Pirotte (1996), Dries Vanysacker (1996), Ria Christens (2003), Carine Dujardin (2003) and Ruben Mantels (2006) – all authors who have published on this theme elsewhere as well. Congregations ensured their own histories were recorded, for instance in the chapters by Frans Bontinck and Wim Goossens in Verhelst, Daniël, and Daniëls, Hyacint, eds., *Scheut vroeger en nu. Geschiedenis van de Congregatie van het Onbevlekt Hart van Maria C.I.C.M.*, Universitaire Pers Leuven, Leuven, 1991 and Deneef, Alain e.a., eds., *De la mission du Kwango à la province d'Afrique centrale. Les jésuites au Congo-Zaïre cent ans d'épopée*, AESM Éditions, Brussels, 1995. In this chapter I also mention Loffman, Reuben, *Church, State and Colonialism in Southeastern Congo, 1890-1962*, Palgrave, Basingstoke, 2019; Maxwell, David, 'Continuity and Change in the Luba Christian Movement, Katanga, Belgian Congo, c. 1915-50', *Journal of Ecclesiastical History*, 69, 2018, 2, p. 326-344; and Nkay Malu, Flavien, *La mission chrétienne à l'épreuve de la tradition ancestrale (Congo-belge, 1891-1933)*, Karthala, Paris, 2007. In 2021, I published a Dutch monograph on the history, memory and decolonization of missionaries: *Missionarissen: geschiedenis, herinnering, dekolonisering*, Leuven, LannooCampus.

Notes

1 Cleys, Bram, De Maeyer, Jan, Dujardin, Carine, and Vints, Luc, 'België in Congo, Congo in België. Weerslag van de missionering op de religieuze instituten', in Viaene, Vincent, Van Reybrouck, David, and Ceuppens, Bambi, eds., *Congo in België. Koloniale cultuur in de metropool*, Universitaire Pers Leuven, Leuven, 2009, p. 151-152.
2 Delathuy, A.M., *Missie en staat in Oud-Kongo 1880-1914. Witte paters, scheutisten en jezuïeten*, Epo, Berchem, 1992, p. 217. The conversion was done using https://statbel.fgov.be/nl/themas/consumptieprijsindex/consumptieprijsindex#panel-13 (consulted on 26 November 2019): 100 Belgian francs in 1914 was worth approximately 25,000 (and therefore 625 euros) in 2019.
3 Delathuy, *Missie en staat*, p. 307-308 and 121.
4 26,000 around 1906 according to Foutry, Vita, and Neckers, Jan, *Als een wereld zo groot waar uw vlag staat geplant. Kongo 1885-1960*, BRT-Instructieve Omroep, Brussels, 1985, p. 139; 60,000 in 1911 according to Delathuy, *Missie en staat*, p. 174.
5 Markowitz, Marvin D., *Cross and Sword: The Political Role of Christian Missions in the Belgian Congo, 1908-1960*, Hoover Institution Press, Stanford, 1973, p. 59.
6 Markowitz, *Cross and Sword*, p. 25-26.

7 Vanthemsche, Guy, *Congo: de impact van de kolonie op België*, Lannoo, Tielt, 2007, p. 55; and Foutry and Neckers, *Als een wereld zo groot*, p. 133.
8 Stengers, Jean, *Congo. Mythes et réalités. 100 ans d'histoire*, Éditions Duculot, Paris-Louvain-la-Neuve, 1989, p. 194 (p. 209 in the reissue by Racine, Brussels, 2007).
9 Vanthemsche, Guy, 'Le Saint-Siège et la fin du Congo belge (1958-1960)', *Revue d'Histoire Ecclésiastique*, 109, 2014, 1-2, p. 209.
10 Stengers, *Congo*, p. 191-192 (p. 206 in the 2007 edition).
11 Vansina, Jan, *Being Colonized: The Kuba Experience in Rural Congo, 1880-1960*, University of Wisconsin Press, Madison, 2010, p. 283.

MAARTEN LANGHENDRIES AND
REINOUT VANDER HULST

22. Health Care

The Jewel in Belgian Colonization's Crown?

'But the Belgians built all those hospitals in the Congo, didn't they?' This is an argument that regularly pops up in discussions about the 'benefits' of colonization. Moreover, the introduction of 'Western' medicine is sometimes portrayed as the most laudable legacy of Belgian colonialism. It is true that – especially after the Second World War – the colonizing power created a substantial medical infrastructure in the Belgian Congo. However, the complex story of colonial health care cannot be confined to its material aspects alone. Instead, we should think in terms of questions. Such as, how available was Western health care to the average Congolese individual? Can the medical system in the Congo be regarded as a mirror image of its Belgian version? After all, the very notion of *public* medical care simply did not exist for the majority of the colonial era. What is more, all the actors involved had their own agendas, with health care always explicitly serving another objective. This had far-reaching consequences when it came to decisions about who was to be treated by whom and in what way. So, what were the different colonial players' underlying motives for offering medical care? Over the next few pages, we will try to sketch a more nuanced picture of 'Belgian' colonial medicine by focusing on these different actors, challenges and evolutions.

Who Cured Whom?

It should be stressed that, during the colonial era as well as during other times, Congolese people who became ill were first and foremost looked after by their fellow countrymen and women. 'Western' medicine never acquired a monopoly in Central Africa. And contrary to what Belgium had hoped, numerous local medical traditions continued to exist. These had a complex structure, in which bodily care and the preservation of social relations were blended. The Bakongo made use of different therapeutic roles, for instance. Alongside the *nganga mbuki*, the herbalist and general curer, and the *nganga bilau*, the healer of mental diseases, there was also the *nganga nkisi*, who looked after the spiritual wellbeing of the community. It was precisely because of this spiritual dimension that the Belgians labelled local medical cultures as 'superstition', 'magic', 'witchcraft', etc.; and considered the Congolese totally ignorant in the domain of illness and health.

Nevertheless, the Belgians were regularly forced to call on the local population to provide medical care. The colonial apparatus often lacked sufficient manpower; for example, in 1891, the Congo Free State counted only eight European doctors, with the result that the colonizer slowly incorporated a small number of Congolese workers into its healthcare system. These jobs were initially administrative ones, for instance conducting censuses. It was only in 1917 that the growing need for trained medical personnel led to the foundation of the first nursing school in Boma. Twenty years later, in 1936, the government set up a more in-depth training-course for male indigenous medical assistants (*assistants médicaux indigènes*), a function halfway between nurse and doctor. It was in this period that developing Congolese medical personnel became an extremely important aspect for the practical execution of Belgian colonial policy. However, it was not until 1954 that Lovanium University was finally established and introduced a medical degree course, and it would take until 1961 before the first two Congolese doctors, Félicien Ilunga Bitokwela and Marcel Tshibamba, graduated. This was relatively late compared to other African territories. Even before the Second World War, the British and French had instituted training for African doctors in Senegal, Uganda and Nigeria.

The colonial government was the most active player within Belgian health care. During the Congo Free State era, physicians remained part of the military apparatus and first and foremost had to ensure the physical well-being of the *Force Publique*. This rudimentary medical corps shared an international background with other members of the colonial administration, for instance engaging Italian doctors for their expertise in the treatment of malaria. After the Belgian state had taken over the colony, the medical structure in the Belgian Congo continued to be characterized by its military and international nature.

The medical system expanded only very gradually. The government set up the Indigenous Medical Assistance Service (SAMI), but this service only came under the direct authority of the governor-general in 1922. SAMI enabled the colonial government to coordinate the work of the various health care institutions more efficiently, but towards 1929, the medical corps (excluding nursing staff) comprised a mere 241 doctors, 122 health care officials and 10 pharmacists (for an area covering some 75 times the size of Belgium, that is). Moreover, health care remained extremely utilitarian, which meant that access to medical care was restricted to Congolese people who were considered important in the eyes of the government, such as soldiers and auxiliary personnel.

In addition to the state, the industrial sector created its own private health care system for its own workers. Railway companies such as the CFC erected hospitals for Congolese workers around their large yards in Bas-Congo from 1893 onwards, and other industrial players followed suit. The company with the most comprehensive health care policy was indubitably the UMHK. In order to diminish child mortality and compensate for staff shortages in the labor camps, the UMHK began to focus on the children of its workers through the so-called *goutte de lait* ('milk scheme') from 1924 onwards. The company doctor linked the mother's food rations to her willingness to feed her child with the powdered milk offered. This led to a very strict system, whereby the mothers had to report several times a day. Using medical provisions, the company thus exercised far-reaching control over its employees' family life (see Chapter 10).

The third player in the classical colonial triumvirate, the mission system, organized health care as well. Unlike the government and companies, the missions were more attentive to the needs of the ordinary rural Congolese people. However, Catholic missionaries were not medically trained, or very minimally so, and were for the most part only able to provide medical assistance at an extremely rudimentary level. The recruitment of mission doctors slowly began to take off during the interwar years, but in 1939 the medical corps of the Catholic missions amounted to a mere eighteen doctors (see Chapter 21). Neither could the underlying motive for Christian health care be described as philanthropic. Missionaries used biomedicine as a tool for the evangelization of the African population. They tried to recruit converts by amazing them with new physical treatments and medications. Missionaries wanted to increase the rate at which people were converted initially through medicine, with the idea that the soul could be reached via care for the body. The development of missionary health care was thus also in part a consequence of the competitive battle for Congolese souls between Catholics and Protestants, whose greater medical expertise made the Catholics green with envy for quite some time. Protestant congregations often relied on professionalized care providers. By 1930, they engaged thirty missionaries with a medical degree (see Chapter 21).

Despite the missionary propaganda about the caring and public nature of its medical services, the line between missionary and utilitarian state medicine tended to be wafer-thin. In practice, missionary doctors had to take part in government-led health campaigns just as often as they were able to consult patients on their own account. Remote mission posts in rural areas thus served as an extension to the selective and rudimentary health apparatus of the state. They did not offer a public and accessible form of healthcare. Nor were their therapeutics particularly caring. Both Catholic and Protestant doctors had no qualms about sporadically resorting to violence in order to get Congolese individuals to visit the white physician. The British Protestant doctor Clement Chesterman, for instance, was notorious for wielding the *chicotte* alongside his stethoscope at times.

Pre-War Challenges to Western Medicine

In the first place, the Belgians introduced diseases rather than healthcare into the Congo. Leopold II's cruel regime had severely weakened the Congolese population, which made it very susceptible to all kinds of infections. In addition to forced labor and malnutrition, forced migration and refugee flows gave a further boost to infectious diseases (see Chapter 7). Diseases that were already present in Central Africa, such as malaria, could thus develop into real epidemics. White doctors had little or no experience with these infections. In order to treat intensively the diseases that they were familiar with – chicken pox, tuberculosis and measles, for instance – the Belgians generally lacked time, money and equipment. Besides, the medical corps was extremely selective about the diseases it treated. Attention was focused primarily on epidemics that formed a threat to the economy.

Because sleeping sickness created the highest number of victims among Congolese workers, it caused the Belgian regime the greatest concern during the colonial period. Sleeping sickness or trypanosomiasis – transmitted by the tsetse fly – first causes headaches, fever and nausea and, if untreated, leads to inevitable death. A scientific expedition by the Liverpool School of Tropical Medicine diagnosed the outbreak of a sleeping sickness epidemic in large parts of the Congo as early as 1904. Initially, the government tried to stop the spread by isolating infected people or by moving healthy sections of the population. When the first experiments with Atoxyl yielded positive results, large-scale injection campaigns were introduced. The occasional violence that would accompany this would often lead to fear and repulsion amongst the Congolese (see Chapter 16).

Vertical public health programs, with mobile medical teams actively tracking and treating one or more diseases in a specific geographical area, formed the core task of the Queen Elisabeth Fund for Medical Assistance to Indigenous People (FOREAMI), set up in 1930. This semi-governmental organization, partly financed by a personal gift from Queen Elisabeth, became the most important medical institution in the Belgian Congo. When sleeping sickness infections witnessed a steady decline during the late 1930s, the Fund abandoned its exclusive focus on this epidemic. It was only then that FOREAMI and similar organizations began to concentrate on other diseases. Leprosy, for instance, became a concern during this period, first for the missionaries and later also for the Red Cross. In 1939, a national organization, the Father Damien Foundation for the Fight against Leprosy (FOPERDA), was set up in order to intensify the 'battle' against Hansen's disease.

Postwar Ambitions

Only after the Second World War did the government aspire to a broader and more permanent form of health care. In a context in which colonialism was increasingly questioned, the Belgians foregrounded healthcare to legitimize their presence in the Congo. In 1947, emulating the British Native Welfare Fund, the government founded the Fund for Indigenous Wellbeing (FBEI). Financed with Belgian reimbursements from Congolese war investments and with income from the Colonial Lottery, after eleven years the fund had 11.5 billion Belgian francs at its disposal. Rather than combatting diseases, the FBEI wanted to boost public health by investing in drinking water supplies in rural areas. This emphasis on rural communities reappeared in the Van Hoof-Duren plan, which was named after two high-ranking health officials in the Ministry of Colonies. The plan was part of the Ten-Year Plan (see Chapter 13) and could count on financial support from the FBEI. In each of the 120 administrative districts, Van Hoof and Duren wanted a fully-equipped medical-surgical center, supplemented by local hospitals.

The medical infrastructure was thus further developed and in 1954, the Belgian Congo was home to 2,164 care institutions (hospitals, maternity hospitals, dispensaries, leper colonies, etc.). This translated into one care bed per 186 inhabitants, making the Belgian Congo perform better than its neighboring colonies. The British Federation of Rhodesia and Nyasaland (present-day Zimbabwe, Zambia and Malawi) and French Equatorial Africa (present-day Gabon, Congo-Brazzaville, the Central African Republic and Chad), offered just one bed per 369 and 364 people at that particular point in time. Increased financial scope for colonial health care also resulted in an extension of the medical corps. In this respect, the Belgian colony could present far less spectacular figures. With one doctor per 20,138 inhabitants, the degree of medicalization was approximately on a par with French Equatorial Africa (23,028), but almost 50 per cent lower than in the Federation of Rhodesia and Nyasaland (10,736).[1]

Moreover, health care policy in the Belgian Congo was grounded throughout on a racial and paternalistic worldview. Hospital infrastructure in the average-sized city of Coquilhatville served as a good example of this. Starting in 1931, the city proudly erected two large medical complexes: the *Clinique Reine Élisabeth* for white colonials, and the less sophisticated *Hôpital Léopold II* for its black inhabitants. Only in the 1950s was it decided that the Congolese deserved a better-equipped hospital, and that the Belgians should start to build a new complex. This took till 1962 to complete, while the *Clinique Reine Élisabeth* dealt with a severe lack of patients. The hospital did not admit Congolese patients until 1960, after independence. Stories like these show that, behind numbers, a grubby, segregated reality lurked.

Conclusion

During colonization, Belgium was attentive to Congolese healthcare, but for a major part of the colonial era this was primarily at the service of economic, military or religious ambitions. By and large, it was an ad hoc by-product of colonial initiatives. Medical care was initially a privilege for white Europeans and their subordinates. Later, doctors focused on the treatment of specific diseases amongst certain groups in society, such as workers or mothers, or they limited themselves to particular regions and epidemics. The sleeping sickness epidemic, absorbing the majority of Belgian money, time and manpower, was for the most part a direct consequence of colonization itself. It would therefore attest to a certain cynicism to present these medical endeavors as an 'accomplishment' on the part of the colonizer. What is more, despite the sleeping sickness campaigns and postwar efforts in health care, the number of doctors and hospitals remained relatively small. Nor did biomedical medicine manage to replace local medical practices, something the Belgians had fiercely hoped would happen. The Congolese dealt very pragmatically with the care they were offered and called on multiple forms of medicine. For a large part of the populace, the medical aspect of colonization barely had any impact. When the population came into contact with health care, this 'care' could take on an extremely segregated or even violent form. Worse still, medicine was maybe the domain in which the separation between white colonizer and its black colonized counterpart was the greatest. That individual doctors were sometimes genuinely concerned about the wellbeing of Congolese people does therefore not mean that the colonial medical system was altruistic or even caring.

Bibliography

British and American historians in particular have conducted pioneering studies into the medical history of the Belgian Congo. Maryinez Lyons has carried out ground-breaking research into sleeping sickness, notably in Lyons, Maryinez, *The Colonial Disease: A Social History of Sleeping Sickness in Northern Zaïre, 1900-1940*, Cambridge University Press, Cambridge, 1992. Nancy Rose Hunt did the same for mother-and-child care (see: Hunt, Nancy Rose, '"Le Bébé en Brousse": European Women, African Birth Spacing and Colonial Intervention in Breast Feeding in the Belgian Congo', *The International Journal of African Historical Studies*, 21, 1988, p. 401-432; and Hunt, Nancy Rose, *A Colonial Lexicon of Birth Ritual, Medicalization, and Mobility in the Congo*, Durham, Duke University Press, 1999). In Belgium, Jean-Luc Vellut was a trailblazer (see Vellut, Jean-Luc, 'La médecine européenne dans l'État Indépendant du Congo (1885-1908)', in Janssens, P.G., et al., eds., *Médecine et hygiène en Afrique centrale de 1885 à nos jours*, Fondation Roi Baudouin, Brussels, 1992, p. 61-81). Research into missions was done amongst others by Sokhieng Au (Au, Sokhieng, 'Medical Orders: Catholic and Protestant Missionary Medicine in the Belgian Congo 1880-1940', *BMGN – Low Countries Historical Review*, 132, 2017, 1, p. 62-82). Recently, less archetypal topics have received attention, such as architecture (Geenen, Kristien, 'Categorizing Colonial Patients: Segregated Medical Care, Space and Decolonization in a Congolese City, 1931-62', *Africa*, 89, 2019, 1, p. 100-124) and the pharmaceutical industry (Mertens, Myriam, *Chemical Compounds in the Congo: Pharmaceuticals and the 'Crossed History' of Public Health in Belgian Africa (ca. 1905-1939)*, doctoral thesis, Universiteit Gent, 2014). The authors would also like to thank the KU Leuven students who took part in the bachelor try-out seminar on illness and health in the Belgian Congo (2018-2019).

Notes

1 Bouvier, Paule, *L'accession du Congo à l'indépendance*, Éditions de l'Institut de Sociologie, Brussels, 1965, p. 49.

MARC DEPAEPE AND
ANNETTE LEMBAGUSALA KIKUMBI

23. Colonial Education in the Congo

More than a Paternalistic One-Way Street?

In the aftermath of Congolese independence, many Belgians harbored the view that, in terms of colonial education, they had not done too badly. As public opinion saw it, the Congo's educational provisions could serve as a model for other colonies. Yet it very much remains to be seen whether this positive view is correct.

There appears to be some academic proof for this. Some studies, including one by UNESCO, suggested that half-way through the 1950s, the Belgian Congo was the most literate country on the African continent (despite the fact that 60 to 65 per cent of its populace was still illiterate). Only South Africa with 10 per cent fewer illiterate people performed better.[1]

Such statistics are not very reliable, however. It was almost impossible to gather correct data about an area as vast and difficult to access as the Congo. Congolese educational historians such as Pierre Kita therefore qualify this kind of quantitative data. Kita differentiated three colonial spheres of influence in tropical Africa around the time of independence: British, French and Belgian. In these three spheres of influence, around 1960, there were respectively 6,200, 4,400 and 10,500 pupils in primary, 740, 260 and 230 in secondary, and 14, 15 and 6 in higher education per 100,000 inhabitants.[2] If Belgium was not doing too badly, then this was almost exclusively at the primary education level.

Belgian colonial education policy can be summarized, at least for the first half of the twentieth century, in the following way: (1) support from the Catholic network of missionary schools; (2) almost exclusive focus on primary education, with an emphasis on moral upbringing, rather than on acquiring knowledge; (3) preference for the use of indigenous *linguae francae* over French (and Dutch); (4) fundamental pedagogic attitude of paternalism, which implied a one-way channel from Belgium for the concrete materialization of schools, whereby (5) the voice of the Africans was not heard. Emancipation was not on the agenda in the colony, especially before the Second World War. Only during the 1950s can a coherent strategy of colonial education policy be discerned, albeit piecemeal.

It is not always easy to find out what Belgian educational activity on behalf of the Congolese achieved in exact educational results. Apart from perhaps hugely diverse individual experiences, there is a systemic absence of relevant source material for the entire colonial period. The archives contain few personal recollections from the pupils themselves – which moreover tend to be colored by opinions from and interventions by the organizers – but instead contain rather normatively-charged texts and rules about educational objectives and values in the mission congregations' educational institutions. The first thing that stands out here is the fact that these educational attempts followed on naturally from the government's colonial project and were regarded as the humanitarian complement of colonization and evangelization.

The Congo Free State's Legacy (1885-1908)

The collaboration between the colonial authorities and the Catholic missions goes back to the time of the Congo Free State. Right from the start, Belgian missionaries were mobilized in Leopold's project (see Chapter 21). That the Catholic Church seized the missionary assignment to extend its power in Central Africa goes without saying. Just as in the 'motherland', where it managed to create a subsidized network of non-state schools in the wake of the nineteenth-century school funding battle, during the first half of the twentieth century it tried to push through this dominance as well. Yet, aside from the major cultural differences, the situation was very different from that in Belgium. In the Congo, the Catholic Church not only had to start implanting education from scratch, it also had to compete with foreign Protestant missions which Leopold II, partly because of the latter's' criticism of his regime, wanted to sideline.

On 26 May 1906, the Congo Free State and the Holy See concluded a convention which, more symbolically than actually, underscored the Catholic missions' preferential treatment. In return for more practically-oriented education, the state offered all kinds of material benefits, including land and the supply of so-called wards of court which were allocated to the school colonies that the state contracted out to the free Catholic missions (including the Jesuit 'chapel farms'). The wards of court tended to be purported orphans and children that had been taken away following military raids and punitive expeditions during Leopold II's rule. Yet cooperation between state and Church, and more specifically between civil servants and missionaries, was far from smooth. Mutual distrust was great, even though the principle of cooperation was never questioned.

The Belgians did not have a high opinion about the Africans' educational capacities. They regarded them as not theoretically-minded and lazy by nature, passionate, lewd, polygamous and so on. Yet they wanted to lift them onto a higher level from a Christian 'civilization' perspective, so that they would be able to carry out useful work in service of the colony. That is why strict discipline, manual labor and agriculture were at the core of the educational institutions of the time.

The High Point of the Catholic Missionizing Offensive in the Belgian Congo

After the Congo had become a Belgian colony in 1908, the collaboration between Church and state was continued. Yet this was not ratified officially, because too tight a policy framework was perceived as burdensome. The Colonial Charter only adopted the principle of education from the Belgian constitution. In practice this meant that the Catholic missions, at least until the outbreak of the Second World War, were able to go about their business unhindered. This led to an expansion of what was being offered in terms of education and to the Catholic institutions acquiring a quasi-monopoly.

Leaving education to Catholic missions was in some sense a solution of convenience. From the beginning, the missionaries had been loyal to the colonial project: what is more, they were relatively cheap, partly because they were satisfied with less than colonial officials. That many of them were also more or less familiar with the local languages made the support to the Catholic mission acceptable to non-believing politicians in Belgium, despite internal tensions. Most Belgians saw religion and the resultant moral principles as a steppingstone to Western civilization and, more specifically, as a sop to the indigenous population.

At the end of the 1920s, on the basis of several drafts (including those by the Franck commission and the resulting De Jonghe conventions, named after the liberal Minister of Colonies Louis Franck and the Catholic civil servant of that same Ministry Edouard De Jonghe respectively), a new settlement with the missions was introduced. That this had been so long in coming was not only related to the political instability at the time; above all, it was the result of the unwillingness of the Catholic missions to subject themselves to the authority of the government inspectorate. They got their way in the end, and it was agreed that the Catholic mission schools could oversee themselves. Additionally, it was laid down that only 'national' missions were eligible for subsidies, which gave the (chiefly foreign) Protestant mission schools a significant handicap.

The 'yellow brochure' – as the 1929 program was commonly known – developed the five policy principles summarized in this chapter's introduction. The Belgians wished to work broadly rather than in depth, and set up primary schools comprising two years of study organized in school days lasting four to five hours. The curriculum was focused on fostering practical skills and willingness to work so that individuals could be self-supporting. As regards content, the emphasis was on religion, math, reading and writing, singing and PE, handicrafts and agriculture, and for the girls on domestic science and modest conduct. In terms of method, the curriculum recommended intuitive and occasional education able to respond to all manner of themes deemed relevant. In urban centers and larger mission posts a second phase (lasting two years) was introduced for selected pupils. Because this was also preparation for office clerk, teacher and craftsman training, contact with European culture could be pursued. It is clear that all these aspects placed the Belgian colonizers' 'successes' – the creation of primary education and even the high literacy – in perspective.

For girls, even fewer initiatives were taken than for boys. On the eve of independence, their share in the Congo's entire school population amounted to a mere twenty per cent. What is more, education for girls was placed in a separate learning stream, which only allowed access to specific care professions, such as nun, teacher, monitor, (assistant) nurse and/or (assistant) midwife. This suggested a colonial mentality that assigned Africans solely an assisting role, but also dovetailed with Western gender views of the time, and with the pedagogic orientations for vocational training in the 'motherland'. In Belgium, up until the 1960s, parenting and education were focused on obedience, accepting authority, finding your place in the social order and above all to conforming to socially desired norms and values, which, as far as girls were concerned, was inextricably bound up with motherhood ideology. Nonetheless, discipline and subjugation made itself felt much more strongly in the Congo than in Belgium. Western culture – which was considered superior and which the Europeans used to justify their authority and hierarchy – had, according to the prevailing views, to be realized rapidly and within a context portrayed as hostile.

Psychopedagogic Principles

Even though hardly any research was conducted into this until the 1950s, from the end of the nineteenth century, strong views existed on the 'psychology of the (African) negro'. Based purely on impressions and memories, many were adamant that 'the black race' showed a clear intellectual disadvantage. This led to a paradoxical question: how should the colonial project, which presupposed a minimal form of adjustment to European norms and values, be realized if the Congolese proved to be difficult to educate, if at all?

In practice, the missionaries ignored this and, as required, they invested massively in primary education. In the end, it would take until the 1938 reforms, and de facto until those of 1948, for the education of a Congolese elite to be given full attention. In the education program of 1948, selection mechanisms were drawn up (whereby the missionaries themselves were able to decide the number of candidates per selection grade). The spectrum of vocational training which linked in with primary education was expanded. Levels were extremely variable, but that was the intention. The elite, which the Belgians wanted to create for their self-labelled 'harmonious development of the colony', did not necessarily have to be intellectual. The so-called *évolués* (see Chapter 18) should really be more a kind of artisan middle-class, not only essential to the local economy, but to safeguard the postwar Congo against revolts and revolutionary ideas, both from the inside and beyond. In as far as education played any role in this, this was much greater in further vocational training than in higher education, let alone university education.

Thus, the educationalists tried to solve a fundamental problem within the colonial system. On the one hand, an introduction into 'modern' thinking and value patterns was vital for the success of the colonial project; on the other, too much education was risky because it could fuel the indigenous populace's revolutionary potential. The question 'how far can/should/may we go?' was never far away, all the more because the massive broadening of primary education bolstered a craving for 'more' education. The frequently heard one-liner *Pas d'élite, pas d'ennuis* ('No elite, no trouble') caught on less and less. After the Second World War, the rapid social changes, such as the increase in wage labor and the concentration of the population in the Congolese cities, undermined the all too simplistic colonial expectations. The call for university education sounded ever louder, while the Catholic educational monopoly came more and more under attack. Belgian liberals and socialists wanted to take an active part in colonial policy and began to create a more laicized state education system.

The Crucial 1950s

The official network only began to be organized in 1954 when a socialist-liberal government took office. Over four years, three hundred 'official' (in other words state) schools would be set up, including the first 'interracial' state secondary school (*atheneum*). The report by a ministerial mission, which criticized the Catholic mission's educational standards, based this decision on a need for higher-quality education. The missions obviously disputed the report's conclusions but were not able to halt the scaling-back of mission schools' subsidies.

This measure led to a Congolese battle over school funding, in the margin of the Belgian one, in practice more with word and pen than in actual conflicts. In 1955, afraid of a collapse of the Congolese education system, the Government caved in and scrapped some cost-cutting measures. This did not mean the end of the conflict. A new storm erupted over (construction) subsidies for schools, which was solved through a new compromise. The subsidies were allocated to state, Catholic and Protestant schools in a ratio of a 45:45:10 per cent.

The Government's involvement in education led to a significant increase in the number of school attendees in the Congo. Between 1954 and 1957, this grew by more than fifty per cent (from 1,112,562 to 1,692,218). Yet state education's share remained rather small. In 1958, a mere three per cent of the primary school population attended a state school, while in secondary education the proportion was 14 per cent. In vocational schools and higher education (training of clerical staff and other 'assistants'), this percentage rose to 42 and 45 respectively, but the actual numbers were small. More than 95 per cent of pupils in 1957 were in pre-school (4 per cent) and primary education (91.3 per cent), the vast majority of which were in first level (which in most rural areas constituted the full extent of schooling).[3]

Likewise, the presence of 'indigenous' pupils in so-called interracial education in larger urban centers should be put firmly into perspective. According to Jean-Marie Mutamba, their share in the official secondary schools in 1957 did not rise above 1.5 per cent (59 pupils out of a total of 4,138)[4], which shows that this kind of education was not primarily meant for Africans, but for the white children of colonials. Meanwhile, the introduction of official education resulted in the Catholic network, partly out of competition, feeling forced to 'metropolize' its programs further, i.e. bring it into line with the Belgian programs. To the Congolese, this essentially opened better perspectives for participation in (general) secondary education, but we should not exaggerate this. In 1957, the number of Congolese pupils in secondary schools following the Belgian curriculum (both Catholic and state) was still a mere 5 per cent.[5]

Higher education was in even worse a state. Lovanium only opened its doors as the first university in the Congo in 1954 (see Chapter 25). There had been training courses for medical and agricultural 'assistants' since 1932, but those completing them were never considered true university graduates. In its first academic year, Lovanium University had 33 students, only 11 of which were Congolese… In 1956, the first official university of the Belgian Congo and Ruanda-Urundi was erected as a counterpart to the Catholic university. This nonetheless was not able to undo the effects of the biased policies from the past fifty years. A paltry 0.1 per cent of the Congolese school population followed higher education in 1960. This was four times less than the 0.4 per cent for the whole of Africa at the time and thirty per cent less than for the entire world.[6]

Conclusion

Although some opinionmakers, both ecclesiastical and civil, showed understanding for Congolese complaints, they avoided a wholesale opening of the flood gates for the development of the indigenous population through education. From a colonial perspective, education still meant 'looking after' and therefore taking decisions for those who as yet were not allowed to do so for themselves. Not wanting to relinquish this patronizing strategy accelerated – paradoxical as it may sound – the downfall of Belgian paternalism. Continuing to patronize only increased disaffection with colonization. As one *évolué* put it: *Le plus élevé des Noirs était encore en dessous du plus petit des Blancs* ('The most elevated black was still below the lowest white') (see Chapter 17).

It should therefore not surprise us that the Congolese in Kinshasa and in the Brussels neighborhood of Matonge who were interviewed by us entertained mixed feelings about the late colonial period. On the one hand, there was some positive appreciation for what could be acquired via the Belgians in general and the missions in particular; but on the other the entire educational enterprise could be assessed as one big, missed opportunity. It is no surprise that colonial (mission) education did not prompt critical thinking – something that has been the subject of little pedagogic research until now. On the other hand, it should not be forgotten that late 1950s Belgium pedagogic principles were not at all focused on liberation, autonomy and freedom of speech, and that so-called emancipatory pedagogics only gained ground during the late 1960s. This does not alter the fact that the initial question of whether the colonial Congo was a pedagogic Eldorado, must be answered largely in the negative. The Belgians' constant emphasis on proper conduct and discipline meant the mental space opened for the Congolese for personal development was in the end extremely limited.

Bibliography

This chapter was largely based on Depaepe, Marc, 'Colonial Education in the Congo – a Question of "Uncritical" Pedagogy Until the Bitter End?', *Encounters in Theory and History of Education*, 18, 2017, p. 2-26. Additional information can be found in, amongst others, Depaepe, Marc, and Van Rompaey, Lies, *In het teken van de bevoogding. De educatieve actie in Belgisch-Congo (1908-1960)*, Garant, Leuven-Apeldoorn, 1995; Kita Kyankenge Masandi, Pierre, *Colonisation et enseignement. Cas du Zaïre avant 1960*, Éditions du Ceruki, Bukavu, 1982; Mutamba Makombo Kitatshima, Jean-Marie, *Du Congo belge au Congo indépendant, 1940-1960. Émergence des 'évolués' et genèse du nationalisme*, Publications de l'Institut de Formation et d'Études Politiques, Kinshasa, 1998; Tshimanga, Charles, *Jeunesse, formation et société au Congo/Kinshasa 1890-1960*, L'Harmattan, Paris, 2001; Kita Kyankenge Masandi, Pierre, and Depaepe, Marc, *La chanson scolaire au Congo belge. Anthologie*, L'Harmattan, Paris, 2004; Vinck, Honoré, Briffaerts, Jan, Herman, Frederik, and Depaepe, Marc, 'Expériences scolaires au Congo Belge. Étude explorative', *Annales Aequatoria*, 27, 2006, p. 5-101; Briffaerts, Jan, *'Als Kongo op de schoolbank wil'. De onderwijspraktijk in het lager onderwijs in Belgisch Congo (1925-1960)*, Acco, Leuven-Voorbrug, 2007; and Tödt, Daniel, *Elitenbildung und Dekolonisierung. Die Évolués in Belgisch-Kongo 1944-1960*, Vandenhoeck & Ruprecht, Göttingen, 2018.

Notes

1 Cf. Bouvier, Paule, *L'Accession du Congo belge à l'indépendance*, Éditions de l'Institut de Sociologie, Brussels, 1965, p. 43-44; Depaepe, Marc, and Van

Rompaey, Lies, *In het teken van de bevoogding*, Garant, Leuven-Apeldoorn, 1995, p. 213-214. Additional numbers can be found in Depaepe and Van Rompaey, *In het teken*, p. 209-215 and 153-185.
2 Kita Kyankenge Masandi, Pierre, *Colonisation et enseignement. Cas du Zaïre avant 1960*, Éditions du Ceruki, Bukavu, 1985, p. 260.
3 Cf. Depaepe and Van Rompaey, *In het teken*, p. 211; Kita Kyankenge Masandi, *Colonisation et enseignement*, p. 253. These numbers are based on Vander Elst, G., *Population des écoles au Congo belge avant l'indépendance*, Cemubac, Brussels, s.a. [1960], p. 12-13.
4 Mutamba Makombo Kitatshima, Jean-Marie, *Du Congo belge au Congo indépendant, 1940-1960. Émergence des 'évolués' et genèse du nationalisme*, Publications de l'Institut de Formation et d'Études Politiques, Kinshasa, 1998, p. 78.
5 Depaepe and Van Rompaey, *In het teken*, p. 212. Based on Kita Kyankenge Masandi, *Colonisation et enseignement*, p. 237.
6 Depaepe and Van Rompaey, *In het teken*, p. 213. Based on Ekwa bis Isal, Martin, *Congo et l'éducation: réalisations et perspectives dans l'enseignement national catholique*, Bureau de l'Enseignement National Catholique, Léopoldville, 1965, p. 75.

MATTHEW G. STANARD

24. Colonial Propaganda

The Awakening of a Belgian Colonial Consciousness?

On 30 June 2018, Patrice Lumumba Square was inaugurated in Brussels. It was a victory for Afro-Belgian activists and their Belgian sympathizers critical of their country's colonial past. Barely three hundred meters away, Leopold II's equestrian statue remained in place unperturbed. That monument is a tribute to the Congo Free State's sovereign, the great-uncle of King Baudouin, who was on the throne when Lumumba was killed – a murder that occurred just a few months after its colony became independent and in which Belgium played an active part (see Chapter 6). That these two monuments are located a stone's throw apart speaks volumes about the political, social, historical and cultural complexity of the recent debate about the colonial past. It also shows how propaganda has left its mark on Belgian public space, in the shape of colonial monuments, among other things.

All colonial powers used propaganda to legitimize themselves and to communicate their 'civilizing mission' to the public. Just as in other countries, Belgian propaganda services wanted to promote colonialism and its 'accomplishments' in Africa amongst the country's people, in particular the young, so that future generations would acquire a 'colonial consciousness'. This propaganda, which was disseminated through all kinds of channels (media, events, monuments, and so on), made use of (and thus reinforced) assorted racist clichés and prejudices about African inferiority. Just like their colonizing neighbors, the Belgians focused a great deal on the battles which accompanied their overseas conquests, sketching an epic, brave and heroic image of their past violent military actions in Central Africa.

Belgian colonial propaganda nonetheless displayed some specific features. First and foremost, there was the central role assigned to one key figure, namely Leopold II. This was unique in Europe, because nowhere else in the realm of European colonial propaganda can such a personality cult be detected. A further peculiarity is related to the fact that Belgium only acquired a colony relatively late. Unlike the French, English or Portuguese, the Belgians had no tradition of expansionism. That is why the country 'nationalized' its Leopoldian past, in an attempt to create a colonial tradition.

History can be ironic: after 1908, the Congo Free State era was thus 'rehabilitated' to justify the Belgian presence in Central Africa, while it was the Congo Free State's misrule and illegitimacy in the eyes of the international community that had forced Leopold II to hand over 'his' Congo to Belgium in the first place.

In this chapter, we will examine to what extent Belgium created propaganda to spread a particular image of its Central African colony. Which interests lay behind these attempts to bring home the 'colonial body of thought' to Belgium? Which individuals or groups of people were the target audience? And, to conclude, can we say with any certainty what the effect was of the various forms of colonial propaganda?

Royal Colonial Enthusiasm versus General Belgian Indifference

Pro-colonial propaganda began with Leopold II's initial expansionist activities. Because the Belgian general public had little interest in overseas colonies, the King made efforts to rouse a colonial sentiment among his subjects. Alongside direct appeals to industrialists, missionaries and financiers, step by step, the King and his staff tried to engender a colonial consciousness in the wider public. They launched the journal *Le Mouvement Géographique*, the Chief Editor of which, Alphonse-Jules Wauters, specialized in Central Africa – without ever having been there. This journal soon became a reference point, not only in scholarly circles. Just like quite a number of other journals from the time, it published letters by missionaries, officers and civil servants operating in the Congo Free State, so that their voices were also heard outside academic circles. These 'everyday' testimonies acted as unofficial promotional channels for the 'civilizing mission'.

The various international and world fairs held in Belgium from the late nineteenth century onwards were also used for colonial propaganda. During the Leopoldian era (and subsequently during the time of the Belgian Congo) there were colonial pavilions at the universal expositions in Antwerp (1885, 1894, 1930), Liège (1905, 1930), Ghent (1913) and Brussels (1897, 1910, 1935, 1958). The most remarkable was the colonial section of the 1897 international exposition in Tervuren. For the event, hundreds of Congolese people were housed in several reconstructed 'indigenous villages' in Tervuren Park, seven of whom died during that summer. Thousands of Belgian and European visitors came to marvel at these Africans in their 'natural habitat', as if they were animals in a zoo (see Chapter 14). This exhibition also offered the Congo Free State's authorities the opportunity to build a 'Palace of the Colonies', where it could house its growing collection of objects and materials from the Congo.

Following the end of the fair in 1897, the Palace of the Colonies was transformed into a permanent Museum of the Congo, conceived as a window onto and a showcase for the Central African colony. This museum, which opened its doors in 1898, became *the* place in Belgium for collecting and keeping all kinds of expertise, objects and 'specimens' from Africa; it also became a popular science exhibition space (see Chapters 25 and 26). In the museum, which had been set up and managed by the colonial authorities, the Congo and the Congolese people merely featured as 'content' – until 1958 none of its directors had any experience in the Congo itself. The institute propagated an image of the Congo as an exotic country where time had stood still since prehistory and which was populated by a variety of 'ethnic groups' and 'tribes'. A veil was drawn over the colonial regime's 'unpleasant aspects'.

While the colonial propaganda machine gathered momentum in Belgium, exploitation of the Congo continued unabated, which led to criticism that would have a major impact on the direction propaganda would take (see Chapter 2). Around the turn of the century, international protest against the atrocities in the Congo meant criticism was directed increasingly at Leopold II's regime, resulting in a counter-offensive by the King himself who launched a veritable propaganda deluge in defense of his Congolese rule. The King bribed several journalists into silence and paid others to depict his colony in a positive light both in Belgium and on the international stage. Thus, Leopold commissioned and paid British author Demetrius C. Boulger to write *The Congo State, or The Growth of Civilization in Central Africa* (1898), a richly illustrated volume intended to emphasize the merits of Leopoldian rule in the Congo: 'modern' transport infrastructure, a disciplined colonial army, well-educated Africans, plantations, and so on. The King also initiated the *Fédération pour la Défense des Intérêts belges à l'Étranger* ('Federation for the Defense of Belgian Interests Abroad'), a front organization that published a trilingual propaganda magazine in English, French and German disseminating a positive image of the Congo.

The First World War: A Watershed in Colonial Perception

For some, Belgium's takeover of the Congo in 1908 meant the beginning of a new era. The official call to take part in the 1913 World Fair in Ghent expressed a greater colonialist attitude than ever: 'For the first time [...] Belgium will reveal itself to other countries, as a colonial power. A Congolese pavilion will show the glorious effort realized by the Belgian people in its large African domain.'[1] Despite all the propaganda for the Congo Free State, there are clear indications that Belgians were still unable to summon much enthusiasm for the colony, and that Leopold II, until his death in 1909 – and possibly afterwards as well – was not very popular. On the international stage, Belgium retained its image as a 'black sheep' on account of its dark colonial history. 'Leopold's ghost' was not expelled until the First World War. Because of the Belgian army's valiant resistance against the advancing Germans in 1914 and its subsequent merciless occupation, Belgium was now seen as a victim country, whereas before it had been associated with acts of violence in the Congo Free State. The Leopoldian past was thus 'erased', creating new mental space offering fresh opportunities for colonial and nationalist propaganda, whereby the African colonial possessions were presented as a reason for national pride.

During the interwar years, the Belgian people began to show increasing interest and pride in their Congolese colony. Two factors played an important part in this: first, Belgian nationalism, which had been given new zeal as a result of the war, and secondly the fear that the colony might be confiscated by enemies. Before the war, the English seemed to present the biggest threat in that sense, but now the greatest danger came from the Germans. It was feared that Germany wanted to take its revenge on Belgium (which had been allocated the former German colonial territories of Ruanda-Urundi) and wanted to establish itself anew in Central Africa. This fear, coupled with cranked-up nationalism, induced the Belgians to publish a host of publications to prove that they held (and would continue to hold) absolute sway over their colony.

Immediately after the First World War, government propaganda about the Congo snowballed. During the interwar years, the Museum of the Congo in Tervuren – now renamed the Museum of the Belgian Congo – welcomed tens of thousands of visitors, a remarkable number considering the size of the country's population. The Ministry of Colonies acquired an additional department which designed and orchestrated all forms of colonial propaganda in the 'motherland': the Colonial Bureau (later to become the

Information and Documentation Centre for the Belgian Congo and Ruanda-Urundi, and finally *Inforcongo*, the Belgian Congo and Ruanda-Urundi's Information Center). The Belgian Government once again used the two interwar world fairs to showcase the colony. More than four million visitors admired the Belgian Congo pavilion at the 1930 Antwerp World Fair, and almost 3,250,000 visited the colonial pavilion at the 1935 World Fair in Brussels. Aside from these large-scale events there were temporary exhibitions such as the *quinzaines coloniales* ('colonial fortnights'), organized by the Colonial Bureau between 1925 and 1939. Tours by the royal family also played a major part in the propaganda of this era. Albert I and Elisabeth made a state visit to the Congo in 1928, followed in 1932 by an informal visit by the King. Crown Prince Leopold (later Leopold III) went to the colony in 1926 and in 1933. These royal visits tended to be followed closely by the press, reinforcing even more in the national consciousness the association between colonialism and the Belgian dynasty.

Other actors made efforts to disseminate a pro-colonial message in an unofficial or semi-official way, via specialized journals, exhibitions about the colony, newspaper articles by missionaries, films, and so on. Various colonial enterprises financed films such as *Sabena: l'aviation* (1925-1926) and *L'Union Minière du Haut-Katanga* (1928), both directed by Ernest Genval. The message behind these productions was clear: Belgium brought technological, economic and cultural progress to a 'primitive' region, which of necessity led to the rational exploitation of the Congo's natural resources and to the transformation of Congolese people into productive, well-educated workers. During this period, the Church was not yet involved in making promotional films, but many missionaries wrote articles to rouse enthusiasm and raise funds, while priests sang the praises of the 'civilizing mission' from the pulpit. The major Belgian newspapers only intermittently published articles about the colony, but there were several specialized colonial publications, such as the official, bilingual magazine *L'Illustration Congolaise*, which bulged with exotic photos of the colony and the pleasant lives led by the white people who had settled there.

Before 1908, there were few colonial monuments in Belgium, but after the First World War, a large number were added. This development was linked to the increased nationalism postwar and to the surge of monuments for those killed in action. *The Ligue du Souvenir Congolais* ('League for the Congolese Memory') asked every municipality in which at least one inhabitant had died in the Congo before 1908 to erect a memorial to the person or people concerned. Other prominent colonial monuments were built, including two large equestrian statues of Leopold II: one on the *Place du Trône* in Brussels (1926), the other on the seaside esplanade in Ostend (1931). The busts, statues and commemorative plaques for the 'pioneers' of colonial conquest (in particular Belgian *Force Publique* officers) propagated a heroic image. During the 1920s, hundreds of memorials were put up, and some 170 streets were given a name referring to the Central African colonies. The tone at the inauguration ceremonies of these monuments was at times almost religious, suggesting that the colony had become a sacred institute with a 'holy' mission. When the fallen were honored, colonial veterans raised the 'Tabora Flag' to commemorate the 1916 victory over the German troops in German East Africa, sometimes in the presence of *Force Publique* detachments who had been brought to the 'motherland' especially for the festivities (see Chapter 4). At local level, many (ex-)colonials clubbed together in *cercles coloniaux*, the purpose of which, in addition to offering a social and supportive role, was to promote the colonial cause. Their activities, which were imbued with a positive outlook on the Belgian presence in the Congo, may not have been of decisive importance, but they did contribute to a positive appreciation of the colonial past, which makes itself felt to this day.

A few things can be noted about this propaganda. What stands out first and foremost is the 'nationalization' of the Leopoldian past. Although the Congo Free State had been the King's 'personal' colony and despite the fact that he had frequently worked with foreigners because of Belgians' scant interest in the project, history books, exhibitions and commemorations now presented this past as entirely Belgian, with the aim of justifying the present colonial regime. The propaganda machine depicted Leopold II as a visionary colonial genius. From the onset of Belgian colonialism, propaganda underlined how inferior and 'different' the Congolese people were. According to that logic, Central Africa was one of the most remote, dangerous and exotic regions in the world, populated by backward, helpless black folk (not able to stand up against Arab slave traders, for instance). In photos, films or even on monuments, Congolese individuals tended to be represented naked or half-naked, while Europeans were clothed. In *Tintin in the Congo*, retitled *Tintin in Africa* in 1954, all the black characters speak imperfect French (unlike Tintin's dog, Snowy) and are depicted as primitive, superstitious and easily hoodwinked. In direct contrast stood the Belgian accomplishments in the Congo: railways, dams, mines, bridges, mission posts and cities. Not only were the Belgians 'civilizers' who had brought religion, technology and an 'efficacious' administration, it was also insinuated that the Africans themselves were not capable of cultivating their own land or exercising efficient control over it. Such images and stories reinforced the Belgian population's latent racism, which justified the 'civilizing mission' and, by extension, Belgium's presence in the Congo.

The propaganda in Belgium itself undoubtably played a significant part in the development of opinions about the Congo and Belgian colonial action, but the colonial state also conducted rigorous control over back-and-forth migration between the 'motherland' and the Congo (see Chapter 14). For many Belgians, these propaganda images were the only 'contact' they had with the colony. The number of missionaries grew steadily, but there continued to be a general lack of interest in other colonial careers, even though the ties between Belgium and its colony were generally strengthened.

The 1950s: The Heyday of Propaganda

During the Second World War, the colonial propaganda machine in Belgium fell quiet, but after the conflict, and especially during the 1950s, it spun faster than ever before. Each summer, 'colonial days' were organized, during which the Belgian people hit the streets to celebrate their African colony. Revellers included numerous schoolchildren, indicating that young people were still an important target for propaganda. Not only did history books paint a laudatory picture of Leopold II and the colony's pioneers, the Ministry of Colonies also frequently sent speakers to schools across the entire country to highlight the Founder-King's virtues and the importance of the 'Belgian Empire'.

Belgian dailies continued to report little about what was happening in the colony, but there were more colonial journals than ever. King Baudouin's tour of the Congo became an extremely important event, which was followed closely by the press and about which a remarkable propaganda film was shot, a true 'classic' in its genre, *Bwana Kitoko* (1955). In fact, most Belgian colonial films date from the 1950s, and many filmmakers made dozens of 'colonial' films, some of which were aimed at Congolese viewers, others at a European audience. These films focused on Belgian accomplishments in the fields of engineering, infrastructure, urbanization and education, and gave the impression that these had all penetrated to the colony's farthest corners. Those in charge thus wanted to show that the tiny Belgian population in the Congo was carrying out 'the work of giants' and was making the colonial Congo 'thriving' and 'modern' (see Chapters 12 and 13). For its part, the Museum of the Belgian Congo in Tervuren continued to fulfil its dual function as 'window on' and 'showcase for' the Congo to the many visitors it received each year. The Catholic congregations organized 'mission expos' with objects and photos from the Congo to raise money for the missions. And finally, throughout the 1950s, monuments were inaugurated in honor of Leopold II and his associates all over the country: in Arlon (1951), Hasselt (1952), Ghent (1955), Forest/Vorst (1957), Mons (1958) and Namur (re-erected in 1958). Colonial tourism, too, which had originally been conceived as an instrument for colonial propaganda, gradually blossomed.

By repeatedly confronting the population with propaganda – in schools, cinemas or around monuments – the authorities wanted to bring home the message that Belgium, as lawful heir of the colonial genius Leopold II and present ruler of a colonial empire, could be proud of its excellent work in the Congo, where it had brought the 'primitive' indigenous population into contact with civilization. The same applies to the 1958 Brussels World Fair at the Heysel plateau which attracted millions of Belgian and international visitors. 'Expo 58' pulled out all the stops with an entire section devoted to Belgian 'accomplishments' in the Congo and Ruanda-Urundi (obviously in extremely positive terms), comprising seven large pavilions, an exotic garden and a so-called 'native village'. A bronze bust of Leopold II graced the entrance to the main pavilion, with, above it, a remark by the King sketching an extremely flattering image of himself: 'I have undertaken work in the Congo in the interest of civilization and for the wellbeing of Belgium'.

The question remains whether we can say with certainty what kind of effect this colonial propaganda had. Did this prolonged communication campaign really create a 'colonial consciousness' in Belgium? Often there is only indirect proof of propaganda's effectiveness. An opinion poll amongst Belgians from the 1950s showed that more than 80 per cent of those interviewed considered the Belgian presence in the Congo to be legitimate and that 83 per cent thought that colonialism benefitted the indigenous population. Had the Belgian colonial efforts been worth their while? 'Without a doubt, if you knew what the Congo looked like 75 years ago', 'Without Belgium the Congo would have been somewhere where diseases, superstition and tribal wars had free play', 'There are all kinds of positive effects: hygiene, less superstition, etc.!'[2] These responses suggest that Belgians had become proud of their colony, even though it is hard to assess to what degree propaganda played a fundamental role in the genesis of this 'imperialist consciousness'. What is clear, however, is that the Congolese never participated in the dissemination of these colonial views, and that the positive image pitched of the Congo led to a complete rehabilitation of

Leopold II, while the Congolese people were being infantilized and the Congo depicted as a 'backward' country. It goes without saying that this propaganda paints an extremely limited picture of the Congolese truth and that, a few exceptions aside, all negative aspects of Belgian colonial action were hushed up.

Conclusion

The fact that Congolese independence came as a shock in 1960 is illustrative of the prevailing mentality in Belgium: after a presence in Central Africa lasting more than fifty years and dozens of years of propaganda, it is likely that the Belgians had become used to the idea that their country was a colonial power. Yet it appears that the general public got over this trauma pretty quickly, which we believe points to the fact that colonial consciousness, although most definitely a part of the Belgian sense of identity, never became a deep-seated belief for the majority of the population. Except for a minority, the shock of the Congo's independence was short-lived; which does not alter the fact that, all in all, the memory of the colonial era would be treasured in a somewhat uncritical light.

Colonial propaganda, whether conducted in schools, cinemas, in Tervuren or by means of colonial monuments and exhibitions, constituted a fundamental part of Belgian colonial rule. This propaganda had important consequences in the middle and long term, especially with respect to the rehabilitation of Leopold II and the dissemination of racial stereotypes about African people. After Congolese independence, many Belgians for a long time continued to cherish positive memories of the colonial era. The tools that had contributed to this positive image (museums, books, photos, films, etc.), did not disappear with decolonization; and films, statements and testimonies eulogizing Belgian action in the Congo continued to circulate. Thus, the positive image of Leopold II, the explorers and the so-called civilizing mission lived on in history and geography lessons. Apart from a few rare exceptions, colonial monuments remained in place – signs of commemoration and silent witnesses of a 'heroic' time. For dozens of years, nothing changed at the Museum of the Belgian Congo in Tervuren, in 1960 renamed the Royal Museum for Central Africa and (again) the AfricaMuseum in 2018, although it did remain one of the country's most-visited museums. It is only recently that the memory of the colonial past – based to a large extent on colonialist propaganda – has become the topic of debate again, thanks to a new militancy among the growing Afro-Belgian population, several important anniversaries and generational change (see Chapter 28). Here we can argue that the recent attacks on public colonial monuments, just like the discussions about the long-awaited renovation of the AfricaMuseum, are each in their own way indicative of what colonial propaganda achieved, and of the difficult relationship Belgium continues to have with its history.

Bibliography

Not much literature exists about Belgian colonial propaganda or what we can refer to as Belgian 'colonial culture'. Three pioneering works merit mention here: Vints, Luc, *Kongo made in Belgium. Beeld van een kolonie in film en propaganda*, Kritak, Leuven, 1984; *Zaïre 1885-1985. Cent ans de regards belges*, Coopération Éducation Culture (CEC), Brussels, 1985; and Jacquemin, Jean-Pierre, ed., *Racisme, continent obscur. Clichés, stéréotypes et phantasmes à propos des noirs dans le Royaume de Belgique*, CEC, Brussels, 1991. The two following works are of vital significance: Viaene, Vincent, Ceuppens, Bambi, and Van Reybrouck, David, eds., *Congo in België: koloniale cultuur in de metropool*, Leuven University Press, Leuven, 2009; and Stanard, Matthew G., *Selling the Congo: A History of European Pro-Empire Propaganda and the Making of Belgian Imperialism*, University of Nebraska Press, Lincoln, 2011. A recent publication is M'Bokolo, Elikia, and Truddaïu, Julien, eds., *Notre Congo/Onze Kongo: La propagande coloniale belge dévoilée*, CEC, Brussels, 2018. On the historiography of Belgian 'colonial culture' and the memory of the colonial past: Stanard, Matthew G., 'Lumumba's Ghost: A Historiography of Belgian Colonial Culture', in Barczewski, Stephanie, and Farr, Martin, eds., *The MacKenzie Moment and Imperial History: Essays in Honour of John M. MacKenzie*, Palgrave, Basingstoke, 2019. In the field of colonial film, in addition to the many important publications by Guido Convents, the classic reference work remains Ramirez, Francis, and Rolot, Christian, *Histoire du cinéma colonial au Zaïre, au Rwanda et au Burundi*, Royal Museum for Central Africa, Tervuren, 1985. Only a few studies have examined how Belgian culture has dealt with decolonization in the long term, namely Buettner, Elizabeth, *Europe after Empire: Decolonization, Society, and Culture*, Cambridge University Press, Cambridge, 2016; Cornet, Anne, and Gillet, Florence, *Congo Belgique 1955-1965: Entre propagande et réalité*, CegeSoma/Renaissance du Livre, Brussels, 2010; and Stanard, Matthew G., *The Leopard, the Lion, and the Cock: Colonial Memories and Monuments in Belgium*, Leuven University Press, Leuven, 2019.

Notes

1 *Exposition universelle et internationale de Gand en 1913. Programme général. Appel aux producteurs. Règlement-Classification*, Brussels, 1911, p. 6.
2 Jacquemyns, Guillaume, 'Le Congo belge devant l'opinion publique', *Institut Universitaire d'Information Sociale et Économique (Insoc)*, 2 and 3, Brussels, 1956, p. 63-72.

25. Science

Belgian Colonialism's Accomplice?

Colonization of the Congo was preceded by science. In September 1876, before the foundation of the Congo Free State, Leopold II organized a 'geographic conference' to commence the scientific exploration of Central Africa. The conference decided to send expeditions to study the climate, soil conditions, natural resources and extent of the territory, and to investigate the local populations' level of 'civilization'. From the outset, scientific enterprises in the Congo had an applied character and formed part of the colonial project. Émile Banning, a senior member of Leopold II's staff, in his *L'Afrique et la conférence géographique de Bruxelles* (1876), described the scientific exploration as an *œuvre de civilization*, a work of civilization.

Did this mean that science was colonialism's accomplice? In the postcolonial era, some believe colonial rulers used science to further their cause. Information about the inhabitants and geographical, biological and physical features of the acquired territory had been necessary in order to govern the area adequately. This leads us into a classic discrepancy: while colonials such as Banning regarded science as an instrument of civilization, Congolese Professor and author Valentin Mudimbe called it a project of domestication and humiliation.[1] Depending on the viewpoint of the beholder – colonizer or former colonized – the notion of 'scientific colonization' acquired a different connotation. Let us examine first how the scientific exploration of Central Africa was conducted.

Pioneers (1885-1914)

Geography paved the way with the conference of 1876, but other disciplines soon followed, including ethnography, geology and botany. Lawyers too had great influence: they steered Leopold II through the establishment of international bodies and the legal legitimization of the Congo Free State, and later also set to work on the codification of indigenous law. Characteristically, the two Catholic University of Louvain/Leuven representatives at the 1876 geographic conference, Theodore Smolders and Joseph Van Biervliet, both belonged to the Law Faculty.

The nature of the colonial project gave science wide powers. The new colony was alien and untouched. It constituted a region that had yet to be mapped in all respects. Scientific motivations, legitimate or not, accompanied military and strategic campaigns sent out under the authority of Leopold II: cartography was wrested with violence, 'discovered' regions turned into colonial possessions, and geological missions, such as those by Jules Cornet in 1891-1893, laid the foundation for the exploitation of raw material in Katanga.

During the pioneering era, science leant heavily on colonization, and consequently on the missions (see Chapter 21). Together with soldiers and adventurers, the missionaries represented the most important 'non-indigenous' group in the young colony. In order to carry out their tasks, the missionaries had to engage in science and become familiar with the languages and customs of the population groups they wanted to convert. As a result, it was primarily the fathers and priests who presented themselves as scientists in colonial practice and who worked as ethnographers, documenting indigenous languages, compiling dictionaries, but also studying Congolese nature. Around the turn of the century, the Jesuit Justin Gillet planted a botanical garden in Kisantu, not far from Léopoldville. Premonstratensian brother Hymelinus Hutsebaut's mission post was in the equatorial rainforest and he acquired expertise as a fauna specialist, on elephants and okapis in particular. His extensive collection of bird species is now at the AfricaMuseum. Scheut missionary Leo Bittremieux found himself with the Yombe in 1907 and would describe their language and culture in various scholarly studies. The Mayombe objects he collected, including the well-known ritual Nkisi Nkondi figurines, ended up in the ethnographic collection of the Catholic University of Louvain/Leuven. Considering their expertise, it is no coincidence that missionaries almost entirely dominated the first edition of *La Revue Congolaise*, founded in 1910. The journal was overseen by a (secular, but Catholic) Professor: Edouard de Jonghe, who taught ethnology at Louvain/Leuven and was an important intermediary between the colonial administration, the missions and the academic world.

Typical for the scientific method of this period were the survey lists and instruction literature drawn up for missionaries or expedition leaders by salon ethnographers and anthropologists. This method had wafted over from sociology. In 1905, Cyrille Van Overbergh, Belgian sociology pioneer, had founded the *Bureau International d'Ethnographie*. This research bureau compiled a vast amount of data about the Congo using a *questionnaire ethnographique*, which was entered onto index cards and formed the basis of twelve descriptive volumes. De Jonghe, a participant in the project, was responsible for the volumes about the Bangala (1907), the Mayombe (1907) and the Mangbetu (1908) and, in 1908, published a *Guide pour la récolte des objets ethnographiques* ('Guide for the collection of ethnographic objects'). The 'data collection' assembled by the ethnographic bureau was transferred to the Museum of the Belgian Congo in Tervuren after the First World War.

Although the colonial sciences were still in their infancy, even before 1900 a process of differentiation took place. Infighting developed between ethnology, ethnography, anthropology and the racially orientated physical anthropology, which pitted De Jonghe's Louvain/Leuven School, the *Société d'Anthropologie de Bruxelles* founded in 1882, the Tervuren museum and the sociologists attached to the *Institut de Sociologie Solvay* in Brussels against each other. At the same time, all these experts shared the view that knowledge about the colonized peoples was a prerequisite for the success of the colonial project. *Nous devons coloniser scientifiquement* ('We must colonize scientifically'), was De Jonghe's motto who, as a senior official at the Ministry of Colonies, put his own words into practice. Negatively put: colonial science was focused on taming, suppressing and breaking the 'wild Congo', a practice which was presented as 'civilizing work'. Scientific knowledge production was at the service of the exercise of power and was executed by the white occupier, even though he needed help from Congolese assistants as guides, translators and knowledge gatherers.

Whereas early ethnography and anthropology were strongly influenced by colonial and racial ideology, other pioneering sciences had a pragmatic character. Widespread mortality amongst the white population of the Congo led to a breakthrough in tropical medicine. Although existing universities showed interest in this, it was decided to bundle knowledge into a new institute: the Institute of Tropical Medicine, located in Brussels when it was founded in 1906. Tropical agriculture on the other hand became a university discipline. The Louvain/Leuven institute in particular, led by Edmond Leplae, acquired a strong reputation. Like De Jonghe, Leplae was a senior civil servant, as well as a Professor. In 1911, he toured Katanga to study the feasibility of agricultural colonization in situ. The agricultural research focused on optimizing crop yields; policy concentrated on its efficiency. In 1917, as Director-General of the Ministry of Colonies, Leplae introduced the system of obligatory crops, which became a yoke for Congolese agriculture and, in practice, gave preference to export-oriented cotton production (see Chapters 9 and 11). Just like De Jonghe, Leplae combined both knowledge and power.

Exploration (1918-1945)

Before the First World War, few scientists went to the colony. They left the fieldwork to the missionaries and adventurers. Brussels botanist Émile de Wildeman, who had become the Director of the National Botanic Garden of Belgium, never set foot in the Congo, but became an expert on Congolese flora on the basis of specimens and herbaria that were sent to him. During the interwar years, this situation changed. The Congo became a more stable environment: more opened up, safer, less threatening and 'healthier'. Consequently, Belgian scientists now traveled in greater numbers to the colony themselves (which did not mean that scientist-missionaries disappeared). In the geological and biological disciplines in particular a culture of scientific missions developed to exploit the Belgian Congo's natural resources. Walter Robyns, Wildeman's successor at the National Botanical Garden, was sent out on botanical expeditions by the Minister of Colonies in 1925 and 1926. Linguistic fieldwork flourished too (see Chapter 20). Africa specialist Amaat Burssens, who would later teach in Ghent, conducted several missions, chiefly in Kasaï and Katanga, in order to study the Luba languages. He documented these study trips himself using diaries, linguistic notes, photos and early audio recordings. An example from the legal disciplines was Guy Malengreau from Louvain/Leuven, who, as *aspirant à titre colonial* ('colonial trainee'), traversed the colony in 1937-1938 for a year to document indigenous customs.

Malengreau carried out his research with funds from the National Fund for Scientific Research, set up in 1928. Institutionalization was indeed a second characteristic feature of colonial research during the interwar years. 'Colonial sciences' constituted a complex grouping of an entire array of scientific disciplines – varying from linguistics to oceanography – that had only one thing in common, namely testing whether and how they could be applied in the Belgian Congo. There was *colonial* law, *tropical* medicine and *African* linguistics, different disciplines that were only connected by their shared geographical context. Because universities were structured into study domains, colonial experts tended to meet in cross-discipline institutes, which thus grew into the places where 'colonial research' concentrated. Aside from the Museum of the Belgian Congo, which focused on both humanities and science, this included the Royal Belgian Colonial Institute (1928), the National Institute for the Agronomic Study of the Belgian Congo (INEAC, 1933) and the Institute for the National Parks in the Belgian Congo (1934).

The INEAC researchers focused on the improvement of rubber, palm oil and coffee cultivation, but also conducted basic research into botany, zoology and soil science (see Chapter 11). For this, they were able to make use of whole swathes of plantations, testing stations, farms and laboratories. INEAC's headquarters in Yangambi was the first scientific institute to build its own large-scale research infrastructure in the colony itself. A few medical (FOMULAC – Medical Foundation of the University of Louvain in the Congo) and agricultural (CADULAC – Agronomic Centers of the University of Louvain in the Congo) institutes had been set up, in Kisantu among other places, but these focused on education. The area around Coquilhatville in Équateur Province was also the home of the botanical gardens of Eala, which had been established by Émile Laurent in 1900. From the 1930s, the site was placed under the authority of INEAC. As a 'breeding ground' for indigenous flora, it was an important reservoir for colonial botany. Just as in the Albert National Park, created in 1925 and a reserve for the natural resources of the Eastern Congo (see Chapter 27), the colony's INEAC sites were well-equipped open-air laboratories for biologists, geologists and agronomists.

All these achievements occurred in a colonial ideology that did not differ all that greatly from that of the pioneering days. In 1923, at the opening of the Colonial University in Middelheim, King Albert called 'the activity of scientific research the proof of a sense of duty towards people we wish to civilize'.[2]

Big Science (1945-1960)

The 1950s can be counted amongst the heydays of the classic triumphal story about civilizing endeavors in the Belgian Congo. The colonial administration was generous with medical health care, education, infrastructure works resulting from the Ten-Year Plan, the successful *paysannats* system and the emergence of an indigenous, Congolese middle-class (see Chapters 11, 12, 13, 18, 22 and 23). On an academic front, knowledge production was on the increase and there was a process of professionalization. An important milestone was the foundation in 1954 of the first Congolese (Catholic) university of Lovanium near Léopoldville, which alongside higher education also developed a program of basic and applied research. In 1956, the inauguration of a second (and the first official) university followed in Élisabethville. In 1959, the first Congolese agricultural engineer graduated: Pierre Lebughe.

Despite the altered relations and scaling up of scientific research, old patterns continued unabated. The figure of missionary-scientist was one example. Jesuit Gaston van Bulck, for instance, published a linguistic map of the Belgian Congo in 1948. The old journal *La Revue Congolaise* had been transformed during the interwar years into *Congo* and in 1947 was rebranded *Zaïre*. 'In the main, it will continue to be a journal in the service of a wide-ranging popularization of science and study center', with contributions primarily about 'African cultural anthropology', the new editors wrote.[3] A further constant was the encyclopedic character of the colonial sciences. In 1947, De Jonghe proposed a plan within the Royal Belgian Colonial Institute to launch a new series of monographic survey studies, in the spirit of the *Bureau International d'Ethnographie* where he had started out in 1905. He described colonial scientific research as a *grande œuvre de civilisation* ('a great work of civilization'), in other words in exactly the same terms Bannings had used at the 1876 geographic conference.[4]

At the same time, new paths were taken. In 1947, Frans Olbrechts, trailblazer of the scientific study of African art, was appointed Director of the Museum of the Belgian Congo (see Chapter 26). A year later he also became the Director of the Humanities Department at the newly established Institute for Scientific Research in Central Africa (IRSAC). By organizing a *Congrès international des sciences anthropologiques et ethnologiques* in 1948, following on from earlier conferences in Louvain/Leuven (1934), Copenhagen (1938) and London (1945), Olbrechts updated classic, descriptive ethnography with international expertise. He sent some of his students – including Daniel Biebuyck, Luc de Heusch and Jan Vansina – to the School of Oriental and African Studies (SOAS) in London and trained them in conducting anthropological field work. The success of this first generation of professional anthropologists spelled the definitive end of the era of index cards and descriptive inventories.

IRSAC was founded to coordinate the multi-disciplinary research that was happening in the Belgian Congo. It had physics, biological science and humanities departments, but above all a modern research spirit. It was much less strongly steered by the government than INEAC and was much further removed from the traditional colonial environment than the Royal Belgian Colonial Institute. Still in the 1950s, the universities of Ghent (*Ganda-Congo*), Liège (FULREAC) and Brussels (CEMUBAC) set up research institutions in the colony. Because of this expansion and scaling up of research, the need for direction grew. In order to coordinate the 'big science' of the national scientific institutes, of the two Congolese universities and of the overseas satellite institutes, the Ministry of Colonies developed plans at the end of the 1950s to synchronize research even more and to shift the heart of research organization to the Congo.

In some academic circles, this awareness had manifested itself earlier. The editors of *Zaïre*, for instance, thought that scientific production should guarantee 'a better future for the 14 million Congolese people'. In progressive legal environments, white activism against the colonial project developed. In Katanga, this led to cooperation between the UMHK and a group of reformist jurists and sociologists. With financial support from the company, they set up the Study Center for Indigenous Social Problems (CEPSI), a research institute that not only wanted to study, but also improve the indigenous populace's socio-political situation. One of CEPSI's achievements was the foundation in 1952 of a psychotherapeutic center for consultancy and research for Congolese UMHK employees.

Another important institute was Lovanium University, where the first generation of Congolese students was educated. But this also went through an evolution. In the beginning, Western knowledge was reproduced – for the 1954 history exam students had to situate the Congress of Vienna and describe the significance of the industrial revolution – and not everyone was able to let go of the spirit of paternalism and patronization. A law faculty was not on the cards, for fear it would train up too articulate a generation of jurists. But spurred on by rector Luc Gillon, who wanted to make Lovanium a Congolese university, and figures such as Joseph Nicaise, historian Benoît Verhaegen and anthropologist Jan Vansina, the climate changed. Vansina, who upgraded Central Africa's oral tradition into historic source material, began to teach Congolese students their own heritage. Even before independence, a licentiate in African Philology was launched at the Faculty of Arts, while within Political and Social Sciences, a special master's program in Cultural Anthropology was introduced. Vansina was involved in both course units. The Faculty of Theology held a debate about the feasibility of an African theology and sent *vota* to the Second Vatican Council about 'adaption' and respect for indigenous religions. In Medicine likewise, reform of the medical curriculum took place in 1959, which meant that Congolese students were able to obtain a full diploma in Tropical Medicine. During that same year, the long-awaited Law Faculty opened. Meanwhile the best students from the first cohort were deployed as assistants in education and research.

This evolution was also visible in study themes. The first monograph in the series *Publications de l'Université de Lovanium* was dedicated to Plato, but this changed quickly. Innovative research was conducted in the *Institut de Recherches Économiques et Sociales* ('Institute for Economic and Social Research'), established in 1955, by economist and demographer Fernand Bézy. The work about Kinois youth culture by sociologist Paul Raymaekers took Congolese societal problems as a study object. Showcasing the campus more than anything else was the nuclear reactor which was commissioned in June 1959. This nuclear installation allowed the colony to produce radio isotopes themselves, which, in fact, were shared with researchers from IRSAC, INEAC and the university of Élisabethville. Following independence, the reactor was placed under the surveillance of UN peacekeeping forces.

Conclusion

Post-independence, the colonial science park was given a new name. The Royal Belgian Colonial Institute became the Royal Academy for Overseas Sciences, the Royal Museum of the Belgian Congo became the Royal Museum for Central Africa and after 1971 Lovanium University was incorporated into the *Université Nationale du Zaïre*. The former 'colonial' scientific team was left orphaned. In 1962-1963, the Academy published a three-part *White Paper*, 'from an upsurge of national spirit' and out of hurt pride.[5] The hefty volumes charted their scientific contribution to the development of Central Africa. These had been compiled with the express wish to show that – at least on a scientific front – the Belgian colonizers had taken their responsibilities seriously. Similarly, a directory of Lovanium University alumni (*Université Lovanium de Kinshasa. Annuaire des diplomés de l'Université, 1958-1968*), published in 1969, demonstrated the Congolese nation the efforts the university had put in since its foundation.

These publications reflected the typical mix of pride and bitterness which lingered in the academic world. Many scientists felt aggrieved because their work was seen belonging to a crushed system. This leads us back to the opening question: were the sciences accomplices of colonialism?

The close interconnectedness between the colonial administration and the academic/scientific apparatus – and between power and knowledge – seems to answer that question in the affirmative before it has even been asked. The colonizers believed indisputably in a 'scientific' colonization. On an archival level, it is still possible to discern the entanglement of scientific expeditions and colonial administration. Yet nuance is called for. After the Second World War, scientists gradually liberated themselves from the colonial agenda, even though the pursuit of value-free and independent science was still hampered by colonial practice. Sociologist Nicaise, who supported and supplied the Congolese emancipation movement with intellectual ammunition, also had a 'boy', for example. The fact that the colony and its inhabitants were primarily 'study objects', automatically led to a form of reduction.

This was later denounced by the Congolese. Valentin Mudimbe, who studied at Lovanium University during the 1960s and established himself as a Professor of Comparative Literature, called 'colonial science' a contradiction in terms. Research, after all, was conducted within a relationship of rulers and subjects. He did not hesitate to label the entire library of the Royal Belgian Colonial Institute a work of fabulists, and the colonial scientific apparatus an instrument of 'domestication'.

Bibliography

The basic study about scientific research in the Congo is still Poncelet, Marc, *L'invention des sciences coloniales belges*, Karthala, Paris, 2008. Specifically about the Louvain/Leuven colonial sciences, including Lovanium University, there is Mantels, Ruben, *Geleerd in de tropen. Leuven, Congo en de wetenschappen (1885-1960)*, Universitaire Pers Leuven, Leuven, 2007. People described in this include De Jonghe and Leplae, with a list of sources and a bibliography. About the colonial horizon (and for instance figures such as Jules Cornet and Amaat Burssens) of Ghent University, much material has been collected on www.ugentmemorie.be. The early history of the Tervuren museum, with an extensive scientific-historical discussion about colonial anthropology, is presented in Couttenier, Maarten, *Congo tentoongesteld. Een geschiedenis van de Belgische antropologie en het museum van Tervuren*, Acco, Leuven, 2005. Additionally, Petridis, Constantijn, ed., *Frans M. Olbrechts. 1899-1958. Op zoek naar kunst in Afrika*, Ethnographic Museum, Antwerp, 2001, contains some valuable testimonies and contributions about the emergence of modern anthropology in the context of IRSAC. The KADOC exhibition catalogue *Eenige bijzonderheden: missie en wetenschap*, Leuven, 2006 covers the relationship between mission and science.

Rubbers, Benjamin, and Poncelet, Marc, 'Sociologie coloniale au Congo belge. Les études sur le Katanga industriel et urbain à la veille de l'Indépendance', *Genèses*, 99, 2015, 2, p. 93-112, discusses the CEPSI.

Notes

1 Mudimbe, Valentin, 'La culture', in Vanderlinden, Jacques, ed., *Du Congo au Zaïre 1960-1980. Essai de bilan*, Brussels, 1980, p. 309-390.
2 *Middelheim. Gedenkboek van het Universitair Instituut voor de Overzeese Gebieden*, Antwerp, 1987, p. 112.
3 'Aan onze lezers', *Zaïre*, 1, 1947, p. 5-6.
4 De Jonghe, Edouard, 'Plan d'exploration ethnographique et ethnologique du Congo Belge', *Bulletin de l'Institut Royal Colonial Belge*, 18, 1947, p. 13.
5 *Witboek. Wetenschappelijke bijdrage van België tot de ontwikkeling van Centraal-Afrika*, Brussels, 1962-1963.

SARAH VAN BEURDEN

26. Did the Belgian Colonizer Create, Destroy or Steal Congolese Art?

The debate around the decolonization of colonial collections and the restitution of African art is in the limelight again in Europe. In Belgium, it partly flared up because of the renovation and reopening of the AfricaMuseum in Tervuren. Advocates of a restitution of the colonial collections point to the historical injustice. Africans have too little access to their own patrimony, which was frequently taken from them illegitimately and is now kept in Europe. They link this to the underlying moral question of how Belgium deals with its colonial past. Opponents of restitution argue that these collections cannot be considered illegal and that it is in the interest of all humanity that objects are preserved in proper scientific and conservational conditions (which they believe is not the case on the African continent).

This debate around restitution is by no means new. Even in the run-up to independence, Congolese political leaders asked questions about the Tervuren museum's collections, and these questions were repeated during the 1960s and 1970s with increasing urgency. Between 1976 and 1982, a series of objects was in fact transferred from Tervuren to the Congo.

This chapter discusses the debate from a historical perspective. How did the contested objects leave the Congo during the colonial period? How did they find a place in museums and how were they interpreted? What role did they play in colonial politics? And finally: how has the restitution question been evaluated historically?

The Deceptive Neutrality of 'Collecting'

Already in the early modern era, Europeans were interested in the material cultures of Central Africa. Most objects only reached Belgium from the end of the nineteenth century onwards, however. Their trajectories are closely intertwined with the colonial project. The term 'collecting' has a deceptive neutrality and in reality comprises widely varying practices which were strongly intertwined with the violent and forced character of colonization in Central

Africa. Cultural objects, in addition to flora and fauna specimens, and even human remains, were taken home by soldiers, traders, missionaries, colonial officials, scientists and later also by tourists. At times they did this on their own initiative, at others on behalf of private individuals or scientific institutes (especially in Europe and North America). The motivations likewise were extremely diverse and could be personal, military, professional, political, economic, but also religious.

One of the first groups to collect objects were the soldiers and other representatives of Leopold II and the Congo Free State. They brought objects to Belgium both independently and at the request of Leopold II. These could be spoils of war, but also purchases, objects of exchange or 'gifts'. The items were given various denotations: from trophies and souvenirs to research objects and propaganda material for colonial exhibitions and museums.

Missionaries too showed an early interest in local ceremonial and religious objects (see Chapter 21). Some destroyed these because they symbolized the Congolese people's so-called barbarism and 'superstition'. Others began to collect them in order to understand local cultures better and to use this information in the conversion process, for example. Another group removed objects under duress; yet others returned particular objects with the agreement or cooperation of Congolese communities; and in later phases, after having been christened, local communities even rejected certain objects and took them to the mission posts themselves. All this resulted in large mission collections, which were either exhibited locally (for example in the Scheut Fathers' 'Fetish' Museum in Kangu), or ended up with the congregations in Europe and in the many mission exhibitions in Belgium, and were used to attract attention and funds for mission work. Increasingly greater numbers of missionaries cultivated a scientific interest in local cultures, which led to more focused and better-informed collecting.

Just like the colonial officials and missionaries, scientists were a heterogeneous group (see Chapter 25). The earliest scientific collecting missions were closely bound up with military conquest campaigns. Other scientists were involved in economic exploitations, such as the Hungarian ethnographer Emil Torday, who worked for the *Compagnie du Kasaï*. The Museum of the (Belgian) Congo, founded in 1898, was also active, even though ethnographic expeditions remained extremely rare. Joseph Maes, for instance, head of the museum's ethnographic department between 1910 and 1946, went to the Congo only once. Commercial art dealers initially limited their activities primarily to Europe and North America. They tended to work with African middlemen or traded objects which were already in Europe. Only from the late colonial era onwards did some art traders travel to Central Africa to amass 'merchandise'.

The legality of most 'transactions' is generally not easily established. Quite a few objects were simply bought, but here too there are many questions, partly because of the lack of clarity about the legal regime in which these exchanges took place, the hazy context and, obviously, the prices at which they were purchased. A legal framework was only introduced when, in 1936, for the first time, guidelines were issued for the protection of indigenous Congolese art. This meant that colonial officials could grant sites or objects the status of protected monument. These laws were never implemented, however. What is more, no consensus exists over the question of whether international rules around warfare apply to the era of colonial conquest. Clear international agreements around cultural heritage and trade only came about after the Second World War (for example the 1970 UNESCO Convention on the Means of Prohibiting and Preventing the Illicit Import, Export and Transfer of Ownership of Cultural Property). These were explicitly not retroactive, however; in other words, they could not be applied to the European colonial past.

What was collected depended on who collected it, although it is once again difficult to generalize. Missionaries were usually interested in objects from the religious and spiritual sphere. Soldiers were drawn to weapons and trophies. The most spectacular or 'intriguing' sculptural objects were much sought after by art collectors. This somewhat haphazard form of 'collecting' was decisive for the distorted view of Congolese cultures in Europe and North America. Most collectors were invariably less concerned with objects made by women, usually ceramics or textiles.

The growth in administration and enterprises led to an increase in the number of colonial employees: officials, servants, engineers, doctors, and so on, and of course their families, as well as the number of tourists. This in turn created a growing market in all kinds of souvenir objects, which were made specifically for outsiders. Examples that spring to mind are numerous ivory objects (such as small elephants, decorated tusks, figurines), paintings with rural scenes, masks with newly invented designs, and so on. Several mission posts derived income from the sale of such objects, which were often made by their pupils. The local economy also responded to the demand for 'authentic' art: objects showing no influence from European cultures and purporting to be intended for local use. At least part of current collections in Europe and the US was made purely to be sold to foreigners. Some artists worked for the local market as well as for the Europeans, which shows that 'authenticity' is an unstable notion.

Generally, we know rather little about the specific circumstances under which objects were removed from the Congo. In exceptional cases, this information is available. Émile Storms, Oscar Michaux and Alexandre Delcommune noted their war booty in diaries and reports. Even during later so-called scientific expeditions, those taking part focused more on hurriedly gathering material (believing that artistic traditions were dying out) than its careful documentation. Because of inadequate and biased information in colonial archives, we also know little about the role of the Africans themselves, for example the guides, translators and converts in mission posts who took care of contact with the surrounding communities and thus supplied essential expertise and networks. These Africans were embedded in a complex and subdivided power structure, and this makes forming a judgment about the nature of the acquisitions process rather difficult. Despite the collectors' diverse motivations and the growing trade in objects by the Congolese themselves, it cannot be denied that these transfers took place in politically, socially and economically unequal circumstances, not only within colonialism as a system, but also regarding interpersonal relations. How exactly this inequality played a part is not always clear, but that it did so is a fact, and this is often used as a moral argument by proponents of the restitution of African objects.

Congolese Art in the Promotion of the Colony

Many collected objects somehow or other found their way to colonial museums such as the one in Tervuren. The museums had to promote the colonial initiatives amongst a wider population and convince the public that colonization was a valuable and economically profitable civilizing project (see Chapter 24). The collected objects not only served as exhibition or propaganda material but were also an important source of information about Congolese cultures. This was problematic, because many collections had come about randomly and without contextual background. Moreover, the first generations of scientists rarely went to the Congo themselves. The museums tried to fill these gaps by commissioning focused collection trips or by sending ethnographic questionnaires to colonial officials and missionaries (see Chapter 25). This resulted in knowledge that was disconnected from reality. In particular the tendency to arrange population groups and cultures in a – plainly racist – classification passed over the complex reality. Yet these approaches and views became dominant, not only among the wider public, but also within education at the Colonial University of Belgium.

Some artistic traditions, such as that of the Kuba in Kasaï, were regarded as 'art' by the Europeans since the beginning of the colonial era. Influenced by European artists such as Picasso and Matisse, who found inspiration in African objects, a broader appreciation developed. This in turn increased the art trade's interest in African objects and led to objects being presented and labelled differently in museums. During the 1950s, a modernized gallery for the display of African art was set up in Tervuren by Director Frans Olbrechts. His academic work played a trailblazing role in the global development of an art-historical approach to African art. The focus in the new gallery was on the aesthetic qualities of individual objects and the stylistic features of particular style groups. Like his predecessors, Olbrechts himself did not frequent Africa and only visited the Congo once. His approach was motivated by the conviction that all interesting cultural expressions had taken place in the past and that the colonizer should help to protect and appreciate its heritage.

These classifications and definitions did not necessarily take into account the way in which the objects were regarded in their original cultures. Although the Congolese had an aesthetic appreciation for countless objects, they had not generally created them with this intention, but rather had assigned them a religious, political or simply utilitarian function. Certain categories of objects are still being used, while others have fallen into disuse, even though they continue to dominate the image of African societies. Whereas these cultures were seen as static units with little mutual or global contact, in reality they were extremely dynamic and characterized by the circulation of objects and techniques. This contradicts the image of a static, immutable 'essence' of a particular culture, as museum displays and academic knowledge tend to suggest.

Cultural Policy as Colonization Policy

The growing interest in Congolese art for its part influenced the way in which the colonial system was justified. Contemporary Congolese cultures and societies were portrayed as if they were in decline and in need of protection. Collecting had long been associated with 'salvage anthropology' (the rescuing of the remnants of cultures which were threatened with extinction), but from the 1930s this also manifested itself in the field of policy. A few organizations were set up to stimulate cultural policy and give it more concrete shape, including the Commission for the Protection of Indigenous

Arts and Crafts (COPAMI) in 1935, linked to the colonial administration in Brussels, and the Friends of Indigenous Art (AAI), an association in the Congo itself. The COPAMI tried to organize the market and production of artisan art, so that the latter would remain 'authentic'. It set up workshops supervised by colonial officials who had to safeguard the quality and authenticity of the objects made. The AAI was more involved in setting up and managing museums in the Congo itself, where colonials could become acquainted with Congolese cultures and Congolese people could 'learn to appreciate' their 'ancestral' art. Thus, in 1936, the *Musée de la Vie Indigène* ('Museum of Indigenous Life') was established in Léopoldville; similar initiatives were taken in Élisabethville, Coquilhatville, Boma and Stanleyville. The growing political significance and implications of possessing and 'protecting' Congolese art obviously did not escape the Congolese people's attention. Local leaders – including the Kuba King and *Mwant Yav* of the Lunda – tried to set up local museums, which would be under their control.

The COPAMI and the AAI hoped that such a well-fleshed out cultural policy would check the 'wild growth' in the Congolese society's 'modernization'. Their activities were thus in essence extremely conservative. They regarded the preservation of 'traditional' power structures (that it is to say, under colonial supervision) and the rural cultures as an 'antidote' to the alleged growing politicization of the Congolese urban population and to the emerging independence movements in other colonies (see Chapters 5 and 18). In this way, the 'protection' of Congolese art justified the continuance of colonialism.

Decolonization and Restitution

Congolese individuals not only protested against colonialism but also against the presence of collections in Belgium. In as early as the 1950s, the Tervuren museum staff picked up dissatisfaction from visiting Congolese and Rwandan notables and students. Just as these visitors wanted to manage their country's economic resources themselves, they also demanded that they take possession again of the museum's collections. Following the colonial example, a link was made between the protection of a cultural patrimony and political legitimacy. The request for restitution received a great deal of publicity in Congolese and Belgian circles, but in the end did not feature in the 1960 roundtable discussions in preparation for independence (see Chapter 5). It kept cropping up in the political discourse, however. An exhibition in 1967, *Art of the Congo*, based on the Tervuren collections and shown in several museums in North America, caused considerable resentment in President Mobutu's regime. It showed that Belgium was still capable of representing the Congo internationally and that the former colonizer was simply continuing its role as protector of Congolese art.

Belgium did indeed hang on to the image of the Congo as an immature state incapable of protecting its own patrimony. According to Lucien Cahen, Tervuren museum's Director between 1958 and 1977, restitution was out of the question. Firstly, he pointed to the absence of Congolese legislation to protect the art, obviously passing over the fact that the (former) colonial state itself had failed to do exactly that. Secondly, he regretted that colonial museum infrastructure had suffered badly under the political and military chaos of the 1960s. Thirdly, Cahen asserted that the Tervuren collections had been acquired legally through purchases, donations or scientific expeditions. The Director's argumentation was based on a literal interpretation of the collection's history: it is true that many of the now controversial objects had not been removed from the Congo by the museum *itself*. Fourthly, Cahen pointed to the scientific value of the collections as a whole. According to his reasoning, it was of universal importance that the objects were held for safekeeping in Belgium. This last argument did not take into account the random way in which these collections had been assembled.

Partly to evade the question of restitution, Cahen offered Mobutu an interesting option. A Congolese team could work together with the Belgian museum to create a new museum infrastructure in the Congo. This offer led to the establishment of the *Institut des Musées Nationaux du Congo* ('Institute for National Museums in the Congo') between 1969 and 1971. Cahen became the Director of both museums, and a start was made with building a new collection in the Congo. The initiative dovetailed well with Mobutu's general culture policy, with its emphasis on the value of pre-colonial cultures (*recours à l'authenticité*), even though dissatisfaction arose fairly swiftly about the Belgians' dominant position in the museum institute.

The demand for restitution did not disappear, however. In his famous 1973 speech to the UN, Mobutu condemned the 'systemic plunderings' of African heritage by the colonizers. He no longer aimed his message at his national audience alone, he wanted to acquire international visibility for his restitution campaign. He only had limited success when Zaïre renounced the term 'restitution' and reconciled itself with a 'gift' of objects, Belgium's preferred option. This was more than a difference in nuance. While 'restitution' implies the correcting of a mistake from the past, 'gift' emphasizes the generosity and lack of obligations on the part of the donor. This change in attitude by the Zaireans led to the return of 114 objects from depots of the Tervuren museum to the museum institute in Kinshasa. Although this was an extremely modest consignment compared to Tervuren's complete collection (comprising some 125,000 objects), it was presented by both Belgium and Zaïre as a victory. Zaïre used the transfer to underline Mobutu's influence internationally, while Belgium could award itself the image of benevolent ex-colonizer. The Belgian Government failed to transfer the objects' titles of ownership to Zaire. When a number of the 114 objects surfaced on the international art market in the 1990s in the wake of the unrest and plunderings in Kinshasa, the Royal Museum for Central Africa was able to claim these back again. Some are now in Tervuren once more.

Conclusion

In order to keep Congolese art in European or North American museums, the seemingly neutral term 'protection' is still used today. Yet this notion carries traces of a colonial attitude towards the Congolese. The collections were put together in an arbitrary way and in opaque circumstances, and were given new interpretations in Europe. Academic knowledge and museological representations were marked by the ideology of colonialism. Many European ethnographic museums with 'non-Western' collections are in crisis today, precisely because their institutional and ideological origin is so deeply bound up with colonialism. The restitution debate is just one of the aspects of this crisis, which also includes the need for a reevaluation of exhibition policies, for example.

The arguments for and against in the restitution debate however have changed little over the years. One element is new: the growing public attention for the theme, both in Europe and North America and in Africa. This attention, driven by African diaspora activism and Black Lives Matter protests across the world has in recent years had a tangible impact in the form of policy, legal, academic, and other initiatives around African art restitution. In the case of Belgium, in July 2022 the Government approved a law for the restitution of objects from federally held colonial collections from the Congo (which in practice concerns mostly the collections of the AfricaMuseum) that were either wrongfully obtained or are specifically requested for restitution. Much debate remains, however, about what exactly 'wrongfully obtained' means. For some, this applies to all objects removed during the colonial era, while others believe this should only apply to those removed with physical violence, for example. Provenance research that establishes how objects were removed thus becomes increasingly important. In addition to the law, the Government also provided the AfricaMuseum in Tervuren with a 2.3 million euro budget for research on the provenance of its collections. While such research is an important avenue to learn more about the history of colonialism, it also comes with a serious set of limitations. It is extremely time-consuming and the outcome is not guaranteed. The nature of colonial archives is such that unless there are local memories about the removal of objects, there might not be much information available. In other words, colonialism continues to impact the ways we deal with the past today. In conclusion, even though these recent initiatives represent significant change, many obstacles remain and no real restitutions have taken place so far.

Bibliography

Interesting primary sources for colonial views on Congolese art are the journal *Brousse*, published by the AAI in the Belgian Congo, as well as the extensive oeuvre by COPAMI member Gaston-Denys Périer. Several publications offer critical reflection about the history of the collection of the Tervuren museum, including: Couttenier, Maarten, *Congo tentoongesteld. Een geschiedenis van de Belgische antropologie en het museum van Tervuren (1882-1925)*, Acco, Leuven, 2005; Couttenier, Maarten, 'EO.0.07943', *BMGN – Low Countries Historical Review*, 133, 2018, 2, p. 91-104; Wastiau, Boris, *Congo-Tervuren, Aller-Retour*, KMMA, Tervuren, 2001; Wastiau, Boris, *Exit Congo Museum*, KMMA, Tervuren, 2000; Ceyssens, Rik, *De Luulu à Tervuren. La Collection Michaux au Musée royal de l'Afrique centrale*, KMMA, Tervuren, 2011; Van Beurden, Sarah, *Authentically African: Arts and the Transnational Politics of Congolese Culture*, Ohio University Press, Athens, 2015. For further information about Frans Olbrechts, see Petridis, Constantijn, ed., *Frans M. Olbrechts, 1899-1958. Op zoek naar kunst in Afrika*, Ethnographic Museum, Antwerp, 2001. To learn more about the trajectory and re-interpretations of African art in general, see: Coombes, Annie, *Reinventing Africa: Museums, Material Culture and Popular Imagination in Late Victorian and Edwardian England*, Yale University Press, New Haven, 1997; and Price, Sally, *Primitive Art in Civilized Places*, University of Chicago Press, Chicago, 1989. On the subject of collecting in the Congo, see Schilkrout, Enid, and Keim, Curtis A., eds., *The Scramble for African Art in Central Africa*, Cambridge University Press, Cambridge, 1998.

For more philosophical reflections on the re-invention of Africa through its art, see: Appiah, Anthony, *In My Father's House: Africa in the Philosophy of Culture*, Oxford University Press, New York, 1992; Mudimbe, Valentin, *The Invention of Africa: Gnosis, Philosophy and the Order of Knowledge*, Indiana University Press, Bloomington, 1988; and Mudimbe, Valentin, *The Idea of Africa*, Indiana University Press, Bloomington, 1994.

VIOLETTE POUILLARD

27. Animals and the Environment in the Congo

Was Nature Conservation the Same as Nature Protection?

The DR Congo's environment is often in the news. Newspaper articles report pollution, animal species such as gorillas and okapis under threat, or the uncertain fate of the national parks, for example Virunga and Kahuzi-Biega, both in the east of the country. These parks formed the stage of bloody conflicts between various groups of actors: militias in a region marked by the Rwandan genocide and civil wars, armed park guards occasionally working together with the army – which says a great deal about the militarization of environmental policies –, NGO workers, poachers, rural people who are kept out of the protected areas, and the animals themselves.

In order to better understand these conflicts, we must place them in a wider context. Struggles for access to the Congo's environmental resources and the development of its environmental policy reflect patterns of asymmetrical power relations which partly originate from the colonial era. Both Virunga National Park, created in 1925, and Kahuzi-Biega National Park, which was established after independence, in 1970, have their roots in the period of Belgian rule. The same goes for the belief that gorillas should be protected.

How did Leopoldian and later Belgian colonial authorities appropriate the Congo's environmental resources and how did they manage them? What were the social and ecological consequences? What were the reactions to the real or assumed depletion of these resources perpetrated by both colonials and colonized people? What were the challenges of colonial environmental protection in the Congo, or to put it more simply, what was protected and in which ways? And, as part of broader historiographical issues, should environmental management in the Congo be interpreted in terms of an opposition between colonizing and colonized actors?

The Leopoldian and later Belgian Congo was characterized by a large-scale appropriation of natural resources and at the same time, by the development of an extensive nature conservation policy. The latter came about through historical as well as ecological reasons, such as the high biodiversity and the presence of animal species, for example elephants, okapis or gorillas, which fed colonial mythology.

Because of the centralized nature of Leopoldian and later Belgian rule, natural resources could be cultivated in a systematic way and, to both temper and perpetuate this drain, an arsenal of measures were introduced to 'rationalize' and 'protect' these natural resources.

Environmental Violence

Colonial propaganda about nature conservation, and in particular about the national parks, imprinted on the collective memory an image of wild, unspoiled and pre- or a-historical Congolese landscapes. Environmental historians have shown that this image is false: a landscape takes shape as a result of what lives there, whether animals or people, and nature and culture are therefore inextricably linked. The African 'Eden' is a myth, therefore, as is the literary figure of the 'noble savage'. Landscapes in pre-colonial Central Africa were shaped by highly regionally-diversified activities encompassing the gathering of natural products, hunting, fishing, and agriculture, and by the associated labor and commercial networks. From the Middle Ages onwards, more and more ivory was transported via transcontinental trade routes and, with the expansion of empires, these routes acquired a global character. Rulers such as Tippu Tip and M'siri had developed large-scale ivory extraction and export networks by relying on forced labor and slavery when the Europeans began to colonize Central Africa at the end of the nineteenth century.

The development of ivory exploitation in the Congo of Leopold II drew upon the already eroded social fabric and ecological disruptions caused by pre-colonization ivory collection. The Belgian colonizers reorganized the existing ivory networks to their own advantage and orientated these to the West. They used the fight against the Afro-Arabic slave traders controlling the ivory trade as an excuse to justify morally the conquest of the Congo, although they themselves used a plethora of forced labor to exploit the Congo's natural resources (see Chapter 2). All this led to large numbers of elephants being killed. Patricia Van Schuylenbergh, a specialist in the environmental history of the Congo, estimates that during the Congo Free State era around 10 to 14,000 elephants a year were killed for the official trade.[1]

The economy of the Congo Free State ran on the ruthless exploitation of two export products: ivory and rubber. The latter was tapped off trees and liana and was used as a raw material by the bicycle and car tire industry. The extreme violence perpetrated against the population during forced rubber extraction provoked an international campaign of protest (see Chapter 2). The elephant hunt had the benefit of generating enormous quantities of meat, which formed a protein supplement for militaries, officials and local workers. This hunt could be more easily justified than rubber extraction on a moral level, especially because hunting licenses were sold to Western companies and hunters, who found new hunting grounds in Central Africa after elephants had been practically rendered extinct by colonial hunting practices in South Africa in the late nineteenth century.

The colonial regime soon began to exploit the Congolese soil, the extraction of copper in Katanga from 1907 being one example. This mining industry caused air, soil and water pollution, the destruction of animals and vegetation, afforestation, adverse effects on human health, and it introduced drastic changes to the landscape, which were discernible far into the hinterland. In order to meet the food requirements of the mine workers, hunting, fisheries, and livestock and arable farming intensified. Trees were cut down, watercourses rerouted, hydro-electric power stations built, and transport infrastructure constructed for the production and transport of raw materials and goods. Because the industrial centers needed large numbers of workers, rural areas emptied. This affected the countryside and created overpopulation and epidemics (such as dysentery and enteritis) in the cities and mining centers, which were primarily related to poor water supplies and waste disposal.

The colonizers were aware of the significant social and environmental impact of their policies and they knew that all-out exploitation of natural resources was not sustainable. Rubber production, based on forced labor, dropped steeply as a result of international criticism, but also because the raw material was becoming exhausted and had to be extracted ever deeper in the forest. In 1917, the colonial authorities introduced a system of forced cultivation which also had major social-environmental effects (see Chapter 11). Compulsory cotton production by the Congolese, for instance, was bought by big concession companies that reduced the economic risk of the crop by keeping labor costs as low as possible, leading to wretched living conditions for the Congolese producers (see Chapters 8 and 9). The fact that the colony focused so strongly on monocultures for export, also entailed ecological risks (plant diseases, erosion), put a brake on food crop cultivation and caused food shortages. The extraction activities and intensive production were gradually slotted into policies of 'economic opening up' (*mise en valeur*), 'development' and 'protection', which were intended to facilitate a long-lasting, profitable, and morally justifiable exploitation of Congolese resources.

In the wake of the 1930s crisis and in particular after the Second World War, agricultural reforms were introduced, which were notably aimed at upscaling the *paysannats* (see Chapter 11). The deployment of mechanical, technical and agronomic aids, such as improvements to plant breeding and the use of chemical fertilizers and pesticides, were all tried and tested methods from the 'second agricultural revolution' that had brought about huge rises in production in Europe, but once again entailed social and ecological costs.

Managing and Conserving Resources

The exploitation of raw materials went hand in hand with wildlife management and 'protection' measures. The latter bear testimony to both the scale of the reforms initiated, and the development of the resource exploitation that they permitted. Wildlife protection initially took shape as part of an international movement. Alarmed at the situation of elephants in South Africa, the European countries with colonies in Sub-Saharan Africa met in London in 1900 to agree on measures to put a stop to the depletion of elephants. They signed an international convention which also applied to other animals in the wild. The treaty was not ratified, but the majority of colonial powers cast its principles into law. Leopold II, for instance, issued a decree to protect wild animals as early as 1901. This was the beginning of an entire series of legal texts creating a framework within which two main thrusts could be distinguished that still form the spearheads of environmental policy today: the protection of species (gorillas, for instance) and the protection of areas (such as national parks).

In terms of species protection, animal species considered useful or threatened should be managed 'rationally', not unlike the commercial approach to managing capital, that is to say by generating profit without eroding value. 'Harmful' animal species, such as lions and leopards, on the other hand, could be killed without demur. A few minor adjustments were made in a new international convention signed in London in 1933, and the system on the whole was maintained during the colonial era. The legal protection framework sought to regulate African hunting practices. Among several restrictions, Congolese hunters now had to apply for a hunting license, were no longer allowed to hunt protected species, and saw their usual hunting techniques such as setting traps and snares and netting becoming illegal. Any appropriation that took place outside the legal framework was reframed as 'poaching'. However, special licenses issued for subsistence purposes slightly tempered this exclusion of African rural populations from the hunt.[2] Here too the colonizer's monopoly was given a moral justification. African traps were depicted as 'cruel', even though they were regularly used or tolerated by colonizers, and even though animals were also injured by firearms – many mammals had to live with bullets still lodged in their bodies.

At the same time, the colonial authorities encouraged uses it *did* consider legitimate. They derived income from hunting licenses and duty on the export of animals (or animal parts) and from the possession and sale of firearms and ammunition. Because legislation was reputed to be more liberal in the Congo than in the surrounding colonies, during the interbellum, it was a sought-after hunting ground for Western devotees of big game hunting. Throughout the entire colonial era, even the most protected animal species such as gorillas or okapis were sometimes also hunted in the name of science. Legal exceptions were made for hunters who supplied Belgian or foreign research institutes, museums and zoos. These animals were used, dead or alive, as diplomatic and propaganda tools to enhance the image of the colony, which had been tarnished by the Leopoldian regime's acts of violence, and to publicize the colonial program of wildlife management and protection.

Nature in Reserve

At the heart of the colonial protection policy lay the nature reserves, with different legal status. The colonial authorities set them up first of all to retain control over natural resources and create a reservoir of animal and plant resources in order to utilize these better. Thus, the development of the nature reserves was also underpinned by a utilitarian vision, which has been defined as 'conservation' by historians: an important branch in the protection of nature arguing for 'a rational management of natural resources, which have to be conserved in order to exploit them better'.[3] From the interwar years, the Belgian authorities took a tougher line in the creation of reserves. In 1925, they established Africa's first national park as a result of an international campaign to protect the mountain gorilla supported by King Albert I, after whom the park was named – Albert National Park, now called Virunga National Park.

Thousands of Congolese people lived in the Albert National Park, and several population groups from the surrounding area used it seasonally. Apart from a few exceptions, these users were banned from hunting, fishing, gathering, cultivating crops and grazing livestock in the park. The inhabitants of the domain were evicted, theoretically in exchange for monetary and land compensation. Just a few groups deemed sufficiently 'traditional', such as the Twa or 'Pygmies', were allowed to stay within the park boundaries under strict conditions, since they were regarded as potential study objects for anthropological research. The park became a scientific open-air laboratory for Belgian and international researchers, mainly devoted to biological research.

The exclusion of rural populations was a recurring feature in the other national parks – which were established in the Belgian Congo in the wake of the 1933 London convention – and led to conflicts which continue to play out to this day. Moreover, the creation of reserves also involved environmental effects which were bound up with the social inequality they caused. The setting aside of reserves does not conflict with the further exploitation of natural resources: such policies, by declaring tightly demarcated parts of the territory as protected domain, implicitly validated the belief that everything that fell outside their borders was available for (increasingly intensive) exploitation. Furthermore, the parks did not exclude all people. Thousands of park workers, scientists and tourists were allowed to enter and utilize them for both scientific and touristic purposes, which also involved the development of different forms of infrastructure. Scientific missions collected animals and plants en masse in the parks for inventories and biological or ecological research, and the touristic exploitation of the parks led to territorial and behavioral changes in the animals.

Discipline, Collaboration, and Resistance

The politics of exploitation, 'development' and conservation of natural resources restricted precolonial uses and led to significant changes in land use as well as to the development of new, colonial, uses, even in the most protected nature reserves. Should we therefore address the colonial environmental policy as an expression of the socio-economic inequities resulting from the colonizer/colonized dichotomy?

The heaviest burden of extractive activities (such as rubber harvesting) and the intensive cultivation of export crops (such as cotton) landed on the shoulders of Congolese workers, who were bowed down under the heavy workload. In contrast, rather lax environmental policies resulted in colonizers and colonized instrumentalizing each other in order to regain, keep hold of or increase access to the natural resources. Many colonial actors relied on Congolese hunters to hunt for scientific, commercial or food purposes, because they themselves had insufficient knowledge of the behavior of the animals and had insufficient manpower at their disposal. If many Congolese workers were forced or encouraged to assist, others saw collaboration as a way to reconquer the exercising of rights that had been taken away from them, or to obtain new access to environmental resources.

The colonial authorities, for their part, were not able to realize the monopoly over the hunting grounds they aspired to in part because staffing levels were too low for exercising on-site control in order to enforce the law. This powerlessness encouraged systemic resistance by Congolese rural populations, who secretly hunted protected game or ignored the boundaries of the reserves. After the Second World War, resistance became more open. Just as in other colonies, the resentment associated with the unfair distribution of the Congo's natural resources formed an important ingredient in the claims for independence. During the 1950s, the national parks' infrastructure, personnel and animals were repeatedly besieged.

Protest against the production-oriented exploitation of the living environment rarely featured and was usually shrugged off. Yet some instances can be found. When, in 1948, the Belgian colonial authority set up an expedition to the east of the Congo to catch young gorillas for Western zoos, the expedition leader noted that it was extremely difficult to find the animals, because the local population 'withheld the truth',[4] which seems to point to isolated resistance. On the European side, in 1900, the French jurist Paul Fauchille published an article about the London convention in the propagandist journal *Le Mouvement Géographique* criticizing conservationists' violence which was wrecking humans and animals alike: 'Animals have not yet succeeded in getting humans to understand that they too have a right to live. […] Human interests are not only placed above those of the animal, the interests are also those of white Europeans.'[5] These rare critical noises had little effect on policy. Although colonial policy imposed restrictions on African environmental uses, it was not able to prevent many of these from continuing unabated. Meanwhile new, more intensive, exploitation methods were rolled out rapidly. Towards the end of the colonial era, a broad consensus prevailed in colonial circles about the deteriorating situation of Congolese wildlife resources.

Conclusion

The policy measures which were taken on behalf of the 'rationalization' of exploitation and conservation of nature were generally not successful in protecting the environment, not only because the law was not applied, but also because the law itself sanctioned and encouraged this exploitation. The essence of the most preservationist policies, namely the protection of species and the national parks, shows that the colonial authorities wanted to protect their own ideas about the environment rather than the environment itself. One of these was that the animals had to make way for the 'economic opening-up' and the 'development' of the colony and could continue to exist as memories of a lost 'Eden' in reserves, as scientific specimens in museums, or as representatives of a domestication ideal in zoos.[6] Whilst this policy led to new forms of appropriation of animals, these were far outweighed by the most unbridled forms of exploitation. Nature conservation and economic interests often clashed as a result. National parks and species protection measures, generally supported by the authorities in Brussels, met with opposition from colonial economic actors, and even from the local authorities.

The unbridled exploitation of environmental resources, and its mitigation by protection measures, are not specific to Europe. As demonstrated by the example of ivory, the intensive exploitation of animals predates the Belgian colonial expansion. Several studies have shown that in the pre-colonial era, some environmental protection measures had been introduced in Central Africa, in particular in the shape of protected areas. After independence in 1960, the new Congolese political elites adopted the colonial conservationist policy almost wholesale and expanded it sensitively, not only because the Belgians (and more generally the Europeans) had already given it a solid base in Africa, but also because it fitted the new political and economic ambitions. It enhanced Congolese national identity through the promotion of iconic animals and landscapes, enabled the government to reinforce control over its territory, tapped new sources of income such as tourism and international nature conservation funds and – just as importantly – allowed unabated exploitation outside the borders of protected areas. Mobutu translated colonial rules into Congolese laws and expanded the national parks. In 1970, he transformed former colonial reserves into the Kahuzi-Biega National Park and founded Salonga National Park.

Instead of addressing the issue of exploitation and management of environmental resources in terms of a conflict between colonizers and colonized, between Westerners and Africans, we can also see it in terms of social inequality, which was intensified considerably by colonization and its racist basis. Within these asymmetrical dynamics, the refusal to violently exploit the environment and animals for one's own benefit remains, from the colonial era to this day, largely a personal, individual choice. This does not mean that the colonial era can be reduced to an intermezzo in the Congo's environmental history. Quite the reverse, it was a pivotal point at which natural resources were being exploited at a faster rate than ever before and protection measures were taken which were directly related to this.

Bibliography

The Ministry of Foreign Affairs in Brussels holds the majority of documents about environmental policy in the Congo in its Africa Archive (now gradually being transferred to the State Archives), while the AfricaMuseum possesses personal archives from countless actors who were involved in the scientific 'discovery', exploitation and protection of the Congolese environments. The historian and anthropologist Joseph Nzabandora Ndi Mubanzi has written a seminal PhD thesis on the social and environmental history of national parks in the Congo: *Histoire de conserver: Évolution des relations socio-économiques et ethnoécologiques entre les parcs nationaux du Kivu et les populations avoisinantes (RD Congo)*, doctoral thesis, ULB, 2003. Patricia Van Schuylenbergh has written a doctoral thesis (and various articles) about environmental management in the Congo: *De l'appropriation à la conservation de la faune sauvage. Pratiques d'une colonisation. Le cas du Congo belge (1885-1960)*, doctoral thesis, UCL, 2006. The latter has been published as a book: *Faune sauvage et colonisation. Une histoire de destruction et de protection de la nature congolaise (1885-1960)*, P.I.E. Peter Lang, Brussels, 2020. Lancelot Arzel has written a dissertation and several contributions about human and environmental violence during the Congo Free State era, including 'À la guerre comme à la chasse? Une anthropologie historique de la violence coloniale dans l'État Indépendant du Congo (1885-1908)', in Van Schuylenbergh, Patricia, Plasman, Pierre-Luc, and Lanneau, Catherine, eds., *L'Afrique belge aux XIXe et XXe siècles. Nouvelles recherches et perspectives en histoire coloniale*, P.I.E. Peter Lang, Brussels, 2014, p. 145-162. Several socio-historical works shine a light on the extraction economy, such as in Ngbwapkwa, Te Mobusa, 'L'exploitation du caoutchouc par l'État Indépendant du Congo dans le territoire de Banzyville, district de l'Ubangi (1900-1908)', *Civilisations*, 41, 1993, p. 291-306; and on the 'development programs' in agriculture, such as Likaka, Osumaka, *Rural Society and Cotton in Colonial Zaïre*, University of Wisconsin Press, Madison, 1997. Iva Peša has extensively published on the environmental impact of mining on the Congolese Copperbelt (see for instance 'Mining, Waste and Environmental Thought on the Central African Copperbelt, 1950-2000', *Environment and History*, 28, 2022, 2, p. 259-284). Various historians have explored the history of fauna protection, including Patricia Van Schuylenbergh, Raf De Bont (see for instance: '"Primitives" and Protected Areas: International Conservation and the "Naturalization" of Indigenous People, ca. 1910-1975', *Journal of the History of Ideas*, 72, 2015, 2, p. 215-236) and Violette Pouillard (*Histoire des zoos par les animaux. Impérialisme, contrôle, conservation*, Champ Vallon, Seyssel, 2019). Political scientists too have engaged themselves in this area, including Marijnen, Esther, 'Public Authority and Conservation in Areas of Armed Conflict: Virunga National Park as a "State within a State" in Eastern Congo', *Development and Change*, 2018, p. 1-25. An overview of policy measures after independence can be found in Bashige, Eulalie, et al., *Nature et culture en République démocratique du Congo*, Tervuren, MRAC, 2004. To conclude, the synthesis books by William Beinart and Lotte Hughes (2007) and by Corey Ross (2017) offer an illuminating view on the history of environmental management in Africa, including the Congo.

Notes

1 Van Schuylenbergh, Patricia, *De l'appropriation à la conservation de la faune sauvage. Pratiques d'une colonisation: le cas du Congo belge (1885-1960)*, doctoral thesis, UCL, 2006, p. 177-179.
2 Van Schuylenbergh, *De l'appropriation*, p. 486-488.
3 Definition from Mathis, Charles-François, 'Mobiliser pour l'environnement en Europe et aux États-Unis. Un état des lieux à l'aube du 20e siècle', *Vingtième siècle*, 113, 2012, 1, p. 15-27 (p. 19-20).
4 Africa Archive, Ministry of Foreign Affairs, GG 19339, Jean de Medina, *Rapport… janvier 1948*, p. 4.
5 Excerpt from Fauchille, A., 'La protection des animaux en Afrique', *Le Mouvement Géographique*, 14 Octobre 1900, col. 498, cited in Van Schuylenbergh, *De l'appropriation*, p. 230.
6 See Isenberg, A.C., *The Destruction of the Bison: An Environmental History, 1750-1920*, Cambridge University Press, Cambridge, 2000.

Part V

Afterword

IDESBALD GODDEERIS, AMANDINE LAURO
AND GUY VANTHEMSCHE

28. The Colonial Past through a Belgian Lens

From White Nostalgia to Decolonial Debate

More than sixty years after Congolese independence, the colonial past has yet to be fully processed. After decades of low-profile debates, however, recent years have witnessed an unprecedented acceleration of postcolonial discussions in Belgian public and political discourses. In December 2018, King Philippe could still choose not to attend the reopening of the redesigned AfricaMuseum in Tervuren, because the debate was 'still ongoing', according to the media. In March 2019, however, Prime Minister Charles Michel officially apologized to the mixed-race people born during Belgium's colonization, as well as to their families, for the injustices and suffering they had experienced. In June 2020, King Philippe made a remarkable about-turn and for the first time voiced his opinion about Belgium's colonial past, expressing his 'deepest regrets' in a letter to the DRC President Tshisekedi, something he repeated during his first visit to the DRC in June 2022. In July 2020, in the aftermath of the celebration of the sixtieth anniversary of decolonization and of intense public mobilizations, the Federal Parliament established a Special Commission 'Congo – Colonial Past', an initiative that aimed to examine the history and legacies of the colonial past. The Commission had far-reaching ambitions with little equivalent at the European level, but eventually collapsed without a final conclusion. On top of that, the media also frequently reports on actions and opinions related to Belgian colonial history. What is happening? Why is this topic all of a sudden dominating the societal agenda?

This chapter reflects on the Belgian postcolonial memory: the way in which Belgium has been looking at its colonial past since the Congo obtained independence in 1960. It examines how collective memory and bilateral relations have evolved over the past decades, and comments on the most important debates of recent years. It forms the first part of a conclusion to this book. The second part consists of reflections from a Congolese perspective by Professor Emeritus Isidore Ndaywel è Nziem. A photographic essay (Chapter 30) closes this afterword.

Silence during the First Decades following Decolonization

The independence of the Congo was a shock for the 'motherland'. Many Belgians found it difficult to understand the events because they thought that, more than anything else, the Congolese people felt gratitude for what had been accomplished under Belgian rule. The Congo Crisis that erupted after independence, accompanied by international criticism (see Chapter 6), made it even more difficult to come to terms with decolonization. The tens of thousands of former colonials who returned to Belgium during the weeks and months after 30 June 1960 were often traumatized and could not find a sympathetic ear for their experiences.

Belgians dealt with this new reality in various ways. Some kept silent and tried to forget. Others continued to engage, especially after Mobutu had definitively obtained power in 1965 and the country regained a modicum of stability. Official Belgian development aid, which partly carried on where the former colonial administration had left off, as well as countless private development NGOs (many of which evolved from mission works), focused largely on the former colony. The Belgian King and Queen traveled to the Congo in 1970 for the tenth anniversary of independence.

Further research will have to uncover whether there were significant differences between Flanders and the Francophone parts of the country and how to make sense of them, but it is clear that Congolese independence did not put an end to colonial reflexes within Belgian society. Belgian companies tried to retain their position in the Congo during the 1960s, only to be hit by Mobutu's policies, which included the nationalization of the UMHK in 1966-1967 and the 'Zaireanization' of foreign businesses at the beginning of the 1970s. The Tervuren museum, which had undergone a major refurbishment in 1958, was not given a new overhaul during the first decades after decolonization. The highest-selling Dutch-language literary work about the Congo during the 1960s and 1970s was the autobiographical novel *Black Venus* by former colonial Jef Geeraerts, who reduced black women to sexual objects and glorified Congolese society for is primitiveness.

Geeraerts's portrayal of the colonial administration and its officials was not flattering, however. Other dissenting voices were even more explicit in their criticism. In the early 1970s, Hugo Claus, in his play *Het leven en de werken van Leopold II* ('The Life and Works of Leopold II'), and Paul Brondeel in his novel *Ik, blanke kaffer* ('I, White Kaffir') denounced the rule of the Congo Free State and the 1950s Belgian Congo respectively. A few historians at Francophone universities, most notably Jean Stengers (ULB) and Jean-Luc Vellut (UCL), began to investigate aspects of colonial history, but their results seldom reached the media. From 1985 onwards, Daniel Vangroenweghe and Jules Marchal (under the pseudonym A.M. Delathuy) wrote critical books about the Congo Free State (see Chapter 1). Reference works for secondary education likewise became gradually more and more critical of colonialism within a European context and regarding a further removed past (in particular the first wave of colonization in America during the sixteenth and seventeenth century). Until the late 1990s, however, they remained extremely positive about the Belgian presence in the Congo, and colonial history itself was not a requirement for graduation.

Storms around the Turn of the Century

The first real societal debates about the colonial past only erupted around the turn of the twenty-first century. Firstly, American journalist Adam Hochschild published a book in 1998 in which he shed a crude light on the violence of the Congo Free State regime, stating that ten million Congolese people had died under Leopold II (see Chapters 1, 3 and 7). Although his work did not really break any new ground and had no academic ambitions, *King Leopold's Ghost* became a best-seller and Belgium was no longer able to ignore the international interest. Secondly, in 1999, Belgian sociologist Ludo De Witte exposed the involvement of the Belgian Government in the murder of Patrice Lumumba (see Chapter 6). His book led to a parliamentary inquiry which concluded in February 2002 that several Belgian ministers bore a moral responsibility and that King Baudouin had acted outside his constitutional powers. Minister of Foreign Affairs Louis Michel apologized on behalf of the Government to the surviving relatives and the Congolese people. Belgium did not want to pay any compensation, but did promise to put money into a new Patrice Lumumba Foundation (which never came to fruition).

Louis Michel also expressed his sympathies with the Belgians who had been forced to flee the Congo after independence. These former colonials became a renewed focus of attention thanks to a book by the Flemish journalist Peter Verlinden, and they themselves spoke out against the works by Hochschild and De Witte. They had set up dozens of new associations after their return to Belgium, and established new organizations at the beginning of the twenty-first century – first *Mémoire du Congo* ('Memory of the Congo') (2002), later its Flemish counterpart *Afrika Getuigenissen* ('Africa

Testimonials') (2004). In order to publicize their so-called 'impartial', but in reality, extremely nostalgic truth, they filmed hundreds of testimonials. *CegeSoma* (the Study and Documentation Center for War and Contemporary Society, a federal research and documentation center which was integrated into the Belgian State Archives in 2016) conducted an extensive survey amongst former colonials in the early 2000s, but their networks of influence and connections with Belgian political groups remains to this day little-explored.

Opponents of this colonial version of the past did not abandon the struggle either. Shortly after the Belgian broadcast of the critical BBC documentary *Congo: White King, Red Rubber, Black Death* in April 2004, a hand was cut off from one of the black figures cheering Leopold II's equestrian statue in Ostend. This action was seemingly carried out by a group of activists in reference to a notorious punishment during the Monarch's reign in the Congo, and against the glorifying representation of colonial rule embodied in the many monuments devoted to the country's history of overseas expansion. In 2006, a protest action took place around Congolese memorials in Liège. During the following years, statues of Leopold II were frequently covered in red paint or graffiti, for example in Ekeren (June 2007 and November 2009), Brussels (September 2008), Ostend (November 2008), Tervuren (December 2009) and Namur (June 2011). Spurred on by negative reactions, in particular of the Liège City Council, about a dozen organizations joined forces in 2008 and founded the *Collectif 'Mémoires Coloniales'*, wishing to put the theme of the colonial past and its heritage on the political agenda. A few years later, a new generation of militants of African descent set up the CMCLD (Colonial Memories and Fight against Discrimination Collective), which made an explicit link between limited acknowledgement of the Belgian colonial past and discrimination of black people in Belgium. These organizations took a considerable number of initiatives, the best known of which is probably the campaign for a Patrice Lumumba Square in the neighborhood of Matonge in Ixelles/Elsene (Brussels). Activists repeatedly affixed paper street names (which were removed each time) and, in 2013, managed to get the topic on the City Council's agenda, where they were met with refusal by the liberal ruling majority.

Meanwhile, Belgian national policymakers did not know exactly what line to take towards the Congo in the new millennium. The former colony's place in Belgian foreign trade and in foreign development had shrunk gradually during the first decades after decolonization, and this process accelerated spectacularly following the end of the Cold War. Louis Michel tried to strengthen ties again between 1999 and 2004, and saw this policy confirmed by the DRC

President Joseph Kabila, who in a speech for the Belgian Senate in 2004 praised the work of Leopold II. His successor Karel De Gucht (2004-2009), however, was more critical towards the Kabila Government and as a result became persona non grata in the Congo. King Albert traveled to Kinshasa in 2010 for the celebrations of the fiftieth anniversary of Congolese independence – the first time a Belgian king visited the Congo since 1985 –, but the Government had decided that he should not give an official speech, so that no 'offence' would be caused to anyone.

'Congo Mania' and Nostalgia around 2010

In Belgium itself, the Congo also hit the headlines because of the fiftieth anniversary of decolonization. The debates were notably less fierce (but no less abundant) than during the previous years. Many books were published, and in Flanders in particular, attention was focused on the colonial period, rather than on the Congolese state which was turning fifty. Quite a few books appeared with accounts by former colonials, with titles such as *The Best Time of My Life*. They were all overshadowed by *Congo: The Epic History of a People*, David Van Reybrouck's compelling account of travel through the Congo in the past and the present. The bestseller won numerous prizes and was translated into many languages, including French, German and English.

The dominant narratives also met with criticism, for instance by Ludo De Witte and the CMCLD. However, these counter-voices reached mainstream media and the general public far less than in previous years. Moreover, their influence was mitigated by explicitly positive opinions. In June 2010, Louis Michel – at the time still a Member of the European Parliament – called Leopold II 'a Belgian hero'. On 30 June 2010, Flemish public broadcaster VRT showed André Cauvin's 1955 documentary film *Bwana Kitoko*, one of the classics of colonial propaganda (see Chapter 24; conversely, its Francophone counterpart RTBF broadcasted the film *Lumumba* by Haitian cinematographer Raoul Peck).

Despite years of public debate and decades of critical academic research, the 2010 anniversary was celebrated with much mildness and nostalgia. There might be various explanations for this. Firstly, there had been ten years of polarization, and large groups within society probably sought a new consensus. The fact that many people still had personal memories of the colonial past or of former colonials, and did not recognize themselves in the criticism, might also have played a part. Secondly, this period coincided with a major political and even identity crisis. In 2007, Belgium was led by a federal government lacking full legal capacity for six months, and in 2010-2011 this was the case for no less than eighteen months. In other words, there were concerns other than the memory of the colonial past on the societal and political agenda.

Thirdly, the voice of the postcolonial diaspora has been slow to be heard, especially in Flanders, whereas in other former colonial metropoles, diasporas have often been at the forefront of the development of postcolonial critique. Both during the colonial era and in the first decades following independence, Belgium only allowed a fairly small number of Congolese migrants into the country (see Chapter 14). In 1990, fewer than 20,000 Congolese individuals lived in Belgium; their numbers only rose with the streams of refugees during Mobutu's 'democratization process', Kabila's takeover and the 1998-2003 war (in addition to other fluxes of refugees from Central Africa, notably after the 1994 Rwandan genocide). When the Nigerian-Belgian writer Chika Unigwe (who has been living in the US since 2013) published her debut novel *De feniks* ('The Phoenix') in 2005, it was greeted as the first book by a Flemish author of African origin.

A Decolonization of the Mind?

In recent years, postcolonial debates have been gaining ground again, and the (relative) public hiatus of the 2010 anniversary seems like a thing of the past. An important explanation for this is that Congolese (and other) migrants are a great deal more vocal. In Flanders, a second generation has grown up speaking Dutch and some of them are making careers for themselves in institutional structures. In Francophone Belgium, there is likewise a new generation of intellectuals and militants with a migration background who wish to place the colonial legacy and racial discrimination more explicitly in the media and political spotlight. New associations have been set up, such as Decolonize Belgium or Bamko, among others, and their demands have been picked up by broader organizations as well, including Intal or Hand in Hand.

All these individuals and groups call for a 'decolonization of the mind'. They focus their criticism on several societal domains. 'Old' popular traditions portraying black people in denigrating ways, such as Black Pete, the *Noirauds* ('swarthies') in Brussels and the *Sauvage* ('savage') in Ath, have come under fire. Certain expressions in the Dutch language are being questioned; for instance, increasingly greater numbers of people are arguing for the use of *wit* ('white') instead of *blank* ('white', with the added meanings of 'unblemished', 'fair'), because the latter is associated with purity and therefore has a connotation of superiority. The overrepresentation of white Belgians in prominent positions – from education to the media – and amongst expertise about themes relating to Africa, is being denounced. The reopening of the redesigned AfricaMuseum was accompanied by all kinds of debates about the new display and the restitution of museum objects (see Chapter 26).

It is not only the dominant white view of the colonial past that is being criticized. Parallels are also being drawn with contemporary social phenomena, such as unequal power relations, Eurocentric prejudices, feelings of superiority, and racism. Sociological studies do indeed show that people of African origin are discriminated against in the labor and housing markets. The UN Working Group of Experts on People of African Descent called the inequality 'deeply entrenched', and racial discrimination in Belgian institutions 'endemic'. When the Working Group formulated its first conclusions following its visit to Belgium in February 2019, Prime Minister Charles Michel (the son of the previously mentioned Louis Michel) responded with 'surprise' and 'incomprehension'; when the definitive report appeared in September 2019, the media barely paid any attention to it. It should also be noted that while the report devotes considerable space to the issue of colonial history and calls for a better recognition of this past, it is sometimes strikingly light on historical data, such as the claim that '17 to 25 million Congolese were killed by colonial agents and authorities' in the Congo Free State – an assertion that cannot be maintained in the light of current historical research (see Chapter 7). Public space is often the target of actions, no longer just the monuments and streets commemorating Leopold II, but also a wider spectrum of colonial *lieux de mémoire* (the statue of missionary De Deken in Wilrijk, for example). Scandals around memorials related to the colonial or racist past world-wide generate new protests in Belgium, causing the debate to flare up again; for instance, following the campaign against the statue of Cecil Rhodes in Cape Town in the spring of 2015, or that of Robert E. Lee in Charlottesville, Virginia in August 2017. Awareness has also been growing about the material omnipresence of colonial heritage in Belgian cities, and especially in Brussels, but also in Antwerp, Leuven and Namur, notably thanks to novel guided tours organized by associations from the diaspora.

To some extent, the polarization of debates has led to a radicalization of the arguments. Iconoclasts of the white hegemony brandish unfounded numbers (for example more than 15 million deaths under Leopold II); young right-wing extremists idolize colonialism in repugnant internet memes. But the moderate center likewise does not know what to do about the criticism. Initially, local administrations – including Halle, Wilrijk, Ostend, Geraardsbergen, Ghent, Tervuren, Hasselt and Mechelen – put information signs at the foot of controversial statues, but many of them tend to be so evasive or vaguely formulated that they miss the mark. In September 2017, the Mons City Council decided to compensate for a plaque commemorating former colonials underneath the town hall's porch by hanging next to it a plaque honoring Lumumba and his fight for independence. In May 2018, Charleroi announced Belgium's first *Rue Lumumba*, even though this was a small street outside the city's ring road. A month later, the mayor of Brussels inaugurated Patrice Lumumba Square in a previously nameless remote corner of a square that is for the most part located in the municipality of Ixelles/Elsene. In 2019, the first Leopold II avenues were altered. Dendermonde approved a motion in March that year to rename it Leopold Avenue and Courtrai did the same along with its Cyriel Verschaeve Street, named after a Flemish nationalist priest who has drawn even more criticism for collaboration during the Second World War. On a national level too, politicians swung into action. At the end of June 2016, green Flemish and Francophone Members of Parliament proposed the setting up of a kind of 'truth commission' about the colonial past. They backed down, but gained support from their socialist and communist colleagues for another resolution 'about the implementation of an inquiry in order to establish the facts and acknowledge the involvement of various Belgian institutions in the colonization of the Congo, Rwanda and Burundi'. Later that year, Francophone politicians – including liberals and Christian democrats –, urged on by pressure groups, addressed the issue of the segregation and forced adoptions of mixed-race children. Their action ultimately led to the earlier mentioned apologies made by Charles Michel in March 2019. In July 2019, the new coalition of the Brussels-Capital Region (with socialists, greens, the centrist DéFI party and the Flemish liberals) included in their policy statement an intention to 'launch a thought exercise about the symbols in the public space related to colonization in consultation with the academic world and the associations concerned.'

On the eve of the celebration of the sixtieth anniversary of Congolese independence, the worldwide Black Lives Matter protest that erupted at the end of May 2020 was a new catalyst in this process. Protests against legacies of colonialism and contemporary racism in the streets of Brussels reached a whole new level. The long-standing demands of activists to acknowledge the particularly violent history of Belgian colonialism could finally be heard. For the first time, monuments to Leopold II were removed, inter alia in Ekeren, Mons, Leuven, and Ghent. The Flemish Minister of Internal Affairs and the Brussels-Capital Region commissioned reports about how to deal with colonial heritage in the public space, and several cities, including Halle, Beringen and Mechelen, set up participatory trajectories on this topic. On 30 June 2020 – on the sixtieth anniversary of Congolese independence and at the apogee of the BLM protest –, the Belgian King Philippe in a letter addressed to DRC President Felix Tshisekedi expressed his 'deepest regrets' about the violence and atrocities committed under Leopold II's regime, and the suffering and humiliation in the Belgian Congo; regrets that he repeated in Kinshasa during his first visit to the Congo in June 2022. Also in the summer of 2020, the Federal Parliament established a Special Commission 'Congo-Colonial Past'. First, ten experts appointed by the Commission wrote an extensive report (which was released in October 2021) providing an overview of both the history and the legacies of Belgian colonialism. Afterwards, commission members discussed specific topics with other specialists and members of the civil society – and among themselves – in dozens of lengthy meetings. While these debates offered an unprecedented platform to public discussions about colonialism and its aftermath, they have also been the site of renewed tense political confrontations over the colonial past and how to deal with it. Despite efforts to achieve a consensus among the parliamentary members of the majority on political, memory and material measures, in the end the Commission failed. Significantly, it was the question of the appropriateness of an apology for the violence of colonization (and with it of potential claims for compensation) that stalled the members of the Commission – and met the opposition of the liberals. The 128 recommendations painstakingly negotiated after two years of intense work were not even put to vote.

But the multiplication of initiatives and commissions related to the colonial past, reflecting the fragmentation of the Belgian institutional landscape, shows that the post/decolonial debate will no longer be silenced, even if it seems slow to be translated into concrete measures. The removal, in December 2022, of the *Ducasse d'Ath* ('Fair of the city of Ath') by UNESCO from its List of Intangible Cultural Heritage of Humanity because of the racist depiction of the *Sauvage* character, despite the creation of a local citizens commission to reflect on the issue, is a telling example of the limits of institutional tergiversations. It is also the latest episode in a long list of critical impulses coming from international actors that forced Belgium to tackle its colonial past and postcolonial present. Besides controversial issues of removals, restitutions or reparations, the production of knowledge about the colonial past has also been a key site of recent debates, with multiple calls to facilitate access to colonial archives and to stimulate new research on the history of colonialism.

These steps are considered insufficient by some. The same applies to other measures aimed at breaking through white hegemony. When the AfricaMuseum reopened after more than five years of renovation, it was criticized by many activists and experts because its changes, which had seemed ground-breaking in the mid-2010s, had, by the end of that decade, not gone far enough. The series *Kinderen van de kolonie* ('Children of the Colony'), broadcast by public TV channel Canvas in Flanders in the autumn of 2018, for the first time gave many Congolese testimonials airtime, but was blamed for being selective, partly because most of the interviewees came from the diaspora and would be more negative about the colonial past than Congolese people in the Congo themselves. King Philippe was hailed for taking a critical standpoint on Belgium's colonial past and his predecessor Leopold II, but also met with negative reaction because he only expressed his regrets, and not his apologies. Some scholars strive to adopt non-Eurocentric perspectives; however, they are sometimes criticized for not going far enough to shake up a so-called 'white truth regime'.

These discussions are not a problem in themselves. Quite the opposite, they can have a healing effect and in so doing help the processing of the colonial past; in any case they reveal the vitality of debates around postcolonial issues in Belgium and to the very definition of a post/decolonial agenda. This book also wishes to make its contribution, by placing scientific accuracy once more at the center and by allowing different academic voices to have their say. Historians do not like to pass judgment over watersheds in the present and changes in the future. But somewhere along the line we hope that this book can help in the construction of a new dialogue between Belgium and the Congo, and in the shaping of a taboo-free recollection about the shared colonial past.

Bibliography

In 2019, American historian Matthew G. Stanard published his book *The Leopard, the Lion, and the Cock: Colonial Memories and Monuments in Belgium*, Universitaire Pers Leuven, Leuven, 2019, which was instantly regarded a standard work about the way Belgium has dealt with its colonial past. Vanthemsche, Guy, *Congo. De impact van de kolonie op België*, Lannoo, Tielt, 2007, also devotes attention to Belgian Congolese political and economic relations and development cooperation and has a comprehensive historiographic overview in its introduction. Idesbald Goddeeris has published articles about the recent postcolonial memories and debates, for instance in *Interventions: International Journal of Postcolonial Studies* (2015), *Postcolonial Studies* (2016), *Tijdschrift voor Geschiedenis* (2016), *Zeitgeschichte* (2019), *BMGN – Low Countries Historical Review* (2020) and *Memoria e Ricerca* (2023). In addition, in this chapter we refer to the following works, amongst others: Verlinden, Peter, *Weg uit Congo. Het drama van de kolonialen*, Davidsfonds, Leuven, 2002; Gillet, Florence, 'Congo rêvé? Congo détruit… Les anciens coloniaux belges aux prises avec une société en repentir. Enquête sur la face émergée d'une mémoire', *Cahiers d'Histoire du Temps Présent*, 19, 2008, p. 79-133; Raymaekers, Jan, *Congo. De schoonste tijd van mijn leven. Getuigenissen van oud-kolonialen in woord en beeld*, Van Halewyck, Leuven, 2009; and Catherine, Lucas, *Het dekoloniseringsparcours. Wandelen langs Kongolees erfgoed in België*, Epo, Berchem, 2019. The other books can be easily traced; the quotes are from the *Report of the Working Group of Experts on People of African Descent* (14 August 2019) and the *Gemeenschappelijke Algemene Beleidsverklaring van de Brusselse Hoofdstedelijke Regering en het Verenigd College van de Gemeenschappelijke Gemeenschapscommissie, regeerperiode 2019-2024*. The experts' report of the Special Commission 'Congo-Colonial Past' (2021) and the lengthy auditions led by the Commission remain available on the website of the Belgian Federal Parliament.

ISIDORE NDAYWEL È NZIEM

29. The Colonial Past through a Congolese Lens

From Red Rubber to Red Coltan

Over the past several years, historians have increasingly delved into the subject of the colonial past.[1] Whatever the motivation behind it may be, this curiosity is a sign of the times. In this second part of this book's conclusion, we will focus on the Congolese perception of that past, then and now.

It is common knowledge that the colonial period was not experienced in the same way everywhere. The most significant fault line was between city and rural regions. On the one hand, there were extensive industrial or commercially exploited areas, such as Kinshasa, Bas-Congo, Kivu or Katanga; on the other, there were less urbanized areas with almost no Europeans, except for the local trade agents or missionaries who would visit sporadically. In this vast part of the country, 'the colonial experience' was above all synonymous with taxes, routine tasks and all kinds of obligations, such as health regulations, evangelization and compulsory school attendance.

Also, the perception of the colonial experience, and the awareness arising from it, embodied both opportunities and limitations which evolved over time. In my opinion, at least four periods can be distinguished which clearly differ from each other: the first could be dubbed the 'Red Rubber Era' (a title drawn from the famous words that the French-British author Edmund Dene Morel used to describe the era of Leopold II). This era was followed by the triumphing colonial era, which we will refer to as the '*Ba-Flamands* Era', after the Congolese term for the Belgian colonizers. After independence, the Congo Crisis took on an international dimension, as can be seen in the two subsequent periods: the 'Cold War Era' and the 'Red Coltan Era'. From the end of the 1950s, during the Cold War Era, other powers appeared in addition to Belgium which would play a major role on the Congolese stage, especially the United States and France. It was the time of *Bwana Kitoko* (King Baudouin's nickname), but in particular the trio of Kasa-Vubu, Lumumba and Mobutu.

In the Congolese understanding, 'the colony' – post-independence – had acquired an add-on in neo-colonialism, which would ultimately flow into the last era, the Red Coltan Era, to stay with Morel's metaphor. In this period, the country's natural resources were and continue to be exploited by a large body of traders, including those from Asia and Africa (the new 'predators', as Colette Braeckman described them),[2] acting as proconsuls for oligarchs who have at their disposal all kinds of transcontinental capital.

Another important observation to add is that Congolese consciousness-raising did not necessarily coincide with these eras. Criticism was initially levelled at the Belgian era, and later at the Cold War Era. Gradually, a posteriori, the Red Rubber Era became the target. The basis for many postcolonial disappointments was found in this era and people saw similarities with the Congo's current woes. In this chapter, we will follow the same order: from the initial *Ba-Flamands* empire to the Red Coltan Era, followed by the excesses of Leopold II's Red Rubber Era, echoes of which can be heard in the rule of the Congolese despots in the Cold War and the Red Coltan Eras.

The *Ba-Flamands* Era

During the glorifying colonial era, the whites spoke to each other in their own language when they wanted to keep things secret: *Ki-Flamand*, in the same way that the Congolese used their mother languages. The segregation between white and black people was absolute, in work, housing, religion, public transport, daily life, etc. In the concept of 'white' (*mundele, muzungu*), all kinds of connotations converged related to knowledge, property, power, and body aesthetics, and all those facets seemed to affirm a form of predestined privilege vis-à-vis black individuals. Unlike in the French colonies, no reference was ever made to 'our ancestors the Gauls'. On the contrary, black people were more likely to be descendants of the Biblical Ham, Noah's cursed son.

At least three categories of white people existed. The *Ba-Flamands* included the colonial civil servants and the majority of the missionaries. The 'assimilated' people comprised white individuals from other nationalities, such as Protestant missionaries (Dutch, British, Swedish or American) and trade representatives (Italian, Luxembourger, and so on). At the bottom of the ladder sat a third category, often called Portuguese, but coming from a wider range of countries: white people who ran grocery shops, conducted all manner of small trades, were able to appreciate Congolese cuisine and married local women.

The *Ba-Flamands*, who occupied the best positions of the 'colonial trinity' (state, Church and capital), were conspicuous due to their arrogance. They were fond of handing out blows and kicks and were unsparing with insults and abuse: 'macaque', 'filthy savage', *nondedju* ('darned'), 'damn it'. The 'assimilated' exercised greater restraint and existed more in the margins, because they did not follow the official religious course (non-Catholic missionaries) or because their main concern was commercial profits (company representatives). The 'Portuguese' were looked down on because they were a form of 'inferior whites', a bit like mixed-race people, who were referred to as 'mulattoes' at the time and who constituted an intermediate class.

Congolese individuals who lived through this era themselves had neither the time nor the opportunity to form an opinion about this, because they had no awareness of what the issues really were. They lived and endured, or briefly rebelled. Forced labor under Leopold II was followed by 'colonial taxes' laid down on 2 May 1910 in the 'decree concerning the indigenous regions'. The taxes, which had been collected in kind up to that point, now had to be paid in hard cash. Money was something you were only able to get from the whites, which is why men and women who had enjoyed every freedom of movement henceforth had to set to work as laborers in factories, catechumens in the missions, or as manpower in the city or their own village. This imposed social change was in pursuit of colonial works (mining, industry, the construction and maintenance of roads, state buildings and business hotels, agricultural cultivation, harvesting crops, and so on). It was a profound change, and if you did not meet your obligations, you were dealt with firmly, which often meant a flogging with the *chicotte* or a prison sentence.

There were some misunderstandings about the obligations imposed by the colony. For instance, there was a widespread popular belief that vaccinations were a way to spread incurable diseases and to exterminate the local population. Whites were also seen as cannibals. The oldest missionaries had pot bellies because they liked to tuck into human flesh. Corned beef, the tinned red meat, very popular in expat circles, was regarded as the tangible proof of this gastronomic preference, because the Congolese did not know any local or non-local meat with such a strange color. Another colonial practice – the forced recruitment of manpower – only reinforced this popular belief: Congolese people believed that their white counterparts went out on 'man-hunts'. Many victims were sent to far-away places from which they never returned. Some unfortunate souls, an extremely detailed account tells us, were thrown into deep pits, where they were fattened up and slaughtered, cut into pieces and distributed amongst the whites. Because of this, the recruitment campaigns had a recurring character – purportedly to meet the requirements of the colonial economy, but in reality, because white customers hankered after fresh human meat.

The local populace naturally tried to defend itself in all manner of ways against the 'intruders'. A complete overview of all the methods they used to retaliate has never been compiled, but they were many and varied – from fruitless attempts to 'bewitch' the missionary or priest, to firing poisoned arrows at enemy aircraft to the use of amulets that rendered you invisible or transported you to a different place in a flash or transformed you into a wild animal to outwit your opponent. Some of these invincibility techniques reappeared in a modernized form during the post-independence uprisings.[3]

The most commonly used technique seems to have been a curious potion for evading *Force Publique* recruitment that affected the body weight of the intended recruits in a mysterious way. If you drank the brew and were subsequently 'grabbed' by the army recruiting officer, at the end of the recruitment process you would have to contend with the problem that you weighed almost nothing, even though you appeared to be of quite sturdy build. All officers released these young men, because their low weight rendered them unsuitable for army service.

Colonial excesses obviously provoked recurrent reactions (see Chapter 16). We know a great deal about the uprisings and revolts which accurately illustrate 'indigenous resistance against the colonial occupation'.[4] Much less is known about the messianic resistance movements, not all of which have been unearthed and chronicled, not only because they were extremely diverse but also because they were particularly secret.[5]

Within these movements the first seeds of political awareness blossomed. Their trailblazers tended to have had personal experience of the colony's oppressive regime. Prophetess Maria Nkoy (Maria with the Leopards), for example, had lived through the red rubber reign of terror in her youth. At the beginning of the twentieth century, she propounded the liberation of the country to the Ekonda. Simon Kimbangu was four years old when, in 1891, the construction of the Matadi-Léopoldville railway line began in his area, and eleven when this work was completed. He must have seen terrible scenes involving the maltreatment and assault of Africans. He would go on to predict that the social roles of white and black people would eventually be reversed – 'The whites will take the place of the blacks, and the blacks those of the whites!'[6]

The Cold War Era

The next era ran from the end of the 1950s until the end of the 1980s. This period was marked by three important speeches and one memorable incident. The Congolese call for independence indisputably rang out first in the 'Manifesto', published in *Conscience Africaine*, which was distributed on 30 June 1956. On 28 December 1958, Patrice Lumumba's 'deadly' phrase followed, which he uttered on his return from the All-African Peoples' Conference in Accra: 'The independence we demand should not be considered a gift by Belgium – we are entitled to a right that was taken away from the Congolese people!'[7] This led to the first public protest calling for decolonization on 4 January 1959, in response to the cancelled ABAKO meeting. King Baudouin's famous radio speech on 13 January 1959 completed the circle of the change: 'It is our intention to lead the Congolese people to independence without harmful delay, but also without irresponsible rashness, in prosperity and peace' (see Chapter 5).

And this independence came about on 30 June 1960, following two roundtable conferences, a new constitution and general elections. In the immediate aftermath of the independence, a showdown between the new Republic of the Congo and the former 'motherland' developed, despite the exemplary 'Treaty of Friendship, Cooperation and Mutual Assistance' signed by both states on 29 June, but put into cold storage a mere two weeks later because of the diplomatic 'rift' between the two countries. Prime Minister Lumumba's speech on 30 June pointed to the need for such a necessary 'break' with the 'dreadful' past, which was still fresh in the memory: 'That was our lot for eighty years of colonial rule and our wounds are too fresh and too painful to be forgotten.'[8] Independence was followed by two long periods of crisis, the first stretching from the *Force Publique* mutiny to the reunification with Katanga (1960-1963), and the second from the Mulelist rebellions to the execution of their leader Pierre Mulele.[9]

The secession of Katanga (11 July 1960) and of South Kasai (8 August), the intervention of UN forces in the Congo (14 July), the murder of Patrice Lumumba (17 January 1961), and the United Nations and foreign mercenaries' interventions in Katanga were all factors that pointed to an incipient internationalization of the Congo Crisis (see Chapter 6). The former Belgian Congo grew into one of the major battlegrounds of the Cold War. Jean Ziegler, at the time working for the UN in the Congo, bore witness to this: 'Within the enclosure of *Le Royal*,[10] every day I saw scheming special representatives from South African, Belgian, French, Soviet, Swiss and

American mining companies, who appeared to have at their disposal inexhaustible monetary resources to finance their corrupt deals. The illustrious ONUC (United Nations Operation in the Congo) was infiltrated on all sides.'[11] It is no surprise that this tangle of diverse and clashing interests ultimately led to the killing of the Swedish Secretary-General of the UN, Dag Hammarskjöld, as recent research has shown.[12]

But that was not all. Mulelist rebellions,[13] Che Guevara's support for the Congolese rebels,[14] Mobutu's coup and the Shaba wars during the second half of the 1970s[15] further hampered the postcolonial Congo's relations with the rest of the world. During this 'Cold War Era', two significant symbolic events took place: while Operation *Ommegang* led by Colonel Vandewalle had been going on for some time, on 24 November 1964, Belgian paratroopers supported by the United States landed in Stanleyville; and on 19 May 1978 the second French parachute division intervened, followed by a Belgian airborne operation. The Belgian troops limited themselves to the evacuation of 'Western citizens', while the French went further and 'wished to restore public order'.[16] It is important to note that these interventions, both in 1964 and in 1978, sought above all to protect and evacuate *Western* foreigners.

This sequence of postcolonial crises led to some Congolese people idealizing the colonial period. The Congolese recalled that this era had offered more than whiplashes and racial segregation. It had also been characterized by peace, hygiene, health care, education, work and weekly company food rations. While Mobutu launched *authenticité* as an official creed, the colonial era acquired the aura of a golden age. Everything related to the Belgian Congo was given a kind of hallmark, especially in the field of technology. A driver's license or a diploma from the colonial era had greater credibility, and the initial elites boasted that they had studied in leading schools on an equal footing with those in Belgium. Laurent-Désiré Kabila, who succeeded Mobutu in 1997, imitated the tried and tested colonial model to such an extent that he even reintroduced the *chicotte* and the uniform for his territorial officials. Under his administration, the 'six' provinces from the colonial era were tacitly reinstated through the 'return' of the independence flag, on which the six provinces were represented by six stars, even though this was not a reflection of the territorial reality.[17]

In this context, elements from an earlier discussion resurfaced. Had independence come about too early? The priest and later Cardinal Joseph Malula left no doubt about this during the decisive years before independence. 'The whites want to award independence fifteen minutes too late and the blacks want it fifteen minutes too early. Better fifteen minutes early than fifteen minutes late!' he proclaimed from the lectern on 28 May 1958 at the *Humanisme Chrétien* ('Christian humanism') conference in Brussels.[18] A few decades later, the average Congolese was no longer so sure, and public opinion believed that it should have happened a little later. Historians may point out that no colony in the world had become independent in the way its colonizers had in mind, yet most Congolese stubbornly maintain that everyone should have listened to Jef Van Bilsen. His famous 'Thirty-Year Plan for the Emancipation of the Congo' should have been pursued, and independence should have been deferred until 1985, 'a hundred years after the Berlin Conference', as progressive colonials predicted at the time.

The same public opinion blamed the Congolese delegation at the 1960 political roundtable discussions for refusing to accept King Baudouin as temporary head of state of the Congo. Their thinking is that this could have prevented the conflict between Kasa-Vubu and Lumumba. For instance, some Congolese individuals still regret that, headed by Lumumba, the leading lights of the roundtable discussions refused to grant Congolese nationality to those colonials who sought it, something Moïse Tshombe's CONAKAT had demanded. The Congo would have been a 'rainbow nation' by now, and the economic debacle of 'Zaireanization' would have been avoided.

The Red Coltan Era

The idealization of the colonial era eventually clashed with another line of thought from the West. In the Belgian neo-colonial discourse, decolonization had long been depicted as an enormous 'waste', in which a magnificent structure had fallen into decline at the hands of 'impetuous' and 'inexperienced' leaders.[19] From the middle of the 1980s onwards, the wind suddenly started to blow from an entirely different direction. The West began to point out to the Congolese themselves how much they had been exploited. Colonization had been an inadmissible exploitation; not only that, it had been criminal! These voices to some extent endorsed Lumumba's 30 June 1960 speech, which had been considered iconoclastic and 'offensive' to Leopold II's great-grand-nephew. Obviously, the fact that the 'whites' now admitted as much only fanned Congolese insurgent feelings. Striking up a sincere friendship with the Belgians 'just like that' suddenly seemed an unjust reward for the former 'tyrants'.

The Western discourse can be seen as a Belgian contribution to the decolonization of the Congo.[20] From publications by authors such as Daniel Vangroenweghe, Michel Massoz and Jules Marchal – and later by American author Adam Hochschild –[21] the Congolese learned that their ancestors had undergone unspeakable acts of violence during the Leopoldian era. The macabre memory of the concession companies' reign of terror had been skillfully glossed over; only in the former rubber extraction areas did the memory linger on. These new books opened people's eyes to this painful chapter in Congolese history.

It is a known fact that the Congolese almost blindly believed the ethnographic claims in the writings by missionaries and colonials, who – in the words of Mudimbe – formed the 'colonial library'.[22] The new literature was received in the same way. Scientific information found its way to all layers of society via the rumor mill, a process that continues to this day. The first time Congolese officials referred to this was during a television debate between a Zairean delegation and the Belgian press. Since then, the memory of the 'severed hands' has become common property and visual material has shown 'how bad the whites were'. Even David Van Reybrouck, when he visited rebel Laurent Kundabatware, was challenged: 'Why did the Belgians sever the hands of the Congolese people? Was it to get more coffee ("rubber")?'[23] Meanwhile, Ludo De Witte's 'revelations'[24] about Patrice Lumumba's murder had strengthened the Congolese in their conviction that what they thought they knew about colonization's crimes paled into insignificance compared to the gruesome reality, even though the Westerners had obscured the truth as long as they could with ingenious euphemisms.

All these new books meant that the Congolese began to view colonial history, and in particular the Leopoldian era, in a different light. With mixed feelings of anger, defiance and resignation, they discovered that their natural resources had always been a source of suffering. They felt betrayed by the commitments Leopold II had agreed with other Western superpowers, first and foremost the United States. 'Leopold II sold us to the international community right from the beginning!', Congolese people complain today. And they consider this situation to be irreversible: the Congo will always be an 'international marketplace', a hunk of 'elephant flesh' everyone can help themselves to, to their heart's desire.

The conclusion therefore ultimately sounds as follows: is the Congo's instability, which we are witnessing today, a direct consequence in particular of the strategic position the country occupies, without realizing it, within global geopolitics? In which case, everything that happens in the Congo would be of direct interest to the 'business world'. The Congo would be the victim of its own resources. The fact that the transition from the twentieth to the twenty-first century shows bizarre similarities with the previous turn of the century is often invoked as proof of this argument. During the Leopoldian era, the Euro-American economy was brought into the Congo; today the country has a place in the global economy. During the 'transition' from the first plunder era to the second, Western actors were reinforced by other agents of globalization, who constituted the new 'white tribes'. The most important of these are Lebanese, Chinese and Indians – the term 'Lebanese' referring to everyone from Mashriq to Maghreb; everyone from East Asia is 'Chinese', even if they hail from Vietnam, Laos or Korea; similarly, all individuals from the Indo-Pakistani continent become 'Indian', regardless of their actual nationality.

The 'Chinese' and 'Indians', who are much more adaptable than their Western counterparts – they learn the local languages surprisingly quickly – take part in the unbridled hunt for natural resources in equal measure. Because of their extensive networks of intermediaries in the Congo, Africa and the rest of the world, they have acquired the reputation of being driven only by financial gain. They are not engaged in cultural enterprises or missionary work and instead launch themselves into the plunder and export of minerals, wood and rare animal species with uncompromising voracity. They then shamelessly flood the market with their own products, in the process nipping young local industries in the bud.

Thus, a relentless competitive battle between all kinds of 'foreigners' is fought on Congolese territory over the extraction and export of products which are in high demand on the international market, in particular coltan and cobalt. Just as during the Leopoldian era, the trade war around these ores is accompanied by a total disdain for the local population. This once again translates itself into terrible acts of violence.

Instead of 'blood on the liana' (Daniel Vangroenweghe) referring to the 'red rubber' in the south of Équateur Province, we can now talk of 'blood under the banana trees' in Kivu and Ituri. Just as during the nineteenth century, violence is accompanied by endless international negotiations and fierce accusations, which clearly have no effect and leave the guilty parties unpunished. Meanwhile the Congolese land borders have once more become unstable, because entire regions are divided according to the commercial demands of these foreign 'vultures', just as during the border negotiations era following the Berlin Conference. In 1996, Rwanda lit the fuse by demanding a new 'Berlin Conference', so that the country would recover the territory it had lost to the Congo. Even so, an entirely different narrative could be told about the history of this border. In

1885, the Congo extended to the other side of Lake Kivu. After the 1910 Brussels Conference, it had to cede a part of its territory to Rwanda.

The Belgian Era, 'My Other Congo'

In this context of 'globalness',[25] we should first and foremost try and free Belgian Congolese relations from the 'colonial situation' straitjacket, in the sense that Georges Balandier gives it. It is time that Belgian internal debates stopped acquiescing with the over-emotional tales from colonials and the Congolese diaspora. This debate was initially understandable, because colonialism had created an entirely new state of affairs, because there were still some major, unresolved points of contention between the two countries, and because the 'divorce' passed off a great deal more brusquely than both parties had wanted. But in the final analysis this shared memory is ultimately a common heritage, which, like the attendant infrastructure, needs to be managed efficiently.

These days, in its political and economic choices with regard to the Congo, Belgium presents itself more than anything as a member of the European Union, the seat of which happens to reside on Belgian territory. That the Congo was a former Belgian colony only leads to a heightened emotional sensitivity in Belgium's relationship with the country. Belgium is frequently reminded of this special status, and with a degree of fervor, by the large Congolese migrant community, the dying group of former colonials and a handful of Congo experts from media, academic or cultural circles.

The Congo's situation is more complex. Firstly, the country has an especially unsteady institutional basis as a result of the ongoing turmoil that characterized the initial decades following independence, and then spread like gangrene to all domains of public life: economy, society and culture. Another important difference is that, over the course of this endemic discontinuity since 1960, the Congo has realized that it cannot expect selfless solidarity from the rest of Africa. As it is, it has had to process much disillusionment, from the inexorable expulsion of its citizens (by Angola and Congo-Brazzaville) to the scandalous plundering of its natural resources above and below ground (by Uganda, Rwanda and Zimbabwe), via the shameless succession of unfair contracts (South Africa) and all kinds of attempts to strip it of a part of its territory. The Congolese view the African Union, just as they do the many subregional communities their country is a member of, as no more than a superstructure which convenes politicians and experts on a regular basis, but is not in touch with the people, who for their part cannot see its value.

These people meanwhile experience the perverse consequences of globalization daily. As discussed above, different 'white tribes' have emerged all lustily taking part in the plunder, at times even with the complicity of the Congolese, who have little awareness of these global interests and are happy with the pittance they are handed.

Confronted with this deep 'crisis', the Congolese opinion of the colonial past has become a side issue. In reality, the people who keep the memory of this period alive are just a minority. Not only has the number of Belgians in the Congo shrunk significantly – those remaining are chiefly diplomats and missionaries – but the Congolese migrant community likewise has become a minority group. There are more Congolese in France than in Belgium. If we take into account the full size of this enormous diaspora, with its representatives in Germany, Great Britain and in particular North America, the 'Belgian' Congolese constitute a group that only has weight when taken together with their compatriots in other Western European countries.

On the other hand, this exceptional situation, in combination with Belgium's incapacity to pursue a far-reaching policy with regard to the Congo, such as those pursued by China, India, South Korea, the United States, Canada or the European Union, has turned out to be a winning card for Belgian Congolese solidarity. For the Congo, Belgium is a gateway, a kind of indispensable waiting room, a place where it can re-establish its identity again before taking on the big challenges of today and the future. Belgium, the Congolese President Félix Tshisekedi declared, is my 'other Congo'. If we can believe Congolese politicians, it is a reference point, where all manner of 'reconciliation discussions' and 'consultation conferences' take place, as when the Congolese opposition convened in 2015 in Genval to find a common position. Antoine Gizenga, the Prime Minister who was once reproached for never having visited the Congolese hinterland, defended himself with a surprising historically inspired argument: 'Did not Leopold II rule over the Congo without ever having set foot there?' In the same way President Tshisekedi minimalized the formation of a government that dragged on for months on end by referring to Belgium, where political negotiations in order to form a government often last even longer.

In this context, relations between Belgium and the Congo are far from useless, and they can form an impetus for meaningful solidarity between two communities who share a seventy-five-year history and who are prepared to look this past in the eye together.

This solidarity does not preclude that differences of opinion will continue to exist about particular topics, but these do not need to be accompanied by needless animosity or nostalgia. In the words of King Baudouin, we could tackle the pending colonial points of contention 'without harmful delay, but also without irresponsible rashness',[26] try to come up with new ways of managing Belgian colonial patrimonies, as in the AfricaMuseum in Tervuren, and reinforce Belgian expertise regarding Africa by consistently supporting research 'in the field' in the Congo. Belgium for its part could contribute more to social recovery by facilitating the transfer of this Africa expertise, which has become somewhat meaningless within daily Belgian reality, but in the Congo is still of prime importance. As part of this, retired 'Congo anciens' – doctors, agronomists, engineers and teachers – assisted by their professional networks, could organize 'working holidays' and spend time in Congolese institutions. Likewise, young Belgian 'volunteers', whether of Congolese origin or not, could take part in literacy programs, primary health care or reforestation and environmental education projects. Operation *Tosalisana* (literally: 'Let's help each other'), set up at the end of the 1950s by Belgium to give young Belgian teachers the chance to do their national service in the Congo and work in schools there, would be much more appropriate these days. This humanist perspective is perhaps the 'royal road' for future Belgian Congolese relations.

Notes

1 Cf. my contribution: 'Vous avez dit "passé colonial"?', *Septentrion. Arts, lettres et culture de Flandre et des Pays-Bas*, 2018, 3, p. 5-9. Or, a little longer ago, in my book *L'invention du Congo contemporain. Traditions, mémoires, modernités*, L'Harmattan, Paris, 2017, part 1, p. 139-254 (Chapter II, 'Mutations et quêtes de modernité').
2 Braeckman, Colette, *Les nouveaux prédateurs. Politique des puissances en Afrique centrale*, Fayard, Paris, 2003.
3 See the literature about this topic, in particular the study about the Maniema dossier: Verhaegen, Benoît, *Rébellions au Congo. Tome 2, Le Maniema*, Crisp-Ires, Brussels-Kinshasa, 1969.
4 Ndaywel è Nziem, Isidore, *Histoire générale du Congo. De l'héritage ancien à la République démocratique*, Duculot-Afrique éditions, Brussels-Kinshasa, 1998, p. 298-304, 410-415.
5 The only available publication which attempts this, is Vellut, Jean-Luc, 'Résistances et espaces de libertés dans l'histoire coloniale du Zaïre avant la marche de l'indépendance (ca. 1876-1965)', in Coquery-Vidrovitch,

Catherine, e.a., eds., *Rébellions-révolution au Zaïre 1963-1965*, L'Harmattan, Paris, 1987, part 1, p. 24-73.
6 See Ndaywel è Nziem, Isidore, *Le Congo dans l'ouragan de l'histoire*, L'Harmattan, Paris, 2019, p. 48.
7 Ndaywel è Nziem, Isidore, *Nouvelle histoire du Congo. Des origines à la République démocratique*, Le Cri-Buku, Brussels-Kinshasa, 2010, p. 434-435.
8 Van Lierde, Jean, ed., *La pensée politique de Patrice Lumumba*, Présence africaine, Paris, 1963, p. 198.
9 Ndaywel è Nziem, Isidore, *Nouvelle histoire du Congo*, p. 473 and 497.
10 *Le Royal*, originally a hotel, acted as ONUC headquarters. It housed all services.
11 Ziegler, Jean, *Le bonheur d'être suisse*, Seuil-Fayard, Paris, 1993, p. 143-144.
12 Picard, Maurin, *Ils ont tué Monsieur H: Congo 1961. Le complot des mercenaires français contre l'ONU*, Seuil, Paris, 2019.
13 Verhaegen, Benoît, *Rébellions au Congo. Tome 1, Le Kwilu, Tome 2, le Maniema*, Crisp-Ires, Brussels-Kinshasa, 1966-1969. Pierre Mulele (1929-1968), an associate of Lumumba, was the leader of the Kwilu rebellion (1963).
14 See Galvez, William, *Le rêve africain du Che*, Epo, Berchem, 1998; Che Guevara, Ernesto, *Passages de la guerre révolutionnaire. Le Congo*, Métailié, Paris, 2000.
15 This concerns the Shaba wars (1977-1978) and the Moba wars (1984-1985). These conflicts, provoked by the invasion of Katanga by the *Front National de Libération du Congo*, led to interventions by foreign troops (from Morocco, France and Belgium in particular), who came to the assistance of Mobutu's regime which was under fire.
16 de Villers, Gauthier, *De Mobutu à Mobutu. Trente ans de relations Belgique-Zaïre*, De Boeck Université, Brussels, 1995, p. 73-74.
17 Laurent-Désiré Kabila did not recognise the green flag of Mobutu's Zaïre, but he did not want to have anything to do with the flag adopted at the constitutional meeting in Luluabourg either. The Lumumbist nationalists had not taken part in this.
18 Malula, Joseph, *L'Évêque africain aujourd'hui et demain*, Kinshasa, 1979, p. 42-63.
19 These words by Émile Janssens have the advantage that they are second to none in directness (*J'étais le général Janssens*, Charles Dessart éditeur, Brussels, 1961).
20 In reality, the Congo Free State and Belgian Congo reign of terror had been denounced in literature much earlier, even though this criticism tended to be ignored or dismissed as unimportant. See for example the new translation of Arthur Conan Doyle (*Le crime du Congo belge*, Les nuits rouges, Paris, 2005) or the plea by Jules Chomé (*La passion de Simon Kimbangu*, Les Amis de Présence Africaine, Brussels, 1959).

21 Vangroenweghe, Daniel, *Rood Rubber. Leopold II en zijn Congo*, Elsevier, Brussels, 1985; Massoz, Michel, *Le Congo de Léopold II (1878-1908). Récit historique*, Liège, 1989; *Le Congo des Belges (1908-1960). Récit historique*, Liège, 1994; for the titles of the books by Jules Marchal and Adam Hochschild, see the bibliographies for Chapter 1 and 2, amongst others. Jules Marchal also wrote *L'histoire du Congo 1876-1900, vol. 1, État libre du Congo, paradis perdu, vol. 2, Travail forcé pour le rail*, Paula Bellings, Borgloon, 1996-2000.

22 Cf. Mudimbe, Valentin, *The Invention of Africa*, Indiana University Press, Bloomington, 1988. The contents of the 'Belgian colonial library' have been extensively investigated (Vellut, Jean-Luc, 'Ressources scientifiques, culturelles et humaines de l'africanisme belge', in de Villers, Gauthier, ed., *Belgique/Zaïre. Une histoire en quête d'avenir*, Institut africain CÉDAF-l'Harmattan, Brussels-Paris, 1994, p. 115-144; Poncelet, Marc, *L'invention des sciences coloniales belges*, Karthala, Paris, 2008).

23 Van Reybrouck, David, *Congo, een geschiedenis*, De Bezige Bij, Amsterdam, 2010, p. 545.

24 De Witte, Ludo, *The Assassination of Lumumba*, Verso, London, New York, 2001. See also de Villers, Gauthier, 'Histoire, justice et politique. Propos de la Commission d'enquête sur l'assassinat de Patrice Lumumba, instituée par la Chambre belge des Représentants', *Cahiers d'Études Africaines*, 44, 2004, 1-2, p. 193-220.

25 I have borrowed this term from the Haitian writer René Depestre, who equates the new 'cohabiting on this planet' with the 'humane science' of our daily life (Depestre, René, 'Comment abattre les murs de la barbarie?', in Ndaywel è Nziem, Isidore, and Kilanga Musinde, Julien, eds., *Mondialisation, cultures et développement*, Maisonneuve et Larose, Paris, 2005, p. 36.

26 Baba Kake, Ibrahima, ed., *Conflit belgo-zaïrois. Fondements historiques, politiques et culturels*, Présence Africaine, Paris, 1990.

PEDRO MONAVILLE

30. Photographic Essay

Many historians, art historians and artists have showed interest in photographic archives from the colonial Congo in the past few years. This closing chapter explores some of the questions raised by this new body of work. In order to do so, we have gathered fifteen images from different sources: photos taken by humanitarian workers or missionaries, commercial photographs, propaganda images and ethnographic and artistic representations. We did not select these images as simple illustrations of colonial history, but rather as invitations to reflect: in what way did photography act as an instrument of control in the hands of the colonizer and did it offer colonized people the opportunity to bear witness to their own personal experience?

Images, Gazes and Colonialism

Photography was invented in the middle of the nineteenth century, on the eve of European colonial expansion in Africa. The new medium's promise to control the material world by recording 'absolute reality' on photographic material appealed to the colonizers. Soon, all kinds of European and American explorers, soldiers and missionaries headed for the colonies, equipped with cameras and the necessary technical baggage to take photographs. Photography was more than a documentation tool in colonial Africa. It was also an instrument of subjugation and control. Because photography claimed to reproduce reality, it forced both Europeans and Africans to look and present themselves in new ways, and it laid bare the relationship between knowledge and power, as historian Isabelle de Rezende persuasively showed recently.

The two images here are from the AfricaMuseum's extensive colonial photo archive in Tervuren. They were part of the dozens of photographs selected by photographer Carl De Keyzer and architectural historian Johan Lagae for their exhibition *Congo belge en images* (2010). One of the key thoughts behind the exhibition was that the camera itself, even if it was used as an instrument of control,

PHOTOGRAPHIC ESSAY 349

Fig. 1. Bas-Congo, Mayumbe. Marsh-crossing on the border with Portuguese Congo (Cabinda), 1898. (AP.0.0.16972, RMCA Tervuren collection; photo Cabra Mission)

Fig. 2. Moma District. Elephant skulls being sent to the Museum, c. 1924. (AP.0.0.35857, RMCA Tervuren collection; photo S. Molin; all rights reserved)

gave the African individuals captured on camera the opportunity to convey a subjective experience which clashed with colonial contexts of interpretation.

Bibliography

De Keyzer, Carl, and Lagae, Johan, *Congo belge en images*, Lannoo, Tielt, 2010; Colard, Sandrine, *Photography in the Colonial Congo*, doctoral thesis, Columbia University, New York, 2016; and De Rezende, Isabelle, 'Ambivalent Mediations: Photographic Desire, Anxiety, and Knowledge in Nineteenth-Century Central Africa', in Hayes, Patricia, and Minkley, Gary, eds., *Ambivalent: Photography and Visibility in African History*, Ohio University Press, Athens, 2019, p. 35-55. See also: Colard, Sandrine, ed., *Recaptioning Congo. African Stories and Colonial Pictures*, Acc Art Books, New York, 2022.

See also Chapters 12, 26 and 27.

The Atrocities of Leopoldian Rule and Humanitarian Photography

Fig. 3. Alice Seely Harris, Nsala from Wala in the Nsongo District, 1904.

This is one of the best-known images from the Congo Free State era. It shows a man looking at two human remains: the hand and foot of a child. The photo's caption gives the name of the man, Nsala, and explains that the hand and foot belonged to his five-year old daughter, who was killed and 'eaten during a cannibal banquet' organized by the militias of a concession company that was responsible for the rubber extraction in Équateur Province.

The image was taken by Alice Harris, a British Protestant missionary who, from 1905 onwards, had been very active in the protest campaign against the Leopoldian rule's atrocities in the Congo. Her photos of the Congo – she took many others in addition to the one of Nsala, often showing mutilated children – traversed the whole of Great Britain as part of awareness-raising campaigns. These images contributed to the genesis of a wide popular movement that protested against the situation in the Congo Free State.

A trailblazer of the modern humanitarian movement, Harris used photography as a tool for criticizing the malpractices of colonial exploitation. The composition of her images and the accompanying texts, which were permeated with Christian moralism, nonetheless removed the suffering of the 'red rubber' victims from its context and left certain aspects of colonial violence out of the picture, such as sexual violence against women. The pressure group Harris belonged to, the Congo Reform Association, lobbied for Leopold II's regime to be replaced by a colonial administration that would respect the rights of the indigenous population, but had no fundamental difficulty with colonization itself.

Bibliography

Grant, Kevin, 'The Limits of Exposure: Atrocity Photographs in the Congo Reform Campaign', in Fehrenbach, Heide, and Rodogno, Davide, eds., *Humanitarian Photography: A History*, Cambridge University Press, Cambridge, 2015, p. 64-88; and Hunt, Nancy R., 'An Acoustic Register, Tenacious Images, and Congolese Scenes of Rape and Repetition', *Cultural Anthropology*, 23, 2008, 2, p. 220-253.

See also Chapters 2 and 7.

Shanu and the Beginning of African Photography in the Congo

He cuts a cool figure in his *col cassé*, a three-piece suit and finely-carved walking stick, she in her velvet and corset dress, crocheted mittens and fan: the clothes this couple are wearing, captured by Herzekiah Andrew Shanu in Boma, are perfectly in tune with the etiquette and fashion of the Western bourgeoisie at the time. The people depicted in this studio portrait, G.I. Samuel and his wife, belonged to the West African community in the Congo Free State. These 'Afro-Victorians', who were recruited in Dakar, Freetown or Lagos to work as civil servants or employees of private companies, played an important role in the nascence of an African urban culture in the Congo. An aura of respectability – that this image emphatically exudes, according to the codes of the time – was crucial to these people, who saw their status in the colony permanently threatened by European racism. Photographer Shanu came from Nigeria himself and belonged to the small West African colony in the Congo; he had landed in Central Africa as an employee of the Congo Free State and subsequently established himself as an independent photographer and trader. Shanu's suicide in 1905 shows how vulnerable people in his community of black expatriates were: an active critic of the Leopoldian rule's atrocities, he had been cast out by Boma's white establishment, which had resulted in the bankruptcy of his businesses.

PHOTOGRAPHIC ESSAY 353

Fig. 4. Herzekiah Andrew Shanu, portrait of G.I. Samuel and his wife, c. 1893.
(HP.1965.14.273, RMCA Tervuren collection; photo H.A. Shanu)

Colonialism allowed little space for groups and individuals who fell outside the binary logic of European racism. At the beginning of the twentieth century, for instance, the colonial authorities imposed a ban on American Churches sending black missionaries to their missions in the Congo. Yet, despite censure, derision and discrimination, a lively African alternative modernity continued to thrive throughout the entire colonial era.

Bibliography

Morimont, Françoise, 'H.-A. Shanu: photographe, agent de l'État et commerçant africain (1858-1905)', in Vellut, Jean-Luc, ed., *La mémoire du Congo: le temps colonial*, Snoeck, Ghent, 2005, p. 213-217.

See also Chapters 2 and 17.

'All Best Wishes from the Colony': Postcards and Colonial Iconography

From the late nineteenth century, illustrated postcards became an important medium for the circulation of photographs from the Congo. These Congolese postcards were produced for commercial as well as propagandist reasons. There were various genres: photos of European-looking interiors, official buildings, city centers, natural landscapes and hunting trophies. There were obviously also many images of Congolese people, often in the context of missionary work or within the genre of 'type'-photograph, which reflected colonial ethnography's urge to categorize people and cultures. Many postcards were also of a self-proclaimed humorous nature – primarily aimed at mocking African subjects.

Bibliography

Geary, Christraud M., *In and Out of Focus: Images from Central Africa, 1885-1960*, Philip Wilson Publishers, London, 2002.

See also Chapters 12, 24 and 27.

Fig. 5. Congo – *Annoncez la bonne Nouvelle*. DRC, c. 1910. (*Les Franciscaines Missionnaires de Marie en Mission*; Postcard, collotype, b&w, 14 x 9 cm.; EEPA Postcard Collection, CG-39-05; Eliot Elisofon Photographic Archives; National Museum of African Art; Smithsonian Institution)

Fig. 6. *Sergent indigène et son domestique*. DRC, c. 1910. (*La Mission des Pères du St.-Esprit à Kindu, Congo-belge*; Postcard, collotype, b&w, 14 x 9 cm.; EEPA Postcard Collection, CG-38-18; Eliot Elisofon Photographic Archives National Museum of African Art; Smithsonian Institution)

Fig. 7. *Documentation du Ministère des Colonies de Belgique/Cyclistes sur le pont brisé.* DRC, c. 1910. (*Publiée au bénéfice de l'œuvre: 'Asiles des Soldats Invalides Belges', Cabinet de Mr. le Ministre Vandervelde*, France (Seine Inférieure); Postcard, collotype, b&w, 9 x 14 cm.; EEPA Postcard Collection, CG-47-95; Eliot Elisofon Photographic Archives; National Museum of African Art; Smithsonian Institution)

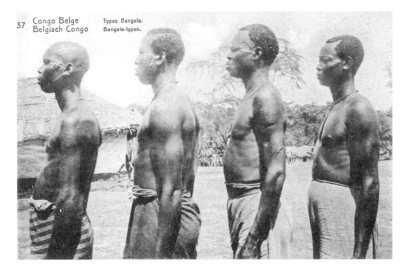

Fig. 8. *37. Congo Belge/Types Bangala.* DRC, c. 1910. (*Congo Belge – Belgisch Congo*; Postcard, collotype, b&w, 9 x 14 cm.; EEPA Postcard Collection, CG-20-20; Eliot Elisofon Photographic Archives; National Museum of African Art; Smithsonian Institution)

Empathy, Humanism and Colonial Rule

Figs 9a-c. Casimir Zagourski, three photos from the series *L'Afrique qui disparaît*. Boa Sword (© The History Collection/Alamy); *Femme Mongo portant ses charges sur le dos* (EP.0.0.8954, RMCA Tervuren collection; photo C. Zagourski, 1929-1940); *Mangbetu un type*.

In 1924, Casimir Zagourski, a former pilot in the Tsarist army from an aristocratic Polish family, established himself as a photographer in Léopoldville. Until his death in 1944, he photographed the customs, traditions, institutions and material culture of the Central African populations. His best-known work is the series *L'Afrique qui disparaît* ('Disappearing Africa'), first shown in the Belgian pavilion at the 1937 Paris colonial exhibition. The series encompassed more than four hundred images. Although Zagourski's work is often referred to on account of its aesthetic qualities and the empathetic view of African individuals it manifests, he himself took an active part in the colonial project. His interest in all kinds of African political and cultural traditions that were 'threatened with extinction', dovetailed with the colonial humanist trend of the interwar years. This regretted the consequences of the European conquest, but nonetheless believed that the colonial system, when it allowed itself to be inspired by the principles of 'indirect rule', would be the only possible solution for stopping Africa's cultural decline.

Bibliography

Geary, Christraud M., *In and Out of Focus: Images from Central Africa, 1885-1960*, Philip Wilson Publishers, London, 2002.

See also Chapters 17, 18, 20, 21 and 26.

The Congo of Tomorrow: Propaganda and Auto-Representation after the Second World War

Fig. 10. Joseph Makulu, 'A family of Congolese *évolués* in Léopoldville, 1956'. (HP.1956.32.671, RMCA Tervuren collection; photo J. Makulu (*Inforcongo*), © RMCA Tervuren)

Joseph Makula, born in Stanleyville in 1929, learned the craft of photography when serving with the *Force Publique*. In the early 1950s, he was hired by the colonial information service set up to promote the 'new' postwar Congo, the Congo of the Ten-Year Plan, modern industrial infrastructure, and *évolué* families. Together with Henri Goldstein, Makula was one of the leading photographers of *Congopresse* (the Congolese section of *Inforcongo*, the Belgian

Congo and Ruanda-Urundi Public Information Service). He contributed significantly to the image of an increasingly urbanized Congo, that looked to the future and in which Africans were no longer depicted as ethnic subjects, but more in the light of their integration into colonial society. *Inforcongo* engaged in colonial propaganda, but as art historian Sandrine Colard has shown, Makula's work should also be seen as a form of auto-representation: he called himself an *évolué* and was the favorite photographer of this now iconic class from the 1940s and 1950s, which was the colonizer's preferred interlocutor and yet remained the victim of the hierarchical colonial system.

Bibliography

Colard, Sandrine, *Photography in the Colonial Congo*, doctoral thesis, Columbia University, New York, 2016; Tödt, Daniel, *The Lumumba Generation: African Bourgeoisie and Colonial Distinction in the Belgian Congo*, De Gruyter, Berlin, 2021

See also Chapters 13, 18 and 24.

The Impossible Community

During the 1950s, one of *Inforcongo*'s aims was to produce a visual translation of the concept of 'Belgian Congolese community' – the project of a reformed colonial rule which would have been stripped of its worst racist traits and would encourage mutually advantageous harmonious relations among black and white people. Despite the colonial authorities' efforts, this soon proved to be a mirage. The contradictions were too great, and the Congolese opted en masse for the independence struggle, rather than a community which promised little progress with respect to their social status and daily life.

Although Congolese society remained segregated right up to the very end of the colonial era, *Inforcongo* and *Congopresse* tried to create an image of a peaceful, fraternal and egalitarian society with photos picturing black and white individuals alongside each other. This image of black and white children (including a barefoot girl) next to *Sinterklaas* ('St Nicolas', a counterpart of Santa Claus) is emblematic of this vision. The racial dimension of this Belgian popular tradition (with Black Pete as *Sinterklaas*'s helper who is tasked with punishing naughty children) speaks volumes about the thoroughly

Fig. 11. In the Belgian Congo. The General Colonial Administration's information service in Léopoldville organizes a *Sinterklaas* party for the children of its staff, 1957. (HP.1957.1.949, Collection RMCA Tervuren collection; photo C. Lamote (*Inforcongo*), © RMCA Tervuren)

rotten foundation on which the colonial authorities wanted to build this Belgian Congolese community.

See also Chapters 5 and 17.

Buffalo Bill in Léopoldville

Various independent African photographers followed in the footsteps of H.A. Shanu and went to work in the Congo during the colonial era. One of the most important of these was arguably Jean Depara, a man of Angolan origin. In 1951, he opened his own studio in Léopoldville. In addition to his portraits, he was known for his photos of nightlife, 'free women', rumba orchestra vocalists and young bodybuilders. His images reveal a specific urban culture which shirks colonial norms and control. One of Depara's subjects during the 1950s were the 'Bills', young Congolese men who were enthralled by Westerns and paraded through Léopoldville dressed up as cowboys.

Fig. 12. Andrada's gang of Bills (© Photo Jean Depara, from the series 'Night & Day in Kinshasa', DRC, c. 1955-1965/Courtesy Estate of Depara – *Revue Noire*, Paris)

The subculture of the Bills was radically transgressive and consisted of small groups of young men who smoked cannabis and dealt in drugs. The pursuance of masculinity was a central ingredient, and the gangs were notorious for the many rapes and assaults they committed on young girls.

The image here shows a gang of Bills. Gang leader Andrada, a mixed-race boy, is on the left; the young man to his right is Hubert Kunguniko; and the two girls crouching are Meta (left) and Thérèse Muyaka (right). As historian Didier Gondola has recently pointed out, the unique feature of Andrada's gang was that it included two girls. Thérèse Muyaka in particular became a mythical figure in the urban subculture of Kinshasa, and the subject of many rumba songs.

Bibliography

Gondola, Ch. Didier, *Tropical Cowboys: Westerns, Violence, and Masculinity in Kinshasa*, Indiana University Press, Bloomington, 2016.

See also Chapters 16 and 19.

The Plural Time of the Colonial Photo Archive

Sammy Baloji, born in 1978 in Lubumbashi, is a leading contemporary artist. Much of his work investigates the social-historical heritage of Southern Katanga, the mining region which, from the 1910s onwards, was one of the cradles of colonial capitalism. Baloji often uses colonial archive images in order to document the temporal rupture in which Katanga has been finding itself since the collapse of *Gécamines* in the 1990s. *Gécamines* was the powerful descendant of the UMHK, which controlled the economy of the entire province and had shaped the identity of the local population for decades.

Fig. 13. Sammy Baloji, Untitled, from the 'Mémoire' series, 2006.

This photo forms part of the 'Mémoire' series, which is emblematic for Baloji's work. The series consists of a group of images in which Baloji combines archival photographs (here a naked young worker, shot from behind during a medical examination) with images of the post-industrial landscape of present-day Katanga. In its confrontation of colonial and postcolonial temporalities, the series avoids any trace of nostalgia. Its archival fragments display the violence of colonial extraction (with images of forced or child labor) and the violence of the colonial photographic act itself; while the industrial ruins in the background of the images raise questions about the impasse of the present.

Bibliography

Jewsiewicki, Bogumil, 'Imaginaire collectif des Katangais au temps de la désindustrialisation. Regard du dedans et regard d'en dehors: la photographie de Sammy Baloji et le rap de Baloji Tshiani', *Cahiers d'Études Africaines*, 198-199-200, 2010, p. 1079-1111.

See also Chapters 8 and 10.

Timeline

12-14 September 1876	A 'geographic conference' is held in Brussels at the request of Leopold II, the starting signal for the Monarch's initiatives in Central Africa.
October 1882	Foundation of the AIC, the organization secretly led by Leopold II that launches expeditions to the African interior, initially to trade, later to acquire sovereignty as well.
26 February 1885	Signing of the General Act of the Berlin Conference. During the course of and in the margins of this international diplomatic meeting about Africa, through successive declarations from the participating powers, the AIC is recognized as a new state, the Congo Free State.
1 June 1885	Leopold II is officially recognized as the Congo Free State's head of state.
27 December 1886	Foundation of the CCCI, the 'elder' amongst Belgian colonial public limited companies.
1892-1894	The so-called Arab campaigns, military operations with which the Congo Free State's *Force Publique* eliminates the Arab-Swahili rulers and traders, particularly in the east of the Congo.
4 July 1895	Beginning of *Force Publique* troop revolts in Luluabourg; the last groups of insurrectionists are only eliminated during the first years of the twentieth century.
1897-1898	Brussels International Exposition and establishment of the *Palais des Colonies* in Tervuren; more than 260 Congolese people are 'exhibited' at the fair's 'Colonial Section'. A few months later, the *Palais des Colonies* is converted into the Museum of the Congo (from 1910: Museum of the Belgian Congo; since 1960: the Royal Museum for Central Africa; since 2018: AfricaMuseum).

March 1904	Foundation of the Congo Reform Association in Great Britain, which wages a fierce campaign against the abuses in the Congo Free State.
23 July 1904	Leopold II sets up a commission to investigate the allegations against the Congo Free State.
October/November 1906	Foundation of the UMHK, *Forminière* and the BCK, powerful colonial enterprises.
19 December 1906	The Belgian Parliament sets up the so-called Commission of XVII, tasked with working out the details of Belgium's takeover of the Congo Free State.
15 November 1908	The Congo Free State is dissolved, and the Congo becomes a Belgian colony: the Belgian Congo.
1914-1918	During the First World War, Belgian colonial troops take part in the fight against the Germans in Cameroon, Northern Rhodesia (now Zambia) and German East Africa (now Tanzania). In the process, Ruanda and Urundi are also occupied and, after the war, entrusted as a 'mandate' to Belgium by the League of Nations.
30 August 1919	Foundation of the *Union Congolaise*, the first association set up by Congolese individuals on Belgian soil, on the initiative of Paul Panda Farnana.
12 September 1921	Arrest of the prophet Simon Kimbangu, who is sentenced to death a few days later. On 22 November of that year, his sentence is commuted to life imprisonment. He dies in prison in 1951.
1929	Léopoldville succeeds Boma as the new capital of the Belgian Congo.
May-September 1931	Uprising by the Pende (in the Kwango region), which is met with bloody suppression.
1940-1945	The Belgian Congo sides with the Allies in the fight against Nazi Germany and its allies. The colony is an important supplier of raw materials for the Allied war effort.
March-July 1941	The Belgian colonial troops inflict a defeat on the Italians in Abyssinia (Ethiopia).
4 December 1941	A strike by black workers in Élisabethville is quashed in a bloody fashion.
1945	Foundation of *La Voix du Congolais*, the 'official' periodical for the Congolese who are called *évolués*.

1 July 1947	Foundation of the Fund for Indigenous Wellbeing (FBEI), a public organization focused on healthcare.
1949	Launch of the Ten-Year Plan for the economic and social development of the Congo.
1954	Foundation of Lovanium University in Léopoldville.
December 1955	Jef Van Bilsen publishes his Thirty-Year Plan for the independence of the Congo.
30 June 1956	Publication of the 'Manifesto' in the journal *Conscience Africaine*, the first document in which the Congolese publicly announce their determination to gain political emancipation.
December 1957	First local elections in some urban centers; the black population is able to take part.
4 January 1959	Beginning of fierce riots in Léopoldville that last three days and are met with bloody repression.
January-February 1960	The Belgian Congolese roundtable conference in which the political parties of both countries discuss the future of the colony and reach an accord about the independence of the Congo.
22 May 1960	First parliamentary elections in the Congo. The result of this poll means that Patrice Lumumba becomes the Prime Minister and Joseph Kasa-Vubu the President of the country.
30 June 1960	Independence of the Congo.
17 January 1961	Prime Minister Lumumba, who had been deposed and imprisoned earlier, is killed in Katanga, together with two of his supporters.
1 July 1962	Independence of Rwanda and Burundi.

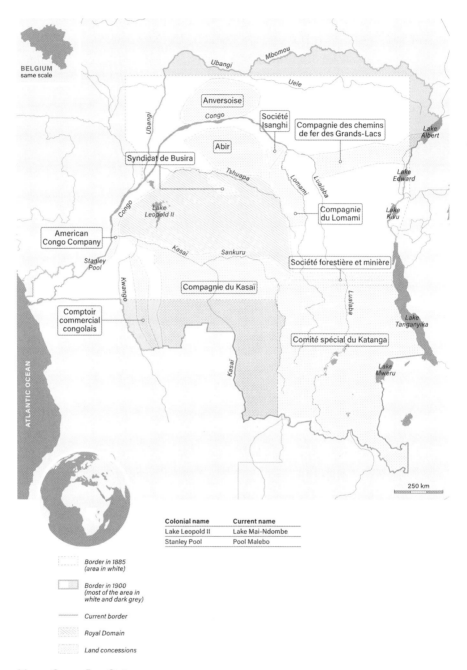

Map 1. Congo Free State, c. 1900

Map 2. Belgian Congo, c. 1950

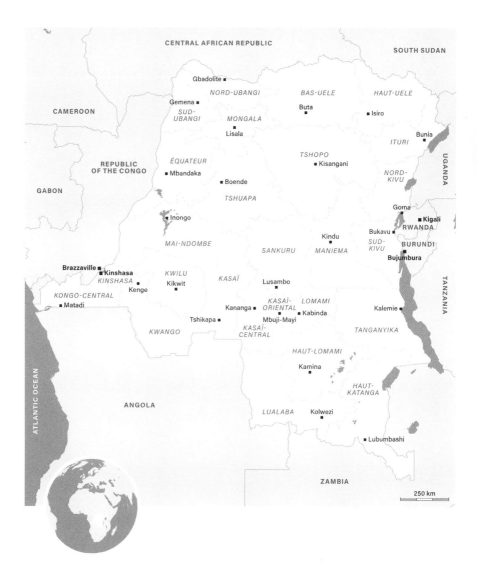

Map 3. Democratic Republic of the Congo, c. 2020

Abbreviations

AAI	*Amis de l'Art Indigène* (Friends of Indigenous Art)
ABAKO	*Alliance des Bakongos* (Alliance of the Bakongo)
ABIR	Anglo-Belgian India Rubber Company
ABVV	*Algemeen Belgisch Vakverbond* (General Labor Federation of Belgium) (see also FGTB)
ACV	*Algemeen Christelijk Vakverbond* (Confederation of Christian Trade Unions) (see also CSC)
AIC	*Association Internationale du Congo* (International Association of the Congo)
ANC	*Armée Nationale Congolaise* (National Congolese Army)
Anversoise	*Société Anversoise du Commerce au Congo* (Antwerp Society for Trade in the Congo)
APIC	*Association du Personnel Indigène de la Colonie* (Association of Indigenous Staff from the Colony)
ARSOM	*Académie Royale des Sciences d'Outre-Mer* (Royal Academy of Overseas Sciences) (see also KAOW)
ASSORECO	*Association des Ressortissants du Haut-Congo* (Association of Citizens of Haut-Congo)
Auxilacs	*Société Auxiliaire Industrielle et Financière de la Compagnie des Chemins de Fer du Congo Supérieur aux Lacs Africains* (Industrial and Financial Auxiliary Society of the Upper Congo to the African Great Lakes Railway Company [CFL])
BALUBAKAT	*Association Générale des Baluba du Katanga* (General Association of the Baluba of Katanga)
BBC	British Broadcasting Corporation
BCK [*Bécéka*]	*Compagnie du Chemin de Fer du Bas-Congo au Katanga* (Bas-Congo to Katanga Railway Company)
Bécéka	See BCK
BTK	*Bourse du Travail du Katanga* (Katanga Labor Office)
CADULAC	*Centres Agronomiques de l'Université de Louvain au Congo* (Agronomic Centers of the University of Louvain in the Congo)
CAPA	*Centre d'Accueil pour le Personnel Africain* (Reception Center for African Staff)
CCCI	*Compagnie du Congo pour le Commerce et l'Industrie* (Congo Company for Commerce and Industry)

CÉDAF	*Centre d'Étude et de Documentation Africaines* (African Study and Documentation Center)
CegeSoma	*Centre d'Étude Guerre et Société / Studie- en Documentatiecentrum Oorlog en Hedendaagse Maatschappij* (Study and Documentation Center for War and Contemporary Society)
CEMUBAC	*Centre Scientifique et Médical de l'Université libre de Bruxelles en Afrique Centrale* (Scientific and Medical Center of the ULB in Central Africa)
CEPSI	*Centre d'Études des Problèmes Sociaux Indigènes* (Study Center for Indigenous Social Problems)
CEREA	*Centre de Regroupement Africain* (African Regrouping Center)
CFC	*Compagnie du Chemin de Fer du Congo* (The Congo Railway Company)
CFL	*Compagnie des Chemins de Fer du Congo Supérieur aux Grands Lacs Africains* (Upper Congo to the African Great Lakes Railway Company)
CGS	*Confédération Générale des Syndicats* (General Confederation of Trade Unions)
CGSC	*Confédération Générale des Syndiqués du Congo* (General Confederation of Unionists from the Congo)
CIA	Central Intelligence Agency
CIC	*Comité Intérieur Colonial* (Colonial Interior Committee)
CIE	*Conseil Indigène d'Enterprise* (Indigenous Works Council)
CK	*Compagnie du Katanga* (Katanga Company)
CMCLD	*Collectif 'Mémoires Coloniales et Lutte contre les Discriminations'* ('Colonial Memories and Fight against Discrimination' Collective)
COGERGO	*Compagnie de Gérance du Coton* (Cotton Management Company)
Cominière	*Société Commerciale et Minière du Congo* (Commercial and Mining Company of the Congo)
CONAKAT	*Confédération des Associations Tribales du Katanga* (Confederation of Tribal Associations of Katanga)
COPAMI	*Commission pour la Protection des Arts et Métiers Indigènes* (Commission for the Protection of Indigenous Arts and Crafts)
Cotonco	*Compagnie Cotonnière Congolaise* (Congolese Cotton Company)
CPAS	*Centre Public d'Action Sociale* (Public Center for Social Welfare)
CSC	*Confédération des Syndicats Chrétiens* (Confederation of Christian Trade Unions) (see also ACV)
CSCC	*Confédération des Syndicats Chrétiens du Congo* (Confederation of Christian Trade Unions in the Congo)
CSK	*Comité Spécial du Katanga* (Katanga Special Committee)

DéFI	*Démocrate Fédéraliste Indépendant* (Democratic, Federalist, Independent)
Diamang	*Companhia de Diamantes de Angola* (Angola Diamond Company)
DRC	Democratic Republic of the Congo
FBEI	*Fonds du Bien-Être Indigène* (Fund for Indigenous Wellbeing)
FGTB	*Fédération Générale du Travail de Belgique* (General Labor Federation of Belgium) (see also ABVV)
FGTK	*Fédération Générale des Travailleurs du Kongo* (General Federation of Workers from the Congo)
FNRS	*Fonds National de la Recherche Scientifique* (National Fund for Scientific Research)
FOMULAC	*Fondation Médicale de l'Université de Louvain au Congo* (Medical Foundation of the University of Louvain in the Congo)
FOPERDA	*Fondation Père Damien pour la Lutte contre la Lèpre* (Father Damien Foundation for the Fight against Leprosy)
FOREAMI	*Fonds Reine Élisabeth pour l'Assistance Médicale aux Indigènes* (Queen Elisabeth Fund for Medical Assistance to Indigenous People)
Forminière	*Société Internationale Forestière et Minière du Congo* (International Forestry and Mining Company of the Congo)
FRS	*Fonds de la Recherche Scientifique* (Fund for Scientific Research)
FULREAC	*Fondation de l'Université de Liège pour les Recherches Scientifiques en Afrique Centrale* (Foundation of the University of Liège for Scientific Research in Central Africa)
FWO	*Fonds voor Wetenschappelijk Onderzoek* (Research Foundation – Flanders)
Gécamines	*La Générale des Carrières et des Mines* (General [Society] of Quarries and Mines)
Géomines	*Compagnie Géologique et Minière des Ingénieurs et Industriels Belges* (Geological and Mining Company of Belgian Engineers and Industrialists)
ICOMOS	International Council on Monuments and Sites
IFEP	*Institut de Formation et d'Études Politiques* (Institute of Political Formation and Studies [Kinshasa])
ILO	International Labor Organization
INEAC	*Institut National pour l'Étude Agronomique du Congo Belge* (National Institute for the Agronomic Study of the Belgian Congo)
Inforcongo	*Office de l'Information et des Relations Publiques pour le Congo Belge et le Ruanda-Urundi* (Belgian Congo and Ruanda-Urundi Information and Public Relation Office)
IRSAC	*Institut pour la Recherche Scientifique en Afrique Centrale* (Institute for Scientific Research in Central Africa)

JOC	*Jeunesse Ouvrière Chrétienne* (Young Christian Workers) (see also KAJ)
KADOC	*KADOC Documentatie- en Onderzoekscentrum voor Religie, Cultuur en Samenleving* (KADOC Documentation and Research Center on Religion, Culture and Society)
KAJ	*Kristelijke Arbeidersjongeren* [previously *Kristelijke Arbeidersjeugd*] (Young Christian Workers) (see also JOC)
KAOW	*Koninklijke Academie voor Overzeese Wetenschappen* (Royal Academy of Overseas Sciences) (see also ARSOM)
KBUOL	*Koninklijke Belgische Unie voor de Overzeese Landen* (Royal Belgian Union for Overseas Countries) (see also UROME)
KMMA	*Koninklijk Museum voor Midden-Afrika* (Royal Museum for Central Africa) (see also MRAC; currently AfricaMuseum [Tervuren])
KU Leuven	*Katholieke Universiteit Leuven* (Catholic University of Leuven [Louvain])
KVHV	*Katholiek Vlaams Hoogstudenten Verbond* (Catholic Flemish Students Union)
Milacs	*Compagnie Minière des Grands Lacs Africains* (African Great Lakes Mining Company)
MNC	*Mouvement National Congolais* (National Congolese Movement)
MNC/K	*Mouvement National Congolais/Kalonji* (National Congolese Movement/Kalonji)
MNC/L	*Mouvement National Congolais/Lumumba* (National Congolese Movement/Lumumba)
MRAC	*Musée Royal de l'Afrique Centrale* (Royal Museum for Central Africa) (see also KMMA; currently AfricaMuseum [Tervuren])
NATO	North Atlantic Treaty Organization
NGO	Non-governmental organization
ONUC	*Opération des Nations Unies au Congo* (United Nations Operation in the Congo)
OTRACO	*Office des Transports Coloniaux* (Colonial Transport Office)
PNP	*Parti National du Progrès* (National Progress Party)
PSA	*Parti Solidaire Africain* (African Solidarity Party)
PUNA	*Parti de l'Unité Nationale* (National Unity Party)
REPCO	*Régie des Plantations de la Colonie* (Public Enterprise of the Plantations of the Colony)
RMCA	Royal Museum for Central Africa (Tervuren) (see also KMMA and MRAC)
RTBF	*Radio-Télévision Belge de la Communauté Française* (Belgian Radio and Television of the French Community)

Sabena	*Société Anonyme Belge d'Exploitation de la Navigation Aérienne* (Belgian Limited Company for the Exploitation of Aerial Navigation)
SAFRICAS	*Société Africaine de Construction* (African Construction Company)
SAMI	*Service d'Assistance Médicale Indigène* (Indigenous Medical Assistance Service)
SIBÉKA	*Société Minière du Bécéka* (Mining Society of the BCK)
SOAS	School of Oriental and African Studies
UCL	*Université Catholique de Louvain* (Catholic University of Louvain-la-Neuve; since 2018 UCLouvain)
ULB	*Université Libre de Bruxelles* ([Francophone] Free University of Brussels)
UMHK	*Union Minière du Haut-Katanga* (Mining Union of Haut-Katanga)
UN	United Nations
UNESCO	United Nations Educational, Scientific and Cultural Organization
UNIMO	*Union Mongo* (Mongo Union)
UROME	*Union Royale Belge pour les Pays d'Outre-Mer* (Royal Belgian Union for Overseas Countries) (see also KBUOL)
US[A]	United States [of America]
USSR	Union of Socialist Soviet Republics
UTC	*Union des Travailleurs du Congo* (The Congo Workers' Union)
VRT	*Vlaamse Radio- en Televisieomroeporganisatie* (Flemish Radio and Television Organization)

About the Authors

Frans Buelens is a Senior Researcher at the University of Antwerp.

Bas De Roo obtained his doctorate from Ghent University on the history of the Congo Free State and is currently a Researcher at Geheugen Collectief, an independent center for historical research.

Marc Depaepe is Full Professor Emeritus at KU Leuven, Faculty of Psychology and Educational Sciences, Kortrijk Campus (KULAK) and Leading Researcher at the University of Latvia (Riga).

Donatien Dibwe dia Mwembu is Full Professor Emeritus at the University of Lubumbashi, Faculty of Arts and Humanities, Department of History.

Mathieu Zana Etambala was born in Congo and has lived in Flanders since 1962. He obtained a PhD in History from KU Leuven and worked as a Researcher at the AfricaMuseum in Tervuren, section History and Politics, until his retirement in February 2020.

Emmanuel Gerard is a historian and Full Professor Emeritus at KU Leuven, Faculty of Social Sciences.

Idesbald Goddeeris is a Full Professor at KU Leuven, Faculty of Arts, research group Modernity and Society 1800-2000 (MoSa), and teaches colonial history and migration history, among other things.

Didier Gondola, the author of *Tropical Cowboys* (2016) and *Matswa vivant* (2021), is a Full Professor at Johns Hopkins University, Department of History, and a recipient of a Fulbright Scholarship and several fellowships, including the prestigious European Institutes for Advanced Study (Eurias).

Benoît Henriet is an Associate Professor at the VUB, Faculty of Arts and Philosophy, and a member of the research group Social History of Capitalism (SHOC).

ABOUT THE AUTHORS

Johan Lagae is a Full Professor at Ghent University, Faculty of Engineering and Architecture.

Maarten Langhendries obtained his doctorate from KU Leuven in 2022 with a dissertation on Catholic doctors and reproductive medicine in Belgium and the Belgian Congo (1900-1968).

Amandine Lauro is a Research Associate of the FRS-FNRS at the ULB, where she teaches on African, gender and colonial history.

Annette Lembagusala Kikumbi obtained her doctorate in Educational Sciences at KU Leuven and teaches at the Institut *Supérieur Pédagogique of Kikwit* and at the *Université du Grand Bandundu*.

Ruben Mantels is a historian and affiliated with the Ghent University Library.

Michael Meeuwis is a Professor at Ghent University, Department of African Languages and Cultures, where he teaches and conducts research on Lingala and on missionary and colonial linguistics.

Pedro Monaville is an Associate Professor in History at McGill University in Montreal.

Jean-Marie Mutamba Makombo is Full Professor Emeritus at the University of Kinshasa, Faculty of Arts and Humanities, Department of History.

Isidore Ndaywel è Nziem is Full Professor Emeritus at the University of Kinshasa, Faculty of Arts and Humanities, Department of History, and is Full Member of the Congolese Academy of Sciences and of the African Academy of Religious, Social and Political Sciences.

Jean Omasombo Tshonda is a PhD in Political Science (ULB, 1987), Researcher at the AfricaMuseum in Tervuren and Professor and Director of the *Centre d'Études Politiques* at the University of Kinshasa.

Violette Pouillard is a Permanent Research Fellow at the French National Center for Scientific Research (CNRS), affiliated with the LARHRA (UMR 5190) and a Visiting Professor at Ghent University.

Jacob Sabakinu Kivilu († 2021) was a Full Professor at the University of Kinshasa, Faculty of Arts and Humanities, Department of History, and an Honorary Corresponding Member of the Belgian Royal Academy of Overseas Sciences.

About the Authors

Jean-Paul Sanderson is a Researcher at the UCLouvain, *Centre de Recherche en Démographie*. He teaches at the University of Lille, Department of Sociology, and at the University of Paris 1 Panthéon-Sorbonne, Institute of Demography.

Yves Segers is Director of the Interfaculty Center for Agricultural History (ICAG, KU Leuven) and Associate Professor of Rural History at KU Leuven, Faculty of Arts, research group Modernity and Society 1800-2000 (MoSa).

Julia Seibert taught Modern African History at the American University in Cairo and at the Humboldt-Universität in Berlin. She currently works as a development consultant and consults at several universities in the Great Lakes region.

Matthew G. Stanard is Professor of History at Berry College (Georgia, USA).

Daniel Tödt is a Researcher at the Konstanz Universität. His dissertation on African elite formation in the Belgian Congo (2015, published 2018, English translation 2021) received prizes from the ZEIT-*Stiftung* and from the *Börsenverein des Deutschen Buchhandels*.

Sarah Van Beurden received her PhD from the University of Pennsylvania and is an Associate Professor of History and African American and African Studies at Ohio State University.

Leen Van Molle is Full Professor Emeritus at KU Leuven, Faculty of Arts, research group Modernity and Society 1800-2000 (MoSa).

Reinout Vander Hulst obtained his doctorate from KU Leuven with a dissertation on colonial medicine and is currently a Postdoctoral Researcher at the State Archives of Belgium.

Guy Vanthemsche is Professor Emeritus of Contemporary History at the VUB.

Georgi Verbeeck is Professor of History at KU Leuven and Associate Professor of Modern History and Political Cultures at Maastricht University.